# Information & Communication Technologies in Action

## Linking Theory & Narratives of Practice

# Information & Communication Technologies in Action

## Linking Theory & Narratives of Practice

Larry D. Browning

Alf Steinar Sætre

Keri K. Stephens

Jan-Oddvar Sørnes

Routledge
Taylor & Francis Group

NEW YORK AND LONDON

This volume originally published 2005 by CBS Press

This revised edition published 2008
by Routledge
270 Madison Ave, New York, NY 10016

Simultaneously published in the UK
by Routledge
2 Park Square, Milton Park, Abingdon, Oxon OX14 4RN

*Routledge is an imprint of the Taylor & Francis Group, an informa business*

First edition © 2005 CBS Press
Revised edition © 2008 Taylor & Francis

This book has been prepared from camera-ready copy provided
by the author.

Printed and bound in the United States of America on acid-free paper
by Sheridan Books, Inc.

*Library of Congress Cataloging in Publication Data*
Browning, Larry D.
Information and communication technology in action : linking theory and
narratives of practice / Larry Davis Browning, Alf Steinar Saetre,
Keri K. Stephens.
p.  cm.
ISBN 978-0-415-96546-0 -- ISBN 978-0-415-96547-7 --
ISBN 978-0-8058-1630-3   1. Telecommunication systems.   I. Steinar
Saetre, Alf.   II. Stephens, Keri K.   III. Title.
TK5101B745 2007
621.382--dc22
2007036660

ISBN10: 0–415–96546–2 (hbk)
ISBN10: 0–415–96547–0 (pbk)
ISBN10: 0–203–93244–7 (ebk)

ISBN13: 978–0–415–96546–0 (hbk)
ISBN13: 978–0–415–96547–7 (pbk)
ISBN13: 978–0–203–93244–5 (ebk)

# Contents

C

Preface .................................................................................................................. xiii

Introduction ......................................................................................................... xv

    *Stories as Sources of Information* ........................................................................ *xvi*
    *The Narrative Approach* .................................................................................. *xvi*
    *Concepts in the book* ...................................................................................... *xviii*
    *Practical Questions — Stories/Concepts* .............................................................. *xx*
    *Story Summaries* ............................................................................................ *xxii*

1. Media Choice and ICT Use ............................................................................ 27

    *Determinism or Social Construction?* .................................................................. *27*
    *Technological Determinism: Richness and Conscious Choice* ................................... *28*
    *Figure 1-1: Visual Representation of Media Richness Theory* ................................. *28*
    *The Social Construction of ICTs* ....................................................................... *30*
    *Figure 1-2: Social Influence Model* ................................................................... *30*
    *Figure 1-3: Dual Capacity Model* .................................................................... *31*
    *Comparing Deterministic and Social Constructionist Perspectives* ........................... *33*
    *Pulling Theory Together to Guide an Understanding of Narratives of ICT Use* ......... *34*

2. The Role of Credibility and Trust in ICT Studies:
   Understanding the Source, Message, Media, and Audience ........................... 37

    *Source Credibility* ........................................................................................... *37*
    *Message Credibility* ........................................................................................ *40*
    *Media Credibility* .......................................................................................... *41*
    *Audience Considerations* .................................................................................. *42*
    *Fluid Model Depicting Credibility Considerations* .............................................. *42*
    *Relating Theory to Practice* ............................................................................. *43*
    *Figure 2-1: Factors Affecting Overall Perceptions of Credibility* ............................ *43*

3. Rogers' Diffusion of Innovations ................................................................... 47

    *Figure 3-1: Rate of Adoption* .......................................................................... *48*
    *Opinion Leadership and Peer Leadership* .......................................................... *49*
    *Examining ICTs as an Innovation in Norway and the U.S.* ................................. *50*
    *The Relativity and Uncertainty of Innovations* .................................................. *51*
    *Boosterism and Criticism in Diffusion Research* ................................................. *52*
    *Characteristics of an Innovation* ...................................................................... *52*
    *Communication Channels as a Special Type of Innovation* ................................... *53*
    *Summary* ...................................................................................................... *55*

4. A Garbage Can Model of Information Communication Technology Choice ............... 57

   *Problems* ........................................................................................................... *59*
   *Solutions* ........................................................................................................... *59*
   *Participants* ...................................................................................................... *60*
   *Choice Opportunities* ......................................................................................... *61*
   *The Status and Application of Garbage Can Theory* ........................................... *61*
   *Garbage Can Patterns in the Cases* .................................................................... *62*

5. Impression Management and ICTs ............................................................. 65

   *Manipulation and Ethics in Impression Management* .......................................... *66*
   *Goffman's Work on Impression Management* ....................................................... *67*
   *Impression Management and ICTs* ..................................................................... *69*

6. Enactment and Sensemaking in Organizations ........................................ 73

   *Weick's Theory of Organizing* ............................................................................. *74*
   *Ecological Change, Enactment, Selection and Retention* ..................................... *75*
   *Sensemaking* ...................................................................................................... *76*
   *Figure 6–1: Sensemaking and Enactment* .......................................................... *77*
   *Table 6–1: Seven Properties of Sensemaking* ...................................................... *77*
   *Coupling ICTs and Enactment* ........................................................................... *78*
   *Figure 6–2: The relationship between Enactment and ICTs* ................................ *79*
   *The Enactment of Cause Maps* ........................................................................... *80*
   *Figure 6–3: Roos and Hall's Cause Map of the Policy Domain of an ECU* ......... *81*
   *Figure 6–4: A Composite Map of Three Cases* .................................................... *82*
   *Summary* ........................................................................................................... *83*

7. Giddens' Structuration Theory and ICTs ................................................. 85

   *Reflexivity and the Duality of Structure* ............................................................. *86*
   *Adaptive Structuration Theory* .......................................................................... *88*
   *Time-Space Relations* ........................................................................................ *90*
   *Summary* ........................................................................................................... *91*

8. Complexity Theories and ICTs .................................................................. 93

   *Complexity and Organizations* ........................................................................... *94*
   *Fundamentals of Complexity: Nonlinearity and Self-Organization in Complex Adaptive Systems* ........ *96*
   *Nonlinearity* ...................................................................................................... *97*
   *Complex Adaptive Systems* ................................................................................. *97*
   *Characteristics of CAS* ....................................................................................... *98*
   *Table 8–1: Four Characteristics of CAS and their Relevance to Organizations* ..... *99*
   *Emergence* ......................................................................................................... *100*
   *Bifurcation Points and Prigogine's Theory of Dissipative Structures* ................... *101*
   *Dissipative Structures* ........................................................................................ *101*
   *Table 8–2: The Formation of Dissipative Structures* ........................................... *102*
   *Conclusion* ......................................................................................................... *103*

9. ICT and Culture ......................................................................................... 105

   *The Relationship Between Culture and ICTs* ...................................................... *106*
   *Organizational Culture* ...................................................................................... *107*
   *Subcultural Influence* ......................................................................................... *109*
   *National Culture – Hofstede's Perspective* .......................................................... *111*
   *Hofstede's Four Dimensions of Cultural Differences* ........................................... *112*
   *Table 9–1: Norwegian and U.S. scores on Hofstede's 4 Dimensions* ................... *113*

*Power Distance Index (PDI)* .......................................................................... *113*
*Uncertainty Avoidance Index (UAI)* ............................................................. *113*
*Individualism/Collectivism (IDV)* ................................................................. *114*
*Materiality/Sociality Index (MSI)* ................................................................. *115*
*Reflexivity of ICTs and Culture* ..................................................................... *116*
*Relating Theory to Practice* ........................................................................... *116*

10. **The Frustrated Professor** ........................................................................ **119**

*Gunnar's Goals and Intentions* ....................................................................... *120*
*The Web-Based Learning Arena* ..................................................................... *121*
*Students Resist Web Learning* ......................................................................... *122*
*Gunnar's Payoff* .............................................................................................. *123*
*Fear of Being the "Old" Professor* .................................................................. *124*
*Follow the Leader?* .......................................................................................... *125*
*Conclusion* ...................................................................................................... *125*
*Questions for Review or Discussion* ................................................................. *126*

11. **Teaching the Good Old Boys New Tricks: Taking ICTs to the Bank** ........ **127**

*A CFO's ICT Use* ............................................................................................ *128*
*Extensive Use of Email* ................................................................................... *128*
*Occasional Use of Other Media* ...................................................................... *129*
*Extensive Use of the Web in Her Job* .............................................................. *130*
*ICT Preference Differences Are OK* ............................................................... *132*
*Banking Changes Create a Need for a New Banking Culture* .......................... *132*
*Conclusion* ...................................................................................................... *134*
*Questions for Review or Discussion* ................................................................. *135*

12. **From Blunt Talk to Kid Gloves: The Importance of Adaptability Across Culture** ..... **137**

*Openness About Ecological Practices* ............................................................... *138*
*Creating a New Corporate Culture at NorFood* .............................................. *139*
*Karen's Communication Strategies* ................................................................. *140*
*Communicating With People To Demonstrate Their Value* .............................. *142*
*Conclusion* ...................................................................................................... *144*
*Questions for Review or Discussion* ................................................................. *145*

13. **Slowing Down in the Fast Lane** ............................................................... **147**

*Be Conscious of the Person Receiving Your Communication* ............................ *149*
*Choose an ICT that is Adaptive and Move On* ................................................ *150*
*Shape the Behavior of Peers to Match Your Preferences* .................................. *150*
*Have Strategies to Get You Better Information* ............................................... *151*
*Communicate Efficiently in a Slowed-Down World* ........................................ *152*
*Conclusion* ...................................................................................................... *152*
*Questions for Review or Discussion* ................................................................. *153*

14. **Serving the Customer Locally Without Moving There:
How to Use ICTs to Project a Local Presence** .......................................... **155**

*Working Across Different Business Cultures and National Regulations* ............. *155*
*Projecting a Local Presence* ............................................................................ *158*
*Distance and Media Usage* ............................................................................. *159*
*Organizational Learning and Emergent Strategy* ........................................... *160*
*Conclusion* ...................................................................................................... *162*
*Questions for Review or Discussion* ................................................................. *163*

15. Overloaded But Not Overwhelmed:
    Communication in Inter-Organizational Relationships ........................................... 165

    *What Causes Information Overload?* ................................................................... 165
    *Strategies for Handling Overload* ...................................................................... 167
    *Conclusion* ......................................................................................................... 171
    *Questions for Review or Discussion* .................................................................. 172

16. Depending on the Kindness of Strangers:
    Using Newsgroups for Just-in-Time Learning ...................................................... 173

    *Just-in-Time Learning* ...................................................................................... 173
    *Asking Questions on a Newsgroup* ..................................................................... 174
    *Role of Culture* ................................................................................................. 175
    *Socialization of Fresh Newsgroup Members* ....................................................... 176
    *Conflicting Rules* .............................................................................................. 177
    *Who Are the Digital Philanthropists?* ............................................................... 177
    *Conclusion* ......................................................................................................... 178
    *Questions for Review or Discussion* .................................................................. 179

17. Building a Medical Community Using Remote Diagnosis:
    The Story of DocNet .............................................................................................. 181

    *Starting DocNet* ................................................................................................ 182
    *Excitement in Spite of Struggles* ....................................................................... 184
    *Defining the Success of DocNet* ......................................................................... 184
    *Sharing of Knowledge* ....................................................................................... 186
    *Security Issues* .................................................................................................. 186
    *Conclusion* ......................................................................................................... 187
    *Questions for Review or Discussion* .................................................................. 188

18. Don't Get Between Me and My Customer:
    How Changing Jobs Shifts ICT Use ...................................................................... 189

    *Working in the Virtual Office* ............................................................................ 190
    *Using ICTs for Sales and Marketing* ................................................................. 191
    *ICT Changes Resulting from a Different Career* ................................................ 193
    *Conclusion* ......................................................................................................... 195
    *Questions for Review or Discussion* .................................................................. 196

19. Fighting Uncertainty With Intelligence ................................................................ 197

    *NorthCell's Challenge* ....................................................................................... 198
    *The Nature of Competitive Intelligence* ............................................................ 198
    *Ambiguity and Uncertainty* .............................................................................. 198
    *Responding to the Requirements of Uncertainty and Speed* ............................... 200
    *CI Information Dissemination and Media Choice* .............................................. 205
    *Conclusion* ......................................................................................................... 206
    *Questions for Review or Discussion* .................................................................. 206

20. Close Up . . . From a Distance:
    Using ICTs for Managing International Manufacturing ........................................ 207

    *Using a Third Party to Manage Confidentiality* ................................................ 207
    *An Example of the Order Process* ...................................................................... 208
    *Selective Communication and the Need to Know* ............................................... 210
    *Communication Within His Own Company* ...................................................... 211

Deciding When to Use Different ICTs .................................................. 213
Conclusion .................................................................................... 214
Questions for Review or Discussion .................................................. 215

21. Over the Hill but on Top of the World: An Atypical Salesperson .............................. 217

Overcoming the Odds with Adaptability and Honesty ........................... 217
Resourceful Usage of ICTs ............................................................... 219
Strategies for Overcoming Remoteness ............................................... 220
Optimizing Media Usage with Suppliers ............................................. 221
Using the Web to Enhance Credibility ................................................ 222
Conclusion .................................................................................... 223
Questions for Review or Discussion .................................................. 224

22. The Role of ICTs in Maintaining Personal Relationships
Across Distance and Cultures ................................................... 225

Media Preferences Across Cultures ................................................... 226
Distance and Media Choice .............................................................. 227
The Primacy of Email Over Other Media ............................................ 227
Managing Private Relationships ........................................................ 228
The Internet as a Two-Way Source .................................................... 229
Email Etiquette .............................................................................. 230
The Richness of Face-To-Face Communication .................................. 231
On Being Constantly Available and Modern Office Spaces ................... 231
Conclusion .................................................................................... 232
Questions for Review or Discussion .................................................. 233

23. One in the Hand is Worth Two on the Web:
Relying on Tradition When Selling Financial Services ......................... 235

The Client Strategy ........................................................................ 235
Displaying Information ................................................................... 237
Website Interaction ........................................................................ 237
Learning From the Pizza Guy ........................................................... 237
Increasing Website Visitors—Lurkers vs. Clients ................................ 238
Partnerships .................................................................................. 239
The Structure of Ed's Firm and the Integration of His Personal Life ...... 240
Conclusion .................................................................................... 240
Questions for Review or Discussion .................................................. 241

24. Do What You Do Well and Outsource the Rest...
Even Guarded Information ....................................................... 243

CommMeets as Useful ICTs ............................................................ 244
The Importance of Face-to-Face Communication in Sales .................... 246
Partnering for Trust ....................................................................... 246
Conclusion .................................................................................... 248
Questions for Review or Discussion .................................................. 249

25. Orchestrating Communication:
The Process of Selling in the Semiconductor Market ......................... 251

The Web of Behind-the-Scenes Relationships .................................... 251
Using ICTs to Overcome the Imperfect Organizational System ............ 253
Conclusion .................................................................................... 257
Questions for Review or Discussion .................................................. 258

26. Nothing Fishy Going on Here:
    Tracing the Quality of the Seafood Product ............................................. 259

    *Fisheries: a Vital Part of Norway's Economy* ............................................ 259
    *The Regulatory Problem* ............................................................................ 260
    *The Commercial Problem* ........................................................................... 260
    *The Technical Problem* ............................................................................... 261
    *Solutions* ..................................................................................................... 262
    *The Value of Automating the Production Process* ..................................... 264
    *The Doubled-Edged Sword of Traceable Information* ............................... 265
    *Conclusion* .................................................................................................. 266
    *Questions for Review or Discussion* ........................................................... 266

27. From Information to Emotion:
    The Changing Use of ICTs Following the 9/11 Tragedy ......................... 267

    *The Case* ..................................................................................................... 267
    *StrategyFirst's Work Culture* ..................................................................... 268
    *Barbara's Role in StrategyFirst* .................................................................. 268
    *Barbara's Use of the Internet* ..................................................................... 269
    *Barbara's Private Business and Social Use of ICTs* ................................... 270
    *Barbara in New York City After 9/11* ....................................................... 270
    *Barbara in New York City After 9/11* ....................................................... 272
    *Questions for Review or Discussion* ........................................................... 273

28. Give Me a Cellphone and I'll Give You Trouble:
    Technology Usage in a Young Start-Up ................................................... 275

    *Using Email and the Internet Productively* ............................................... 276
    *The Unintended Consequences of ICT Use* ............................................... 278
    *Communication Technologies in the Public and Private Domain* ............ 280
    *Conclusion* .................................................................................................. 281
    *Questions for Review or Discussion* ........................................................... 282

29. Information Will Get You to Heaven ...................................................... 283

    *Banned From Pursuing His Own Family Genealogy* ................................. 283
    *Networking as a Key Source of Information* .............................................. 284
    *Email for Sharing Information* ................................................................... 285
    *His Elaborate Storage and Backup System* ............................................... 286
    *The Challenge of Collecting Credible Information* ................................... 287
    *Conclusion* .................................................................................................. 289
    *Questions for Review or Discussion* ........................................................... 290

Postscript: The Source of Our Stories .......................................................... 291

Index ............................................................................................................... 293

About the Authors .......................................................................................... 302

# Information & Communication Technologies in Action

## Linking Theory & Narratives of Practice

# Preface

p

Lawrence Summers, President of Harvard University, has said, "One good example is worth a thousand theories."[1] Kurt Lewin, meanwhile, the famous social scientist, contended that "there is nothing so practical as good theory." We think both contentions contain major, but partial, truths. Our book combines 20 vivid stories (examples) with a selection of nine good theories-some mainstream, some emerging. For more details on our research methods, see the note at the end of the book. The stories let you meet a set of bright, articulate individuals talking about how they communicate today via information and communication technologies (ICTs). And the theories, which we have designed to make accessible, illuminate the implicit patterns in these stories. We hope that our mix of stories and theories will lead you to say, "Oh, so that's why people do that!"

Our examples are as diverse as they are memorable. One of them, for instance, will introduce you to the world of fish-industry management 75 miles north of the Arctic Circle. Another will introduce you to a banker who must drive past 20 central Texas ranches to the small town where she works. The book also contains somber stories of how the 9/11 disaster changed the ICT use of two women. One was in New York City the day of the disaster, and the other worked with many who died in the Twin Towers that day. Other stories are less emotionally wrenching and report ecstatic moments of professional achievement via ICTs. Our purpose in this book is to demonstrate how and why these technologies are used under myriad circumstances.

One thing that you'll quickly note as you read this book is that the conventional understanding of ICTs has been expanded by the storytellers themselves. Although our interview protocol focused on how they communicate via electronic means, almost to the person they told us that their most important-and preferred-means of communication was face-to-face. Our talks with them also showed that they treat face-to-face as a technology-that is, a method with specific steps to follow, much as with other technologies.

---

[1]  Friedman, T. L. (2003, October 12). Courageous Arab Thinkers. The New York Times, Editorial Page.

As a group of four authors spread across two continents, we have more production tales than there is room for in this preface, but let's simply say that intense work sessions at 9,000 feet in the Colorado Rockies, on the Lofoten Islands 40 miles off the coast of northern Norway, in Trondheim, Bodø, Oslo, and Austin have left all of us (and some of our children) with enough stories to last a while.

Several people have been instrumental in the completion of this project. First, we'd like to thank Hewlett-Packard sponsors for the research grant and encouragement they gave to our effort. This allowed us to conduct, transcribe, and analyze the interviews that became the stories for our book. John Trimble, a Distinguished Teaching Professor in the Department of English at the University of Texas at Austin, helped us get our writing clearer as he reviewed our drafts of cases and theory chapters. Victoria Hoch, Christine Sætre, and Tab Stephens proofread and gave constructive comments on early drafts of many of the stories. Tab Stephens acted as a technical advisor and meeting facilitator for a crucial four days early in the project, as did Wencke Sørnes in the later stages. Christine Sætre's creative vision and energy engendered the book's layout. Stephanie Hamel, Frode Soelberg, and Amy Schmisseur were instrumental in arranging interviews and helpful in the early analysis of the data.

We would also like to acknowledge Scott Poole for his recommendation to diversify our interviewees. In year two of data collection, we took his advice and many of the stories that appear here are a direct result. We would like to thank Ron Bassett, Steve Corman, Bruce Garrison, Leslie Jarmon, Ron Rice, and Everett Rogers for reviewing our manuscript. A thanks also goes to David Paul for help in securing interviewees.

Most of all, we want to thank our spouses—Victoria, Christine, Tab, and Wencke—for their moral support over the duration of this project. Special thanks go to Keri and Jan-Oddvar's respective children, Sarah, Kyle, Vegard, and Nora, who were asked to have more patience than one could reasonably expect.

Austin, Texas
Trondheim and Bodø, Norway

# Introduction

Larry D. Browning, Alf Steiner Sætre, Keri K. Stephens, & Jan-Oddvar Sørnes

i

This book offers a series of 20 stories about how people from different professions and industries use Information and Communication Technologies (ICTs). Our purpose is to show how people integrate organizational communication with ICTs. Since around 1990, when the Internet and email became common technologies, the work environment has changed dramatically. For example, one of our interviewees said, "If our server goes down and we can't get email, we might as well go home." Our goal is to explore the many and often unpredictable ways that individuals communicate with one another at work via email, phone, or face-to-face meetings. (We include face-to-face communication in this report as an ICT use because our interviewees frequently report the use of face-to-face as a communication technology that has functional strengths and weaknesses much like electronic technologies do.)

We have chosen professionals in two countries: the U.S. and Norway. The U.S. is an obvious choice because of its premier position in the world economy and because of its technological sophistication. Norway, though it has only 4.5 million inhabitants, boasts the highest Internet penetration in the world. Indeed, according to The Economist (quoting OECD), Norway is the only county in the world with a higher GDP per capita than the U.S. The diffusion of advanced ICTs is among the highest in the world in Norway and the United States. Since the late 1980s, Norway has engaged in an ambitious program for telecommunications reform. While previously lagging behind the U.S., they have managed to narrow this historical gap considerably (Bauer, Berne & Maitland, 2002). Norway issued its "National Action Plan for IT" in 1987, making it one of the first countries in Europe to do so, and shortly thereafter many other European countries followed suit, as did the U.S. with its "Agenda for Action" (1993). Norway and the United States are the top two nations in the world in productivity per capita, which is attributed to the countries' use of ICTs.

*Our goal is to explore the many and often unpredictable ways that individuals communicate with one another at work via email, phone, or face-to-face meetings.*

## Stories as Sources of Information

Our premise here is that stories of technology use, drawn directly from individual accounts across a variety of professions, will inform readers about ICT use and how they might make decisions in similar circumstances. We use the story as the device for conveying what we have learned from our interviews because the individual accounts not only contain a compelling human-interest quotient, but provide readers with different opportunities for learning from different parts of a story. Depending on their own level of knowledge and interests, some readers will identify with one theme in the story, others with a different theme in the same story.

*We use the story as the device for conveying what we have learned from our interviews because the individual accounts not only contain a compelling human-interest quotient, but provide readers with different opportunities for learning from different parts of a story.*

For example, one of our interviews from Norway is with a woman who manages her company's internal Webpage. It turns out that she is a virtual gatekeeper for the company with respect to what it communicates to its employees about what it is doing. She describes her efforts to build a credible source of information that keeps employees updated on substantive issues (e.g., the cost and availability of product) and to do so while managing a sensitive and ethical part of organizational knowledge. For instance, she avoids the possibility of insider trading by never posting confidential market information until it's already listed publicly on the Stock Exchange. In still another instance, she tells of a morale problem in one of their South American production units—a problem stemming from the employees' disappointment with their medical benefits. She says the company resolved that problem simply by attending to reports from employees about what they needed in order to be more satisfied with their job. In a third instance, she tells how she implemented a company consultant's plan for improving the company by establishing a style of communication that fosters both employee respect and customer openness. These are a few of the main sub-plots within the story; different readers will naturally relate more to some sub-plots than others.

## The Narrative Approach

Most studies of technology employ the questionnaire as the tool of choice for studying usage. That tool allows a wide sampling because of the ease of collecting questionnaire data with paper-and-pencil tests or over the Internet. But getting a wide sample wasn't our chief goal here. Even though our total data set includes 67 transcribed interviews, of which the 20 we showcase are the richest and most compelling, our approach focuses on individual users—on what narrative theorists would call the "point of view of the narrative actor."

*Our approach focuses on individual users—on what narrative theorists would call the "point of view of the narrative actor."*

Jerome Blumer, in his chapter "Possible Castles" in *Actual Minds, Possible Worlds,* tells of two physicists, Heisenberg and Bohr, visiting the Kronberg Castle in Denmark and commenting on how the castle changes from a structure of stones as soon as one imagines that Hamlet lived there. These physicists could only imagine life in castles, but in our interviews, we could actually ask people how they live with their ICTs—and get answers! We were curious about what it's like to work in a given information environment. We were also interested in giving people great latitude to talk about that experience; we hoped to spontaneously elicit surprising revelations that we'd never have gotten using a more structured approach. One image of the process and effect of in-depth interviewing is that a person's mind is like a container stored in the attic—you can never tell what's going to tumble out of it when you lift it up.

*One image of the process and effect of in-depth interviewing is that a person's mind is like a container stored in the attic-- you can never tell what's going to tumble out of it when you lift it up.*

We will thus showcase specific examples from 20 in-depth interviews where people tell how they use technology—and how they're influenced by it. Because these people were asked only three open-ended questions (e.g., "Would you walk me through a day of your use of the computer?"), they were free to talk about a wide assortment of issues, many of which could never have been anticipated. For instance, when we asked "Gina," a staff person at a U.S. international business consulting company, how extensively ICTs are used in her firm, she dropped a bombshell: In 2002, computer technology is rarely used by the top consultants in her company. Instead, the old-fashioned telephone is the communication medium of choice for giving advice to the CEOs of their client corporations. She stressed that the Internet and email documents have a very low priority in how consultants communicate their advice to CEOs. Such surprises in these cases serve as anchors for other ideas within them.

**Worth Noting**

Concept Pieces

The purpose of the *concept pieces* is to draw the reader's attention toward elements in the stories that they might otherwise have missed. How do the concepts inform an understanding of the stories, and how do the stories illustrate concepts? For example, the chapter on "impression management" identifies the ways in which individuals in organizations strategically "put their best foot forward" when communicating with people whose judgment is important to them. While it is possible to detect these strategies from many instances in our cases, it will be easier still to identify them after having read the impression management piece.

The stories, on the other hand, were written from a distinctly different point of view. They describe a person's experience with ICTs with little or no attention to any conceptual framing of them. We present a table showing some of the links between stories and concepts. Feel free to identify other links between concepts and stories. The stories are presented horizontally and the concepts are laid out vertically. We have also included the country and gender of the interviewee from each story.

One way to use this book is to read all or several of the cases that contain examples of a particular concept. In this way you can learn more about a specific theoretical perspective through multiple stories. For example, if you are studying the concept of "credibility," you can first read that concept chapter and then refer to the grid on pages *xx* and *xxi* and choose the related stories. If you read the chapter, "Over the Hill But on Top of the World: An Atypical Salesperson," you will learn why credibility is considered important by a small business owner and how he uses the Web to search for information to build his credibility in front of his customers.

To see a different view of "credibility", you can also read the chapter titled "Information Will Get You to Heaven." In this narrative, a minister collects historical information by using many different ICTs. Through his research using ICTs, he has accumulated a deep knowledge that he has parlayed into credibility with many of the town's most prestigious members. Still another angle on "credibility" is found in the chapter titled, "From a Distance: Using ICTs for Managing Manufacturing." Here an engineer discusses how he establishes credibility while managing a complicated production process—half a world away.

As you can see from these example cases, credibility is important for people in many different occupations. By reading these three cases you will see actual examples of how credibility is established. These individuals use some ICTs in similar ways, such as turning to the Web when a research tool is needed, to accomplish their credibility objectives. But much diversity is illustrated in the stories since often different ICTs are used to accomplish similar objectives.

## Concepts in the book

The nine concepts of the book are listed below by noting the phrase that most represents the idea and then giving an idea of what the concept is about.

*Rogers' diffusion of innovations* (Rogers, 2003, 1995). The diffusion of innovations research conceptualizes and tracks the way new ideas, both technical and conceptual, are adopted by a group of people in a culture or a community. The research in this area focuses on both the people who adopt innovations—whether they are early or late to take up the practice—and the qualities of an innovation that make it likely to be adopted.

*Weick's organizational enactment* (Weick, 1995, 2001). Karl Weick developed the term "enactment," which is central to his theory of organizational sensemaking. The idea accounts for the way that an organization responds to and shapes its environment through action. He uses the term enactment as a part of a four-stage model of organizing that includes ecological change, enactment, selection and retention. Weick views the organization as extracting equivocal information from its environment, and trying to make it meaningful. As such, organizations learn as they make sense of their environments and themselves.

*Goffman's impression management* (Goffman, 1959). This concept refers to the way an individual or an organization consciously shapes the impressions others have of them by selectively presenting information that will place them in a favorable light. While Goffman's idea was originally limited to the control of face-to-face interactions, the array of media available to individuals who are communicating has resulted in the application of his ideas to ICTs. Impression management is accomplished by anticipating the response of the target of influence and providing a message that impresses them.

*Gidden's structuration theory* (1984). Structuration theory addresses the age-old question of whether individuals have power over organizations or are instead controlled by them. The theory answers the query by taking a middle ground that suggests power swings like a pendulum. At one instant, we are subject to the structures we are in, in another instant we set up our structures by the way we communicate to arrange them. Giddens calls the back-and-forth of this interplay "reflexivity" and he asserts that ICTs allow us to stretch organizational structures across time and space in a manner different from the past.

*Complexity theories* (Anderson, 1999; Holland, 1995). Complexity theories address the circumstances where non-linear relations, and thus surprises, provide the best account for how a system is operating. Complexity theories include such ideas as the emergence of novel outcomes—self-organizing, and unanticipated consequences that result from novel combinations of elements. A key feature of complexity theories is that systems operate in far-from-equilibrium conditions. This refers to the balancing point between the stability of the system and the novelty that provides new information and hence enables it to innovate.

*Organizational and national cultures* (Hofstede, 1980). The concept of culture accounts for differences within nations, organizations, and sub groups. One group of people may do things differently than another group, even though they have the same responsibilities. The simple definition, "how things are done here" is aptly used to highlight how organizational cultures differ.

*Communicator credibility* (Metzger, Flanagin, Eyal, Lemus, & McCann, 2003). This concept addresses how and why the messages of some individuals and organizations are held in high regard and others are not. The classic definition of credibility is a combination of two features: expertness—the person has the professional and technical knowledge to be taken seriously, and trustworthiness—the person can be trusted to consistently speak the truth that he or she knows, even in circumstances where their personal interests might be aided by a different answer than the one they know to be true.

*Garbage can theory* (Cohen, March & Olsen, 1972). The garbage can theory of organizational choice lays out three conditions that make organizations—according to the authors' playful and pejorative term—into "garbage cans." First there are uncertain goals because individuals differ over purpose. Second, there are uncertain preferences since technologies and practices are valued differently. Third, organizational membership changes; people come and people go. As a result of these conditions, four definable entities float in and out of contact in the garbage can. There are problems, solutions, participants, and choice opportunities; furthermore, these entities cohere or slip apart in a temporal rather than a logical manner.

## Practical Questions — *Stories/Concepts*

How do you implement a virtual learning arena to supplement classroom learning?
*Chapter 10. The Frustrated Professor*

How do you get the right mix of personal and ICT skills?
*Chapter 11. Teaching the Good Old Boys New Tricks: Taking ICTs to the Bank*

How do you manage public and private information for a Website?
*Chapter 12. From Blunt Talk to Kid Gloves: The Importance of Adaptability across Culture*

How much should you use ICTs when balancing personal and professional life?
*Chapter 13. Slowing Down in The Fast Lane*

How do you use ICTs to communicate a local presence?
*Chapter 14. Serving the Customer Locally Without Moving There: How to Use ICTs to Project a Local Presence*

How do you adapt to internal and customer preferences across time zones?
*Chapter 15. Overloaded but not Overwhelmed: Communication in Inter-Organizational Relationships*

How do you take advantage of free software and join a worldwide community of technology users?
*Chapter 16. Depending on the Kindness of Strangers: Using Newsgroups for Just-in-Time Learning*

How do you get everyone to use a method provided in an Internet service?
*Chapter 17. Building a Medical Community Using Remote Diagnosis: The Story of DocNet*

What is the symbolic nature of ICT use?
*Chapter 18. Don't Get Between Me and My Customer: How Changing Jobs Shifts ICT Use*

How do you focus on speed and quality to stay ahead of your competitors?
*Chapter 19. Fighting Uncertainty With Intelligence*

What are the ICT choices for managing manufacturing in a global environment?
*Chapter 20. Close Up...From a Distance: Using ICTs for Managing International Manufacturing*

What is the best ICT to use when ease and preference are important?
*Chapter 21. Over the Hill But on Top of the World: An Atypical Salesperson*

When does national culture not make a difference?
*Chapter 22. The Role of ICTs in Maintaining Personal Relationships Across Distance and Cultures*

How important is face-to-face communication in a Web-based business?
*Chapter 23. One in the Hand is Worth Two on the Web: Relying on Tradition When Selling Financial Services*

How do you handle the issue of information confidentiality?
*Chapter 24. Do What You Do Well and Outsource the Rest... Even Guarded Information*

How do you communicate with a technical customer?
*Chapter 25. Orchestrating Communication: The Process of Selling in the Semiconductor Market*

How much information is it useful to have about the product?
*Chapter 26. Nothing Fishy Going on Here: Tracing the Quality of the Seafood Product*

Using ICTs, how do you communicate to people who have experienced personal tragedy?
*Chapter 27. From Information to Emotion: The Changing Use of ICTs Following the 9/11 Tragedy*

What is the role of ICTs in defining public and private communication?
*Chapter 28. Give Me a Cellphone and I'll Give You Trouble: Technology Usage in a Young Start-Up*

How do you quickly become the person at the center of communication?
*Chapter 29. Information Will Get You to Heaven*

| Credibility | Enactment | Garbage Can | Impression Mgmt. | Structuration | Complexity | Diffusion of Innovation | Culture | Media Choice | USA / Norway | Gender: F / M |
|:---:|:---:|:---:|:---:|:---:|:---:|:---:|:---:|:---:|:---:|:---:|
| 2 | 6 | 4 | 5 | 7 | 8 | 3 | 9 | 1 | | |
| ■ | ■ | | ■ | | | | | ■ | NO | M |
| ■ | ■ | | | | | ■ | ■ | ■ | U.S. | F |
| | | | ■ | | | ■ | ■ | ■ | NO | F |
| | | ■ | ■ | | ■ | | ■ | ■ | U.S. | F |
| ■ | | | ■ | ■ | | | ■ | ■ | NO | M |
| | | | | ■ | | ■ | | ■ | U.S. | M |
| ■ | | | | | | ■ | ■ | ■ | NO | M |
| ■ | | ■ | | | | ■ | ■ | ■ | NO | M |
| | ■ | | | | | ■ | | ■ | U.S. | M |
| | | ■ | ■ | | | | | ■ | NO | M |
| ■ | ■ | | ■ | | ■ | | | ■ | U.S. | M |
| ■ | ■ | | ■ | | | ■ | ■ | ■ | U.S. | M |
| | | | ■ | | | | ■ | ■ | NO | F |
| ■ | | | ■ | | | | | ■ | U.S. | M |
| ■ | ■ | | | | | | | ■ | U.S. | M |
| | | | | ■ | ■ | | ■ | ■ | U.S. | M |
| ■ | | ■ | | | ■ | | | ■ | NO | M |
| ■ | | | ■ | | ■ | | ■ | ■ | U.S. | F |
| | ■ | ■ | | ■ | ■ | ■ | ■ | ■ | NO | M |
| ■ | ■ | | ■ | | | | ■ | ■ | U.S. | M |

## Story Summaries

*The Frustrated Professor (Chapter 10)*

This is the story of Gunnar, an award-winning teacher at a business school in Norway. His story illustrates his attempt to implement ICTs in order to increase the value of his courses and decrease the resistance students displayed toward his efforts at innovation. The cat-and-mouse game between Gunnar and his students eventually resulted in his practices spreading to other courses in the business school.

*Teaching the Good Old Boys New Tricks: Taking ICTs to The Bank (Chapter 11)*

Ms. Galvin, the Chief Financial Officer (CFO) of a bank located in an oil-wealthy Kansas community, explains a move toward considerable use of ICTs as a result of consolidation and on-line services in the banking industry. She details why the shift occurred, the struggles she faced while retraining her employees, and the ICTs she now uses to communicate both internally and externally.

*From Blunt Talk to Kid Gloves: The Importance of Adaptability Across Cultures (Chapter 12)*

This story from Norway is about Karen, the Chief Information Officer for NorFoods, a multi-national corporation. She characterizes Norwegians as having a direct and succinct style that is easily misinterpreted by people from other cultures. Being a digital gatekeeper who manages news releases to employees and the outside world, she modifies messages to reduce misinterpretation by other national cultures within the corporation.

*Slowing Down in the Fast Lane (Chapter 13)*

Gina Botticelli is a consultant with an international strategy-consulting firm called "Northwest Associates." She insists on the efficient use of ICTs when working with others in her company. It is Gina's belief that the incessant use of ICTs during the economic surge of the dotcom bubble had become a mindless and numbing routine. Six months after 9/11, she now feels that people are backing off and focusing on their personal lives in a more balanced way.

*Serving the Customer Locally Without Moving There: How to Use ICTs to Project a Local Presence (Chapter 14)*

This story is about InterStock, a small Norwegian firm that uses ICTs heavily to not only serve their customers' brokerage needs but also to qualify as a broker on new stock exchanges as they take their operations into new markets. InterStock uses ICTs to project a local presence into different national markets, when in fact the entire organization is physically located in Oslo, Norway.

*Overloaded but not Overwhelmed: Communication in Inter-Organizational Relationships (Chapter 15)*

In this case, a semiconductor salesperson, Stan Silverthorne, tells us how he has adapted to different ICTs. Stan's company is head quartered in California, but he himself lives two time zones away and works primarily out of his home. Stan explains the different ICTs he must use to communicate within his own organization as well as with his many customers.

*Depending on the Kindness of Strangers: Using NewsGroups for Just-in-Time Learning (Chapter 16)*

This narrative introduces you to several gurus who use newsgroups as the primary source for their just-in-time learning. For small organizations, easy access to experts around the world provides a critical learning link that costs very little. The information received via newsgroup is often of top quality, yet they rarely know much about the actual contributors. These contributors—digital philanthropists—are few and far between, but their advice spans cultural and national boundaries.

*Building a Medical Community Using Remote Diagnosis: The Story of DocNet (Chapter 17)*

This story concerns a small group of enthusiastic pathologists who, quite unaware of the many obstacles facing them, formed an organization they call "DocNet," a Web-based service for all practicing pathologists in Norway. In spite of the potential of this idea—other branches of medicine have already copied it—they have experienced slow adoption rates driven by two factors. Not only are many senior pathologists set in their ways, there is a concern for the security of patient records.

*Don't Get Between Me and My Customer: How Changing Jobs Shifts ICT Use (Chapter 18)*

While many previous studies of ICT use assume that preferences are somewhat fixed, Darrell Urbanski illustrates how different job roles necessitate a changed mix of ICTs. Darrell explains that in his previous job as the director of an international technology association, he used ICTs that kept him connected—a Palm Pilot and scheduling software. Now, as an entrepreneur, he has given up his Palm Pilot because it distracts from communication with his customers and distributors — he now uses a legal pad to take notes at meetings.

*Fighting Uncertainty with Intelligence (Chapter 19)*

The ever-growing popularity of the Internet has revamped the way businesses select, collect, process, analyze, and distribute highly specific and timely information concerning industry rivals. This is the story of Trond Horn, a consultant in a Norwegian cellphone service organization and the strategies he uses for communicating findings to company decision makers, so the company can stay ahead of their competitors.

*Close Up ... From A Distance: Using ICTs For Managing International Manufacturing (Chapter 20)*

Jeff Smith is an engineer who manages a portion of the production process for a U.S. Technology Company that subcontracts its manufacturing of communication hardware to a Pacific Rim company. Jeff says his use of ICTs takes various forms, including phone calls, regular conference calls, some use of video conferences, and the production of videos by its Asian partner, which are streamed onto a Website to display the details of how the product is being made. This level of detail allows Jeff's company to closely monitor intricate production processes from a distance.

*Over the Hill, But on Top of the World: An Atypical Salesperson (Chapter 21)*

Ron Klein is a retired schoolteacher who is now a self-employed water-purification sales-and-service businessman. Ron's distinctive ability consists of drawing expert information and documentation from the Web and communicating it to clients. He has been described as "the worst salesperson," because he refuses to sell equipment that does not serve his customers' long term interests even if they ask for it. Despite this, he has more referral business than he can handle.

*The Role of ICTs in Maintaining Personal Relationships Across Distance and Cultures (Chapter 22)*

Ann Eidsvik is an energy-policy advisor at Energia, a government agency charged with increasing the awareness in Norway of energy conservation and alternative energy sources. She has a worldwide network of personal relationships both from her international schooling and from her work experiences. She notes that "the differences are often greater within a culture than between them," and that people are frequently controlled by technologies, rather than taking personal control of them.

*One in the Hand is Worth Two on the Web: Relying on Tradition When Selling Financial Services (Chapter 23)*

This is the story of Ed, a young entrepreneur who runs a firm that offers investment advice over the Web. Although he uses the Web to market his financial services to potential clients, his story concerns how he develops credibility with his clients by visiting with them face-to-face. This demonstrates his understanding that people prefer direct contact when important deals are being made.

*Do What You Do Well and Outsource the Rest… Even Guarded Information (Chapter 24)*

Bob Reynolds is a marketing specialist in a U.S. software firm that provides information-security for high-tech companies, both in the States and abroad. The firm has found a way to isolate clients' sensitive financial information so that their employees, and others, can't access it and use it improperly. Bob explains how customers are introduced to the software product through Web site visits that allow them to see how the product actually performs.

*Orchestrating Communication: The Process of Selling in the Semiconductor Market (Chapter 25)*

This story details the communication practices of an engineer, Elliott McGuire, who works as a sales specialist in the computer chip manufacturing industry. Three themes help to summarize his practices. He uses ICTs to overcome the geographical distance between the U.S. and Japan, to communicate frequently with a large number of people in his own company who also serve the customer, and to automate details so that human communication can focus on emerging issues.

*Nothing Fishy Going on Here: Tracing the Quality of the Seafood Product (Chapter 26)*

Polar Seafood, a fish-farming company in Norway, is introducing ICTs in every stage of the value chain to ensure better quality, cut cost, and provide better customer service. Arne is a young marine biologist charged with bringing Polar Seafood online. Because seafood is a perishable product, much attention is placed on providing a record of its quality to the many stakeholders in the value chain.

*From Information to Emotion: The Changing Use of ICTs Following the 9/11 Tragedy (Chapter 27)*

Barbara is a staff specialist in an international technology and strategy-consulting firm that serves the chief executive officers of corporations—exclusively. As a researcher and writer she provides technical reports for the company's knowledge base. Barbara tells of her work for this company, her private real estate business, and the use of ICTs to retain a sense of community following the 9/11 tragedy.

*Give Me a Cellphone & I'll Give You Trouble: Technology Usage in a Young Start-Up (Chapter 28)*

This is the story of ICT use, and abuse, of the company cellphones and other ICTs in a small entrepreneurial venture called "Portfolio" that provides large corporations with software for knowledge management within the organization. This story focuses on the company's gift of cellphones to employees and how this action contributed to the blurring of the boundaries between work and private life.

*Information Will Get You to Heaven (Chapter 29)*

This is the story of a minister of a church in a rural community in Arkansas who has established himself as the "local historian" by using the Internet as an information source when he searches family history for members of the community. In this case, we detail how the minister has created genealogies of the families in his community and in doing so gained the favor of his parishioners.

## References

Anderson, P. (1999). Complexity theory and organization science. *Organization Science*, 10(3), 216-232.

Bauer, J. M., Berne, M, & Maitland, C.F. (2002). Internet access in the European Union and in the United States. *Telematics and Informatics*, 19, 117-137.

Cohen, M. D., March, J. G., & Olsen, J. P. (1972). A garbage can model of organizational choice. *Administrative Science Quarterly*, 17, 1-25.

Giddens, A. (1984). *The constitution of society.* Berkeley, CA: University of California Press.

Goffman, E. (1959). *The presentation of self in everyday life.* New York: Doubleday.

Hofstede, G. (1980). *Culture's consequences: International differences in work related values.* Newbury Park, CA: Sage.

Holland, J. H. (1995). *Hidden order: How adaptation builds complexity.* Cambridge, MA: Helix Books/Perseus Books.

Metzger, M. J., Flanagin, A. J., Eyal, K., Lemus, D. R., & McCann, R. (2003). Credibility in the 21st century: Integrating perspectives on source, message, and media credibility in the contemporary media environment. In P. Kalbfleisch (Ed.), *Communication Yearbook 27*, (pp. 293-335). Newbury Park, CA: Sage Publications.

Rogers, E. M. (1995). *The diffusion of innovations* (4th ed.). New York: The Free Press.

Rogers, E. M. (2003). *The diffusion of innovations* (5th ed.). New York: The Free Press.

Weick, K. E. (1995). *Sensemaking in organizations.* Thousand Oaks, CA: Sage.

Weick, K. E. (2001). *Making sense of the organization.* Malden, MA: Blackwell Publishers.

# Media Choice and ICT Use

1

Keri K. Stephens & Alf Steinar Sætre

"Media choice" is a term acknowledging that, when communicating, we often have a variety of media available and that our choices reflect many variables. For example, some people choose to use email instead of voicemail. But why? And why do different national and organizational cultures view technologies each in their own way? Why is face-to-face preferred when building a relationship? The 20 narratives in this book illustrate how expert ICT users both choose and use particular ICTs, alone and in combination. For example, they tend to prefer face-to-face in ambivalent and emotionally sensitive situations. While that preference seems to be nearly universal, these same expert users are often inconsistent with respect to their preference for email versus the telephone. In this chapter, we will introduce you to the various theories and research findings that try to explain media-choice behaviors.

## Determinism or Social Construction?

Current theories of ICT use tend to fall into two camps.

The first is openly deterministic. Theorists who subscribe to this view assume that media choice is invariably rational and thus predictable. For example, they contend that the very features embedded in a particular technology— say, in a fast or slow Internet connection—automatically predict how individuals will browse the Internet.

*Does technology itself determine how it is used, or do we determine for ourselves how we use communication technologies?*

The rival camp's theory is social construction. Theorists who subscribe to this view assume that technology features and social factors are intertwined, and thus together influence ICT use. To extend our example above, a social constructionist would argue that social variables— e.g., the personal desire to access a certain Web site—are often more important than whether one has a fast or slow connection. In the theory section that follows, we present some of the most popular views on ICT choice and use, looking first at the deterministic views and then at the socially constructed ones.

## Technological Determinism: Richness and Conscious Choice

Communication researchers often postulate face-to-face communication as the gold standard and compare all other modes of communication to it. Face-to-face has been considered the ideal communication "channel" because it supposedly has certain unchanging features embedded in it, making it wonderfully versatile. One such feature is the presence of nonverbal cues—for example, facial expressions and hand gestures. Several theories, all of them deterministic, assume that these cues alone make face-to-face the ideal channel (e.g. Short, Williams, & Christie, 1976).

**Key Theory**
Media
Richness

But another deterministic theory, called "media richness" (Daft & Lengel, 1984; Daft, Lengel, & Trevino, 1987; Trevino, Daft, & Lengel, 1990), posits a more comprehensive view of communication channels. According to media-richness theory, a "rich" channel like face-to-face actually has four useful features:

1.  The ability to transmit multiple signals (e.g., nonverbal cues, voice intonations, and the verbal message itself).

2.  The possibility, if not guarantee, of immediate feedback from the receiver.

3.  The opportunity to tailor the message to the real-time situation.

4.  The ease of incorporating conversational language such as slang and ambiguous references.

A "lean" channel like email, on the other hand, is essentially stripped down and thus lacks these four features. Empirical studies employing this theoretical stance like to rank-order ICTs along a continuum of richness. Face-to-face normally ranks the highest, and text-based ICTs, like email and letters, rank the lowest. But while being "lean" can be a serious handicap, there are occasions when "leanness" is actually preferred.

To decide which kind of channel—rich or lean—is preferable in a given case, media-richness theorists use the criterion of "equivocality." This umbrella term, which is itself a bit equivocal, is applied to two different situations: *uncertain* ones and *ambiguous* ones. Uncertain situations are ones where you simply need more

*Figure 1-1: Visual Representation of Media Richness Theory*

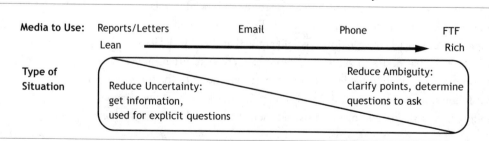

information before you can answer a particular question or complete a task. Ambiguous situations, on the other hand, require you to actually *interact* with someone—perhaps to explore a next direction, to clarify points, or even to determine what points need clarification. (See Figure 1-1 for a visual representation of this theory.)

Let's take an example of each situation. Say you want to remodel your house, and you hire an architect. Handling the project with her strictly by email is likely to be unwise. You'll want to meet face-to-face, study preliminary sketches, hash over likes and dislikes, and then work out a final plan. To achieve all this, a rich channel is ideal—maybe even essential.

But suppose you merely need to tell her that you've now chosen granite for your kitchen countertop rather than Formica. Here you're simply providing a detail to resolve an explicit issue. While you could go to the trouble of arranging a face-to-face meeting to communicate that choice, media-richness theory would remind you that that channel, while effective, would be grossly inefficient here—in effect, overkill.

On the surface, media-richness theory seems eminently logical, in fact incontestable. And it certainly simplifies our thinking about ICTs. We can put them on a nice little menu of if- this, then-that. For example, "If a communication situation is emotional (ambiguous), use face-to-face"; "If you're conveying an instruction or request, use email." Such prescriptions guide people to choose the "right" ICT for the job.

Ah, would that it were that simple!

A decade ago, ICT studies using the various deterministic theories began themselves to be scrutinized (Walther, 1992). What we've now learned is that there is no clear agreement as to how ICTs should be rank-ordered according to richness. Many things can account for these differences. One variable is national culture. Various studies (e.g. Straub, 1994) comparing media perceptions have found that different cultures can perceive channels very differently. (Rice, D'Ambra, & More, 1998 are an exception because they found very few cultural differences.) In Japan, for example, the fax is considered richer than in the U.S. And some cultures highly value the telephone and business memo.

We've also learned that the often-assumed superiority of face-to-face communication over computer-mediated communication (CMC) is actually overstated. Some people who are more practiced using a given ICT will rate it as "richer" than other media, even including face-to-face. And, more surprising still, they report being able, over time, to get a clearer impression of their communication partners that way than if they had actually sat down with them. Furthermore, not all communicators prefer having access to nonverbal cues (Walther & Parks, 2002). Also, in certain situations, asynchronous communication can actually be an advantage. For example, responding via email allows us to ponder, and appropriately time, our response. This will often enhance its quality and thus make email communication ideal.

## The Social Construction of ICTs

In the late 1980's and early 1990's scholars began to look beyond the rational-choice models to consider the potential influence of social and contextual variables on ICT use. An excellent survey of these theories can be found in *Organizations and Communication Technology* (Fulk, Schmitz, & Steinfield, 1990). There, scholars criticize rational-choice models for failing to recognize social contexts, task considerations, and organizational variables. But of course including these extra variables makes the social-construction theories both "messier" and more complex, since now we cannot say flatly that a certain channel is always good for a certain situation. As you read the cases in this book, reflect on your own experiences with ICTs and you'll probably see that you use email differently, at least in some situations, than some other people you know. Social and contextual variables may well explain why that happens.

**Key Theory**
Social
Influence

*Social influence.* One theory in this vein is that of social influence (Fulk, Schmitz, & Steinfield, 1990). Fulk and her associates depart from prior deterministic theories in two primary ways. First, they assume that variables influencing media choice are socially constructed, and second, they claim that the features of both ICTs and tasks are variable. To see how these two major considerations function during ICT choice, we will walk you through their fairly elaborate model.

*Figure 1-2: Social Influence Model*

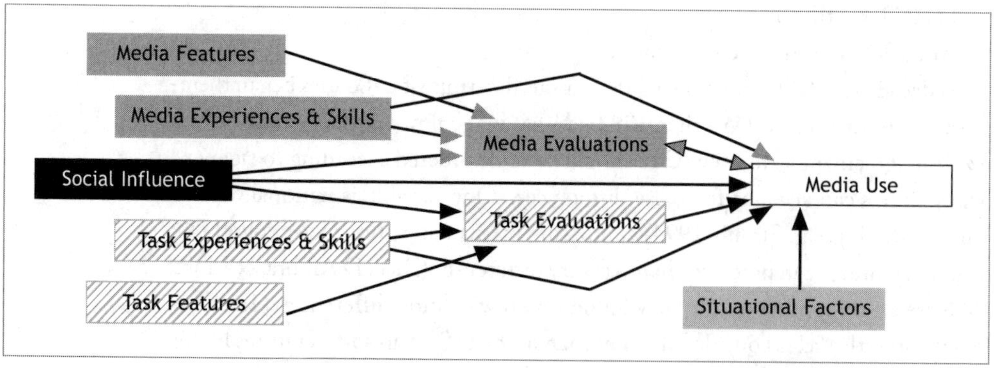

Media Features

Media Experiences & Skills

Social Influence

Task Experiences & Skills

Task Features

Media Evaluations

Task Evaluations

Media Use

Situational Factors

First, you will see that they believe, like deterministic theorists, that some features are embedded in both a medium and a given task, but Fulk and her associates also believe that these features can vary. Further, they believe that an individual's experience with both a task and a medium will influence the medium they choose. For example, if you have used text messaging on a mobile phone for over a year, that experience probably influences if and when you use it in the future. You will not necessarily keep using it more, nor even necessarily better, but you will probably use it more familiarly—and sometimes more wisely. (We say "sometimes" because sheer habit can make prisoners of us all.) Situational variables such as availability of an ICT also influence use. So if you work on an assembly line and never access a computer at work, you probably don't send and receive work-related email.

Finally, at the core of the social-influence model is the claim that social variables influence media use. Social variables include things like (a) overt comments concerning media made by coworkers, (b) the group norms that informally control media choices, (c) how individuals observe others and vicariously learn about media use, and (d) the fact that rationality is itself socially constructed because it is subjectively influenced by others. In one case in this book you will meet a consultant who explains her organizational culture as "a voicemail culture." When she joined her current company, she quickly learned that almost all client-centered communication with CEOs happens via telephone. Because her job involves consulting with clients, it is easier to bill them later when they have been present real-time for the communication exchanges. When they've been on the phone, clients will more likely recall the actual time spent with the consultant because they were involved in the entire process. Emails tend to be problematic from a billing perspective because the client does not simultaneously experience the time the consultant spends handling a request.

In summary, the social influence model says that task and media features, personal experiences, situational factors, social influences—all work together to determine which ICT is chosen for a given situation. As you can see, this departs considerably from media-richness theory. Interestingly enough, empirical research provides only limited support for the social influence model. This support is usually found in qualitative studies, while experimental and survey research find little effect.

*Symbolic meaning of an ICT.* While we now see how social variables can influence media use, several scholars—Sitkin, Sutcliffe, and Barrios-Choplin (1992)—have added another variable to the mix: *channels themselves will develop shared symbolic meanings over time.* For example, face-to-face is a rich medium of communication, but it also silently conveys the message (a symbolic "meaning") that the person arranging the face-to-face meeting considers the topic important enough to justify their physical presence. Sitkin *et al.* therefore developed what they call the Dual Capacity Model showing that every ICT is "a carrier of both data and meaning" (p. 564). Their model is laid out in Figure 1-3 below.

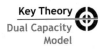

**Key Theory**
Dual Capacity
Model

As you see, their model includes five elements that influence media choice. The first four are similar to what we saw with the Social Influence Model:

*Figure 1-3: Dual Capacity Model*

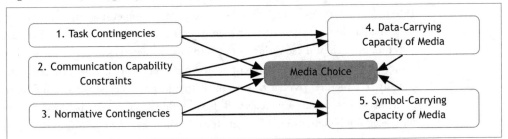

1. *Task Contingencies*: our actual task can influence our choice.

2. *Communication Capability Constraints*: our own strengths and weaknesses, plus those of our communication partners and the organization itself, limit and enable our communication efforts.

3. *Normative Contingencies*: our organization's norms for media use place expectations on us.

4. *Data Carrying Capacity of the Media*: the physical features of a given channel will influence its use.

The fifth element—the *Symbolic Carrying Capacity of Media*—is the new contribution to our understanding of how people choose their media. This element suggests, as we saw a minute ago, that media can send symbolic (silently perceived) messages that are independent of the message itself (the data). This suggestion has been studied by Trevino, Webster, and Stein (2000), who found that respondents actually can articulate the symbolic meanings of their media choices (face-to-face meetings signal a desire for involvement and teamwork, letters signal formality, and fax signal urgency). And they found that these perceptions are consistent over time. But they also found, curiously, that the symbolic view of email has changed in the past decade. When first used, it symbolized a low-priority response. That is no longer universally true. (In the chapters ahead, we will see just how complex this issue is.)

*Organizational culture can determine the symbolic meaning of an ICT.*

Trevino *et al.* made another important discovery, namely, the symbols carried by the various ICTs don't necessarily cross organizational borders: "Depending upon the organizational culture…meetings may represent teamwork in one setting and time wasted in another" (p. 179). O'Sullivan (2000) offers a reason for this: ICTs can "embody symbolic meaning reflecting the codes and values of the organization" (p. 412).

*Structurational influences.* While the social influence model and the concept of symbolic meaning have taught us how ICT use is shaped by social interaction, these theories don't account for how ICT use in turn shapes organizational structures (Contractor & Eisenberg, 1990; Rice & Gattiker, 2000). Essentially, many of the theories we have discussed thus far fail to consider that media choice and use inevitably change over time. To understand more about the interaction between ICTs, their users, and the organization, and how all this interaction causes change, scholars are relying on something called "structuration theory" (Giddens, 1984). "Structuration" deals with how the parts of something are interrelated. Take media choice. We have just seen in this chapter how many variables can affect it. So each of these variables needs to be considered as a part of the media-choice process. A major component of structuration theory is what Giddens calls "duality of structure." What this means is that just as social structures influence individuals, these same individuals will also be influencing social structures. "Structure" need not be something physical. It can include general procedures that span time and space (Giddens). The way people use ICTs, for example, can fall under

**Key Theory**
Giddens'
Structuration
Theory

the rubric "general procedures." So "duality of structure" reminds us that ICT use is not a one-way street. While users clearly rely on structures (norms, expectations, "rules") to guide their ICT use, they also have the ability to change those very structures.

Structuration is especially useful when studying groups because it helps us understand how they interact with technology. For example, it's often been observed that when the same ICT is introduced to multiple groups, they'll use it differently and often in ways contrary to the original design. In "Adaptive Structuration Theory" (AST), Poole and DeSanctis (1990) call such modifications "ironic appropriation," underscoring the sometimes amusing incongruity between what inventors of an ICT expected its use to be and how it is actually used. Let's say two workgroups, one in accounting and one in sales, get the same off-the-shelf software program—maybe Microsoft PowerPoint. Invariably they will use it in different ways. The accountants might import their graphs into PowerPoint and then use the program for formal group presentations. The salespeople, meanwhile, needing to prepare snazzy presentations for customers, might import lots of pictures of products, use fancy animation techniques, and then email the presentation to the client. Studies of groups have found that ICT users decide the "appropriate" use of a given technology for themselves. Orlikowski (2000) calls these "technologies in practice" (p. 407) and argues that technologies themselves change over time, which might explain why people use technology differently if they change jobs or have new communication responsibilities.

## Comparing Deterministic and Social Constructionist Perspectives

These non-deterministic perspectives challenge some of the central tenets of media richness. Consider your own use of email. While email was designed for simple information exchange, today you might also use it for task management (e.g., creating a "to do" list based on your morning's emails) and for archiving (e.g., creating folders to organize and save messages). The application of these additional features of email and their meanings are socially constructed.

The social-constructionist perspective illustrates that ICT use is more complex than the deterministic theories would suggest because we are not simply relying on specific features of an ICT to guide us in how we *Using ICTs is complex.* "should" use them. The term "social construction" better explains how the social variables interact with technology over time and preclude us from creating a simple "How to Communicate with ICTs" guide.

You will notice in our stories that follow that individuals are not always consistent in how they use the same ICT. Indeed, they are often even unaware of the choices they make. And these "choices" might not even deserve the name "choices." For example, Trevino and associates (2000) found that attitudes toward an ICT and behaviors weren't related. While they found this puzzling at first, they explain the finding by suggesting that ICT use is not voluntary, especially in an organizational context. This is why a person's having a negative attitude toward an ICT such as meetings might not let us predict their decreased use if meetings are expected in their organization. Typically, an organization's norms rule. (But not always! As we've seen, users can be stubbornly independent.) You can see, then, that the term "choice" is at least a bit illusory. That is why, in this book, when speaking of people's ICT preferences, we prefer the verb "use" over "choose." It quietly acknowledges the social construction of ICTs. While "use" includes the element of conscious individual choice, it still allows for situations where choice is either unconscious or non-voluntary.

Having discussed a few theories that have been advanced concerning ICT use, let's look at another possible explanation for why subsequent testing has not always supported them. Isolating ICT use from actual practice, as many studies have done, obscures our ability to see how people typically use ICTs in combination. Walther and Parks (2002) theorize that "communication efficiency may rest on sequences or combinations of media rather than on isolated choices about a single medium" (p. 534). You will notice in many of the cases that people clearly describe using an ICT such as email first and then picking up the phone to see if the email was received. Walther and Parks further speculate that communicators may not search for the "best" or most optimal ICT for a given task. The reason, they suggest, is that one task in isolation does not provide us with the entire picture of a user's communication strategies. So a user might send a hasty email, sloppily composed, and then flesh out their ideas in a subsequent meeting that same morning because that task is part of a larger strategy. If we only studied the email or the face-to-face meeting in isolation, we'd miss how the task was fully accomplished. So, as we study ICT use in the future, we need to focus on how people *actually* use ICTs, not just how they *say* they use them.

### Pulling Theory Together to Guide an Understanding of Narratives of ICT Use

The theoretical background above should encourage you to explore the stories in our book from multiple perspectives. Although it's tempting to read the chapters simply as a how-to guide for using ICTs—and we expect it will in fact prove instructive in that regard—we urge you always to ponder the *variables* that might influence each person we showcase. And there are many. These stories offer abundant examples of how organizations themselves both help and hinder their employees' use of ICTs. In addition, individuals bring to their ICT use certain preferences based on their prior experiences, personality, or specific tasks. And, no less important, each individual will vary in how fully conscious they are of their recipients' needs. By reading the narratives using a broad lens, you can learn much more than just "What is email good for?" Keep in mind, the technologies we discuss here are ever-changing, ever-evolving. Some, like the once popular fax, have now nearly disappeared. So it's important for us all to focus on general principles about ICT use—principles that we can then apply to future technologies as they arrive on the scene.

*The stories in this book show examples of how organizations both help and hinder their employees' use of ICTs.*

# References

Contractor, N.S., & Eisenberg, E.M. (1990). Communication networks and new media in organizations. In J. Fulk and C. Steinfield's (Eds.), *Organizations and communication technology* (pp. 143-172). Newbury Park, CA: Sage.

Culnan, M.J., & Markus, M.L. (1987). Information technologies. In F.M. Jablin, et al. (Eds.), *Handbook of organizational communication. An interdisciplinary perspective* (pp. 420-443). Newbury Park CA: Sage.

Daft, R.L., & Lengel, R.H. (1984). Information richness: A new approach to managerial behavior and organization design. In B.M. Staw & L.L. Cummings (Eds.), *Research in organizational behavior* (Vol. 6), (pp. 191-233). Greenwich, CT: JAI.

Daft, R.L., Lengel, R.H., & Trevino, L.K. (1987). Message equivocality, media selection, and manager performance: Implications for information systems. *MIS Quarterly, 11*, 355-366.

Fulk, J., Schmitz, J., & Steinfield, C.W. (1990). A social influence model of technology use. In J. Fulk and C. Steinfield's (Eds.), *Organizations and communication technology* (pp. 117-140). Newbury Park, CA: Sage.

Giddens, A. (1984). *The constitution of society*. Berkeley, CA: University of California Press.

Orlikowski, W.J. (2000). Using technology and constituting structures: A practice lens for studying technology in organizations. *Organization Science, 11*, 404-428.

O'Sullivan, P.B. (2000). What you don't know won't hurt me: Impression management function of communication channels in relationships. *Human Communication Research, 26*, 403-431.

Poole, M.S., & DeSanctis, G. (1990). Understanding the use of group decision support systems: The theory of adaptive structuration. In J. Fulk and C. Steinfield (Eds.), *Organizations and communication technology* (pp. 173-193). Newbury Park, CA: Sage.

Rice, R.E., D'Ambra, J., & More, E. (1998). Cross-cultural comparison of organizational media evaluation and choice. *Journal of Communication, 48*, 3-26.

Rice, R.E., Gattiker, U. (2000). New media and organizational structuring. In F. Jablin & L. Putnam (Eds.), *New handbook of organizational communication* (pp. 544-581). Newbury Park, CA: Sage.

Short, J., Williams, E., & Christie, B. (1976). *The social psychology of telecommunications*. London: Wiley.

Sitkin, S.B., Sutcliff, K.M. & Barrios-Choplin, J.R. (1992). A dual-capacity model of communication media choice in organizations. *Human Communication Research, 18*, 563-598.

Straub, D.W. (1994). The effect of culture on IT diffusion: E-mail and fax in Japan and the U.S. *The Institute of Management Sciences, 5*, 23-47.

Trevino, L.K., Daft, R.L., & Lengel, R.H. (1990). Understanding managers' media choices: A symbolic interactionist perspective. In J. Fulk and C. Steinfield's (Eds.) *Organizations and communication technology*. Newbury Park, CA: Sage.

Trevino L.K., Webster, J., & Stein, E.W. (2000). Making connections: Complementary influences on communication media choices, attitudes, and use. *Organization Science, 11*, 163-182.

Walther, J.B. (1992). Interpersonal effects in computer-mediated interaction: A relational perspective. *Communication Research, 19*, 52-90.

Walther, J.B., & Parks, M.R. (2002). Cues filtered out, cues filtered in: Computer-mediated communication and relationships. In M.L. Knapp and J.A. Daly (Eds.) *Handbook of interpersonal communication* (pp. 529-563). Thousand Oaks, CA: Sage.

# The Role of Credibility and Trust in ICT Studies: Understanding the Source, Message, Media, and Audience

Keri K. Stephens & Alf Steinar Sætre

**2**

In many business situations today, face-to-face communication can feel essential. One reason is that regardless of the occasion—a prospective sale or merger, a debate over internal restructuring, an issue involving some co-worker's grievance—we're constantly searching for truth. To evaluate the veracity of another, we often depend on what we glean from non-verbal communication. We'll look for nervously blinking eyes, sweating skin, and uncomfortable body movement, even though we want to believe that people would never lie to our face.

But of course, face-to-face communication is not always practical. In place of it, a variety of ICTs are used to send, receive, search for, and filter information. This complicates our search for truth. How can we assess the credibility of that information? In the present chapter we focus on the issue of credibility, examining it from four perspectives: source, message, media, and audience.

*When using ICTs, how do we assess the credibility of information or people?*

## Source Credibility

The credibility literature has a rich past reaching all the way back to Aristotle, who first popularized the term "ethos" in his seminal study of effective argumentation, *On Rhetoric*. Ethos is a person's trustworthiness, or credibility. Aristotle saw it as a composite of their perceived (1) intelligence, (2) character, and (3) goodwill. For centuries after Aristotle, it was felt that he had really had the last word, so few advancements were made. Then, during World War II, credibility research surged in the U.S. because the government sought to persuade its citizens to support yet another war. Psychology professor Carl Hovland and his associates at Yale University became involved in this effort and studied how perceptions of credibility affected attitude change—an area of inquiry now called "persuasion research". They found that a source's credibility is evaluated using two criteria: their expertise and their perceived *trustworthiness*. These findings parallel two of Aristotle's original beliefs concerning credibility, since expertise is similar to intelligence and trustworthiness is a strong component of character.

**Key Theoretical Contribution**

*For the past several decades McCroskey and his colleagues have determined that trustworthiness and expertise are two critical components of source credibility.*

Whereas credibility is a perception composed of many variables, the two variables most commonly discussed are expertise and trustworthiness. In his studies of source credibility, McCroskey (1966, 1982) has developed a fairly reliable survey instrument that consists of dichotomous items to measure both expertise and trustworthiness. Expertise consists of measures such as intelligence, training, and competence. Trustworthiness includes traits denoted by adjectives such as "ethical," "honest," "moral," and "genuine."

*Trust.* Of these two variables, trust has been researched from many different disciplinary perspectives and is most relevant to the study of ICTs. In 1998, the Academy of Management Review created a special topic forum to discuss the interdisciplinary nature of trust. Rousseau, Sitkin, Burt, and Camerer (1998), after extensively reviewing the trust literature, concluded that people can experience trust when they are in at least a slightly vulnerable situation and have confident expectations in the outcome. Sheppard and Sherman (1998) also added to this definition by concluding that risk and interdependence are necessary conditions of trust, and risk perceptions change as interdependence increases. The final root assumption shared by all disciplines is that trust is psychological and important to organizational life (Rousseau et al.).

There are two types of trust relevant to a discussion of ICTs: *knowledge-based trust* and *initial trust formation* (McKnight, Cummings, & Chervany, 1998). Knowledge-based trust is established over time. For example, if you access a Website, purchase a product there, and have a positive experience with the product, you are using historical data to help you decide if you trust the Website and the organization it represents. Initial trust formation is different. According to McKnight and his associates, when people have no prior knowledge about a source, they use a combination of psychological and environmental factors to ascertain its trustworthiness. This perspective is grounded in four theories:

1.  Personality-based trust, which asserts that one's ability to trust is formed in childhood (Bowlby, 1982; Erickson, 1968).

2.  Institution-based trust, which contends that our environment affects our security (Shapiro, 1987).

3.  Cognition-based trust, which privileges first impressions over ongoing personal interactions (Brewer, 1981).

4.  Economics or calculative-based trust, which contends that individuals make trust choices based on rationally derived costs and benefits (Lewicki & Bunker, 1995; Shapiro, Shepard, & Cheraskin, 1992).

In the research literature, studies of how teams work together often explore how people assess trustworthiness when ICTs are used. These findings show us how trust is developed despite geographical barriers. In their study of geographically dispersed computer-mediated teams, Meyerson, Weick, and Kramer (1996) found that high levels of computer interactivity reduced both ambiguity and un-certainty while strengthening trust. In high-trust teams, this interactivity is mani-fest through a combination of frequent communication and meaningful feedback (Jarvenpaa, Knoll, & Leidner, 1998).

Having discussed a major component of credibility, trust, let's return to the overarching concept and its implications for ICT use.

*Evaluating source credibility.* In the years following the identification of trust and expertise as core components of credibility, many studies, primarily with paper-and-pencil questionnaires, began to explore how people evaluate source credibility. The findings varied with respect to the characteristics seen as influencing credibility-characteristics such as likeability (e.g., McCroskey, 1966), safety (Berlo et al., 1969), extroversion (McCroskey), dynamism (Berlo et al.), and similarity to the speaker (Atkinson, Brady, & Casas, 1981). While everyone agreed that credibility is important, researchers disagreed over what actually constitutes it and influences it.

Then, in 1999, McCroskey and Teven returned to Aristotle's original conceptualization and explored his third element, *goodwill.* Aristotle vaguely de-fined goodwill as the positive feeling toward another that in some way has earned our respect. Using statistical analyses, McCroskey and Teven found that goodwill has three distinct ingredients: (1) understanding, (2) empathy, and (3) responsiveness. They also concluded that goodwill can be an enor-mously helpful characteristic when people need to open communication channels. Of particular importance to studies of ICTs is the ingredient they term "responsiveness." McCroskey and Teven defined "responsive-ness" as "involv[ing] one person acknowledging another person's commu-nicative attempts," and said "it is judged by how quickly one person reacts to the communication of another, how attentive they are to the other, and the degree to which they appear to listen to the other" (p. 92). When people communicate asynchronously using ICTs such as email, voicemail, TM (Text Messaging), and IM (Instant Messaging) and SMS (Short Message Service), responsiveness is important. If someone receives an email and then responds several days later, the initial sender might be frustrated and thus interpret that slow response negatively. McCroskey and Teven concluded that goodwill is a "meaningful predictor of believability and likeableness and should take its place in the conceptual and operational future of communication research dealing with ethos and source credibility" (p. 101).

*Recently McCroskey and Teven have re-examined the goodwill component of credibility, a concept originally introduced by Aristotle.*

While most credibility research focuses on interpersonal credibility, scholars suggest that the concept also extends to organizations (Gass & Sieter, 1999). In the cases discussed in this book, both individual-level and organizational credibil-ity are present. When we move into the organizational realm, there are several considerations that relate to credibility. First, organizations normally want to project a positive image, and they attempt to do this in such departments as public rela-tions, advertising, and sales and marketing. Maintaining a good public image is so critical that some researchers are now studying how organizations can restore a tarnished image (Benoit, 1995).

## Message Credibility

*In addition to source credibility, a message's content, structure, and delivery also affect perceptions of credibility.*

Whereas credibility is something that an organization or an individual might have, what people say-the actual message-also influences how their credibility is perceived. Historically, credibility research has focused mostly on assessing the source. But researchers (e.g. Hovland, Janis, & Kelley, 1953; Metzger, Flanagin, Eyal, Lemus, & McCann, 2003) suggest that we also consider the credibility of the message itself. The main considerations here are a message's content, structure, and delivery:

1.  **Content** concerns issues such as: "What is the topic? Is the message news, political, entertainment, or interpersonal?"

2.  Message **structure** concerns the clarity of its organization.

3.  Message **delivery** concerns how the source presents the message. This includes such things as the rate, enunciation, and word choices used in delivery.

While the first two elements—content and structure—are directly applicable to all types of ICTs, delivery—i.e., speech rate or enunciation—is specific to an individual's oral communication. Since the cases in this book are written, not spoken, delivery, as defined in this context, cannot easily be assessed. For this reason, here we focus only on the first two elements. The cases that follow exemplify several types of information content: *commercial*, *leisure*, and *reference*. Commercial content involves something being sold. Leisure content, also broadly called "entertainment," involves leisure activities and hobbies. Reference information, meanwhile, involves sources being queried to provide solutions for business problems or to help individuals learn more about their jobs.

Organizations also cast messages that are evaluated based on content considerations. We mentioned previously that times of crisis are critical credibility tests for an organization. Coombs (1999, 1995) studies crisis message strategies—the content—and believes that organizations often try to shift the blame, deny, offer assistance to victims, or use credible outside sources to boost their own credibility.

While the message content will normally differ with the organization, the value to an organization of maintaining credibility over time is similar to that of an individual. Imagine being forced to defend your actions when someone starts a vicious rumor about you. Now imagine that you tell your best friend one story and a family member another. When they talk and discover your inconsistencies, your credibility is questioned. Similar things also happen to organizations. Scholars suggest that organizational responses, especially during a crisis, should be consistent across all stakeholder groups (Barton, 2001; Coombs, 1999; Ogrizek & Guillery, 1999) because consistency is critical for credibility-building (Coombs) and for maintaining organizational legitimacy (Massey, 2001). This means that the messages displayed on an organization's Website must be the same as what they separately communicate to the media.

People also rely on their past knowledge of the organization to help them assess the veracity of crisis information. Cowden and Sellnow (2002), studying Northwest Airline's image-repair strategies after a pilots' strike, found that "audiences are likely to reject organizational messages during a crisis situation that are inconsistent with past actions" (p. 215). So people listen to the content of messages and are cognizant of consistency over time.

Besides content, the structure of the message affects its perceived credibility. Think back to the last Webpage you visited that contained too much disorganized information. Were you angry at the organization that created the site? Did you leave the site in search of an alternative? Several of the narratives in this book elaborate on these feelings, corroborating that disorganization is ill-tolerated. We look for Websites that are well-organized and easy to use. By providing us structure, these sites communicate credibility.

## Media Credibility

As we examine ICTs that participate in the communication process, we should also look to prior literature that examines how people project credibility onto different ICTs. While this view assumes a deterministic view toward a given ICT, it provides one lens for evaluating how people assess credibility. Most mass-communication literature is based on comparisons of media prior to the birth of the Internet. Research has compared the perceived credibility of newspapers verses TV and has found that as TV has become more diffused in the U.S., it has become more believable (Roper, 1991).

The credibility of the Web has also received some attention. Metzger et al. (2003) reviewed this literature and concluded that when comparing the Web to more traditional media, (1) people use similar criteria for evaluation, and (2) the Web is not ranked considerably higher or lower in credibility. But there are still very few studies on Web credibility, and these early conclusions might change over time.

Another challenge with these research findings is that with source, message, and media becoming intertwined, it's hard to sort out what is influencing perceptions of credibility (Chaffee, 1982). This makes sense when we adopt a social-constructionist view of credibility and begin to see it as co-created between a user and a given situation.

Many studies have focused their media-credibility assessments on one type of message content, the news. Why? Because they have been funded by news-related organizations. But many other types of message content are important, too, especially with respect to newer ICTs as information sources. As we move into studies of the Web, scholars like Flanagin and Metzger (2001) are expanding the content to include genres such as entertainment, commercial, and reference information. Even with this expansion in content, though, the studies to date have achieved mixed results across several cultures (e.g., Flanagin & Metzger; Kim, Weaver, & Willnat, 2001; Mashek, 1997; Online News Association, 2001; Schweiger, 2000), and it's not clear that the Internet as an ICT has an embedded amount of credibility.

Similar issues exist with other ICTs. For example, Shin and Cameron (2003) studied how journalists and public-relations practitioners in the U.S. and Korea perceived the credibility of 20 different ICTs. They found both cultural and professional differences in the perceptions of many ICTs. One explanation for these differences is that there are raw cultural differences between the U.S. and Korea (Shin & Cameron). If they are correct, then it's quite possible that credibility does not rest inside an ICT; rather, it is a perception that will change depending on individual and social variables.

## Audience Considerations

Until now we have presented the different factors that can influence credibility; however, without an audience, the other factors essentially float in a pool of possibilities. After all, credibility is a perceived trait. It is the audience that evaluates the source, message, and media to determine overall credibility. Not only do different people have varying attitudes, knowledge, and involvement with respect to a given issue, but all of these issues can change over time. Imagine that you have just heard a news broadcast about some manufacturing company that is using child labor to make its products. Depending on your view of child labor, you might react in several different ways: (1) you decide to do nothing and continue using the product; (2) you stop using the product, but say nothing to anyone else; or (3) you not only stop using the product, but you become vocal about your distaste for this practice. Chances are that your personal views on the issue will color how you view the credibility of this manufacturing organization. On the other hand, of course, if you never listen to the news, you remain ignorant of the company's practice and are thus unaffected by it. Now imagine yet another scenario. Imagine that your family is from the very same country where the children are being forced to work, and five years ago you immigrated to Norway to escape this condition. In this latter case, you are heavily involved in the issue. You can see, then, how an audience's attitudes, knowledge, and involvement with the issue (Petty & Cacioppo, 1986) all contribute to perceptions of credibility.

*Ultimately, the audience decides if a source, message, and medium are credible.*

Audience factors are particularly relevant for ICT use. Even though our study focuses on expert users, you will still notice that they often perceive the credibility of a given ICT differently.

## Fluid Model Depicting Credibility Considerations

To help us visualize the intertwined nature of source, message, media, and audience, see Figure 2-1. This is not the first time that scholars have suggested that at least some of these areas overlap (Chaffee, 1982; Kiousis, 2001), but the diagram illustrates the importance of how they overlap when looking at many ICTs. Metzger et al. (2003) describe the complex situation with the Internet as "offer[ing] a mind-boggling array of information from a mélange of providers" (p. 31). As information increases, perhaps the message area of this diagram expands and assumes a dominant role. In other situations, the source may be the primary contributor; thus, the diagram should be viewed as fluid and capable of increasing or decreasing in the overlapping areas. To appreciate the interaction between these variables, consider the following scenario:

> In one of the narratives that follows, a minister (source) is using ICTs (media) as a way to collect and distribute genealogy information (message) to members of a community (audience). This process results in his own credibility being enhanced. But it's hard to disentangle the four factors and pinpoint which one is most responsible for this desirable outcome. Certainly the nature of his job contributes some source credibility. And his proficiency with ICTs also lends him credibility, since this is a coveted asset. Knowledge, after all, is power. But who's to say if his ICT skills would be valued with a different audience? Furthermore, if he were distributing a different type of information (e.g., health, as opposed to genealogy), it's also unclear how that might affect his credibility.

*Figure 2-1: Factors Affecting Overall Perceptions of Credibility*

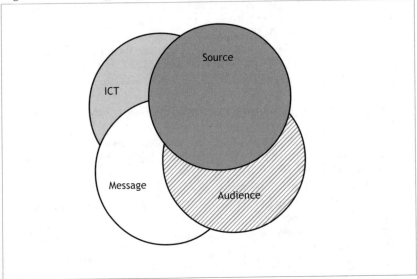

## Relating Theory to Practice

Armed with this discussion of the history of credibility and the four different considerations for ICTs, you should be ready to delve into the narratives. With respect to source credibility, keep in mind that credibility rests on how we evaluate the source's expertise, trustworthiness, and goodwill. While these statistically-derived factors of credibility were derived from studies of human-speaker credibility, there are certainly opportunities to use them as a frame to examine ICT use. We also introduced the idea that since message and media credibility are intertwined-indeed, often with source credibility as well—they are helpful, but not necessarily meant to be stand-alone ways to evaluate credibility. Finally, any discussion of credibility is incomplete without acknowledging the key role of audience perceptions. These four components work together to co-create the perception of ICT credibility.

# References

Atkinson, D.R., Brady, S., & Casas, J.M. (1981). Sexual preference similarity, attitude similarity, and perceived counselor credibility and attractiveness. *Journal of Counseling Psychology, 28,* 504-509.

Barton, L. (1993). *Crisis in organizations: Managing and communicating in the heat of chaos.* Cincinnati, OH: Southwestern Publishing.

Benoit, W.L. (1995). *Accounts, excuses, and apologies: A theory of image restoration.* Albany: State University of New York Press.

Berlo, D.K., Lemert, J.B., & Mertz, R.J. (1970). Dimensions for evaluating the acceptability of message sources. *Public Opinion Quarterly, 33,* 563-576.

Bowlby, J. (1982). *Attachment and loss. Volume 1: Attachment.* New York: Basic Books.

Bradley, B.E. (1974). *Fundamentals of speech communication: The credibility of ideas.* Dubuque, Iowa: WM.C. Brown Company Publishers.

Brewer, M.B. (1981). Ethnocentrism and its role in interpersonal trust. In M.B. Brewer & B.E. Collins (Eds.), *Scientific inquiry and the social sciences* (pp. 214-231). San Francisco: Jossey-Bass.

Chaffee, S.H. (1982). Mass media and interpersonal channels: Competitive, convergent, or complementary? In G. Gumpert & R. Cathcard (Eds.), *Inter/Media: Interpersonal communication in a media world* (pp. 57-77). New York, NY: Oxford University Press.

Coombs, W.T. (1995). Choosing the right words. *Management Communication Quarterly, 8,* 447-477.

Coombs, W.T. (1999). *Ongoing crisis communication: Planning, managing and responding.* Thousand Oaks, CA: Sage.

Cowden, K., & Sellnow, T.L. (2002). Issues advertising as crisis communication: Northwest Airlines' use of image restoration strategies during the 1998 pilot's strike. *Journal of Business Communication, 39,* 193-219.

Erickson, E.H. (1968). *Identity: Youth and crisis.* New York: Norton.

Flanagin, A.J., & Metzger, M.J. (2001). Perceptions of Internet information credibility. *Journalism and Mass Communication Quarterly, 77,* 515-540.

Gass, R.H., & Sieter, J.S. (1999). *Persuasion, social influence, and compliance gaining.* Needham Heights, MA: Allyn & Bacon.

Hovland, C.I., Janis, I.L., & Kelley, H.H. (1953). *Communication and persuasion.* New Haven: Yale University Press.

Jarvenpaa, S.L, Knoll, K., & Leidner, D.E. (1998). Is anybody out there? Antecedents of trust in global virtual teams. *Journal of Management Information Systems. 14,* 29-64.

Kim, S.T., Weaver, D., & Willnat, L. (2001). Media reporting and perceived credibility of online polls. *Journalism & Mass Communication Quarterly, 77,* 846-864.

Kiousis, S. (2001). Public trust or mistrust? Perceptions of media credibility in the information age. *Mass Communication & Society, 4,* 381-403.

Kramer, R.M., & Tyler, T.R. (1995). *Trust in organizations: Frontiers of theory and research* (pp. 166-195). Thousand Oaks, CA: Sage Publications.

Lewicki, R.J., & Bunker, B.B. (1995). Trust in relationships: A model of trust development and decline. In B.B. Bunker & J.Z. Rubin (Eds.) *Conflict, cooperation and justice* (pp. 133-173). San Francisco: Jossey-Bass.

Massey, J.E. (2001). Managing organizational legitimacy: Communication strategies for organizations in crisis. *Journal of Business Communication, 38*, 153-183.

McCroskey, J.C. (1966). Scales for the measurement of ethos. *Speech Monographs, 33*, 65-72.

McCroskey, J.C. (1982). *An introduction to rhetorical communication.* Englewood Cliffs, NJ: Prentice-Hall.

McCroskey, J.C. & Teven, J.J. (1999). Goodwill: A reexamination of the construct and its measurement. *Communication Monographs, 66*, 90-103.

McKnight, D.H., Cummings, L.L., & Chervany, N.L. (1998). Initial trust formation in new organizational relationships. *Academy of Management Review, 23*, 473-490.

Metzger, M.J., Flanagin, A.J., Eyal, K., Lemus, D.R., & McCann, R. (2003). Credibility in the 21st century: Integrating perspectives on source, message, and media credibility in the contemporary media environment. In P. Kalbfleisch (Ed.), *Communication Yearbook 27*, (pp. 293-335). Newbury Park, CA: Sage Publications.

Meyerson, D., Weick, K.E., and Kramer, R.M. (1996). Swift trust and temporary groups. In R.M. Kramer and T.R. Tyler (Eds.), *Trust in Organizations: Frontiers of Theory and Research* (pp. 166-195). Thousand Oaks, CA: Sage Publications.

Online New Association. (2001). *Digital journalism credibility survey.* Retrieved April 25, 2003 from http://www.journalist.org/Programs/ResearchText.htm.

Ogrizek, M., & Guillery, J.M. (1999). *Communicating in crisis: A theoretical and practical guide to crisis management.* New York: Aldine de Gruyter.

Petty, R.E., & Cacioppo, J.T. (1981). *Attitudes and persuasion: Classic and contemporary approaches.* Dubuque, IA: William C. Brown.

Roper Organization. (1991). *America's watching: Public attitudes toward television.* New York: Author.

Rousseau, D.M., Sitkin, S.B., Burt, R.S., & Camerer, C. (1998). Not so different after all: A cross-discipline view of trust. *Academy of Management Review, 23*, 393-404.

Schweiger, W. (2000). Media credibility—experience or image? A survey on the credibility of the World Wide Web in Germany in comparison to other media. *European Journal of Communication, 15*, 37-59.

Shapiro, S.P. (1987). The social control of impersonal trust. *American Journal of Sociology, 93*, 623-658.

Shapiro, D.L., Sheppard, B.H., & Cheraskin, L. (1992). Business on a handshake. *Negotiation Journal, 3*, 367-377.

Sheppard, B.H., & Sherman, D.M. (1998). The grammars of trust: A model and general implications. *Academy of Management Review, 23*, 422-437.

Shin, J.H., & Cameron, G.T. (2003). The interplay of professional and cultural factors in the online source-reporter relationship. *Journalism Studies, 4*, 253-273.

# Rogers' Diffusion of Innovations

**3**

Larry D. Browning & Jan-Oddvar Sørnes

Information and communication technologies like the Internet have revolution-ized how we work with information and communicate with others. The high rate of adoption of such technologies, at least in the Western world, has turned both the workplace and the household into arenas where we increasingly depend on these technologies in our daily tasks.

We now use email and SMS (Short Message Service) to stay in touch with suppliers, customers, colleagues, or students, when we earlier used technologies such as fax, telephone, or just an old fashioned letter or banner on the info board for the same tasks. Similarly, the Web is used to publish information about our company, products, university courses, and selves, when we previously used bro-chures, catalogs, handouts, and resumes. We substitute new ICTs such as the Internet for what were our existing communication practices. To be more specific, ICTs are perceived as more efficient, cheaper, faster, and perhaps more accurate ways of carrying out existing communication tasks. But the unprecedented possi-bilities offered by ICTs can leave both people and organizations overwhelmed with the information available "just in time" and with the rich repertoire of new ways to communicate throughout the world. The combination of innovation and the market stimulate the search for new tools and methods. They also help organizations transform data and information into business advan-tage.

*The diffusion of innova-tions theory addresses the evolution and rate of tech-nological development by tracking the types of people who innovate.*

In this chapter we will introduce Rogers' Diffusion of Innovations Theory (2003, 1995). This influential social-science research theory helps illuminate the interplay between society and technology. It's perspective enjoys widespread influence not only in studies of technology, but in such areas as hybrid seed corn in the United States (Ryan & Gross, 1943), birth control techniques in India (Rogers, 1995), psychoanalysis in Ar-gentina (Plotkin, 1998) and the spread of the Internet (Rogers, 2003). In a nut-shell, the diffusion of innovations theory addresses the evolution and rate of tech-nological development by tracking the types of people who innovate. The idea helps to contextualize ICTs in relation to human actions.

The best known component of the theory is the typology of five personality types appraised by their readiness to innovate. The five categories of innovation types are a major contribution to marketing and organization theory, and offer a reliable forecast of how an innovation is increasingly implemented by a population-a factor called the "Rate of Adoption:"

*Figure 3-1: Rate of Adoption*

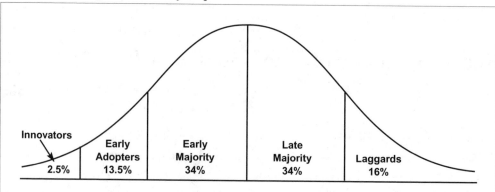

*Innovators* are eager to try new ideas. Their "interest leads them out of a local circle of peer networks and into more cosmopolite social relationships" (Rogers, 1995, p. 263). "Venturesomeness is almost an obsession with innovators" (Rogers, 2003, p. 282).

*Early adopters* are more locally oriented than innovators and are "a more integrated part of the local social system" (1995, p. 264). They often have more years of education and are considered the "individual to check with" (2003, p. 283) before trying out a new idea. They also have more change agent contact than later adopters. As such, they often help trigger the "critical mass" necessary for an innovation to be widely adopted (2003, p. 283).

*The early majority adopters* pick up the idea just before the average member of a social system does though they seldom hold leadership positions (Rogers, 2003). They are an important part of the diffusion of innovations in that "they provide the interconnectedness in the system's networks" (Rogers, 1995, p. 265). Because they are more deliberate in choosing to adopt an idea, their decision period is "relatively longer" than the earlier two types of adopters (2003, p. 284)

*The late majority adopters* come on board just after the average member does, prompted by increasing network pressures. Peer pressure is often necessary to motivate this group (Rogers, 1995, p. 265). Because their resources are more scarce than the earlier adopter types, they are more skeptical and require more uncertainty to be removed before they adopt (Rogers, 2003)

*The laggards'* point of reference is the past (Rogers, 2003). They often will adopt an innovation after early adopters have already moved on to a new innovation. Basically, they are suspicious of innovation and change agents. Like the late majority adopters, they have less resources than earlier adopters and wait until they are certain a new idea will not fail before they adopt (Rogers, 2003).

## Opinion Leadership and Peer Leadership

To understand the value of knowing the rate of adoption, we need to consider how organizational leadership affects people's adoption within firms. Rogers characterizes leadership, as it applies to adopting technology, as essentially falling into two types: *Peer leadership*, where people innovate and learn from each other to continually build their competence at ICT use, and *opinion leadership*, where early adopters demonstrate and compel others to use the technology as they do. Let's look more closely at these two types.

Opinion leadership consists of one person influencing others' use of ICTs. Rogers defines opinion leadership as "the degree to which an individual is able to influence other individuals' attitudes or overt behavior informally in a desired way with relative frequency" (Rogers, 2003, p. 27). Peer leadership, meanwhile, occurs when a big enough group of people has achieved expertise such that their joint level of competence sets a standard that everyone else adopts. In some of our cases, interviewees report how they have influenced others' use of ICTs, but the tone of the interviews suggests that they are actually communicating with peers who are equally sophisticated. There is substantial peer influence on technology use in our stories. For example, now that email is more than a decade old, there is a fairly wide level of highly confident use. Rogers says that peer-to-peer relationships create the level of sharing that causes the technology to be widely used. These two approaches to technology leadership inform us not only about leadership types but also about two models for diffusion that operate simultaneously.

*Rogers defines opinion leadership as "the degree to which an individual is able to influence other individuals' attitudes or overt behavior informally in a desired way with relative frequency."*

One type of diffusion is the *linear model*—which is a one-way diffusion instance wherein a person or organization acts as a change agent by informing a "potential adopter about a new idea" (Rogers, 1995, p. xvi). The linear model is consistent with "opinion leadership" because it is maintained by the individual's technical competence, social accessibility, and conformity to the system's norms" (p. 27). System norms in our cases are represented through ICT use. There is ample evidence that customer expectations help shape these norms.

**Linear Model**
Person or organization acts as a change agent.

In general, when opinion leaders are compared with their followers, we find that they:

1.  "are more exposed to all forms of external communication," (Rogers, 1995, p. 27)

2.  are more cosmopolite,

3.  "have somewhat higher social status" (p. 27), and

4.  "are quite innovative" (although the exact degree of innovativeness depends, in part, on the systems norms) (p. 27).

Our cases show signs of opinion leadership in that most of our interviewees are exposed to all forms of external communication via ICTs, but nothing indicates that they are more cosmopolitan or have higher social status than others referred to in their interviews; they seem to communicate with their equals. Peer leadership emerges to account for more of their practices than their own individual innovation. Another possibility, and the one that fits our cases, is the convergence model. "Decentralized diffusion systems more closely follow a convergence model of communication, in which participants create and share information with one another in order to reach a mutual understanding" (p. 365). This level of sharing is prominent in our cases. For most of them, the authoritative decisions to install ICTs occurred some time earlier for the people in our cases. Our interviewees give the impression that they now are responsible for decisions about use. Rogers would call these "optional innovation-decisions" (p. 28), or "contingent innovation-decisions" (p. 30)—decisions made only after a prior innovation decision.

**Decentralized Diffusion Systems**
Participants create and share to reach mutual understanding.

In a decentralized diffusion system, decisions are broadly shared by clients and likely adopters; here, innovations spread through horizontal networks among the clients (Rogers, 1995, p. 365). Where hierarchy is evident in a few of our stories, most of them take place in horizontal networks.

## Examining ICTs as an Innovation in Norway and the U.S.

One impetus for studying the diffusion of ICTs in the workplace is the fact of their ubiquitousness. From 1990, a time that one of our interviews marks as the beginning of the use of email, to a dozen years later, when our last interview was completed, we saw a dramatic change in the use of the Internet. One interviewee called this a "grand innovation" that, from the earliest part of this time period, changed the way people communicate, especially in organizations, in most of the Western world, including Norway and the U.S. (Rogers' own tracking of the Internet, 2003, identifies approximately the same date for the "Internet's rise").[1] This change is especially true for professionals, for whom the now-standard Internet communication devices and groupware such as PowerPoint, Excel, and of course, Word, became commonplace in Norway and the United States.

*The diffusion of advanced ICTs is among the highest in the world in both Norway and the United States where more than half the population use the Internet daily, which is certain to affect communication patterns and lifestyles.*

The diffusion of advanced ICTs is among the highest in the world in both Norway and the United States where more than half the population use the Internet daily, which is certain to affect communication patterns and lifestyles (Lundby, 2002). There is also a similarity between the U.S. and the Nordic countries on structural, regulatory, and competitive variables in the telecommunications sector (Bauer, Berne, & Maitland, 2002). These two countries are similar in having advanced information societies, which serves to lessen the often confounding effects of differential digital-divide issues and user-experience levels (Henten & Kristenson, 2000).

---

[1] The same interviewee also noted that beyond the Internet as a single innovation, there have been no major innovations in ICTs since that time. While there have been incremental improvements, nothing comes near the effect of that initial innovation.

The implementation of ICTs in Norway and the U.S. has been produced by a "diffusion effect" which is the "cumulatively increasing degree of influence upon an individual to adopt or reject an innovation, resulting from the activation of peer networks about the innovation in the social system" (Rogers, 1983, p. 245). In other words, in a business or organizational performance context, whether in the public or private sector, people tend to adopt the innovation because people important to them, whether customers or peers, communicate via ICTs.

## The Relativity and Uncertainty of Innovations

Even though ICTs have diffused in these two countries, their range of use may be quite varied. This would not surprise Rogers who quotes a critic of relativity by saying "Perhaps the most alarming characteristic of the body of empirical study of innovation is the extreme variation among its findings, what we call instability" (Rogers, 1995, p. 104 citing Downs and Mohr, 1976). Yet Rogers acknowledges that innovation is a "relative" dimension in that one has "either more or less of it than others in a social system" (Rogers, 1983, p. 245).

*In these cases, people offer many different strategies for sequencing the use of the phone, email, and face-to-face communication.*

Our examples are "relative" and show a lot of differences from person to person on how ICTs are used. In these cases, people offer many different strategies for sequencing the use of the phone, email, and face-to-face communication. For our work, the relativity of ICTs is not a methodological failing because ICTs are put to such varied uses with lots of different strategies. Also, innovation is a relative or local concept in that it only needs to be seen as new by the individual or the unit doing the adoption. As Rogers says, "it matters little, so far as human behavior is concerned, whether or not an idea is 'objectively' new as measured by lapse of time since it's first use or discovery" (Rogers, 1995, p. 11).

Relativity is also caused by uncertainty that can be generated by the innovation itself. Because an innovation is defined as "an idea, practice, or object that is perceived as new by an individual or another unit of adoption" (Rogers, 1995, p. 11), its original or best application may be unknown to those using it.

Rogers' theory is also relevant in that it allows us to study the broader social contexts of diffusion as well as its practical effects. He says, "A social system is defined as a set of interrelated units that are engaged in joint problem-solving to accomplish a common goal" (Rogers, 1995, p. 24). For example, our case on competitive intelligence at the Norwegian telecom provider shows the social context of the teams who have been assembled to solve company problems. Their statements about the trust they have in relying on each other's opinion are a good indication of social context.

*"Diffusion is a kind of social change, defined as the process by which alteration occurs in the structure and function of a social system."*

A "diffusion is a kind of social change, defined as the process by which alteration occurs in the structure and function of a social system" (p. 6). So a "technological innovation can increase uncertainty (about the consequences of its use) while reducing uncertainty by the particular information base (or channel) of the technology" (p. 13). This suggests that diffusion is fluid and can be seen in many different ways.

## Boosterism and Criticism in Diffusion Research

Rogers critiques his own work by raising the idea of boosterism or a "pro-innovation bias" (Rogers, 1995, p. 100; Rogers, 2003, Chapter Three, "Contributions and criticisms of diffusion research") which assumes that all innovation should be diffused and adopted by all members of a social system, that it should be diffused more rapidly, and that the innovation should be neither re-invented nor rejected. He has incorporated this concern in the last 20 years of his work by offering analyses of the negative and unintended consequences of technology. His concern for an even-handed treatment of innovation causes him to define unanticipated consequences as "changes due to an innovation that are neither intended nor recognized by the members of a social system" (1995, p. 419). He also expands the possible outcome of an innovation by characterizing the decision that produced it as being desirable or undesirable, direct or contingent, or anticipated or unanticipated (p. 30-31).

*Rogers defines unanticipated consequences as changes due to an innovation that are neither intended nor recognized by the members of a social system.*

Diffusion of Innovations theory makes use of the idea of uncertainty and information, when uncertainty is the number of alternatives in relation to the number of possibilities. "Uncertainty implies a lack of predictability of the future" (Rogers, 1983, p. xvii). Uncertainties open up the possibility of the effects of individual power when diffusions of innovations occur. As Rogers says, "Every innovation has some degree of "status conferral" (p. 217). Articulating a set of effects of diffusion as social, status-giving, and capable of producing unintended consequences opens up the theory to assess all kinds of diffusion effects, both positive and negative.

## Characteristics of an Innovation

Another major contribution of Rogers is the delineation of an innovation's characteristics. His listing is considered classic knowledge because it accurately details what is necessary for an innovation to be implementable. Following an example for classroom analysis offered by Contractor, Stohl and their associates (2003), we use Rogers' characteristics of an innovation to review the Frustrated Professor case in this book.

1.  "Relative advantage" is the degree to which an innovation is better than the one it supersedes (Rogers, 2003, p. 229). For example, in the college professor case in this book, a course Website offers an efficient warehouse for instructional material related to a course because it replaces the need to distribute paper copies and it can be easily updated and circulated to the students (Contractor, Stohl, et al. 2003). "The degree of relative advantage is often expressed in economic profitability, in status giving, or in other ways" (Rogers, 1995, p. 212).

2.  "Compatibility" is the degree to which an innovation is consistent with the practices, values, and past experiences of the potential adopter (2003, p. 240). Again, in the professor case, course Web tools permitting faculty to upload documents previously created in word processors are more likely to be adopted than Web tools that require instructors to re-type course-related materials.

3.  "Complexity" is the extent to which an innovation is perceived as difficult to comprehend, implement and use (Rogers, 2003, p. 257). Technologies tend to be adopted in learning environments if they are easily adaptable (low in complexity). In the professor case, a Web authoring system called ClassFronter is used, and the system provides the professor with considerable flexibility to customize a course Website without having to learn advanced programming (Contractor, Stohl, et al. 2003).

4.  "Trialability" is the extent to which an "innovation can be experimented with on a limited basis" (Rogers, 2003, p. 258). Again, using the professor case, it takes the professor a short period of time to learn the basics of a course Website, but to fully exploit the software would take months of regular application (Contractor, Stohl, et al. 2003). This level of difficulty makes trialability moderate in the Professor story; in reality, his nerd-like skill with the computer made his experimentation go without a hitch.

5.  "Observability" is the degree to which an innovation's results are generally apparent (Rogers, 2003, p. 258). The results of some ideas are easily observed and communicated to others, whereas some innovations are difficult both to observe and to describe. In the case of the professor, the use of on-line courses is very visible to both students and fellow colleagues, and is hence more apt to be adopted by others who see its advantages.

These five characteristics show that successful innovations are adopted because they are seen as viable substitutes for existing practices.

## Communication Channels as a Special Type of Innovation

The term "channel" is a crucial term for studying innovation because it has a widely diverse set of applications, yet a very specific set of meanings. Does channel mean "I am channeling a great spirit," or "you can find it on Channel Five," or "the invasion took place across the English Channel." For the Oxford Dictionary a channel is "The course in which anything moves" (1993, p. 371). For innovations there is at least a dual meaning.

A channel, in innovation parlance, can be the means for adopting the new thing or the channel can be the innovation itself. An innovation might be the

*The term "channel" is a crucial term for studying innovation because it has a widely diverse set of applications, yet a very specific set of meanings.*

means or ends of another innovation.  For example, a new device carried over the Internet can be both a new channel and the carrier of new content.  Support for this concept shows up in Rogers' statement: "Diffusion is the process by which an innovation is communicated through certain channels over time among members of a social system" (Rogers, 1995, p. 5).  In this definition, three things are under consideration; the innovation, the channel and the social system. The most complex situation would be when all three of these are new.  In the case of the Web as an ICT, two of these components can be new simultaneously—a new ICT to communicate a new innovation.

*Diffusion is the process by which an innovation is communicated through certain channels over time among members of a social system.*

ICTs are channels, so they are both innovations and carriers of innovations. As mentioned previously, an innovation is broadly defined as an idea, practice, or object that is perceived as new.

Diffusion of innovations is useful for studying the cases in this book because the idea matches the kinds of ICTs that Rogers studies. He says that one of the advantages of communication research is that it can analyze any type of innovation.  His work on channels is useful for analyzing cases in this book because he sees a distinction between mass-media channels, such as radio and newspapers, and interpersonal channels, which usually involve a face-to-face exchange between individuals. He sees that "interpersonal channels are more effective in persuading an individual to adopt a new idea, especially if the interpersonal channel links two or more individuals who are near-peers" (Rogers, 1995, p. 18).

For example, in our cases, face-to-face communication is often described by our interviewees as a special communication technique that is usually limited in access, in most instances, because other forms, such as the phone and email, are easier and less expensive.  A channel, like face-to-face communication, is also a technology because our cases show that individuals have rationales, recipes, and rules for using it as a social technology.  By Rogers' own definition of a channel, face-to-face certainly qualifies. He says, "A communication channel is the means by which messages get from one individual to another" (Rogers, 2003, p.18).  Here, the innovation is the change in the channel itself—it is reflexive—that is, we use an innovation to select the channel, and the use of the channel changes our innovation choices. For example, we use the Internet to select email and if we find that email introduces faster responses, we then increase our use of the Internet, our innovation. Channels are the only type of innovation that is not only an innovation itself, but also plays an important role as an innovation carrier.

*A communication channel is the means by which messages get from one individual to another.*

## Summary

Rogers' Diffusion of Innovations theory is applicable to the cases in this book because the rate of technological change experienced by the interviewees is substantial. While they advocate and speak for the technology they use, they are also willing in some cases to identify specific negative effects of ICTs. One notable characteristic is the substantial variance in the cases—there is no single preferred use of the technologies.

## References

Bauer, J. M., Berne, M., & Maitland, C. F. (2002). Internet access in the European Union and in the United States. *Telematics and Informatics*, 19, 117-137.

Contractor, N. S., Stohl, C., Monge, P. R., Flanagin, A., & Fulk, J. (2003). Communication in the global \workplace: Advanced E-quad collaboration tools to support multi-university cooperative learning and teaching. Working paper: http://www.spcomm.uiuc.edu/users/nosh/manuscripts/equad.pdf

Downs, G. W., Jr., & Mohr, L. B., (1976). Conceptual issues in the study of innovations. *Administrative Science Quarterly*, 21, 700-714.

Henten, A., & Kristensen, T. M. (2000). Information society visions in the Nordic countries. *Telematics and Informatics*, 17, 77-103.

Lundby, K. (2002). The networked Nordic region: Connections and community. *ICA News*, September, 8-9.

Plotkin, M. (1998). The diffusion of psychoanalysis in Argentina. *Latin American Research Review*, 33, 271-277.

Rogers, E. M. (2003). *Diffusion of innovations* (5th ed.). New York: The Free Press.

Rogers, E. M. (1995). *Diffusion of innovations* (4th ed.). New York: The Free Press.

Rogers, E. M. (1983). *Diffusion of innovations* (3rd ed.). New York: The Free Press.

Ryan, B., & Gross, N. C. (1943). The diffusion of hybrid seed corn in two Iowa communities. *Rural Sociology, 8*, 15-24.

# A Garbage Can Model of Information Communication Technology Choice

**4**

Larry D. Browning & Alf Steinar Sætre

In 1972, Cohen, March, and Olsen, three scholars from the United States and Norway, introduced what they called the "Garbage Can model of organizational choice." Many real-world observers believe that this model, besides being theoretically provocative, accurately describes the factors affecting organizational choice (Bendor, Moe, & Shotts, 2001). We agree. And we believe it offers a unique angle on technology and problem-solving, which are prominent in our cases.

The "Garbage Can" metaphor is meant to focus attention on the sheer messiness of organizational life, at least with respect to the various choices that participants make. Decisions, problems, opportunities, and participants are all mixed together in a single container, so to speak, which limits the ability to control any one of them.

This messiness is created by three initial conditions.

The first is "inconsistent and ill-defined preferences" (Cohen, March, & Olsen, 1972, p. 1), which means that decision-makers often disagree among themselves about their "organization's goals" and thus find it difficult to act on them in concert. Compounding matters, individual decision-makers will themselves change their minds about goals over time, even though preferences are expected to be stable (March & Olsen, 1986, p.15). In fact, preferences are notably unstable. Organizational goals have a habit of changing once needs are met. For example, Sematech, a U.S. computer consortium, was created in 1987 to help America regain market share in the production of computer chips–a market that had been lost to Japan in the mid-1980s. By 2002, Sematech had changed its name to International Sematech and had included Asian countries, including Japan, to set world standards for chip production. Why? Because its initial goal had been achieved, which allowed it to envision a more expansive international goal (Browning & Shetler, 2000). This is an example of the Garbage Can because what was a part of the problem (Japan) now became part of the solution (an international standard).

*Decisions, problems, opportunities, and participants are all mixed together in a single container, so to speak, which limits the ability to control any one of them.*

The second condition is "unclear technology" (Cohen et al., 1972, p. 1), which means that even if there were complete agreement among decision-makers on how best to reach goals, which there is not, the preferred technology to accomplish these goals cannot be known in advance, but instead must be found through trial and error. This makes the organization an even messier place, because people learn chiefly through making choices and failing—but eventually learn from their mistakes (Sitkin, 1992). That reality is acknowledged in such corporate slogans as IDEO's "fail often in order to succeed sooner." Because an organization's members must regularly take action under conditions of uncertainty, their day-to-day ICT use is in fact a "practice" much the same as medicine is commonly called a "practice"—that is, one must often act before knowledge of the results can be known for sure.

*Because technology is unclear, organizations constantly search for the best way to do things, including non-electronic methodologies (like TQM) and ICT tools (like PowerPoint).*

Because technology is unclear, organizations constantly search for the best way to do things, including non-electronic methodologies (like TQM) and ICT tools (like PowerPoint). Models of effective performance have half-lives, just as products do, and frequently change over time (Peters, 1992). How and why methods change is a key question of how individuals innovate—or, in some cases, refuse to. For example, laggards, fearful of change, prefer old ways, whereas innovators eagerly pick up new ways, if only to try them out. Having an unclear technology means that arguments over the "best way" among organizational members are usually legitimate. They're ultimately healthy, too. Such arguments force decision-makers to regularly articulate and reaffirm their preferences.

The third Garbage Can condition is "fluid participation" (Cohen et al., 1972, p. 1), which means that organizational members often change jobs, be it within departments or between firms. And even within firms, participants will vary in how much time and effort they'll give to different organizational problems. Because of this variation in participation, some members of the organization may be even less involved than outsiders, such as vocal customers influencing upgrades of a software program. There are several examples of this in our cases, where people work more closely with people in different countries than they do with colleagues sitting in the next office. This makes the participation boundary of the organization uncertain and sometimes causes changes to occur capriciously.

*Lots of messy processes, unstructured relationships, warring goals, and uncertain results.*

These three conditions make up the reality of organizational life. Whereas the traditional model postulates neat flow charts, dependable reporting structures, clear managerial goals, and predictable outcomes, the Garbage Can postulates just the opposite: lots of messy processes, unstructured relationships, warring goals, and uncertain results. And it emphasizes the flux within every organization-new things are constantly getting added, with old things getting dumped out. Some things get tangled and connected; others get separated and remain distant.

The three conditions of organizational life that we have just identified create four "streams of variables," say Cohen, March, and Olsen. Let's look at these four factors now: problems, solutions, participants, and choice opportunities.

## Problems

Problems are the concerns of people, both inside and outside the organization (Crecine, 1986), that require attention. The term "problems" is the anchor dimension for Garbage Can theory because it acknowledges what every CEO knows: resources should go chiefly to the problem-solvers. But first someone has to decide what things are problems. Deciding implies a selectivity of attention and probable intergroup conflict over whose problems count the most, as well as what solutions are best.

A common theme in problem-solving is deciding who "owns" the problem, because the owner will be responsible for taking action to solve it while others may give it only marginal attention, even though they are affected by the end-result. In short, just as there is a division of labor, there is a division of "problems" to be sorted and assigned for action. Another theme in problem-solving is deciding whether the resources allocated are the right amount and mix for the job. In most instances, when a problem is viewed as complex and uncertain, greater resources will be directed toward solving it.

## Solutions

Solutions are answers actively looking for questions, just as, say, a plumber is searching for leaks or an editor is combing for grammatical mistakes. This notion may be the most creative component of Garbage Can theory, because it reverses traditional wisdom. Instead of viewing individuals in organizations as problem-solvers, it views them as solution-marketers. A solution is somebody's product, be it a new consumer product or a new process for performing some work routine. By this way of thinking, a new ICT, say, is not merely a solution to a problem but a source of identity to its originator, who will keep marketing that same product in new places by "actively looking for a problem to which it is a solution" (Crecine, 1986, p. 84). So, for example, when Bob Noyce, founder of Intel, created the microchip, it was far more expensive to manufacture than the simple transistor it aimed to replace. Noyce's strategy was to temporarily sell chips at a loss in order to popularize them and prove their greater effectiveness. Here, then, was an instance of providing a solution even before there was a perceived problem.

*A solution is somebody's product, be it a new consumer product or a new process for performing some work routine.*

The original archetypes for Garbage Can theory were large, non-profit institutions like religious organizations, hospitals, and educational programs, the reason being that they tend to have more abstract goals that are subject to varying interpretations. But later researchers found that the theory also applies to for-profit organizations. For example, one overarching goal in high tech is to provide the "next big thing"—some solution that either sparks a new product, like Texas Instruments' pocket transistor radio in the 1950s, or an entire communications medium like the Internet.

Garbage Can Theory makes "offering solutions" a key organizational action and suggests such an orientation is ingrained because most people aspire to progress, to "move ahead." An organization is "a collection of choices looking for problems, issues and feelings looking for issues to which they might be an answer, and decision-makers looking for work" (Cohen et al., 1972, p. 2). All the interviewees for this book told us how they themselves used the Web and ICTs as business or personal solutions. The examples are wonderfully varied. In one instance, a technician uses ICTs to track the quality of salmon in a Norwegian fish-farming operation. In another setting, a banker in a small Kansas town manages her office via email because it lets her avoid time-consuming small talk (a local tradition) and frees her up for other things. In still another instance, a consultant uses the Internet while working on an international consulting team to conceptualize a new Internet product that needed inventing. Another person provides legitimating Internet research for risky strategic decisions for a corporate board. And yet another person, a stock trader, describes how he runs his firm over the Internet. In all these cases, someone is offering a solution through the use of technology, and they define themselves through their solutions.

*In all these cases, someone is offering a solution through the use of technology, and they define themselves through their solutions.*

## Participants

Participants vary in participation. First, of course, they simply "come and go" (Cohen et al., 1972, p. 3). But they also have limited attention spans as well as varying interest in the multiple tasks they face, so they must choose to allocate their attention based on how much time they have to participate. "Participation in a particular choice situation is constrained by other demands on a participant's time and attention" (Crecine, 1986, p. 85).

Garbage Can theory uses the term "participants" for an organization's members because it focuses on the varying degree of investment that members have in their work. The use of the term "participants" appears quite conscious. Calling them "agents" would have emphasized their organizational ties. Calling them "players" would have emphasized the game-like finesse required for working in the politics of a complex, often tumultuous organization. Calling them "social actors" would have emphasized the influence of their local culture and the requirements of living in a changing world. But "participants" draws attention to their individual involvement or investment in their work environment. Organizations (Garbage Cans) can be evaluated in part by what participants do in response to the uncertain conditions they face. One advantage of ICTs is their integrative potential-their ability to make participation in the organization's life available to more people (Stohl, 1995). Participation is particularly applicable to ICTs because sharing information is a dramatically different activity than participating with other kinds of resources, information not being a "limited" resource. As Stohl (1995) observes:

**Participation**
ICTs allow more people to participate in an organization.

> *Information is a different type of resource than rubber or gold. Information is shared rather than exchanged (i.e., when I give it to you, we both have it), diffuse rather than limited (i.e., when it leaks, there is more rather than less of*

*it), and it cannot be owned (i.e., you may own a book but you cannot own the facts, ideas, and content contained within). (p. 135)*

While there are many instances in our interviews where individuals treat their information as scarce and share it only under certain conditions, the larger picture of participation is one of a less constrained culture of information-sharing and cooperation. For example, one person solves a problem in a production plant in South America only because she has learned of it from a local supervisor's Internet message and then worked on that same Net to solve it.

One of Garbage Can's theoretical positions that helps us properly understand the term "participants" is its emphasis on the role of *choice*, which focuses on people moving *toward* what they prefer, as opposed to *decision-making*, which implies people eliminating alternatives until only one possibility remains. The idea of participation suggests that an individual chooses whether to be involved in the various tasks at hand. Introducing ICTs into an organization's culture clearly affects participation because it lowers the threshold for involvement.

**Involvement Threshold**
Choice vs. Decision-making

## Choice Opportunities

"Choice opportunities" are occasions when an organization is expected to produce a decision: "People must be hired, promoted, or fired; money spent; and responsibilities allocated" (Cohen et al., 1972, p. 3). These examples imply a hierarchy, or power structure, that allocates resources and legitimizes making choices. Choice opportunities are less apparent in this book than the other three features of Garbage Can theory because our cases offer few examples of organizational control through a supervisor directing an employee's behavior. But since our ICT users report taking many significant actions, we believe that choice opportunities have drifted down the hierarchy. Instead of being prompted by a hierarchical structure, deadline pressures and cultural norms often prompt action, and an individual's feeling for doing "the right thing."

If one accepts these four conditions as realistic, then it's easy to view an organization in Garbage Can terms. Given its emphasis on individual involvement (participation), how technology is used (solutions), what technology is directed toward (problems), and the amount of freedom that the individual now has, thanks to ICTs, to make decisions (choice opportunities), this theory throws a lot of emphasis on individual practices and methods under conditions of uncertainty.

## The Status and Application of Garbage Can Theory

The Garbage Can concept, including the conditions and factors that produce it, has significantly influenced our understanding of organizations as institutions (Bendor, Moe, & Shotts, 2001). By the fall of 2003, there were already over 750 references to the term "Garbage Can" in the management literature since 1980. It is especially popular in studies of organizational strategy, organizational decision-making, organizational communication, and, most of all, computer simulation of organizational processes. It's popular because the Garbage Can conditions are suppositions for "Bounded Rationality," which is a key idea in explaining why decision-makers are only somewhat rational about the choices they make. The three conditions within the Garbage Can that we've been discussing create uncertainty, which in turn causes a limited (or bounded) amount of knowledge from which to operate-hence messiness.

This messiness makes applying rationality to the Garbage Can difficult, since the Garbage Can is driven by timing (the co-occurrence of events) rather than by rationality. As March and Olsen say,

> *Rather than relying on a consequential order to form linkages within decision making, garbage can models of decision-making assume a temporal order. That is, problems, solutions, and participants are assumed to be connected by virtue of their simultaneity (1986, p. 11).*

Management paradigms depend on offering usable solutions, and the ones offered by the Garbage Can—*spend time, persist,* and *interpret history* (Cohen & March, 1986)—can appear self-evident to students as well as seasoned managers. But these ideas affirm the need for knowing and telling the organization's story. One problem with Garbage Can theory is that it is a Grand Theory (that is, it applies to most organizations) but its authors remind us that its use is actually limited because it is just one view among many (March & Olsen, 1986; Olsen, 2001).

## Garbage Can Patterns in the Cases

Cohen, March, and Olsen's Garbage Can Theory of organizational choice allows us to look for the following patterns in the cases we'll be presenting here:

1. Problems and solutions are prominent, whereas choice opportunities and participants (other than the protagonist) are less easy to distinguish, but in most cases are tied to the problem-solution pairing.

2. Technology, while appearing predominantly as a solution looking for a problem to solve, also appears as a problem itself because of the wide variation in beliefs about how ICTs are best used. While the two dimensions of problems and solutions are independent in the theory (Olsen 2001), they are reflexive and interchangeable to participants.

3. People tend to avoid identifying problems until a solution for them exists or is anticipated. Such patience makes decision-making safer.

4. Problems and solutions are inseparable; in the language of another concept piece in this book on "enactment," a problem combined with a solution amounts to a reflexive pairing. The identification of one is almost always accompanied by the other.

5. Since a *person* must make the problem/solution pairing through cognitive and communicative action, problems and solutions remain as separate facts or entities until the actor brings them together.

6.    Participants (who are they?) and participation (what is their access to decision-making?) become entwined. ICTs routinely make participation easier, and remove excuses for a participant being "too busy to respond."

7.    The ability to participate is also determined by one's competence with ICTs. A person unskilled with them is kept out of participation or is humored as an anomaly who requires special and usually redundant technologies.

8.    A person's skill level changes their reason for not participating. Instead of its being the "demands on participant's time," as the Garbage Can theory states (p. 3), it's determined by technological competence.

*Organizational reality is seldom as linear, structured, rational, and predictive as many theories of organizational choice and decision-making would have us believe.*

Cohen, March, and Olsen's Garbage Can Model of organizational choice focuses our attention on the fact that organizational reality is seldom as linear, structured, rational, and predictive as many theories of organizational choice and decision-making would have us believe. The cases presented in this book are based on rich qualitative data and reflect much of the complications and complexities of everyday life in these organizations—a life that the Garbage Can Model is well suited to explain.

## References

Bendor, J., Moe, T. M., & Shotts, K. W. (2001). Recycling the garbage can: An assessment of the research program. *American Political Science Review, 95,* 169-190.

Browning, L. D., & Shetler, J. C. (2000). *Sematech: Saving the U.S. Semiconductor Industry.* College Station, TX: Texas A & M University Press.

Cohen, M. D., March, J. G., & Olsen, J. P. (1972). A garbage can model of organizational choice. *Administrative Science Quarterly, 17,* 1-25.

Cohen, M. D., & March, J. G. (1986*). Leadership and ambiguity: The American college president.* Boston: Harvard Business School Press.

Crecine, J. P. (1986). Defense resource allocation: Garbage can analysis of procurement. In J. G. March and R. Weissinger-Baylon (Eds.*), Ambiguity and command: Organizational perspectives on military decision making.* Marshfield, MA: Pittman Publishing.

March, J. G., & Olsen, J. P. (1986). Garbage can models of decision making in organizations. In J. G. March and Roger Weissinger-Baylon (Eds.), *Ambiguity and command: Organizational perspectives on military decision making.* Marshfield, MA: Pittman Publishing

Olsen, J. P. (2001). Garbage cans, new institutionalism, and the study of politics. *American Political Science Review, 95,* 191-198.

Peters, T. (1992). *Liberation management.* New York: Alfred Knopf.

Sitkin, S. B. (1992). Learning through failure: The strategy of small losses. *Research in Organizational Behavior, 14,* 231-266.

Stohl, C. (1995). *Organizational communication: Connectedness in action.* Thousand Oaks, CA: Sage Publications.

# Impression Management and ICTs

**5**

Larry D. Browning & Keri K. Stephens

The concept of "impression management" assumes that our outcomes in life are significantly affected by others' impressions of us. The consequences of being perceived positively—as capable, amiable, decent, and charming, for example—differ significantly from the consequences of being regarded askance. This being demonstrably true, most of us will try to communicate impressions that we hope will help us obtain our goals. This kind of strategic self-consciousness, combined with our attempts to actively control others' impressions of us, is widely known as "self-presentation" or "impression management" (Leary, Nzlek, Downs, Radford-Davenport, Martin, & McMullen, 1994).

"Impression management" then, refers to the *process* by which people try to influence the image others have of them (Rosenfeld, Booth-Kewley, Edwards, & Alderton, 1994). The idea of impression management is often applied to organizations because they, possibly even more than the average person, spend considerable resources trying to shape what the public, as well as their own members, think of them. When one manages impressions via ICTs, it is necessary to be aware of the symbolic meaning of the channel one is choosing (covered in Chapter One). Impression management behaviors in the workplace have been discussed in various contexts. These include the study of accountability (Frink, 1998), organizational citizenship (Bolino, 1999), leadership (Lord, 1985), exchange relationships (Wayne, 1993), control of behavior (Burger, 1989), managing crises (Allen & Caillouet, 1994), and managing relations with bosses (Rao, 1995).

> *"Impression management" refers to the process by which people try to influence the image others have of them.*

The concept is used as a lens for our own ICT cases because they offer so many examples of people presenting a particular view of themselves, even during their interview for this book. And it's really not surprising. Our interviewees were selected precisely because *they have a reputation for being effective*, which means they are good not only at completing tasks but also at self-presentation.

A review of the book's cases shows that these people explain what they say and do to convey a variety of impressions. Here are some of the things we see them doing as part of their job:

1. Constructing a Website that makes their company appear to be a local and familiar operation when it's actually located far away—in fact, in another country! To further manage the impression of "local," they also employ people who speak the client's own language fluently.

2. Emphasizing the importance of reviewing competitors' home pages to make certain that one's own Webpage has all the right fancy jargon to "prove" the company's expertise in a particular sub-field of management consulting.

**Used as a Lens**

Cases in this book are viewed in the light of impression management.

Another lead-in example that caused us to think of impression management as applicable to our cases is a story where a person manages impressions by traveling to meet potential clients and sitting down with them in person. The owner of this small firm emphasizes managing his clients' impression of him because he knows he looks very young, and this youthfulness might undercut his credibility. Since he sells financial services, he needs to build the relationship face-to-face—in short, he needs first to sell himself. In fact, most of the book's stories show how these ICT users represent themselves to others.

### Manipulation and Ethics in Impression Management

In business, "managing impressions" normally involves someone trying to control the image that a significant stakeholder has of them. In the literature on this subject, the ethics of impression management is a hotly debated issue. Should we see it as honorable or as dishonorable? As effective self-revelation or as cynical manipulation? Because ICTs offer an array of communication possibilities, it's fair to say that there are more ways of misleading than ever before. But some writers insist that impression management can indeed be used for authentic purposes, such as revealing a "truer" version of the self, as our person aimed to do in the financial services example. He knew he looked young, and to reassure his clients, he met with them to show his respect, demonstrate his personableness, and prove his professionalism. Is this form of impression management ethical? Probably so, because he actually shows more of himself and the way he thinks in this personal display. By addressing his youth directly, he avoids the worry that his clients might, on some future occasion, see him in person.

*Some writers insist that impression management can indeed be used for authentic purposes, such as revealing a "truer" version of the self.*

In another of our stories, an American engineer manages the production of hardware by a supplier in Asia who produces the part and then puts the American brand name on it. This engineer works out many technical details through email and audio conferences. He uses transparency—a kind of openness—as an impression management technique when he provides background information to his supplier. For example, he makes several levels of information accessible on the computer to help the Asian managers who supervise the making of his product. He is also adaptable—when he hears his phone listeners whipping out their calculators to test the numbers he has provided, he notes this and in future meetings provides the math formulas he used to produce the results. Because transparency can be provided so easily and because it produces information of value to the audience, it changes the nature of impression management from being cynically manipulative to being a kind of useful adaptation.

## Goffman's Work on Impression Management[1]

While earlier communication theorists (e.g., Burke, 1950; Hart & Burks, 1972) offered perspectives on the person as a strategic performer, Goffman (1959) was the first to develop a specific theory concerning self-presentation. In his well-known work, *The presentation of self in every day life*, Goffman created the foundation and the defining principles of what is commonly called "impression management." Laying out a purpose for his work, Goffman proposed to focus on how people in daily work situations present themselves and, in so doing, what they are doing to others. Goffman was particularly interested in how a person guides and controls how others form an impression of them and what a person "may or may not do" while performing before them (p. xi).

Impression management, as originally conceptualized by Goffman, requires the physical presence of others. Performers, seeking certain ends in their interest, must work to adapt their behavior in such a way as to "give off" the correct impression to a particular audience (Goffman, 1959, p. 2). Performers implicitly ask that the audience take their performance seriously. They also expect others, who are also putting on a show, to help them prepare for the performance and to cover for them when the performance falls short. Goffman argued that impression management reveals the moral character of our everyday lives because it reflects whatever standards we have agreed to live by—as such, moral character is reflected in our norms. In addition, he saw impression management as essentially dialectical: because people wish to appear moral, they spend much of their life on the amoral act of keeping up the show.

*Goffman argued that impression management reveals the moral character of our everyday lives because it reflects whatever standards we have agreed to live by—as such, moral character is reflected in our norms.*

Goffman's 1967 book, *Interaction ritual,* expands on his theory of impression management. People participate in social interactions, he says, by performing a "line," or "pattern of verbal and nonverbal acts," which expresses their view of the situation—the circumstance they find themselves in (1967, p. 5). Such lines are created and maintained by both the performer and the audience. By enacting a line effectively, a person gains positive social value or "face." The success or failure of an interaction depends largely upon the performer's ability to maintain face. Managing impressions is typically a cooperative effort with benefits that extend to those beyond the indi-

---

[1] An earlier version of this review of Goffman's ideas appears in Dillard, C., Browning, L. D., Sitkin, S. & Sutcliffe, K. (2000). Impression management and the use of procedures at the Ritz-Carlton: Moral standards and dramaturgical discipline. Communication Studies, 51, 404-414.

vidual performer. Goffman's rule of "self-respect" and rule of "consideration" mean that the person tends to conduct himself during an encounter in such a way as to maintain both his own face and the face of the other participants (Goffman, 1967). As a result, a person is required to display a kind of character. He must be seen as a dependable player; he must be "someone who can be relied upon to maintain himself as an interactant, poised for communication, and to act so that others do not endanger themselves by presenting themselves as interactants to him" (Goffman, 1967, p. 77).

*When one displays a "good showing" from a duty to one's self, we call it "pride." When one does so because of a duty to some wider social unit, such as an organization, and receives reciprocal support for doing so, we call it "honor" (Goffman, 1967, pp. 9-10).*

While Goffman tends to focus on those people who are physically present in a particular interaction, the social dimension of impression management certainly extends beyond the specific place and time of engagement in the organization. For example, an individual can make a good impression "for his profession or religion by making a good showing for himself" (1967, p. 5). Impression management is a social activity that has individual and community implications. When, in our society, one displays a "good showing" from a duty to one's self, we call it "pride." When one does so because of a duty to some wider social unit, such as an organization, and receives reciprocal support for doing so, we call it "honor" (pp. 9-10).

Another approach to moral standards that Goffman (1967) pursues is the notion of "rules of conduct," which can be partially understood as obligations or moral constraints. Once these rules are learned and embodied, a person is able to obey them even without consciously deciding to do so. Rules of conduct may be substantive (involving laws, morality, and ethics) or ceremonial (involving etiquette).

**Rules of Conduct**
Important in symmetrical/ hierarchical relationships.

Rules of conduct play a particularly important role when a relationship is asymmetrical and the expectations of one person toward another are hierarchical. Such relationships are of course quite common in organizational settings. In these circumstances, there's an implicit promise that the subordinate will treat the superior deferentially during their encounters. Acts of deference function as a symbolic, and reliable, way of expressing appreciation towards a recipient. Such exchanges call for appreciation and politeness, though their honorific tone is "in many ways more complimentary toward the recipient than the actor's true sentiment might warrant" (Goffman, 1967, p. 60).

Because impression management was originally conceptualized for face-to-face interactions, it resembles a drama. Indeed, Goffman says performers use dramaturgical discipline as a defense to ensure that the "show" goes on without interruption. Specifically, good performers will discipline themselves to play their roles fully even while maintaining an ability to recognize and react to unexpected and possibly detrimental occurrences. Goffman (pp. 216-218) contends that dramaturgical discipline includes:

1. coping with dramaturgical contingencies;

2. demonstrating intellectual and emotional involvement;

3. remembering one's part and not committing unmeant gestures or faux pas;

4.  not giving away secrets involuntarily;

5.  covering up inappropriate behavior on the part of teammates on the spur of the moment;

6.  offering plausible reasons or deep apologies for disruptive events;

7.  maintaining self-control (for example, speaking briefly and modestly);

8.  suppressing emotions to private problems; and

9.  suppressing spontaneous feelings.

In a study of the use of these techniques for impression management at a Ritz Carlton Hotel by the first author and his colleagues (Dillard, Browning, Sitkin, & Sutcliffe, 2000), they demonstrated that all nine rules, except for number four (keeping secrets), were in use. Computers allowed customers' preferences to be collected, stored, and communicated electronically so their next visit would allow still more personal service. In addition, electronic communication was used to enhance face-to-face encounters.

## Impression Management and ICTs

We now turn to how impression management occurs with ICTs. Early researchers on ICTs and impression management expressed some doubt about the extent of their effects. It was assumed that ICTs would provide less "social presence" and would filter out essential cues for interpreting what was going on, and thus would be less rich media than face-to-face communication. Yet there is a growing collection of studies showing that people can use "lean" media for effective social interactions; also, that long-distance partners often use ICTs to maintain a satisfactory social relationship that rivals, or even exceeds, the level of satisfaction achieved via face-to-face interactions (Walther, 1992).

Since ICTs can be used as part of self-presentation, we now demonstrate how ICTs are used in a consciously strategic way for impression management (O'Sullivan, 2000). O'Sullivan's model is based on an "information management framework" that shows individuals managing what information about them is known, or isn't known, to control others' impression of them. The assumption is that "through habit or conscious design" (O'Sullivan, p. 406) each person manages the impression they leave with people who are important to them. Anyone who has given the bathroom a quick cleaning when they anticipate the arrival of their mother-in-law (or date) has managed their impression. For an example from ICT use, inviting you to view my Webpage before a face-to-face meeting may predispose you to view me a certain way when we actually meet. In both these examples, the ability to sequence another's information and to make it rich or lean is a way to regulate one's self-presentation.

The main theme of O'Sullivan's (2000) seminal analysis is the dimension of "openness" vs. "closedness," which we treat as a relative variable. Being completely open or completely closed with information about oneself is neither possible nor

*The main theme of O'Sullivan's (2000) seminal analysis is the dimension of "openness" vs. "closedness," which we treat as a relative variable.*

desirable. Others can always find out something about us, and no one will know everything about us. The relative desirability of being open or closed is also applicable here. Who has not taken a long plane or bus trip and had to hear more disclosures from their seatmate than they ever wanted to ("Thanks for sharing!")? On the other hand, who has not occasionally wished their friend or spouse had provided more details about their feelings? Clearly, effective disclosure is relative to the person and circumstances. ICTs allow for regulating "the amount, nature, and timing" (O'Sullivan, p. 407) of information exchange as a way of managing appropriate disclosure.

Again, we will draw on examples from O'Sullivan's research (2000, pp. 408-409). He points out that leaner channels, such as electronic mail, can be used in various ways that benefit the message sender. They can be used to:

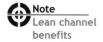

**Note**
Lean channel benefits

1. make more ambiguous, or obscure totally, embarrassing details that would be useful to mask from the receiver;

2. provide limited details about oneself to anticipate and preempt a negative response;

3. manage the intensity felt by the receiver of particular messages, such as leaving a phone message to dampen the feelings aroused by a particular piece of information; and

4. give the receiver control over how and when they respond via asynchronous channels.

The more options for ICT use available to the sender, the more they are able to control the sequence of information about themselves to the receiver.

If rich media are desired from the respondent, via face-to-face or over the phone, using such a technology allows the message sender to:

**Note**
Rich media benefits

1. highlight his or her dramatic use of voice tone or inflection;

2. emphasize conversational dialogue;

3. detect deception, which might increase credibility;

4. give immediate responses and control the damage that might otherwise occur from a particular message; and

5. speak directly and have the opportunity to give immediate and positive feedback to the live message.

## Summary

All of these possibilities demonstrate the pervasiveness of impression- management techniques with ICTs. While granting that the conscious and unconscious attempts can be unethical, our society now recognizes that redirecting attention to desirable issues is not only ethical but also important for individuals and organizations. Surely it is fair to put one's best foot forward, is it not? When reviewing the narratives in this book, ask yourself how individuals are using ICTs to enhance their own image or their organization's. The narratives are intended to give you some awareness as to how you yourself use ICTs for impression management.

*Our society now recognizes that redirecting attention to desirable issues is not only ethical but also important for individuals and organizations. Surely it is fair to put one's best foot forward, is it not?*

## References

Allen, M.W., & Caillouet, R.H. (1994). Legitimate endeavors: Impression management strategies used by an organization in crisis. *Communication Monographs, 61*, 44-62.

Bolino, M.C. (1999). Citizenship and impression management: good soldiers or good actors? *Academy of Management Review, 24*, 82.

Burger, J. M. (1989). Negative reactions to increases in perceived personal control. *Journal of Personality & Social Psychology. 56*, 246-256.

Burke, K. (1950). *A rhetoric of motives.* Berkley, CA: University of California Press.

Dillard, C., Browning, L. D., Sitkin, S., & Sutcliffe, K. (2000). Impression management and the use of procedures at the Ritz-Carlton: Moral standards and dramaturgical discipline. *Communication Studies, 51*, 404-414.

Frink, D. D. (1998). Accountability, impression management, and goal setting in the performance evaluation process. *Human Relations, 51*, 1259-1284.

Goffman, E. (1959). *The presentation of self in everyday life.* New York: Doubleday.

Goffman, E. (1967). *Interaction ritual: Essays on face-to-face behavior.* Chicago: Aldine.

Hart, R. P., & Burks, D. M. (1972). Rhetorical sensitivity and social interaction, *Communication Monographs, 39*, 75-91.

Leary, M. R., Nzlek, J. B., Downs, D., Radford-Davenport, J., Martin, J., & McMullen, A. (1994). Self-presentation in everyday interactions: Effects of target familiarity and gender composition. *Journal of Personality and Social Psychology, 67*, 644-673.

Lord, R. G. (1985). An information processing approach to social perceptions, leadership and behavioral measurement in organizations. In L. L. Cummings & B.M. Staw (Eds.), *Research in organizational behavior, 7*, (pp. 87-128). Greenwich, CT: JAI Press.

O' Sullivan, P. B. (2000). What you don't know won't hurt me: Impression management functions of communication channels in relationships. *Human Communication Research. 26*, 403-431.

Rao, A. (1995). Upward impression management: goals, influence strategies, and consequences, *Human Relations, 48*, 2, 147-168.

Rosenfeld, P., Booth-Kewley, S., Edwards, J. E., & Alderton, D. L. (1994). Linking diversity and impression management. *American Behavioral Scientist, 37*, 672–682.

Walther, J. B. (1992). Interpersonal effects in computer-mediated interaction: A relational perspective. *Communication Research, 19*, 52-90.

Wayne, S. J. (1993). The effects of leader-member exchange on employee citizenship and impression management behavior. *Human Relations, 46*, 14-31.

# Enactment and Sensemaking in Organizations

**6**

Alf Steinar Sætre & Larry D. Browning

Imagine that your boss has asked you to prepare a PowerPoint presentation of a project you've been working on. He plans to present it to some executives who tend to favor slick, ICT-based presentations. You ask him, "What would you like me to focus on? And what are your preferences for layout and design?" He says, "Oh, anything that fills 20 minutes is fine." But you work hard anyway to make a truly professional-looking pitch and then give it to him. He looks at it, then at you, and says curtly, "No, no, that's not it. You need to change the color scheme and fix the layout. Oh, and kill these two slides, and find a place to work in these four new ones."

Depending on how you choose to react to this directive, your work environment could be affected in several different ways. Perhaps you suddenly feel unappreciated and rebuked, and resent what you take to be your boss's irrational behavior, so you yell "Now you tell me!" and storm out. Or perhaps you just say, "Yes, sir," and do what he has asked, contenting yourself with a muted grumble. On the other hand, perhaps you, too, were secretly unhappy about how your presentation looked and just needed him to tell you, so you say "No problem" and go fix it. The point of this example? What you notice, how you interpret what you notice, and how you behave in the stream of experience—all *enact* (i.e., help bring about) the very environment you subsequently encounter.

*In many ways, you enact your own work environment.*

In this one little incident we have all the elements of *enactment* and *sensemaking*. You and your boss have jointly enacted (co-created) a working environment over the PowerPoint presentation. You reacted to his criticisms (reactions) just as he reacted to the job you did. This "joint reaction" is what Karl Weick (1969) calls *enactment*. Enactment is a continual process, as people react to one another. Say you initially *made sense* of (interpreted) his criticism by thinking that he is irrational, but you retrospectively decide that, no, it was simply "because he was stressed." Revised (retrospective) interpretations are commonplace; they show that sensemaking, and hence enactment, is dynamic. Our example sets the tone for this chapter on enactment because one form of it is seen in how people use ICTs.

This chapter lays out the theoretical foundations for understanding the enactment of ICTs.

## Weick's Theory of Organizing

Karl Weick has been writing about organizing for over 30 years. His key contribution to organizational communication was his recognition that organizations, rather than operating like rational planning systems, with plans and attitudes preceding and determining how people behave, often operate in the reverse sequence. That is, some event or behavior will occur, and people will adjust their attitudes to match what happened as well as to make sense of it. In our little PowerPoint scenario, for example, we noted three or four interpretations (meanings) that you

*Action precedes meaning.* might have chosen to make sense of the event. This focus on action determining meaning is at the heart of enactment. Throughout the present chapter, we will be expanding on Weick's theory to show how *action precedes meaning*.

In his influential book *The social psychology of organizing* (1969, 1979), Weick's focus on organizing (a verb) instead of organizations (a noun) provided him an original and provocative point of view. Previously when thinking about organizations people tended to view them as containers in which communication and interaction happen. Weick says that, actually, behaviors create the organization rather than occurring within it, and that the communication—both structures and stories—*are* the organization.

Smircich and Stubbart (1985, p. 725) point out that "The words 'organization' and 'environment' create a dichotomy that profoundly shapes thinking" about organizations and management. This dichotomy had led us to think of organizations and individuals as being at once embedded in an environment *and* as having an independent and external existence outside that same environment. Weick's view that people in part actually *choose* their environment emphasizes organizations as being dynamic, changing entities that live via action and sensemaking.[1]

This conceptualization is even more important for the people "living" in these organizations—the people doing the organizing—than it is for researchers. Weick contends:

> [T]here is not *some kind of monolithic, singular, fixed environment that exists detached from and external to these people. Instead, in each case the people are very much a part of their own environments. They act, and in doing so create the materials that become the constraints and opportunities they face. There is not some impersonal "they" who puts these environments in front of passive people. Instead, the "they" is people who are more active. (Weick, 1995, p. 31)*

[1] Likewise, instead of thinking of organizing and communication as separate and distinct, we ought to think about them as intertwined processes that continually and mutually influence each other (Miller, 2002). Accepting such thinking is not merely to embrace a vague conceptual stance; it affects palpable things, such as who has power in any given dyadic relationship (e.g., the lower-level person will have significant influence in affirming or disaffirming the power of a boss) and how misunderstandings occur (the more people a single message passes through, the more likely it is to be distorted at the end of the process).

The stories in this book show that *people affect their own environments*—indeed, actively construct them, if often unconsciously. They have goals, strategies for achieving them, and ideas about the strengths and weakness of any given choice. Their stories can be examined as a series of action-meaning sequences. For example, how a person uses ICTs to monitor the environment affects their ICT skills, which in turn determines what that particular technology "allows" them to make sense of.

*People affect their own environments—indeed, actively construct them.*

## Ecological Change, Enactment, Selection and Retention

*Enactment drives everything else in an organization.*

Let's attempt a summary of Weick's theory of organizing, showing the centrality of enactment to his theory. *Enactment* is a concept that captures the role of action in organizing and sensemaking, and is the second of a four-element sequence—ecological change, enactment, selection, and retention. Enactment is pivotal in this scheme because rather than having an "external environment," a person "enacts an environment." Since all social actors (people and organizations) are involved in it, enactment is a crucial process for individuals and firms alike. Weick (2001, p. 187) claims that "enactment drives everything else in an organization. How enactment is done is what an organization will know." The same holds true for individuals. Enactment is central because it contains "doing (what is the action?) and meaning (what sense does that person make of the action?)." Briefly stated, Weick's (1969, 1979) theory of organizing is as follows:

- *Ecological change* is an alteration in the flow of experience of social actors. These alterations or differences in experience provide opportunities for social actors to make sense of them, to reduce ambiguity. As research on cognition shows, exceptions are what people tend to monitor to register change (Einhorn & Hogarth, 1986). "Ecological changes provide the enactable environment, the raw materials for sense-making" (Weick, 1979, p. 130). The introduction of a new ICT into the organization illustrates one such change.

**Key Theory**
Weick's 1969 Theory of Organizing

- *Enactment* is the intersection between the activities of social actors and ecological (environmental) changes. Weick states that "enactment is to organizing as variation is to natural selection" (1979, p. 130). This is an apt analogy, for the activities of social actors take different forms in different contexts (variation). Differences generate new possibilities. Yet, over time, certain activities seem to prevail at the expense of others. For example, if someone in the year 2008 spends two hours a day doing email on their computer and they were doing none of this 20 years earlier, a form of "natural selection" has taken place—a very different work environment has been enacted simply through the introduction of an ICT. The term "enactment" refers to actions of both social actors and their environment, and implies a co-creation of activities, thus focusing our attention on change and movement.

- *Selection* involves some kind of arranging of the enacted experiences to reduce their equivocality.[2] This arranging or structuring can be represented in the form of cause maps, or sequences, built on the enacted (past) experiences. A "cause map" is a picture of how someone perceives elements to be causally and sequentially related (Weick, 1995). Over time, certain cause maps gain priority because they reduce equivocality more consistently than do other cause maps, even across different contexts.

- *Retention* involves the storage of the products of successful sense-making or equivocality-reducing activities. What people store are "preferred" cause maps that illustrate how variables are related. Weick uses "the terms *enacted environment* and *cause map* to refer to retained content" (1979, p.131). The term "cause map" is fairly broad and encompasses social actors understanding how "things" fit together. Cause maps are thus central to both organizing and sense-making.

Sensemaking and organizing take place through the processes of ecological change, enactment, selection, and retention. Different ICTs exemplify the raw materials used in sensemaking. Yet environmental change (or what Weick calls "ecological change") frequently arises in connection with some action on the part of the social actor. These changes or alterations make up our enactable environments. The capacity for people to both create their own environment through action as well as respond to it by giving it meaning is central to our understanding of how people enact their work environment when using ICTs.

## Sensemaking

Sensemaking is an important part of organizational life, since members must daily strive to comprehend their rapidly changing environment and any ensuing ambiguity that they face. Both sensemaking and organizing are mindful activities; that is, they require conscious thought. In Weick's (1979) theory of organizing, the driving force behind our organizing stems from how we make sense of our surroundings. How we do that, in turn, comes from the question: "How can I know what I think until I see what I say?" (p. 133). Weick's phrase "what I say" is easy to extend to ICTs. For example, when we are drafting an email, the phrase changes to "what I write and to whom I send it." This question is laid out in Figure 6-1 on the following page.

Paraphrasing Weick's "How can I know what I think" question, here is how the four components of social actor, enactment, selection and retention fit into this sensemaking process:

How can we (social actors) know what we said (retention) until we see and hear (selection) what we say and do (enactment)?

---

[2] Equivocality describes a situation where different significations of events or experiences feel equally appropriate or plausible.

*Figure 6-1: Sensemaking and Enactment*

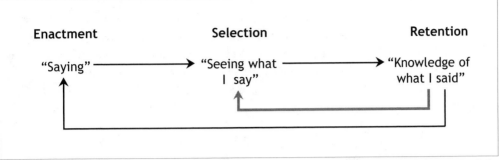

*Adapted from Weick (1979, p. 134).*

Comparing our paraphrase to Weick's model will show that the sequence of the selection-enactment-retention process is not static but has feedback loops since it is a continually re-accomplished activity. It is never really complete.

In his 1995 book *Sensemaking in Organizations*, Weick lists seven properties of sensemaking that help clarify the concept. Table 6-1, below, lists these seven properties along with our summaries of them:

*Table 6-1: Seven Properties of Sensemaking*

| Sensemaking is: | Summary of Property: |
|---|---|
| 1. Grounded in identity construction | Weick argues that to define "what is out there" is also to define one-self. How we make sense of our environments is driven by who we are, and who we are is in many ways colored by how we see our environment. In other words, individuals' perceptions of themselves are influenced by how they think others perceive them. Or: "How can I know who I am until I see what they do?" (Weick, 1995, p. 23). How we use new ICTs, such as mobile messaging systems, defines who we are, but how can we know how they make us feel until we try them? |
| 2. Retrospective | If we view reality as a "stream of experience," the only way we can make sense of this stream is to momentarily step out of it and direct our attention to it. But the only part of the stream we can see has already passed. Hence, "To learn what I think, I look back over what I said earlier" (Weick, 1995, p. 61). We are more conscious of what we have done than of what we are doing. |
| 3. Enactive of sensible environment | As social actors, we receive stimuli as a result of our own activity. When we are engaged in sensemaking, we are also enacting the very environment that we are trying to make sense of. Stimuli are received as a "consequence of an activity of the individual" (Follet, 1924, p. 61). |

*(Table 6-1 continued on next page)*

| Sensemaking is: | Summary of Property: |
| --- | --- |
| 4. Social | The conduct of social actors in organizations hinges on the conduct of others. Meanings are based on words and language, and language is socially constructed. What a social actor focuses on and concludes is in part determined by socialization and by the anticipated audience of the conclusions he or she reaches. Sensemaking is an intersubjective activity. |
| 5. Ongoing | The actions of a social actor are spread across time and compete for attention with other ongoing projects. Sensemaking is part of a larger context and depends on what has happened previously. How we make sense of things today will affect future sensemaking. As Weick puts it, "People are always in the middle of things" (1995, p. 43). |
| 6. Focused on and by extracted cues | The "what" that people single out and elaborate on as the content of a problem is only a small portion of whatever is relevant to any given situation or context. Furthermore, what social actors notice is high-lighted by what they have previously enacted. We use what is familiar to make sense of what is new. |
| 7. Driven by plausibility rather than accuracy | Social actors need to know enough about what they think in order to get on with their projects, but no more. This means sufficiency and plausibility take precedence over accuracy. |

These seven properties of sensemaking and our elaboration of them show how social actors understand their environments. Sensemaking involves placing novel cues into some pre-existing framework (Starbuck & Miliken, 1988) or construct-ing new frameworks with which to make sense of new stimuli (Ring & Rands, 1989). These frameworks are also called "cause maps." Whether social actors use newly constructed cause maps or modifications of pre-existing maps to make sense of the world, they use these frameworks to figure out, understand, explain, and predict their environments. The concepts of enactment and sensemaking are highly interrelated, for we make sense of our worlds by enacting cause maps. Weick sees enactment as the essence of sense-making and states that "sense-making is about the ways people generate what they interpret" (1995, p. 13). Today, various ICTs figure prominently both in generating and interpreting.

## Coupling ICTs and Enactment

As stated previously, Weick views enactment as consisting of a coupled system of action and cognition—that is, a chain of action-learning-action sequences—where people's own actions help shape the circumstances to which they then ori-ent themselves.

In organizations today, where ICTs permeate almost every process at every level, these very technologies become an integral part of the enactment and sensemaking process. ICTs are important not only in terms of what organizational members have to enact and understand—for technologies change very rapidly today—but perhaps more importantly *how* they do so. That is, people in organizations often use technologies when they communicate and interact with people around them seeking to make sense of their environment. In other words, ICTs are important tools in both enactment and sensemaking.

Figure 6-2, below, illustrates how ICTs are integrated into the process of enacting and making sense of a continually changing environment. The circle shows how people's knowledge (cause maps) affects how they perceive their environment or circumstances, which in turn influences how they frame (understand in context) and retain their knowledge. This again affects the form of subsequent conversations. Or, conversely, people's conversations affect how knowledge is framed and retained, which in turns affects how circumstances are perceived and understood, which in turn affects knowledge construction and thus future conversations.

Inside the circle, the arrows illustrate two points: (1) conversations and the form they take (through what media and in what format) affect not only the construction of knowledge (sensemaking) but also the circumstances/environment (enactment); and (2) how knowledge is framed and retained affects the subsequent construction of knowledge. Knowledge is continuously being transformed and reproduced (enacted) through ICT-based interactions between social actors.

It is important to note that this enactment is cyclical, so that sometimes acting precedes knowing and sometimes it follows (Weick, 1979, 1995; Taylor, Groleau,

*In organizations today, ICTs permeate almost every process and thus become an integral part of the enactment and sensemaking process.*

*Figure 6-2: The relationship between Enactment and ICTs* [3]

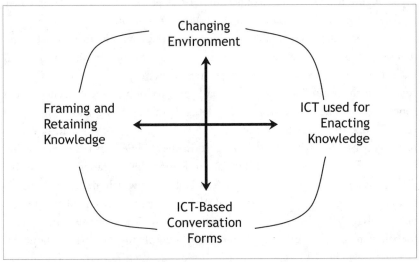

[3] This figure is a revision of Taylor, Groleau, Heaton, & Van Every's (2001, p. 97) figure titled The Consequentiality of Communication.

Heaton, & Van Every, 2001). The link between action and interpretation sharpens the connection between sensemaking and enactment. We shall now turn our focus to a particular sensemaking activity, namely, the creation of cause maps (knowledge).

### The Enactment of Cause Maps

Because cause maps are the product of social actors' enactment and depiction of how various elements are causally related (Weick, 2001), they are a basic form of knowledge. Therefore, sense-making—the enactment of meaning—is the process of making sense of experiences by tracking how events are related. In short, cause maps are enacted frameworks for making sense of our environments. Weick's theory focuses our attention on an enacted environment where activities and experiences are imbued with meaning by organizational members. He also points out that people, both in and outside of organizations, tend to forget this: "They fall victim to this blindspot because of an innocent-sounding phrase, 'the environment.' The word *the* suggests something that is singular and fixed; the word *environment* suggests that this singular, fixed something is set apart from the individual" (Weick, 1995, pp. 31-32). "Both implications," he says, "are nonsense" (Weick, 1995, p. 32). The example of a cause map shown in Figure 6-3 brings Weick's (1995) assertions to life.

*The Environment is not a separate singular and unified entity.*

The following cause map can be seen in Roos and Hall's (1980) analysis of the actions and perspectives of the head of a geriatric unit of a hospital who hoped to move his patients out of their hospital beds and back into society through a program of exercise and dietary improvement. His actions bewildered hospital administrators, who needed senior elderly patients in the hospital to generate income needed to keep the hospital operating. The geriatric head's cause map for his unit differed from other decision-makers' so greatly that they tried to get him fired. Figure 6-3 shows Roos and Hall's (1980, p. 59) cause map of the policy domain of the Extended Care Unit (ECU) that they studied.

In Figure 6-3, policy variables, goals, and performance criteria are labeled and represented as points in the diagram. These concepts are then linked by causal assertions represented by arrows. A positive or negative sign indicates that the concept at the beginning of the arrow has a positive or negative influence on the concept at the end of the arrow. The left side of Figure 6-3 shows the policy variables that the ECU director influences. For example, he can set the budgeted bed occupancy rate (the BBO). The field in the middle shows the intervening variables. For example, the BBO in turn influenced his operating budget (OB). The column labeled "director" shows the variables with which the ECU director is concerned. The OB in part determined the outcome of the cost per patient rehabilitated (CPPR). The far right-hand column shows the Commission's concern for balancing the costs of the ECU and the benefits obtained from it. "The action threshold switches (ATS) represent the turning on and off of various causal relationships as the psychic pressures on the director rise and fall" (Roos & Hall, 1980, p. 60). The ATS is an example of a slight change in pressure that causes the

*Figure 6–3: Roos and Hall's Cause Map of the Policy Domain of an ECU*

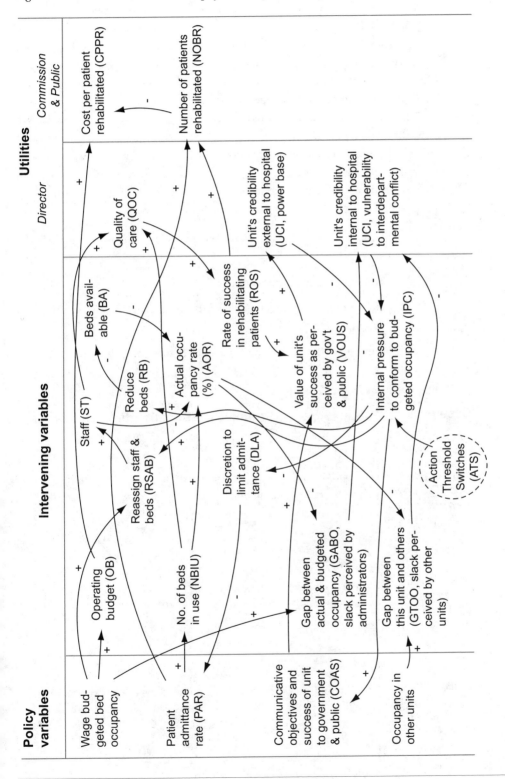

decision-maker to switch his decision. For example, when he has support and credibility in the community, he can focus on quality of care; when he has pressure from administrators in the hospital, he has to increase his unit's bed usage.

So while the director shows autonomy in the example above, he is also dependent on hospital administrators. For example, a drop in the actual bed occupancy rate (AOR) increased the gap between actual and budgeted occupancy, which decreased the unit's credibility within the hospital, which in turn increased internal pressures to conform to the budgeted occupancy rate.

The composite map of Figure 6-4 lists three of the cases in this book. We chose this limited set of cases so as to provide a concrete example of enactment without introducing a large number of variables, or a large number of cases. Our purpose here was to create a simpler, more direct example than that of Figure 6-3.

To create this map, we reviewed each of these three interviews to identify the following features:

1. Behaviors (the actual actions and activities used to accomplish the strategy).

2. Strategy (a larger purpose or goal).

3. Constraints (the forces that undermine the behaviors performed to accomplish the strategy).

4. Outcomes (the interviewees' results after they enact the behavior).

Figure 6- 4: A Composite Map of Three Cases

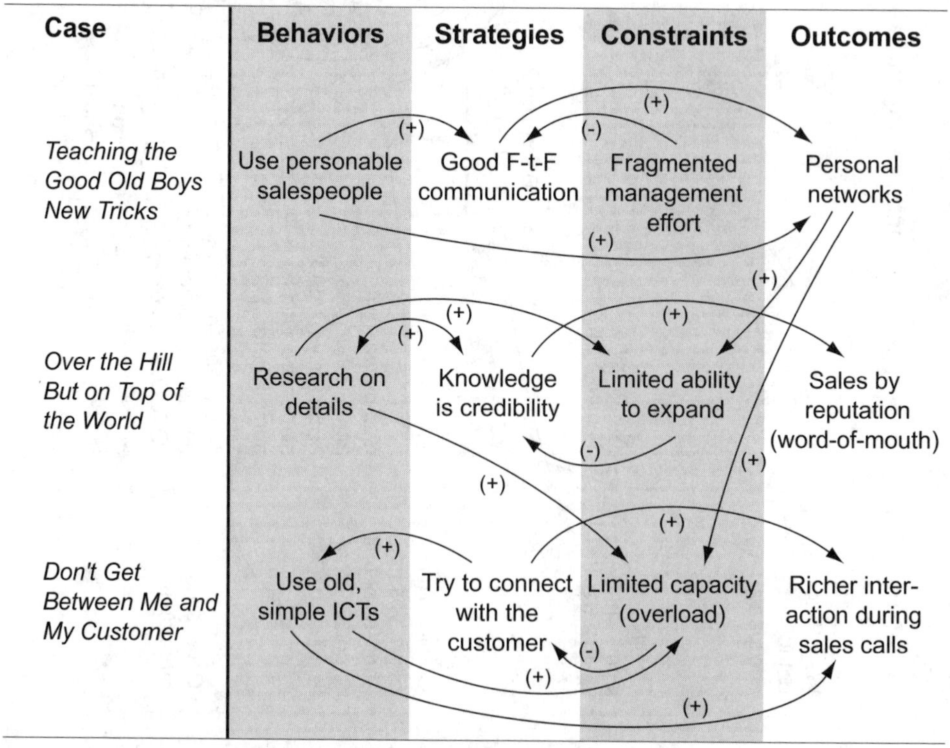

As in Figure 6-3, these concepts are connected by causal relations indicated by arrows. A positive or negative sign shows that the concept at the beginning of the arrow has a positive or negative influence on the one at the end of the arrow.

Although we limited our illustration above to one behavior, one strategy, one constraint, and one outcome for each case, we soon discovered that there were some commonalities between these cases, and this resulted in a few arrows between the three cases.

Here we will just briefly walk you through the reasoning behind the arrows in the "Over the Hill, but on Top of the World" case, which showcases Ron, a retired teacher, who now runs a successful water-purification business. He does a lot of detailed technical research (behavior) on his products. He does this because his philosophy (strategy) is that detailed knowledge gives him credibility; but his sense of being credible also leads him to do still more research. His customers quickly notice that he is very credible and competent, and they happily tell their friends, who then call him themselves to solicit his services. His customers, in other words, become his *de facto* sales staff. Although he has more business than he can handle, his strategy and behavior put severe limits on his ability to expand his business; this is again, at least in part, affected by all the research he does. His detailed research also limits his capacity (overload) to do other kinds of work, such as installing water-purification systems for his clients.

When looking carefully at the cause-map representations in Figure 6-3 and Figure 6-4, it becomes clear that these people enact their own environments through a series of feedback loops and intervening variables. The director's actions in Figure 6-3 affect his own work environment. His enactment of his environment is in turn influenced by what he notices and how he chooses to interpret and make sense of these "concepts," yet he might not be fully aware of all of the feedback loops between all the intervening variables. The same applies to the marketing people in some of our cases represented in Figure 6-4.

## Summary

When people act, "these actions become the raw materials from which a sense of the situation is eventually built" (Weick, 2001, p. 183). Ecological changes (for example, the invention of new ICTs) and people's actions (such as the adoption of new ICTs in the workplace) are both important parts of the raw materials for enactment. As we strive to make sense of our environment and reduce uncertainty and ambiguity through the creation of causal maps, we are in effect enacting context and creating meaning. This reading on enactment and sensemaking captures how people process information by taking action, interpreting the meaning of that action in relation to others, and developing routines, or cause maps, that allow them to act appropriately. In today's organizations, ICT's play an increasingly important role in most processes of enactment and sensemaking.

*People enact their own environments through a series of feedback loops and intervening variables.*

## References

Einhorn, H. J., & Hogarth, R. M. (1986). Judging probable cause. *Psychological Bulletin, 99*, 1-39.

Follett, M. P. (1924). *Creative experience.* New York: Longmans.

Miller, K. (2002). *Communication theories: Perspectives, processes, and contexts.* Boston, MA: McGraw-Hill Higher Education.

Ring, P. S., & Rands, G. P. (1989). Sensemaking, understanding, and committing: Emergent interpersonal transaction processes in the evolution of 3M's microgravity research program. In A. H. Van de Ven, H. L. Angle & M. S. Poole (Eds.), *Research on the management of innovation: The Minnesota studies* (pp. 337-366). New York: Ballinger.

Roos, L. L., & Hall, R. I. (1980). Influence diagrams and organizational power. *Administrative Science Quarterly, 25*(1), 57-71.

Smircich, L., & Stubbard, C. (1985). Strategic management in an enacted world. *Academy of Management Review, 10*(4), 724-736.

Starbuck, W. H., & Milliken, F. J. (1988). Challenger: Fine tuning the odds until something breaks. *Journal of Management Studies, 25*(4), 319-340.

Taylor, J. R., Groleau, C., Heaton, L., & Van Every, E. (2001). *The computerization of work.* Thousand Oaks, CA: Sage.

Weick, K. E. (1969). *The social psychology of organizing.* Reading, MA: Addison-Wesley.

Weick, K. E. (1979). *The social psychology of organizing* (2nd ed.). Reading, MA: Addison-Wesley.

Weick, K. E. (1989). Organized improvisation: 20 years of organizing. *Communication Studies, 40*, 241-248.

Weick, K. E. (1995). *Sensemaking in organizations.* Thousand Oaks, CA: Sage.

Weick, K. E. (2001). *Making sense of the organization.* Malden, MA: Blackwell Publishers.

# Giddens' Structuration Theory and ICTs [1]

**7**

Larry D. Browning & Keri K. Stephens

Structuration theory is an extension of some ideas originally proposed by Anthony Giddens, especially in his 1984 book *The Constitution of Society*, which addresses the fascinating question of how society is structured—and indeed perpetually restructured. For well over three decades, this prolific scholar has advanced, elaborated, and diligently defended a unique conception of how social structures get constituted in day-to-day actions and interactions. Originally, he sought to explain the relationship between the individual and society (Giddens, 1984). Do individuals control social structures through acts of leadership and agency, he wondered, or are they largely passive receivers of social control (Conrad & Haynes, 2001)? This very issue is, of course, central to a study like our own. Do individuals have a determining role in the selection and use of their ICTs, or do cultural preferences select technology?

*Do individuals control social structures through acts of leadership and agency, or are they largely passive receivers of social control?*

Giddens contends that the biggest, or macro, structural features of society result from the *patterned repetition of human interaction*. With respect to ICTs, for example, in what sequence do we typically use them? When we need to communicate with someone who isn't physically present, do we find ourselves automatically picking up the phone, or are we likelier to send them an email? Whichever the answer, over time we are creating a pattern of use. Getting users of the phone, email, face-to-face, etc., to talk about how they use their preferred methods for interaction, and why, can give us insights into how their particular organizations—and even society at large—may be constituted. Constitution, as we use it here, means "to compose or to make up." People's use of ICTs does in fact make up the communication of organizations.

As a counter-example, during the early years of email, it was commonplace at a rural agricultural agency in Colorado for the department secretary to print out

[1] This work draws on papers and articles written by the first author with Jan Beyer, Ron Greene, and Curt Hirsch. These papers and articles are listed in the references. We appreciate the contribution of those papers to this chapter. A special thanks goes to Curt Hirsch for his suggestions on this chapter.

hard copies of all incoming emails and place them in the staff members' physical mailboxes. The staff members would then write out their responses and return them to the secretary, who would then type them into emails and send them out.

The staff members essentially treated email as part of a typing service and did not use the computers on their desks as a communication device. These practices composed the department's organizational communication and indeed helped structure the organization.

*Structuration theory allows us to better assess particular work environments and how people operate there.*

Reviewing structuration theory allows us to better assess particular work environments and how people operate there. What is their sense of space, time, and efficacy under the ICT arrangements? The theory focuses on how "designed transactions," such as technology and processes, both constrain and sanction individual action in organizations. By designed transactions, we mean both the technology, and the steps it offers, and the human consciousness of sequence people use when they anticipate communicating. The idea is attractive to communication and managerial researchers because it helps to explain how different types of communication—here, ICTs—compose the structures in which actors participate. For the stories in this book, our analysis focuses on how individuals use ICTs in the workplace and what structure their use produces.

Beyond Giddens' original formulation, structuration theory has been applied to the study of management and organizational communication for myriad purposes. For example, Browning, Beyer, and Shetler (1995) show that it has been used to:

**Beyond Giddens' original formulation** Structuration theory has been applied to the study of management and organizational communication for myriad purposes.

1. account for the effects of power on organizational arrangements;

2. analyze the interpretive processes that lead people to construct meaning;

3. show how the same technology can produce similar structuring and divergent outcomes and hierarchies;

4. assess how organizational climates change over time;

5. examine dialectical processes in organizational change;

6. understand structuring processes in a research consortium; and

7. understand the use of group-decision support systems (GDSS) as modes of participation in decision-making.

A closer review of some particular aspects of structuration will help you apply Giddens' ideas to ICTs.

## Reflexivity and the Duality of Structure

In Giddens' theory, people (aka "agents") reflexively monitor an ongoing stream of social life and the effect of their (and others') intervening actions upon it. His use of the term agency has a dual meaning; it refers to both the way an agent represents and gets power from organizational affiliation, such as an FBI agent, and how individuals are empowered from self-organization, or the ability to do for one's self. An important part of this monitoring is the capacity of individual agents to rationalize their actions to themselves and others. Such consciousness is particularly possible with several ICTs (email, for example) because using them produces a semi-permanent record of the interaction. Giddens outlines a tripartite system of consciousness, including:

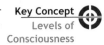

**Key Concept**
Levels of
Consciousness

1.  the unconscious, in which people are unaware of their motives for action;

2.  practical consciousness, in which people can't say what they are doing, yet can put a particular set of rules into operation; and

3.  discursive consciousness, in which people can describe a complex series of communicative and organizational strategies (Browning, Sutcliffe, Sitkin, Obstfeld & Greene, 2000).

These levels of consciousness apply to our understanding of ICT use because while people are free to communicate with relatively few constraints, they are also usually expected to have rationales for what they do (Harre & Secord, 1972).

Giddens explains how individuals constitute societies within societies. In the course of their everyday activities, they consciously or unconsciously "draw upon" the *rules* and *resources* afforded by larger social structures and, in so doing, basically "reproduce" those same societal structures (Hirsh & Browning, 1995).

In applying structuration theory to organizations, Ranson, Hinings, and Greenwood (1980) conceptualize *duality* in terms of frameworks and interaction, and argue that the most fruitful approach is to focus on the interpenetration of the two. How do frameworks, such as syllabi or business plans, influence the way individuals communicate in a class or on the job?

Without rules and resources to draw upon in the course of their interactions, actors would flounder randomly without direction.

*Rules*, according to structuration theory, are the written and unwritten rules of social life, such as the techniques or procedures generally employed to carry out expected social and workplace practices. They might take the form of commandments, protocols, how-to guides, accounting procedures, teamwork norms, and the like. ICT rules, for example, can include both the unalterable ones on a computer (e.g., if you don't spell a file name exactly right, a search for it will prove futile) and more malleable guidelines. These are social norms for action that people enact in different ways.

*How do frameworks, such as syllabi or business plans, influence the way individuals communicate in a class or on the job?*

*Resources*, meanwhile, are of two kinds—authoritative and allocative. *Authoritative resources* derive from the coordination of the activity of human agents. For ICTs, authoritative resources would include a supervisor's right to give direction or a culture's rules for action—in this instance, a rule reflexively becomes a resource to those who use it. For example, a supervisor's power to tell an employee to produce a report in 48 hours is both a rule and a resource. *Allocative resources* result from control of material products or aspects of the material world—finances, hardware, software, infrastructural fixtures of all kinds, physical plants, machines, and of course all electronic ICTs. Allocative resources include the equipment that someone in the organization has provided for another's use. But rules and procedures can't be understood to "structure" anything until actors actually put them into play by implementing them (un-consciously and unreflexively for the most part) in the natural course of their everyday interaction. Social structures, Giddens tells us, are constituted *by* human agency, yet simultaneously are the very *medium* of this constitution. For the purposes of this book, it's important to understand how agents constitute, and are affected by, ICTs.

*Structuration is one of the first serious theoretical attempts to analyze how societal "microfeatures," such as a conversation or an email, can be directly tied to the structure of larger systems.*

All societal forms, says Giddens, are the result of a "duality of structure," with individuals in communicative interaction putting into play the relevant rules and resources afforded by their society. Giddens suggests that this dynamic is the fundamental structural impetus of groups, organizations, and societies. Structuration is one of the first serious theoretical attempts to analyze how societal "microfeatures," such as a conversation or an email, can be directly tied to the structure of larger systems.

Systems of generative rules and resources compose the structures for three modalities outlined by Giddens:

1.  interpretive schemes, which allow for the communication of meaning in interaction (a communication perspective);

2.  norms or "moral rules," which allow agents to apply sanctions in interaction (a sociological perspective); and

3.  facilities or resources, which allow agents the means to deploy power in interactive contexts (a political perspective).

Giddens contends that these three modes are highly interactive, and that in any given interaction, all three structures may be activated.

The rules and resources that compose structure may be regarded as "properties of social systems," which are regularized patterns of interaction involving individuals and groups. Social systems are not structures in themselves; rather, they "have" structures, being ordered by both rules and resources. Structures do not "exist" in time and space except as moments in the constitution of social systems. The practices structured by rules and resources are "deeply layered" in time and space, stretching through many decades and over large or fixed domains that are primary in the structuration of the institutions (Hirsh & Browning, 1995). This means that the history of practices affects contemporary usage; cultures have memory.

*Cultures have memory.*

Now let's apply structuration theory to ICTs.

## Adaptive Structuration Theory

Scott Poole and Gerry DeSanctis have specifically extended structuration theory to the study of ICTs by developing something they call "Adaptive Structuration

Theory," or AST. AST is valuable for analyzing our own cases because it helps explain how people appropriate technology when faced with many ICT options. We can study and understand the role of ICTs in changing organizations by examining the various structures that ICTs themselves provide, as well as the structures that emerge when people interact with technology.

AST
5 Tenets

Five tenets of AST specifically apply to our research:

First, structuration is the process by which groups maintain a system. The process involves the application of structures that might be any of the following; the rules and resources provided by the organization, the task, the organizational culture, the group norms, and the knowledge of the participants. ICTs are certainly a resource, for in these cases individuals report using ICTs to communicate with more people, in more diverse networks, on more specific topics, and with quicker turn-around than they ever did before the present array of communication technologies became available.

Second, AST contends that the potential of any technology is open-ended. Although it's not difficult to list the *intended* functions of a methodology, the uses to which it can actually be put are as varied as the goals it supports. While the individuals in our cases have in common lots of talk about goals, the open-ended nature of ICTs is affirmed in that no two of the interviews offer a particular pattern; instead, there is significant variation among these users about their ICT strategies.

*AST contends that the potential of any technology is open-ended.*

Third, users have *agency*, according to AST, in that they constitute and give meaning to technologies. Until applied by a user in a specific context, technology is "simply dead matter" (Poole & DeSanctis, 1990). Because our own sampling of interviewees required active users, we found no "dead matter" in these reports of practice. All our interviewees reported high use of—and dependence on—ICTs for performance. Sighed one person, for instance, "If the computer is down and you can't use the email, you might as well go home." Yet even there, people have options, no matter how little power they may otherwise wield. Contrary to some social perspectives, structuration theory sees agents as highly knowledgeable and skillful actors who retain some savvy as they operate in the world.

*Until applied by a user in a specific context, technology is simply dead matter.*

Fourth, the recursive interplay among actors, goals, and technologies in an emergent system must account for how specific groups of users assimilate technologies within their own streams of work activity. This accounting for assimilation is registered in our own research here in that our interviewees were asked to offer examples of their ICT use. Our cases show a lot of recursive interplay throughout the data. Even though this group of users varied in their use of ICT technology, they all talked about the rationales they had for the actions they took.

Fifth, "appropriation"—a key term for AST—is the process of bringing structures into practice via interaction. There are three aspects of appropriation: (a) the *amount* of appropriation—i.e., how much a group uses the methodology to complete tasks; (b) the *distribution* of appropriation—i.e., to what degree are members equally likely to use the method in problem-solving; and (c) appropriation *moves*—i.e., whether members use procedures in a textbook way or whether they creatively combine them with other methods or otherwise change them to fit the task (DeSanctis, Poole, Dickson, & Jackson, 1993). The amount of appropriation is substantial in these cases; interviewees use ICTs anywhere from two to eight hours a day. There are examples of both distribution—where people use lots of different methodologies, and density—where Microsoft products such as Word, Excel, and PowerPoint are world-wide universals that ensure that everyone can easily communicate via the same software.

### Time-Space Relations

One feature of Giddens' theory concerns the temporal and spatial attributes of social systems. The idea of time-space relations is especially applicable to organizations because they are capable of stretching over time and space to create a single integrated whole. A prominent feature in many of our cases is face-to-face communication, and Giddens also gives this prominence because the "face" or "presence" is such an important part of social encounters.[2]

*The "face" or "presence" is such an important part of social encounters.*

Giddens asserts that communication with people who are physically absent from an interaction is distinctly different from communication with those who are present because co-presence allows for a kind of moral order via face-to-face communication. But he also sees writing (in our cases, writing on the computer) as bearing a similarity to face-to-face encounters. ICTs are a special case of structuration. They are integrated because "time, space and repetition are so closely intertwined" (Cassell, p. 179). Giddens uses the concept of "positioning" to account for time-space relations:

> *In contemporary societies individuals are positioned within a widening range of zones, in home, workplace, neighborhood, city, nation-state and worldwide system, all displaying features of system integration which increasingly relates the minor details of daily life to social phenomena of massive time-space extension. (Giddens, 1984, p. 85)*

This is Giddens' way of saying, for our stories, that *we are all connected via ICTs and that time and space become subsumed by them.* We are all singular (in positions), yet we are connected and made one via ICTs (integration). Actors, Giddens tells us, are situated in relationship to each other by virtue of their individual time-space paths. Further, he sees the positioning of actors as a social identity that carries with it a "certain range of prerogatives and obligations" (p. 84).

*We are all connected via ICTs and that time and space become subsumed by them.*

For example, ICTs greatly affect the idea of individual positioning in time-space relations because ICTs somewhat negate the drawback of distance. However far apart we are physically, we can be drawn into communication relatively quickly. Take, for example, our writing of this

---

[2] For this book, we have included face-to-face as one kind of ICT because in all our cases, individuals use it as a technology, a particular way of doing things, much as they use electronic communication.

book. Because the four of us have a personal history of face-to-face relations over several years of work and have learned each other's patterns of grumbling, excitement, energy, and conflict, it was possible to complete a number of these cases in real time between Norway and the U.S. by working on them over the phone via NetMeeting.

Such a way of writing illustrates what Giddens calls separating "communication from transportation," in that much of the work was done outside of each other's presence. ICTs replace the need to travel and minimize the "friction of distance" (Cassell, 1993, p. 261), thus reducing the cost and effort of completing a task. Giddens' way of talking about technology is captured by his use of the term "modernity." He sees modern societies as capable of "lifting out" social relations from local contexts and re-articulating them "across indefinite tracts of time-space" (Cassell, 1993, p. 291), which has led to a tremendous acceleration of global connections for communication (see Rogers, 2003, pp. 346-348 for an account of the rapid diffusion of the Internet). An additional feature of modernizing is the development of "technical knowledge" (Cassell, 1993, p. 292), which has validity almost independent of the practitioners and clients who use it. We can use protocols and formats to communicate and thus standardize communication.

If society is indeed constituted, as Giddens says, by individuals positioned in certain social-interaction contexts, the individual and collective capabilities of those individuals will have some strategic impact. But this impact is paradoxical because Giddens also suggests that modern communication, despite the wealth of information, leaves its users insecure and uncertain of themselves as they pursue day-to-day life.

*If society is indeed constituted, as Giddens says, by individuals positioned in certain social-interaction contexts, the individual and collective capabilities of those individuals will have some strategic impact.*

## Summary

Structuration theory is included here to help us address a core question: Do ICTs control their users, or do users control their ICTs? Also, a related question: Do people voluntarily choose their ICTs? The precepts of structuration give us anchors to examine the nature of work life in the time of ICTs and the effects of these technologies.

## References

Browning, L. D., & Beyer, J. M. (1998). The structuring of shared voluntary standards in the U.S. semiconductor industry: Communicating to reach agreement. *Communication Monographs, 64,* 1-25.

Browning, L. D., Sutcliffe, K. M., Sitkin, S., Obstfeld, D., & Greene, R. (2000). Keep 'Em Flying: The constitutive dynamics of an organizational change in The U. S. Air Force. *Electronic Journal of Communication/La Revue Electronique de Communication (EJC/REC), 10* (1).

Cassell, P. (1993). *The Giddens reader.* Stanford, CA: Stanford University Press.

Conrad, C., & Haynes, J. (2001). Development of key constructs. In F. M. Jablin & L. L. Putnam (Eds.), *The new handbook of organizational communication.* Thousand Oaks, CA: Sage, 47-77.

DeSanctis, G., Poole, M. S., Dickson, G. W., & Jackson, B. M. (1993). An interpretive analysis of team use of group technologies. *Journal of Organizational Computing, 3*(1), 1-29.

Giddens, A. (1984). *The constitution of society.* Berkeley, CA: University of California Press.

Harre, R., & Secord, P. F. (1972). *The explanation of social behaviour.* Oxford: Blackwell.

Hirsh, C., & Browning, L. D. (1995, November). Integrating positioning, capacities, and copresence: Structurational elements in the constitution of a greenfield manufacturing operation. A paper presented at the Annual Meeting of the National Communication Association, San Antonio, TX.

Poole, M. S., & DeSanctis, G. (1990). Understanding the use of group decision support systems: The theory of adaptive structuration. In J. Fulk and C. Steinfield (Eds.), *Organizations and communication technology.* Newbury Park, CA: Sage, 173-193.

Ranson, S., Hinings, B., & Greenwood, R. (1980). The structuring of organizational structures. *Administrative Science Quarterly, 25,* 1-17.

Rogers, E. M. (2003). *Diffusion of innovations* (5th ed.). New York: Free Press.

# Complexity Theories and ICTs[1]

**8**

Alf Steinar Sætre & Larry D. Browning

Although an organization may appear a single entity, it is actually composed of many diverse individuals, all more or less autonomous, who communicate with each other, and the world, from their own viewpoints and experiences. In fact, when they use ICTs, their diversity is only amplified by the speed and ease with which they can communicate, since they can now "talk" through a broader range of media with a more diverse set of people than ever before. Clearly, then, a typical modern organization would seem to qualify, at least in normal parlance, as a complex system.[2]

But "complexity" has a more specific meaning within the so-called "complexity sciences," and scholars of this specific kind of complexity are actually divided on whether organizations do in fact qualify. Some scholars insist that they are (Brown & Eisenhardt, 1997; Wood, 1999). Others, like Ralph Stacey, are only willing to see certain limited analogies between organizations and complex systems (Stacey, 2001: Stacey, Griffith & Shaw, 2000).[3] Stacey argues that "the 'system' does not provide an analogy for human action but that the process of interaction does" (Stacey, 2001, p. 70). He goes even further, stating that "complexity theories cannot simply be applied to human action; they can only serve as a source domain for analogies with it" (Stacey, 2001, p. 71).

At the risk of oversimplification, we might state the difference between the two scholarly camps in this way: those who view organizations as systems see organizations as having to react to external elements, such as fluctuations in the economy, whereas those who, like Stacey and his colleagues, view organizations not as systems but as processes, insist that there is nothing outside of the process. And why? Because the organization—if it still makes sense to use such terminology—is itself a part of the economy and thus a part of each fluctuation in it. Hence,

**Note**

There is in fact no such thing as a unified theory of complexity. When scholars talk about Complexity Theory, they are actually referring to Complexity Sciences.

---

[1] We wish to thank Stig Johannessen, Judy Shetler, and Endre Sjøvold for their valuable advice and comments on earlier versions of this chapter.
[2] Part of the difficulty in writing about concepts like complexity lies in the language itself. The term "complexity," while a commonplace word, also has a more precise scientific meaning.
[3] In fact, they even question whether it is appropriate to view organizations as systems at all.

this latter perspective is a radical departure from traditional systems thinking, but perhaps not such a radical departure from Weick's (1979) perspective on enactment and organizing that we present in another chapter in this book.

Our own preference in the present chapter is to view organizations as systems, but since many useful insights can be gained through Stacey's perspective, we will point to important issues where the two viewpoints collide.

## Complexity and Organizations

Most of the theories and models constituting the complexity sciences come from the "hard sciences"— e.g., physics, quantum mechanics, and chemistry. These sciences deal with systems made up of *physical* particles or elements, whereas economists and other social scientists deal with systems made up of social actors or agents—*human* "elements," such as people, firms, and groups. In each case, we have elements reacting to one another. Physicists, unlike their social-scientist counterparts, consider the spatial relations (distance and direction) between their elements. On the other hand, particle elements are dumb, whereas human elements are smart. Particles will react to external stimuli the same way each time, because they have no past, no experience, no future, no goals, no aspirations.[4] This property of their "elements" enables physicists to talk about universal laws, whereas social scientists are hard-pressed to come up with even a single unifying theory of human behavior. Economist Brian Arthur has stated the difference well:

*Most of the theories and models constituting the complexity sciences come from the "hard sciences" such as physics and chemistry.*

> Our [human] particles have to think ahead, and try to figure out how other particles might react if they were to undertake certain actions. Our particles have to act on the basis of expectations and strategies. And regardless of how you model that, that's what makes economics [and the social sciences] truly difficult. (Waldrop, 1992, p. 141)

This statement makes an eloquent argument for the so-called "soft sciences" being the truly "hard sciences," at least in terms of predictability and understanding. The complexity sciences in general hold great promise for the social and physical sciences to share models and theories and to learn from one another.

In this introduction to the complexity sciences, we will try to make these "hard sciences" easier to understand by showing how these rather abstract concepts and theories relate to organizations in general and ICT use in particular. Our chief focus here will be on "complex adaptive systems" (CAS). CAS theory considers the elements operating within a system and formulates models for how these elements interact. In our case, these "elements" are social actors interacting via ICTs.

*The so-called soft sciences are in many ways the truly hard sciences.*

---

[4] Though Einstein, Rosen, & Podolsy devised a theoretical paradox contending that atoms "know" the movement of other atoms, that paradox was later rejected by Bohr. (For a review, see David Bohm's [1980] chapter on "Hidden variables in quantum theory.")

Complex systems, whether they be human bodies or organizations, all have different planes or segments (Deleuze & Guttari, 1988) that work like nested hierarchies of increasingly ordered complexity—e.g., cells á organs á bodies á human organizations. A big organization, for example, consists at the lowest level of individuals who are organized into small work units or teams; these teams in turn constitute a unit; several units in turn make up a larger unit such as a department; several departments make up a business unit, and so on.

For each level we "climb" in these nested hierarchies, the complexity of the system increases because there are more overlapping causes of influence. The system also has different characteristics at higher levels than at lower levels. A complex system, then, is really a system of systems. In other words, there are both (a) interactions among the parts of systems on a given level and (b) interactions across different hierarchical levels. As a result, the communication between subgroups is at times direct and predictable, at other times indirect and unpredictable. With the advent of ICTs, however, organizational boundaries have become far more permeable—even, at times, almost invisible. People routinely use ICTs to send and receive messages without regard to organizational boundaries. Not only have ICTs contributed to the permeability of organizational boundaries (Sætre, 1998), but, more importantly, ICTs have led to a substantial increase in the amount of information and communication within and between organizations. Both the increased permeability of boundaries and the increased amount of communication add to the complexity and unpredictability of modern organizations.

Take yourself as an example. Do you work in a nicely predictable environment?[5] Probably not. In fact, it may sometimes resemble a madhouse. Consider this scenario. Let's say you have a key presentation scheduled tomorrow for a client of your firm. It's almost finished, but due to a social function for that same client tonight, you can't complete it before leaving work, so you take your laptop home with you, thinking you'll finish it before work the next day. Unfortunately, the party drags on into the night, so you go to bed thinking you'll just get up an hour earlier, at 5.30 a.m., and finish it then. You wake up feeling rotten. Worse, when you turn on your laptop, you discover that you'd forgotten to turn it off when you brought it home, and the battery is now flat. Worse still, you left the power cord at work. You dash next door to your neighbor who also has a laptop, wake him up, and ask to borrow his power cord. But as luck would have it, his laptop has both a different plug and a different voltage than yours, which only compounds his irritation at being awakened. Offering a hasty apology, you run back home, take a quick shower, and dash off to the office in hopes of finishing the presentation there. Because your office has unassigned work spaces (increasingly common in many countries), when you arrive you discover the area you had used yesterday is now occupied by someone else, and she has not seen your power cord, so you run around trying to find it. After 12 minutes of frenetic search, you manage to bor-

---

[5] For an example of accident-proneness exacerbating the complexities of getting to work, see Charles Perrow's (1999) book Normal Accidents, pp. 5-6.

row an identical power cord. You work furiously to finish your presentation, then rush into the conference room five minutes late, thoroughly flustered.

If you examine why this "accident" happened, you can see that there are actually multiple *direct* and *indirect* causes. Now multiply these capricious events that happen to one individual by the number of people in an organization and you can begin to see that there are myriad variables at play. Even so, occasionally all the workers in your environment do in fact manage to get to a scheduled meeting on time, and everybody may even come properly prepared for it, and all of the agenda items may get covered in the allotted time. The unpredictable little scenario with the laptop and the missing power cord contains some of the components of complexity theory that we will address here.

*In our lives there are actually multiple direct and indirect causes of accidents.*

### Fundamentals of Complexity: Nonlinearity and Self-Organization in Complex Adaptive Systems

Have you ever noticed that in most public outdoor areas, such as city parks or campus greens, we'll often find well-worn trails created by people who have left the formal walkways—the concrete or cobblestone paths—to cut across those spaces? The formal walkways are like the formal structure of an organization—the official organizational chart. But in organizations, as in parks, people tend to take different pathways than those prescribed for them. In short, they'll use other "channels." Over time, these channels become so routinized that they become part of the actual structure, whether it's a park or an organization.

The well-worn paths illustrate what theorists call "self-organization." With the advent of modern ICTs such as email, text messaging, voicemail, collaborative software, and so on, the opportunity and tools for organizational members to self-organize their activities have reached unprecedented levels.

The essence of self-organization is that system structures—things made up of many parts held together in a specific way—often appear to move toward that *particular* structure without direct pressures from outside the system, although self-organization always occurs as a result of *some* external pressure or perturbation.[6] In our example of the dirt paths, a person who is running late (experiencing pressure) for a meeting is influenced to get to work faster than usual, but how he does it (the "*particular* structure") is improvised, not predetermined. Self-organization is the mechanism that drives the creation of new structures, whether they be worn paths in a park, or new ICT-based communication patterns within and between organizations.

---

[6] Stacey and his associates (Stacey, 2001; Stacey, Griffity & Shaw, 2000) take a different approach, viewing self-organization as a continual process that feeds on itself-i.e., whatever sets the process in motion is a part of the process-thus departing from traditional systems thinking of internal vs. external.

## Nonlinearity

Much of the Newtonian science produced in the last three centuries has rested on the assumption of linearity—that is, it has looked at systems operation in equilibrium (or at least very close to it). Equilibrium is achieved when the sum of all forces affecting a system is zero. Equilibrium is said to be "stable" if small, externally induced forces tend to produce counter forces that return the system to its original state.

But stable equilibrium does not characterize living systems (Capra, 1996). Instead, living systems exist in a state that is termed "far-from-equilibrium," albeit still a stable state. By "stable," we don't mean fixed, nor do we mean that such systems aren't fluctuating, for indeed they are both unfixed and fluctuating. Here is Capra's interpretation of this process:

> *A living organism is characterized by continual flow and change in its metabolism, involving thousands of chemical reactions. . . . Living organisms continually maintain themselves in a state far from equilibrium, which is the state of life. (Capra, 1996, pp. 175-176)*

Living systems in stable but far-from-equilibrium states are described by non-linear thermodynamics. Nonlinear equations usually have more than just one solution, and the higher the degree of nonlinearity, the greater the number of possible solutions. As a result, we live in a world where "the landscape is thickly settled with opinions, positions, and beliefs about the right and wrong way of perceiving and interacting with the world and each other" (Isaacs, 1999, p. 18). Organizations, which consist of social actors involved in multiple complex relationships, and who interact through ICTs, are characterized by nonlinearity. Complex systems, such as organizations, "change inputs to outputs in a nonlinear way because their components interact with one another via a web of feedback loops" (Anderson, 1999, p. 217). And the feedback can drive the system away from equilibrium just as it can move it toward it.

*In a nonlinear system such as an organization, the introduction of new ICTs in one process can dramatically and unpredictably alter the behavior of the whole organization.*

In short, in a nonlinear system such as an organization, intervening to alter one process (variable)—such as introducing a new ICT—can dramatically and unpredictably alter the behavior of the whole system (organization). Nonlinearity and self-organization are common to all complex systems.

Let's now take a closer look at complex adaptive systems and self-organization.

## Complex Adaptive Systems

Key Theory
Complex Adaptive Systems (CAS)

Complex adaptive systems (CAS) consist of heterogeneous agents or populations that seek to further their own interests and, in so doing, adapt to one another (Axelrod & Cohen, 1999; Holland, 1995). Many natural systems (immune systems, ecologies, ant hills, organizations, societies) and many artificial systems (parallel computing systems, artificial intelligence systems) are characterized by complex behaviors that emerge as a result of often nonlinear interactions among a large number of component systems striving to mutually adapt. Unlike Stacey and his associates (Stacey, 2001, Stacey, Griffith & Shaw, 2000), Wood (1999, p.157) believes that organizations are also "complex, adaptive systems comprising physical, cognitive, and socially constructed realities."

Complex adaptive systems often have "many participants, perhaps even many kinds of participants. They interact in intricate ways that continually reshape their collective future" (Axelrod & Cohen, 1999, p. xi). Organizations exhibit complex behavior that is sufficiently organized to ensure stability, but they also exhibit flexibility and novelty. Organizations adaptively adjust to changes in the environment, and this adaptive behavior can be only partially predicted (Brown & Eisenhardt, 1998). Modern ICTs have sped up these cycles of mutual adaptation and enactment[7] of environments as organizations use the Internet to monitor each other's competitive moves. Let's now look more closely at some characteristics of complex adaptive systems.

## Characteristics of CAS

In the two left-most columns of Table 8-1, below, we have laid out four characteristics of complex adaptive systems based on content from Gell-Mann (1994) and Anderson (1999). The two right-most columns show these characteristics' relevance to organizations and their application to ICTs.

Cognitive maps are in many ways shaped through the use of electronic media such as email and the Internet, as these technologies become increasingly important for social actors seeking to make sense of their constantly changing *Complex adaptive systems* environments. ICTs are also crucial as organizational members seek to *have many kinds of partici-* adapt to one another. Seemingly insignificant details, such as each person's *pants that interact in intri-* media preference, can be of great importance, and will vary across differ-*cate ways that continually* ent situations. Yet, in order to be effective, social actors are dependent on *reshape their collective* others not only having access to the same media—email, voicemail, and *future.* so on—but also on their having similar patterns of usage, such as checking their in-boxes regularly and replying promptly. You will see many examples in the various stories in this book.

As organizational members learn their colleagues' preferences, they learn who responds to what and thus learn, for example, to send an email instead of leaving a note in someone's physical in-box, or to send an SMS instead of leaving a voicemail. This knowledge is also used to adapt to new organizational members as they enter the organization, and to retain the relationship with former colleagues who are now working for other organizations. ICTs permeate most, if not all, processes in today's organizations, adding to the complexity of the organization, and speeding up existing processes. This is illustrated in the far-right column of Table 8-1.

In complex adaptive systems, the heterogeneity of multiple components pro-

---

[7] See Chapter 6 on Enactment.

*Table 8-1: Four Characteristics of CAS and their Relevance to Organizations*

| Characteristics | Explanation | Relevance to Organizations | Role of ICTs |
|---|---|---|---|
| 1. Agents with Schemata | Each agent's actions are guided by schemata of its environment. Different agents have different cognitive maps. | Social actors have cognitive maps guiding their behavior (Gioia & Poole, 1984), and these cognitive maps are unique to each individual. | ICTs can be both the subject of schemata or cognitive maps, and the object through which such cognitive maps are formed. |
| 2. Self-Organizing Networks Sustained by Importing Energy | All agents are interconnected to other agents via feed-back loops, so that the behavior of any given agent is dependent on the behavior of some of the other agents in the system. | Social actors are interdependent with other social actors in their own organizational context. Their behaviors are dependent on enacted social and group norms. | The ubiquity of ICTs, combined with their ability to link social actors into widespread networks, makes ICTs crucial both to the formation of these networks and their application for importing new information and energy into the organization. |
| 3. Co-evolution to the Edge of Chaos | Each agent adapts by striving to increase payoff over time. Since agents are continually adapting to one another, the landscape is constantly shifting. The resulting equilibrium is dynamic, not static. | Organizational members strive to succeed in the organization, adapting to shifting performance norms and goals. This constant movement yields a balance that is dynamic, not fixed. | The capacity for speed inherent in most ICTs has only contributed to an acceleration of these dynamic processes. |
| 4. Recombination and System Evolution | Complex adaptive systems (CAS) evolve over time as new agents enter, change, or leave the system. New links and patterns of relationships are formed. | The organization or a department is constantly changing, since new organizational members arrive, existing members learn, and other members leave. New relationships and patterns of interactions emerge. | ICTs add yet another layer of links among organizational members, facilitating the extension of a given unit far beyond its more traditional boundaries. |

vides the variability on which selection can act. These heterogeneous components interact nonlinearly, and self-organize hierarchically into structural arrangements. These self-organized structures in turn determine, and are reinforced by, the flows and interactions among the components (Levin, 1999). Simon Levin's description of complex adaptive systems "begins with the diversity of multiple, individual components, or agents with personal schemata, whose communication provides the interaction potential driving the system" (Shetler, 2002, pp. 24-25). These schemata—often created through the use of various ICTs—include among other things how and when to use a particular communication medium. But simple functional use is not the only thing to consider. According to Sitkin, Sutcliffe, and Barrios-Choplin (1992), each communication medium also carries with it a symbolic meaning that is separate from the actual message conveyed, thereby adding further complexity to the system.[8]

## Emergence

Part of the difficulty in writing about concepts like complexity and emergence lies in the language itself. "Emergent" typifies a commonplace word, like "chaos," long used in several ways, that has now also acquired a precise scientific meaning. For instance, "emergence" had traditionally denoted something of which we have become aware, or which has come into our perceptive focus—as, for example, something is said to "emerge," as from darkness, or from a discussion—although in fact it may have been there long before we became aware of it. In complexity theory, on the other hand, "emergence" refers to something that is genuinely new, not simply perceived as new. [9]

*With CSS-type emergence, a new entity arises that is more than a simple sum of its parts and thus irreversible to its original parts.*

Emergence, so defined, is a fundamental concept in all of the sciences that compose "complex system sciences" (CSS). With CSS-type emergence, a new entity arises that is *more than a simple sum of its parts and thus irreversible to its original parts* (Holland, 1995). Properties of a system that emerges are system properties that aren't evident from each of those parts. In other words, emergence is a higher-level phenomenon that cannot be reduced to its simpler constituents and needs new concepts to be introduced. As long as it retains its identity, it does not

---

[8] See Chapter 1, which covers media choice and media richness.

[9] For example, as one of the authors returned by sailboat from Shetland to the west coast of Norway, the crew witnessed the coastal mountains of Norway emerging out of the North Sea. In this case, Norway did not actually emerge (at least in the CSS sense) out of the ocean, as it has always been there. But in a different boating example, true CSS emergence did occur. In the early hours of November 14, 1963, an Icelandic fisherman named Olafur, when at the helm of a fishing boat, saw massive amounts of smoke near the coast of Westmanna Island. Thinking it was a large ship on fire, he awoke his captain and together they watched as the volcanic island now called Surtsey rose from the ocean. Forty years later, there are over 40 species of vascular plants found on Surtsey, and eight kinds of birds nesting there, not to mention butterflies. Seals now favor the island, too, and are breeding on its beaches. When there was only smoke on the water, it was impossible to predict not only which plants might eventually grow on the island-as some would be brought there by the wind, and others by birds from faraway places-but also the very shape and topography of the island. This is an example of CSS-type emergence. Integral to this type of emergence is the notion of irreversibility.

decompose into its constituent elements, even in a different state. It can disintegrate, but then it is no longer the same thing, just as a living being is not the same as the collection of all its chemical elements. *Irreversibility* is an important distinction between the classical mechanics of Newtonian physics and the nonlinear dynamics of CSS. In Newtonian physics, things were reversible and linear.

## Bifurcation Points and Prigogine's Theory of Dissipative Structures

"Bifurcation" represents a moment when a system's equilibrium is broken. At that moment, participants end their commitment to existing processes and values, and begin something new (Leifer, 1989). Another example of such bifurcation points are the introduction of telegraph and the telephone (Johnson & Rice, 1987). With ICTs, perhaps the most dramatic example of bifurcation was when the World Wide Web became a mainstay of how we communicate in the workplace.[10] Once this happened, our communication was forever altered; it had speed and energy unlike anything we had ever experienced before.

Complexity theory suggests that, following a bifurcation point, the old system may appear to disintegrate in disarray but in the process attains a more complex and appropriate alignment—a new ordering (Gemmill and Smith, 1985). The new emergent patterns from this change are called "dissipative structures" because they dissipate energy or information imported from the environment to continuously renew themselves. In the case of the Web, for example, had value not been gained from implementing it as a technology, it would be a "dead" technology from lack of use. It is to dissipative structures we now turn our attention.

## Dissipative Structures

Dissipative structures are also complex adaptive systems, but dissipative structure theory considers whole systems or populations and constructs mathematical models of their relationships at the macro level. Dissipative structure theory, which earned its developer Ilya Prigogine the Nobel Prize in chemistry in 1977, and the theory of complex adaptive systems both exhibit the central properties of CSS—emergence and nonlinearity.

**Key Theory**
Dissipative
Structures

Table 8-2, on the next page, lays out five steps in the formation of dissipative structures. The contents of the left column are from Stacey, Griffin, and Shaw (2000, p. 94). In the right-hand column we have laid out the analogous application to social systems and organizations.

---

[10] Though bifurcation in dissipative structures is really a point or an instant and thus can't be easily compared to an "instant" that many would argue has taken the better part of a decade, the ramifications are similar, in that there really is no turning back. Most organizations today simply cannot function without using the Internet and other advanced ICT.

*Table 8-2: The Formation of Dissipative Structures*

| The Formation of Dissipative Structures in Chemical Systems[11] | Analogous Formation of Emergent Structures in Social Systems |
| --- | --- |
| 1. A liquid, or gas, is held *far from equilibrium* by some *environmental constraint,* such as heat. | An organization can face major change, such as a merger, a downturn in the economy, or the introduction of a new ICT system. |
| 2. In this condition, small *fluctuations* (that is, variations in molecular movements in the liquid) are *amplified* to break the microscopic *symmetry* of the entities comprising it. | In this situation, organizational members feel tensions, and behaviors and routines are challenged. Disorder is amplified and *breaks the structure* among and within units in the organization. Established communication links are disrupted or even severed. |
| 3. At a critical level of environmental constraint the system reaches a *bifurcation* point. This is a point at which the system becomes unstable and has the possibility of developing along a number of different pathways. | At some critical level the organization can change dramatically. This is a point at which the organization has the possibility of developing along a number of different, and in some cases unknowable, pathways. |
| 4. At this bifurcation the whole ensemble of entities *spontaneously self-organizes,* in effect "choosing" a pathway, one of which could produce a new pattern, such as a laser beam. In other words, long-range *correlations* form between the entities, and a new coherent pattern suddenly *emerges* without any blueprint, one that cannot be explained by, or reduced to, or predicted from, the nature of the system's component entities. | New coherent patterns of interaction and communication can suddenly *emerge in an organization.* These emerging patterns cannot be explained by, or reduced to, or predicted from, the nature of the system's component entities, nor the environmental constraint inducing the change. New communication patterns emerge and thus a new "structure." |
| 5. That pattern is a *dissipative structure,* that is, one that dissipates energy or information imported from the environment, so it continuously renews itself. The structure is an evolving interactive process that temporarily manifests itself in globally stable states taking the form of irregular patterns, and it is essentially a contradiction or paradox: symmetry and uniformity of pattern are being lost, but there is still a structure; disorder is used to create new structure. | In today's organizations, ICTs play a central role in new emergent structures. Previous organizational structures and routines are being irreversibly altered and replaced by temporary *emergent* structures. |

[11] The frequent assumption here is that individual entities or particles of any given type are identical; this is an assumption that clearly does not hold for social systems.

Most organizations are in a constant state of change—or even upheaval. In the environment in which organizations operate, consumer preferences and market conditions are always shifting; new technologies are introduced, and old ones discontinued, augmenting the stress on the system. Old structures—routines, cognitive maps, relationships—are breaking down, and new ones are emerging. The fax machine replaces the telex; then, emailing attachments replaces the fax machine, and electronic bulletin boards replace physical ones. New organizational members bring new knowledge and new ideas to the organization; whole layers of the hierarchy get eradicated (downsized), and remaining organizational members get assigned new roles. Out of this cauldron *emerge* new routines, new relationships, and new media usage—new structures—that could not even have been imagined, much less predicted. These new structures of alteration are continually self-renewing as new ICTs are introduced and new environmental demands are enacted.

## Conclusion

An overarching principle of social systems—and, in particular, organizations—is that instead of following universal laws, they follow complex "rules" unique to a given system (Harre & Secord, 1972). "Near equilibrium we find repetitive phenomena and universal laws. As we move away from equilibrium, we move from the universal to the unique, towards richness, and variety" (Capra, 1996, p. 177). The term for the latter is "far from equilibrium," meaning that the system has both stable elements (that hold it in place) and unstable ones (that create its variety). Uniqueness, richness, and variety indeed characterize living social systems. As you read the 20 cases in this book, you will see patterns of similarity in how social actors use ICTs, but you will also see substantial differences. Most of all, you will notice the richness and variety in their stories. The use of ICTs to build and maintain social interactions is truly a complex phenomenon.

For as long as there have been organizations, the desire for control and predictability of these organizations has been a central notion for practitioners and researchers alike. With the advent of a complexity perspective—transformative or not—the notion of control might have to be at least temporarily abandoned, and replaced by the notion of influence.

*With the advent of a complexity perspective—transformative or not—the notion of control might have to be at least temporarily abandoned, and replaced by the notion of influence.*

## References

Anderson, P. (1999). Complexity theory and organization science. *Organization Science, 10*(3), 216-232.

Axelrod, R., & Cohen, M. D. (1999). *Harnessing complexity: Organizational implications of a scientific frontier.* New York: The Free Press.

Bohm, D. (1980). *Wholeness and the implicate order.* London: Routledge.

Brown, S. L., & Eisenhardt, K. M. (1997). The art of continuous change: Linking complexity theory and time-paced evolution in relentlessly shifting organizations. *Administrative Science Quarterly, 42*(1), 1-34.

Capra, F. (1996). *The web of life*. London: HarperCollins Publishers.

Deleuze, G., & Guttari, F. (1988). *A thousand plateaus: Capitalism and schizophrenia*. London: Athlone Press.

Gell-Mann, M. (1994). *The Quark and the Jaguar: Adventures in the Simple and the Complex*. New York: W.H. Freeman.

Harre, R., & Secord, P. F. (1972). *The explanation of social behaviour*. Totowa, NJ: Littlefield, Adams & Co.

Holland, J. H. (1995). *Hidden order: How adaptation builds complexity*. Cambridge, MA: Helix Books/Perseus Books.

Isaacs, W. (1999). *Dialogue and the art of thinking together*. New York: Currency.

Johnson, B., & Rice, R.E. (1987). *Managing organizational innovation: The evolution from word processing to office information systems*. New York: Columbia University Press.

Leifer, R. (1989). Understanding organizational transformation using a dissipative structure model. *Human Relations, 42*(10), 899-916.

Levin, S. (1999). *Fragile dominion: Complexity and the commons*. Cambridge, MA: Perseus Publishing.

Perrow, C. (1999). *Normal accidents: Living with high-risk technologies* (Updated ed.). Princeton: Princeton University Press.

Sætre, A. S. (1998). Toward a grounded theory of organizing and communicating in the postindustrial economy. *Dissertation Abstracts International, 58*(07), 2464. (UMI No. 9803010)

Shetler, J. (2002). *Complex adaptive systems, attractors, and patching: A complex systems science analysis of organizational change*. Unpublished Doctoral Dissertation, The University of Texas at Austin, Austin, TX.

Sitkin, S. B., Sutcliffe, K. M., & Barrios-Choplin, J. R. (1992). A dual-capacity model of communication media choice in organizations. *Human Communication Research, 18*(4), 563-598.

Stacey, R. H. (2001). *Complex responsive processes in organizations: Learning and knowledge creation*. London: Routledge.

Stacey, R. H., Griffin, D., & Shaw, P. (2000). *Complexity and management: Fad or radical challenge to systems thinking?* London: Routledge.

Waldrop, M. M. (1992). *Complexity: The emerging science at the edge of order and chaos*. London: Penguin Books.

Weick, K. E. (1979). *The social psychology of organizing* (2nd ed.). Reading, MA: Addison-Wesley.

Wood, R. (1999). The future of strategy: The role of the new sciences. In M. R. Lissack & H. P. Gunz (eds.), *Managing complexity in organizations* (pp.118-160). Westport, CT: Quorum Books.

# ICT and Culture

9

Jan-Oddvar Sørnes & Keri K. Stephens

When you hear the word *culture*, what association comes to mind? Is culture something that we have in us? Something we belong to? Something that describes how others are affiliated? People say things like "He's a typical American," "The immigrants brought their culture with them," "IBM has a formal culture that dictates its dress code," "I looked up that company's Website and they must be professional," and "All accountants love numbers." Clearly, such remarks are indicators of culture and show that the term has multiple connotations, varying according to context. As the stories in this book focus on ICT use, the connections between cultures and ICTs need to be explained.

When ICTs are used, culture may both influence them and be influenced by them. Because the imprint of culture is so pervasive, it is also powerful. Leaders often want to change and manage cultures, since once one is established, it's an efficient form of control; the enforcement of cultural practices is often driven by peer assessments and approval. In these readings, we take the structuration view of culture—namely, that people simultaneously control culture and are controlled by it.

> *When ICTs are used, culture may both influence them and be influenced by them.*

For example, in Norway, cellphones have become ubiquitous because Scandinavian countries adopted, early on, a common set of technical specifications and policies, thus giving users the advantage of being able to operate their cellphones across national borders; this in turn promoted among these nations a common cellphone culture. Meanwhile, the very diffusion of cellphone technology has had the effect of making more people more reachable 'round the clock, so it has inevitably begun blurring the boundary between work and home. But easy access has also done something even more insidious: it has turned many Norwegians into *cellphone addicts*, especially if their phones have SMS (Short Message Service). In fact, the SMS capability of cellphones has made pagers obsolete. As a result, all pager services were shut down in Norway as of September 1, 2003. Since the stories in this book are heavily influenced by both ICT use and diverse notions of culture, we need frameworks that help interpret these cultural differences.

We often think of culture in national terms—e.g., American culture, Norwegian culture, French culture. These are examples of *national or societal cultures*, each of which carries stereotypes characterizing the allegedly "typical" attitudes and behaviors associated with it. *Corporate culture* and, more broadly, *organizational culture* are terms used to describe how attitudes are expressed within specific organizations (Schein, 1992). Thus, for example, we speak of the Hewlett-Packard culture, the Telenor culture, the Microsoft culture, the Big Blue (IBM) culture. But even in companies that have a strongly homogeneous culture, it's also useful to identify *organizational subcultures* (Trice & Beyer, 1993), which may consist of individuals sharing either the same occupation or job skills (e.g., engineers or marketers) or hierarchical divisions (e.g., mid-level managers or CEOs). While there are still more subcultures one might explore, such as ethnic, regional, and generational, they are beyond the scope of our present chapter.

### The Relationship Between Culture and ICTs

It's important to study the relationship between culture and ICTs because individuals and organizations in the Western world face the challenge of managing and using a proliferation of new ICTs—e.g., email, voicemail, WWW, cellphones, videoconferencing, etc. As ICTs have become ever-present in organizations, more practices are related to them. Because organizations progressively expand into global markets, critical decisions need to be made about what ICTs will enable successful communication (Ross, 2001). Implementing ICTs effectively within a single organization is a challenge in and of itself, but the task becomes critical when moving to the international scene. To embed a variety of ICTs in organizations requires a meticulous exploration of the dynamics of the particular organizational cultures and, likewise, the cultures of the organizations and countries they will be communicating with (Ross, 2001; Westrup, Al Jaghoub, El Sayed & Liu, 2002).

When we define "culture" according to three main levels—national, organizational, and subcultural—we also need to examine how they each relate to ICT use. Traditionally, this connection can be viewed two different ways. First, technology can affect culture, most obviously on organizational and subcultural occasions. Consider, for example, the way email has changed how people correspond in writing. People no longer rely as much on a fax machine, since attaching documents in an email is both quicker and simpler. As this practice continues, it becomes a new norm in the organization. Voilà, an "email" culture is now established.

Culture can also affect technology use—specifically, in how ICTs are adopted. For example, Orlikowski (2000) studied the implementation of Lotus Notes, a groupware product, into two types of organizations: software and consulting. The software organization implemented Lotus Notes fully and even began to improve it to meet more of its clients' needs. In contrast, the consulting organization only marginally implemented the product and basically left it unchanged. This illustrates how subcultures have different needs and preferences when implementing and using new ICTs. In this case, the norms and rewards for the consultants were independent, so sharing information was not in their best interest.

The existing culture of an organization can also dictate how ICTs are used. In organizations where customers are valued highly, rules such as *"Return every customer call in less than five minutes"* are established. Since organizational culture is often heavily influenced by the founder, leader behavior can shape ICT use, too. For example, suppose the managing partner of a law firm has hundreds of books in her office and no computer on her desk. She sends a strong signal to others in her firm that they should treat books as a first source for information.

## Organizational Culture

Organizational culture, the first level discussed in this chapter, is an organization's patterned way of thinking, feeling, and reacting. The value of an organizational culture is that, in theory, all members of a given community are provided with accepted ways to conform to their beliefs (Trice & Beyer, 1993)— that is, they learn how to behave by expectations. This is both good and bad. It is good because culture can help members fit in and manage uncertainty and ambiguity. It is bad because it can squelch new ideas and indoctrinate all members into group-think.

Organizational culture is not always obvious, and whether it is "changeable" is highly debated. According to Schein (1992), leaders of an organization can shape, direct, and change its culture. He also provides a list of 10 "overt phenomena" that, he says, are associated with organizational culture (see pp. 8-10 for details):

**Key Theory**
Edgar Schein
Organizational
Culture
Ten Overt
Phenomena

1. Observed behavioral regularities when people interact.

2. Group norms.

3. Espoused values.

4. Formal philosophy.

5. Rules of the game.

6. Climate.

7. Embedded skills.

8. Habits of thinking, mental models, and/or linguistic paradigms.

9. Shared meanings.

10. Root metaphors or integrated symbols.

These 10 categories encompass telltale ways of thinking and doing things, so they are especially useful for discerning the differences between cultures. Most of Schein's examples compare one organizational culture with another on a particular dimension. Such a comparison of corporate cultures was possible in an analysis of Sematech, a U.S. semiconductor manufacturing consortium that was created in 1987 to respond to Japan's effort to dominate world chip manufacturing (Browning & Shetler, 2000). The U.S. chip manufacturers, who had had a pitiful history of cooperation with each other and with the companies that supplied them their materials and equipment, established Sematech to overcome their differences and mimic the cooperative relations of the Japanese. The 12 U.S. firms that founded Sematech included IBM, Intel, Motorola, Texas Instruments, and Hewlett-Packard, among others, and constituted 75% of the U.S. chip manufacturers. Delegations from the 12 firms came together in one large building in Austin, Texas, to work on problems of cooperation. A brief account of how they worked together will illustrate Schein's taxonomy of cultural features.

Our comparison begins with contrasting the two dominant forces in U.S. chip manufacturing. One was IBM, which represented the formalistic, East Coast style of work. While IBM's dress code of white shirts and conservative business attire had long passed, they remained "buttoned-down" types habituated to vertical decision-making. It was inevitable, then, that they distrusted their West Coast rivals, such as Intel and Hewlett-Packard, which epitomized the California corporate culture. Those firms had a reputation for being casual and for involving employees democratically in all kinds of business decisions. The West Coast style was epitomized by Bob Noyce, who was named the CEO of Sematech. Noyce implemented high-involvement employee programs because he believed that not to do so meant wasting valuable talent. Over time, Noyce set the tone for how Sematech would operate. He was a charismatic leader, in part because, as a founder of Intel and a co-inventor of the microchip, he had proven his genius.

*Organizational culture can be a powerful force that creates unique identities for companies, but this is simply the macro perspective. Inside the organization one also finds subgroups of employees that form their own distinct cultures.*

Once members of these 12 firms came together and began making decisions that required consensus, they noted some sharp differences. For example, they could spot engineers from each other's firms by the way they handled themselves in meetings. Some engineers would take forever to reach a decision; others, like IBM personnel, would arrive at a meeting with a tight agenda and fret over why others were so disorganized. Some companies, like Hewlett-Packard, had a reputation for having a lot of agreement within their company for any strategy put forth at Sematech; other companies were contentious within their own ranks and thus had little impact on the consortium's agenda. Once they all began operating under a single administrative program at Sematech, individual corporate differences on little things, such as what items were permissible travel expenses, became points of contention. But there were bigger differences, too. Texas Instruments, for instance, had a corporate tradition of guardedness. Having done so much top-secret contract work for the U.S. military, the company was used to being far more secretive than the other members of Sematech; indeed, not surprisingly, some TI leaders staunchly opposed joining Sematech for just that reason. Because of their military contracts, security had long been important in their plants, and their security guards carried pistols—a frightful sight to members of the laid-back California companies. Texas Instruments was also distinguished by its engineering excellence. But the company's very ability to develop engineering talent, together with its reputation for overbearing management, had made it vulnerable to corporate raiding by other Sematech companies such as Motorola, which were run more democratically.

This example demonstrates that organizational culture can be a powerful force that creates unique identities for companies. The individuals inside these organizations carry their broad identities with them as they collaborate with others and as they change jobs. But this example also hints that organizational culture, like Sematech's, is simply the macro perspective, whereas inside the organization one also finds subgroups of employees that form their own distinct cultures.

## Subcultural Influence

Historically, scholars and practitioners have assumed organizational cultures to be fairly homogenous. But more recently they have realized that (1) not all organizations have a single culture, (2) many cultures can exist in a single organization, and (3) there can be an overarching culture along with several other subcultures in a given organization (Trice & Beyer, 1993). Cauldron (1992) has effectively summarized this paradigm shift. In the 1980's, she says, management consultants had focused on convincing corporate America that "corporate culture is a uniform force, a single rudder that guides organizations," whereas in the 1990's these same consultants were now contending that "corporate culture is not a single engine driving the boat; it more closely resembles a collection of oars paddled by employees who have conflicting ideas about the daily course of business" (p. 61).

*Key Concept*
*Organizational cultures are not homogenous.*

While it's important to understand that cultures exist at the organizational level, the narratives in this book show that subcultures will have their own norms with respect to ICTs. Since these narratives regularly illustrate two distinct subcultures—those whose jobs primarily focus on communicating interorganizationally, and those who communicate intraorganizationally—we turn now to the second type of culture discussed in this chapter, subcultures.

Van Maanen and Barley (1985) define "subculture" as "a subset of an organization's members who interact regularly with one another, identify themselves as a distinct group within the organization, share a set of problems commonly defined to be the problems of all and routinely take action on the basis of collective understandings unique to the group" (p. 38). It makes sense that groups like salespeople and software engineers use ICTs differently because, as members of two distinct subcultures, they tend to value different things. Several studies have shown that these two groups differ in their business objectives (Sherriton & Stern, 1997; Workman, 1995), style of dress (Von Meier, 1999), and prior education (Trice & Beyer, 1993). They even tend to stereotype one another to the point of becoming ethnocentric. A marketer explains the concept this way: "Each functional area thinks of themselves as being the company, or at least at the center of it. Engineering sees themselves as being central, with marketing taking their stuff and handing it to sales. Marketing sees themselves as coordinating all the other pieces. They're the ones that set the tone for the company

*Key Concept*
*Subculture*

*Groups like salespeople and software engineers use ICTs differently because, as members of two distinct subcultures, they tend to value different things.*

in general.  Sales people think if you don't get this problem solved by the end of the week, then we're going to lose every sale" (Gregory, 1983, p. 372).  These representations reflect differing work environments, and they spawn different uses for the same ICTs.

In his work on subcultures, Hofstede (1998) labeled these two—the sales people and the engineers—as "customer-interface" and "professional," and noted that customer-interface personnel are (1) more results-oriented, probably because they must constantly respond to market pressures, and (2) more loosely controlled, since they are often off on their own, meeting customers face-to-face. This is why they are often considered interorganizational communicators.

Trice and Beyer (1993) describe "occupations" as "imported subcultures" since they have "their origins outside organizations" (p. 178).  Even members of the same occupation in different organizations can be influenced by their occupational subcultures through friendship networks and memberships in occupationally focused organizations (Trice & Beyer).  With the introduction of some forms of ICTs, the potential interactions that affect subculture formation and existence may be heightened.  For example, email and newsgroups are two forms of ICTs that allow organizational members access to numerous kindred spirits both inside and outside the organization (Trice & Beyer).

**Key Concept**
Occupations are imported subcultures.

Studies that compare ICT use between subunits in a single organization conclude that patterns of use and frequency of use vary among these groups (Markus, Bikson, El-Shinnawy, & Soe, 1992; Rice & Shook, 1990). Rice and Shook (1990) surveyed people in four different organizations to better understand how they use ICTs. These were people in different job categories, too, like clerical, technical, and managerial.  Upon examining how the different groups used ICTs—with formal meetings, face-to-face telephone, and email—Rice and Shook found that the first medium pattern was the same across all organizations—meetings.  But the second medium pattern did change—sometimes email, sometimes phone, etc. Some differences correlated with users' organizational level (e.g., managers and technical staff); other differences correlated with whether users communicated intraorganizationally and interorganizationally.

Fulk and Boyd (1991) believe that computer networks have helped to create new types of interorganizational linkages. Individuals who communicate interorganizationally are affected not only by their own organizations but by other ones as well. Interorganizational communication takes on a different understanding in the context of ICTs because factors such as access, organizational culture, and symbolic meaning might differ. Rice (1993) found some evidence of the differences between these two groups with respect to voicemail use. Studying six organizations, he found that individuals in sales-related jobs tended to rank voicemail as a more appropriate ICT than did individuals in technical and professional roles. Adams, Todd, and Nelson (1993) compared email and voicemail use in a single organization and found that email was considered more useful for intraorganizational communication while voicemail was preferred interorganizationally. In their study of teleworkers, Scott and Timmerman (1999) found that virtual workers used different technologies to communicate with internal audiences than with customers.

As you read the narratives in this book you will notice that they reflect some of these subcultural differences. Salespeople tend to emphasize their use of portable ICTs such as laptop computers and cellphones. Since these workers are typically working out of multiple offices, including their cars, this makes sense. Engineers and software experts talk about how they use the WWW and newsgroups to keep them current in their jobs. Overall, subcultural differences are not always distinct, but they provide an interesting lens through which to examine ICT use.

*Subcultural differences are not always distinct, but they provide an interesting lens through which to examine ICT use.*

## National Culture – Hofstede's Perspective

The term "culture" is commonly used to describe national differences. While we acknowledge that there are many cultural theoretical lenses (see Stohl, 2001, for a review), in the final part of this chapter we focus on Hofstede's (1980) framework. Well-established now after more than 20 years of use, Hofstede's dimensions of national culture are commonly invoked by academics, consultants, and management groups to clarify the differences between national cultures. Relying on an extensive survey involving some 116,000 respondents from over 40 countries, Hofstede created a model that compared different national cultures on four dimensions:

**Key Model** Hofstede's dimensions of national culture.

1.  Power Distance Index (PDI).

2.  Uncertainty Avoidance Index (UAI).

3.  Individualism/Collectivism (IDV).

4.  Materiality and Sociality (MSI).[1]

Hofstede (1980) defines "culture" psychologically and sociologically as "the collective programming of the mind which distinguishes the members in one human group from another" (p. 21). In cross-national research, people from different cultural and ethnic backgrounds are referred to as having "different mindsets," where "mindsets" refers to all those concepts related to cultural similarities and differences (Hofstede, 1991). Hofstede contends that culture is *learned*, not just *inherited*. This is important in a study of ICT use because it suggests that individuals can both learn and unlearn cultural traits based on environmental influences.

*Culture is learned, not just inherited.*

We use Hofstede's concepts for several reasons. First, his model has been shown to be stable and useful for numerous studies across many disciplines (Sondergaard, 1990, Hofstede, 2001). Second, his research and arguments are compelling to or-

---

[1] Hofstede originally coined the term "Masculinity/Femininity" to represent this dimension. We have renamed it "Materiality/Sociality" because such a change reflects that individuals of either the male or female gender might reflect these characteristic.

ganizational researchers because, even before empirical testing, links can be seen between his four dimensions and many aspects of international organizational behavior (Sackman, 1997). Hofstede's "variables" indicate that a given culture's potency varies along each of the four dimensions. Furthermore, his social-psychological categories encompass many of the standard organizational issues like power, participation, information-processing, and social support. For example, familiar organizational constructs such as "decision-making" and "change" can be associated with Hofstede's dimension of "uncertainty avoidance" (UAI). If an organization decides to change its existing company-wide standard from, say, Microsoft software products to Linux, the employees not familiar with this new operating system will experience considerable stress due to uncertainty.

Hofstede's framework also explicitly links national cultural values to communication practices (Merchant, 2002; Samovar, 1981; Stohl, 2001). Since the narratives in this book examine communication practices, particularly in the presence of ICTs, this framework is useful. Hofstede's conceptualization of culture is also no stranger in the ICT literature because several researchers have used it to explain the role of ICTs in the workplace (e.g., Rathod & Miranda 1999; Straub, Loch, Evaristo, Karahanna & Strite, 2002).

## Hofstede's Four Dimensions of Cultural Differences

Since all the data for the narratives in this book were collected in either the United States (11 narratives) or Norway (nine narratives), we will focus the description of Hofstede's four dimensions on similarities and differences between just these two countries.

*Subcultural differences are not always distinct, but they provide an interesting lens through which to examine ICT use.*

To clarify these national-culture considerations, we will first explain each dimension. On the first two dimensions (PDI and UAI), Norway and the U.S. are quite similar; on the third (IDV), they show some difference; and on the final dimension (MSI), they show major differences. Hofstede's study (1980) used 33 questions, focusing on values, that is, "people's more permanent mental programming—that reflect the contribution of the *person* more than the *situation*" (p. 47). Questions such as "Have sufficient time left for your personal or family life?", "Have considerable freedom to adopt your own approach to your job?", and "Have little tension or stress on the job?" were answered on a five-point scale, ranging from "Of utmost importance" to "Of very little or no importance" (see Hofstede, 1980, Appendix 1 for full questionnaire). Based on the 33 questions, each country's scores were factor-analyzed, and correlations were compared. Hofstede concluded that there were four dimensions from both statistical findings and theoretical reasoning. Table 9-1 (opposite page) displays the differences between Norway and the U.S. on each of the four dimensions and gives the range of each dimension.

*Table 9-1: Norwegian and U.S. scores on Hofstede's 4 Dimensions*

| Country | PDI | UAI | IDV | MSI |
|---|---|---|---|---|
| U.S. | 40 | 46 | 91 | 62 |
| Norway | 31 | 50 | 69 | 8 |
| Range (IBM Study) | 11-104 | 8-112 | 6-91 | 5-95 |

## Power Distance Index (PDI)

Hofstede's first dimension (1991), the Power Distance Index (PDI), reveals dependence relationships between people in a country—or, more precisely, the extent to which *less* powerful members of a society accept *unequal* power distribution. Countries scoring on the low side of the PDI, such as Norway and the U.S., show a preference for consultation and cooperation, that is, interdependence between boss and subordinates. Relating this perspective to ICT use, we identified several findings in the existing literature:

1. Employees in low PDI cultures want a sense of participation in the choice and implementation of new ICTs (Veiga, Floyd & Dechants, 2001).

2. Among low PDI cultures, "rich media" such as face-to-face are prevalent, since there are few communication barriers based on status or power issues (Jarvenpaa, Rao & Huber, 1988).

3. In low PDI cultures, "lean media" such as email are used in a number of situations to increase efficiency (Jarvenpaa, Rao & Huber, 1988).

*ICTs reduce power dependence and make participation possible because the cost of scheduling a synchronous electronic meeting is minimal.*

ICTs reduce power dependence and make participation possible because the cost of scheduling a synchronous electronic meeting is minimal. Yet anonymity is also possible through technologies like newsgroups which give some protection to participants who prefer privacy.

## Uncertainty Avoidance Index (UAI)

The second dimension in Hofstede's (1980) original conceptualization is the "Uncertainty Avoidance Index" (UAI), which measures the "extent to which the members of a culture feel threatened by uncertain or unknown situations" (Hofstede, 1991, p. 113). Social psychology frames this concept as "tolerance for ambiguity," which indicates the extent to which a person is willing to let more information accrue before making a final decision. The UAI gauges people's ability to accommodate ambiguity and uncertainty in the workplace. In cultures with low UAI, like Norway and the U.S., there is *less* need for predictability and fewer written and unwritten rules to guide work tasks. When relating this dimension to ICT use, we find the following characteristics:

1. Due to less rule-dependency, low UAI cultures are more trusting (De Mooij, 2000).

2. As early adopters of ICT, low UAI cultures show innovative and advanced usage patterns (Maitland & Bauer, 2001).

3. Low UAI cultures will use multiple ICTs to solve similar working tasks (De Mooij, 2000; Maitland & Bauer, 2001; Veiga, Floyd & Dechants, 2001).

4. In low UAI cultures, employers will seldom try to impose company rules on ICT usage. And if they do, people will likely challenge or break such rules for pragmatic reasons (Veiga, Floyd, & Dechants, 2001).

5. Low UAI countries are more apt to leave tasks and major responsibility in the hands of younger workers (Hofstede, 1980).

6. Unlike managers in high UAI cultures, managers in low UAI cultures don't need to be experts in the field they manage (Hofstede, 1991).

ICT cultures work well when there is trust under conditions of uncertainty because such environments presuppose faith in colleagues' ability to contribute. In low UAI cultures, ICTs enable people at lower levels in the organization to access information previously reserved for higher-level managers. This facilitates more distributed decision-making in organizations and reduces uncertainty since more people are able to use ICTs to search for possible solutions.

**Individualism/Collectivism (IDV)**

Hofstede's (1980) third dimension gauges the "individualistic" or "collectivistic" nature of the country. In "individualistic" societies, individual ties are loose, and people are expected to look out for themselves and their immediate family. In "collectivist" societies, meanwhile, people are integrated at birth into strongly cohesive in-groups beyond their immediate family, and group loyalty lasts a lifetime. In the organizational context, the individualism or collectivism emphasized in a particular culture has a direct bearing on behavior. In Hofstede's study, the United States scores highest of all nations on this dimension, while Norway scores moderately high. When we relate the individualism dimension to ICT use, we find the following:

1. In high IDV countries, the notion that "time is money" is prevalent, causing individuals to manage their time and ICT choice tightly (Trompenaars & Hampden -Turner, 1998).

2. High IDV countries will use ICTs to handle several tasks either simultaneously or sequentially (Veiga, Floyd & Deschants, 2001).

3.  In IDV cultures, new ICTs are more likely to be viewed as useful when they are perceived as enhancing an individual's performance (Veiga, Floyd & Deschants, 2001).

4.  In high IDV cultures, people seem to be innovative and trusting in exchange relationships with external parties (Van Birgelen, Ruyter, Jong, & Wtzels, 2002).

In the stories in this book, you will notice that some people turn out to be high on both individualism *and* on collectivism. While there are several types of ICT use that involve groups of people, the greatest use in these cases occurs on an individual level. This suggests that while high IDV cultures use ICTs to "look out for themselves," individuals will often also be looking out for some larger group, as with bicycle clubs, high-school reunions, political interest groups, and of course the 9/11 support (Sørnes, Stephens, Sætre, & Browning, 2004).

## Materiality/Sociality Index (MSI)

Although Norway and the United States score similarly on the three previous dimensions, they show a stark contrast on the last one—the Materiality/Sociality Index (MSI). In broad terms, "Materiality" pertains to societies where social gender roles are distinct (i.e., "material" countries value assertiveness and focus on material success, whereas "social" countries value modesty, tenderness, and quality of life (Hofstede, 1991). Given the value placed on modesty in more "social" cultures, Triandis (1995) asserts that individuals from such cultures don't like to stick out—that is, be unique or conspicuous—unlike the more assertive, career-seeking individuals found in countries like the United States. The "live in order to work vs. work in order to live" dichotomy is often invoked to illustrate the fundamental difference. The United States scores moderately high in this dimension and is thus labeled "material," while Norway scores extremely low and is thus very "social." The following findings reflect the research that relates this dimension to ICT use:

1.  Leisure and personal activities, such as reading news and maintaining personal relationships using ICTs, may be tolerable in the workplace in social cultures, but unacceptable in material cultures (De Mooij, 2000).

2.  Even though workers in social cultures draw clear boundaries between the workplace and the private sphere, they tend to take work home (and use ICTs from there) just to be with their families (Hofstede, 2000).

These prior findings about ICT use suggest that the material culture of the U.S. is more task-oriented in its ICT use than Norway's social culture. But, interestingly, our cases in this book don't support that inference. ICTs seem to influence the MSI cultural dimension in complex ways such as ICT portability and broad usage. Since a worker in a social culture can do business at home on the computer as well as play or pursue leisure activities when at the office, ICTs appear to blur the differences between work and play.

### Reflexivity of ICTs and Culture

We have just given you a description of Hofstede's four dimensions, shown their usefulness when comparing the national cultures of Norway and the U.S., and offered some examples of what research might predict will happen when ICTs are used. All of this, mind you, focuses solely on how *culture affects ICT use*. But ICTs can also affect culture, and the two variables can interact in complex ways.

**Key Concept**
The relationship between culture and ICTs is reflexive.

It can be difficult to see how ICTs might affect national culture, however, since those changes likely occur over extended periods of time. And also because the relationship between culture and ICTs is reflexive. By "reflexive," we mean that the relationship between organizational cultures and ICTs is not simply causal, with one influencing the other in some fixed, predetermined way, but rather reciprocal (Gudykunst & Ting-Toomey, 1996). One strand of research argues that technical artifacts, such as computers, the Internet, or computer software, carry a DNA-like "technical code" that causes users to act in a certain way (Akrish, 1992; Feenberg, 1995; Flanagin, Farinola & Metzger, 2000). What happens, these authors argue, is that the designers' own values, choices, and assumptions inevitably get built into the things they design. The Internet is a prime example. By examining demographic data, design features, existing policy, and usage patterns, one can readily see that the Internet reflects certain values and norms such as freedom of speech, inclusiveness, open access and sharing of information, decentralized control, and free-market economics (Flanagin et al.). It's hardly surprising, then, that the Internet was created and is shaped predominantly by countries that, like the U.S. and the Scandinavian countries, value democracy and free speech.

*The Internet was created and is shaped predominantly by countries that, like the U.S. and the Scandinavian countries, value democracy and free speech.*

### Relating Theory to Practice

In this chapter we defined and conceptualized culture at three different levels—organizational, subcultural, and national—and showed how culture relates to ICT use in organizational settings. More specifically, we drew attention to the reflexive relationship between culture and ICTs. As you read the stories in this book, you'll discover that many of them have cultural implications. For instance, you will find examples of company policy directly determining how its members use certain ICTs. You will also find cases where certain ICTs are perceived as inappropriate for communicating with people from a different national culture, and even within their own organization. As mentioned previously, culture is complex. Hopefully, this overview sensitizes you to how culture and ICTs are intertwined in modern organizational life.

# References

Adams, D.A., Todd, P.A., & Nelson, R.R. (1993). A comparative evaluation of the impact of electronic and voicemail on organizational communication. *Information & Management, 24*, 9-21.

Akrish, Madeleine (1992). The De-Scription of Technical Objects. In Bijker, W. E. & Law, J. (Eds) *Shaping Technology/Building Society: Studies in Sociotechnical Change*, (pp. 205-224), Cambridge, MIT Press

Browning, L. D & Shetler, J. C. (2000). *Sematech: Saving the U.S. Semiconductor Industry,* College Station, TX, Texas A & M University Press.

Cauldron, S. (1992). Subculture strife hinders productivity. *Personnel Journal, 71*, 60-64.

De Mooij, M. (2000). The future is predictable for international marketers: Converging incomes lead to diverging consumer behavior. *International Marketing Review, 17(2)*, 103-113.

Feenberg, A. (1995). *Alternative Modernity.* Berkeley, University of California Press.

Flanagin, A. J., Farinola, W. J. M., & Metzger, M. J. (2000). The technical code of the Internet / World Wide Web. *Critical Studies in Media Communication, 17*, 409-428.

Fulk, J., & Boyd, B. (1991). Emerging theories of communication in organizations. *Journal of Management, 17*, 407-446.

Gregory, K.L. (1983). Native-view paradigms: Multiple cultures and culture conflicts in organizations. *Administrative Science Quarterly, 9*, 259-376.

Gudykunst, W. B., & Ting-Toomey, S. (1996). Communication in personal relationships across cultures: An introduction. In W. B. Gudykunst, S. Ting-Toomey, & T. Nishida (Eds.) *Communication in personal relationships across cultures*, (pp. 3-16). Thousand Oaks, CA: Sage.

Hofstede, G. (2001). Culture's recent consequences: Using dimension scores in theory and research. *International Journal of cross cultural management, 1(1)*, 11-30.

Hofstede, G. (1980). *Culture's consequences: International differences in work related values.* Newbury Park, CA, Sage.

Hofstede, G. (1991). *Culture and organizations: Software of the mind.* London, UK, McGraw Hill.

Hofstede, G. (1998). Identifying organization subcultures: An empirical approach. *Journal of Management Studies, 35*, 1-12.

Hofstede, G. J., (2000). The information age across culture. *Proceedings of 5th AIM conference - Information Systems and Organizational Change.* CD-Rom, 10pp.

Jarvenpaa, S., Rao, V. S., & Huber, G. P. (1988). Computer support for meetings of groups working on unstructured problems: A field experiment. *MIS Quarterly (December)*, 645-666.

Maitland, C. & Bauer, J. (2001). National level culture and global diffusion: The case of the Internet. In Charles Ess (Ed.), *Culture, Technology, Communication: Towards an Intercultural Global Village*, (pp. 87-128), Albany, NY, State University of New York Press.

Markus, M.L., Bikson, T.K., El-Shinnawy, M., & Soe, L.L. (1992). Fragments of your communication: Email, Vmail, and Fax. *Information Society, 8*, 207-226.

Merchant, J. E. (2002). Communicating across borders: A proposed model for understanding cross-cultural issues for the successful strategic implementation of information systems. *Proceedings of InSITE,* 1031-1040.

Orlikowski, W.J. (2000). Using technology and constituting structures: A practice lens for studying technology in organizations. *Organization Science, 11*, 404-428.

Rathod, M. M., & Miranda, S.M. (1999). Teleworking and psychological distance: The mediating effects of culture and technology in four countries. *Proceedings of ACM SIGCPR,* New Orleans, USA.

Rice, R. & Shook, D. (1990). Relationships of job categories and organizational levels to use of communication channels, including electronic mail: A meta-analysis and extension. *Journal of Management Studies, 27*, 195-229.

Rice, R.E. (1993). Media appropriateness: Using social presence theory to compare traditional and new organizational media. *Human Communication Research, 19*, 451-484.

Ross, D. N. (2001). Electronic communications: Do cultural dimensions matter? *American Business Review, June*, 75-81.

Sackman, S. (1997). *Cultural complexity in organizations: Inherent contrasts and contradictions.* Sage.

Samovar, L.A., Porter, R.E., & Jain, N.C. (1981). *Understanding intercultural communication.* Belmont, CA: Wadsworth

Schein, E. H. (1985). *Organizational culture and leadership.* San Francisco: Jossey-Bass.

Schein, E. H. (1992). *Organizational culture and leadership* (2nd ed.). Jossey-Bass.

Scott, C. R. & Timmerman, C. E. (1999). Communication technology use and multiple workplace identifications among teleworkers with varied degrees of virtuality, IEEE *Transactions on Professional Communication, 42(4)*, 240-260.

Sherriton, J., & Stern, J.L. (1997). *Corporate culture team culture.* New York, NY, Corporate Management Developers.

Sondergaard, M. 1990. Hofstede's consequences: a study of reviews, citations and replications. *Organization Studies, 15(3)*, 447-456.

Stohl, C. (2001). Globalizing organizational communication. In F. Jablin & L. Putnam (Eds.), *The New Handbook of Organizational Communication,* (pp. 323-375). Thousand Oaks, CA, Sage.

Straub, D. W, Loch, K., Evaristo, R., Karahanna, E. & Strite, M. (2002). Toward a theory-based measurement of culture. *Journal of Global Information Management, 10(1)*, 13-23.

Sørnes, J. O., Stephens, K. K., Sætre, A. S., & Browning, L. D. (2004). The reflexivity between ICTs and business culture: Using Hofstede's theory to compare Norway and the United States. *Informing Science, 7*, 1-30.

Triandis, H. C. (1995). *Individualism and collectivism.* Boulder, CO, Westview.

Trice, H.M., & Beyer, J.M. (1993). *The cultures of work organizations.* Englewood Cliffs, NJ: Prentice-Hall.

Trompenaars, F., Hampden-Turner, C. (1998) *Riding the waves of culture: Understanding cultural diversity in business.* London: The Economist Books.

Van Birgelen, M, Ruyter, K.D, Jong, A.D., & Wtzels, M. (2002). Customer evaluations of after-sale service contact modes: An empirical analysis of national culture's consequences. *International Journal of Research in Marketing, 19*, 43-64.

Van Maanen, J. & Barley, S. (1985). Cultural organization: Fragments of a theory, In P. Frost, L. Moore, M. Louis, C. Lundberg & J. Martin (Eds). *Organizational Culture*, (pp. 31-54), Sage, Beverly Hills, CA

Veiga, J.F., S. Floyd & Dechant, K. (2001). Towards modelling the effects of national culture on IT implementation and acceptance. *Journal of Information Technology, 16*, 145-158.

Von Meier, A. (1999). Occupational cultures as a challenge to technical innovation. IEEE *Transactions on Engineering Management, 46*, 101-112.

Westrup, C., Al Jaghoub, S., El Sayed, H., Liu, W. (2002). Taking culture seriously: ICTs, cultures and development. In S. Madon and Krishna (Eds.) *ICTs and Development: New Opportunities, Perspectives & Challenges.* Ashgate.

Workman, J.P. (1995). Engineering's interactions with marketing groups in an engineering-driven organization. *IEEE Transactions on Engineering Management, 42*, 129-140.

# The Frustrated Professor

**10**

Jan-Oddvar Sørnes & Larry D. Browning

Gunnar Pedersen is an award-winning marketing professor at one of Norway's top business schools. Slender, soft-spoken, and yet boyishly enthusiastic, he's at home in deep, animated conversations, but just as capable of drifting off into his own thoughts while conversing. He's clearly a passionate thinker. Students find him sincere, knowledgeable, and charismatic.

**Key Issue** *Finding a workable mix when teaching with technology.*

But Gunnar is a deeply frustrated man. He often feels like a failure because he hasn't yet achieved his two most important goals as a teacher: (1) finding a workable mix of the traditional physical classroom and the new virtual classroom, and (2) imbuing his students with his own excitement about the Web's vast potential for problem-solving.

Most of us can probably remember an apathetic phase in our own education career when we tried to get by with as little effort as possible, and suddenly found ourselves with a teacher who had other ideas for us—a teacher bent on ensuring that we did *all* the work and actually learned something. In this story about Gunnar, this proverbial cat-and-mouse game between student and instructor is acted out over the use of ICTs in the classroom. You will get to know Gunnar from his own perspective. You will hear him explain his teaching goals, learn why they are so vital to him, and come to understand the nature of his fear if he is not successful. You will also see examples of some unexpected side-effects that occurred as Gunnar pursued his goals.

Now in his early 40's, Gunnar has taught marketing to undergraduate and graduate students for almost 15 years. But being a computer-science hobbyist, he is far more technologically savvy than the average marketing professor. In fact, he spends a lot of his free time building his own computers, offering colleagues and friends technical assistance, and consulting on Web services. But for all that, he's careful not to come across as a "techie" to his students. Though he'll freely acknowledge his comfort with technology, he makes sure his students know that his learning goals are not simply cover for a blind infatuation with ICTs. He himself has no patience with people whose lives are driven by technology. "It is important to be in charge of the technology, and not the other way around," Gunnar insists. For him, technology use in a school environment must be pedagogically sound. That is, it must be appropriate to the maturity level of its students, and it must always serve the learning process, not the other way around. For example, his use of email to communicate with students springs not from a delight in finding yet another way to play techie but rather from his conviction that email enhances his ability to communicate with his students more often and more freely. As we will see, however, he also has other, more strategic ways for using ICTs with students.

*He's careful not to come across as a "techie" to his students.*

## Gunnar's Goals and Intentions

Gunnar is eager to exploit the new possibilities that the Web affords. But he's not content to simply transfer traditional learning methods to a new medium. For example, he'll say, "If we use a system where we just post lectures on the Web, we choose to hold the old pedagogic model." Similarly, he sees no real difference between conducting a classroom lecture in person and having distant students follow the same lecture via a two-way videoconference. A videoconference may be a technological marvel, but so what? "One must think alternatively," Gunnar insists, and adds that if you really want to take advantage of the Web, you must wholly rethink the basic conventions of the classroom. The traditional classroom, he says, "is theory-and-fact-oriented. But the Web enables a wonderfully different approach—an approach oriented toward *problem identification*," Gunnar says, emphasizing the words. "To hell with theory in the traditional sense," he adds. When students study virtually, he says, they can develop cognitive skills that will serve them well later in life, when they're on their own. They can become true *thinkers* and *researchers*. Instead of simply getting a problem presented to them, they'll learn to *identify* the problem. And once a problem is identified, they may use the Web to find solutions and support for them. According to Gunnar, this new pedagogic model "turns everything upside down."

*Students can become true thinkers and researchers.*

Gunnar loves being on the cutting edge of things and leading the way. "The motivational factor for me," he says, "is that I actually am up front. I can do something my colleagues can't. I am an innovator." Gunnar is not motivated by the traditional incentive system of getting extra pay; instead, he simply enjoys "taking comparative advantage of being a member of the faculty"—that is, having a license to teach, and the chance to improve the art of teaching. He devoutly believes he is able to offer a better course thanks to all his technological savvy and experience as a freethinker. But it continues to be a struggle for him, and he comes across as a modern Sisyphus. "I am constantly trying and failing," he says. "The system works reasonably well, but not optimally at all."

*"I can do something my colleagues can't. I am an innovator."*

## The Web-Based Learning Arena

The system Gunnar is referring to is called Classfronter, a Web-based virtual classroom consisting of more than 50 tools that promote far greater collaboration between teacher and students via the Web. These tools, all modular, can be combined freely to suit the needs of a course and the teacher's own preferences. "Classfronter is essentially a virtual building, structured into practical 'rooms,'" Gunnar explains. "Each 'room' is equipped with a choice of tools to enable different kinds of asynchronous and synchronous collaboration." The system is structured so that a "room" is open only to students authorized by the teacher, and their rights and privileges within that "room" depend on their various project roles. The idea is to allow teacher and students to collaborate effectively, just as people do in the outside world. Gunnar believes Classfronter gives students the freedom to do things each in their own way:

> For example, they can choose to use it only to get the transparencies before attending the lectures—the bare minimum—and be a traditional student. Or they can be at the other end of the scale and sit at home and be a virtual student—read for themselves, and download transparencies to get an idea about what is happening at lectures. You have all types of students, and that's exactly what I want.

Since there is no attendance policy at most Norwegian business schools, professors can't penalize students for absenteeism. But Gunnar, an ardent teacher, is eager to provide service even to those who aren't especially interested, or who, for whatever reason, aren't able to make it to class. He hopes the flexibility offered by Classfronter will enable students to participate in learning activities more suited to their personal needs and abilities, and eventually make impassioned learners of them.

Gunnar is excited about Classfronter because it focuses on *learning*, not teaching, and facilitates students' learning on their own terms. Class participants have access to everything—lecture notes, assignment lists, teaching material, course-related literature, and, perhaps more significantly, their fellow students. So Gunnar believes that Classfronter is ideal for problem-oriented learning and group collaboration. The system gives every student equal access and possibilities. "What's fantastic is that everyone has access to everything," Gunnar says. "There is not a single student who has advantages in terms of sitting on information, and that is unique." And while Classfronter creates a greater physical distance between Gunnar and his students, he feels much closer to them emotionally: "We have a much better trust relationship. They know they can trust me when I post stuff, and they can use it with confidence." Gunnar feels this is unique, and says, "I have received feedback regarding that from the students. They think it is fabulous."

But Gunnar is very conscious about needing to ease them gently into the Classfronter environment, giving them time to find the best fit of tools. "The students are brought into a completely new world," he says sympathetically, "and

**Key Concept**
The value of the virtual classroom

they don't have any particular qualifications to say very much about it." Being careful not to overload the students, he finds himself concerned about "how much the students accept stuff that is put out over the Net." He is also concerned about "what is justifiable pedagogically." Even though *he* is motivated, he realizes that most of his students will choose the path of least resistance.

Though Gunnar is excited about the possibilities that Classfronter offers, he's bothered by how the software was purchased. The decision to purchase it was made unilaterally by the administration, without input from the teachers themselves. Gunnar bridles at the effrontery of it: "The College has purchased a type of software that is to be the standard for all of us; they provide the solution for us, independent of what we as faculty think of such a system." As much as he loves Classfronter, he apparently cherishes individual freedom even more—and not just for himself.

### Students Resist Web Learning

But despite Gunnar's attempt to create a utopian learning environment—each according to his ability, each according to his interests—he finds that most of his students aren't buying into it, at least to the degree that they might. "They are very selfish," Gunnar complains. Instead of self-reliantly exploring all the details and nuances of a problem, which might allow them to become an expert on it, they take the most direct route possible, "going straight for what they want"— his lecture notes. Gunnar posts them on the Web, and they're one of the most popular features on his Webpage. But this very popularity frustrates him because the students don't show equal enthusiasm when he invites them to participate in an online discussion. He has spent a lot of time, and creativity, designing pedagogically sound learning activities, such as online discussions and useful links for his students, but says, "I feel that I am left with the short end of the stick, because they only want some parts of it, and don't give a damn about the rest." From his perspective, an implicit contract for student involvement is being flouted.

*I feel that I am left with the short end of the stick, because they only want some parts of it, and don't give a damn about the rest.*

One way he's tried to deal with his students' laziness—or is it apathy?—is to compel them to perform certain activities and tasks in a virtual environment rather than in their actual classroom. This new arrangement involves a lot of trial and error for Gunnar and his students, both in how they communicate with each other and how they work with the curriculum. Gunnar approaches this challenge by imposing a specific learning experience on his students. He deliberately reduces the functionality of a previously used virtual environment (his old Webpage) so that the students must use a new software package (Classfronter) to complete some of the course assignments. "They have to go on the Web. They can't get the assignments any other places," Gunnar says. "I think it's important that they learn the new system right away, so I force them to use Classfronter at an early stage, because then it's easier for me to post information and initiate discussions later." Having everyone use the same Website means that Gunnar's priority of equal access to information is met.

But deliberately creating this learning environment had effects that Gunnar didn't anticipate. He discovered that the word traveled fast about his requirements to use Classfronter and that his students monitored whether other professors were enforcing the same requirements. It seems that Gunnar's students loved being able to get transparencies ahead of lectures, and pressured his colleagues to offer the same convenience in their own courses. Gunnar monitored these developments and noted the mounting pressure on his colleagues to follow his lead, which pleased him, since again it placed him "ahead of the game." Also, by raising the expectations of students, Gunnar felt he was being a constructive leader for the university at large, improving the students' education not just in his own courses but, ultimately, throughout his department.

## Gunnar's Payoff

Gunnar is sincerely committed to offering pedagogically sound and flexible learning activities for his students, but he has another motive for steering students to the Net. "The advantage is that I don't have students running down my door," he confides, "and the payoff is that I get the peace to do other things." To avoid sounding too selfish, he adds, "I think that people are more comfortable making contact with me through the Net, rather than coming to my door, and that is exactly what I want."

*I think that people are more comfortable making contact with me through the Net, rather than coming to my door, and that is exactly what I want.*

The way he handles questions from his students illustrates the point. One advantage of online communication, he says, is his Web listing called "FAQ's [Frequently Asked Questions] from students." Whenever he gets a fresh question, he immediately posts it, and his answer, on the Webpage. Many students appreciate this service since it gives them quick answers to questions they probably have themselves, so it saves time all around. But whenever a student fails to check first to see if their question has already been listed, Gunnar will have to point them to the FAQ's when they call or email him. While a Q-and-A procedure is nothing new for interacting on the Web, it definitely is as much of an advantage to Gunnar as to his students, since it gives him much more time for research, which he regards as precious.

Gunnar is constantly looking for procedures that increase both his teaching effectiveness and his control over his time. He finds email particularly efficient "because the communication partners have a greater freedom to choose when they enter." Gunnar believes email is perfect for busy people like himself. He has the flexibility to answer questions whenever he has the time and motivation to do so: "This is the real strength of email," he says, "and in a way the psychological contract that lies in using such a system." His students are aware of both the benefits and the challenges of using email and have learned what to expect of each other by using the ICT.

Gunnar knows, however, that asynchronous ICTs like email aren't appropriate in all situations. In fact, he finds synchronous communication such as face-to-face far more efficient than email when discussing papers and class-projects: "When we are discussing various directions of a project, different approaches, different perspectives, then email is more difficult because it takes a long time." To illustrate the point, Gunnar gives us the scenario of a student who has to write a paper and who emails him about possible perspectives; Gunnar then answers him by email the next day, and then the student replies two days later. Gunnar speculates that this serial communication "might take 14 days before the student has received enough information and direction to pursue the task." To Gunnar this is a paradox with the Web: it can be lightning fast, but if one uses it for asynchronous back-and-forth communication, it can be very slow. He finds this odd, and observes, "With the Web we are independent of time and space, but still it is slow because I might get on today and see a question from the student that was sent two days ago." This example shows that while Gunnar is careful about how he uses his time, he is conscious of the value of face-to-face communication and will spend time doing it when the situation requires it.

*With the Web we are independent of time and space, but still it is slow because I might get on today and see a question from the student that was sent two days ago.*

### Fear of Being the "Old" Professor

Throughout a working day, as Gunnar communicates with both students and colleagues, he recognizes that he deliberately expresses himself differently depending on his audience. He knows he can be more mindless when writing to his students than to his own colleagues. With the latter, the requirements for carefulness and diplomacy are a social pressure that only a blockhead would not acknowledge—his community of colleagues is small, and its memory long. But with students he can be a little more "lax," he says, and even use "smiley faces" as ointment when he is brusque or writes something that might hurt their feelings. When writing to students and commenting on their work from a distance, he worries about eliciting the same feelings that he occasionally does when "answering them in rations," such as when he writes, without preamble or explanation, "No, this is wrong, you have a wrong line of reasoning, the perspective is faulty. Yours truly, Gunnar." While he often answers students this way, he fears being viewed as a grouch. But usually he'll just accept the risk and go on. Still, he worries that his criticism might have an emotional effect, especially when it is stated so bluntly and then dropped on them in an asynchronous email. Gunnar is concerned with appearing like the "old professor" who has everyone scared to death and who stands there at the board with his pointer, a stereotype incarnate.

He is more mindful, he says, when emailing colleagues: "Then I am more thoughtful on what I am actually writing. They also require a more thought-out answer." He is mindful of his receivers and adjusts his communicative efforts according to a standard of how much writing effort to put into his email. Gunnar's writing creates an important part of his own working environment.

## Follow the Leader?

Gunnar wants students to follow his own pedagogical model and behave in a certain way, yet ironically his own attitude and practices remind one of his "non-obeying" students. For example, when faced with a challenge that requires him to learn a certain computer-related skill, he reacts as they might, admitting: "I never look at the manual. I am a trial-and-error kind of guy in that I won't bother to read it; the time investment is too high." He also likes to feel in total control of things; he hates surprises, hates feeling inept and confused. Yet he wants his students to be just the opposite—adventurous, innovative, and eager to enter strange new learning arenas. He admits:

*I never look at the manual. I am a trial-and-error kind of guy in that I won't bother to read it; the time investment is too high.*

> *I am a very cautious person, and I never walk a difficult path if I feel that I am not on top of it. I am also a perfectionist, and must do it right the first time, so if I don't feel that things are right—and am 100% certain of that—then I don't start anything.*

Similarly, when shopping on the Web, he'll do some things that would not be desirable for his students to practice while attending his courses. Gunnar is an avid Web-user and often buys computer components and other products by ordering online from retailers' Webpages. When deciding where to buy products online, Gunnar is meticulous. He's particularly sensitive to the design of the different retailers' homepages, seeing this as a tip-off of their reliability:

> *I see quite quickly how good they are. I see it from their professionalism on the homepage, and how much they have thought through it—that is, if they have thought through the delivery terms well enough. For instance, do they allow the use of credit cards for payment? That is decisive.*

Gunnar's behavior here may help explain why he is so demanding of his students. It appears that Gunnar pursues information diligently even when he casts the rules for information search aside. He wants his students to pursue information with the same tactics, and energy, as he.

## Conclusion

The concept of using ICT to foster more participatory, experimental and collective learning is not new. This case illustrates the benefits and the many challenges facing both students and professors when implementing ICTs in the learning process. While it is difficult to claim that certain ICTs are better, or more suitable, than others when teaching students, this case illustrates the need for a combination of virtual and face-to-face contact in the learning process.

### Questions for Review or Discussion

1. Today people have many options for teaching. From your own perspective, what are the advantages and disadvantage of using Web-based learning environments?

2. Imagine that Gunnar has asked for your advice in getting his students to subscribe to his teaching methods. What would you recommend?

3. Is there a consistency or inconsistency between what Gunnar asks for from students and his own practices?

4. How can ICTs be used for time-management purposes?

5. How does the style of Gunnar's impression management with students differ from the way he communicates with colleagues?

# Teaching the Good Old Boys New Tricks: Taking ICTs to the Bank

Keri K. Stephens & Alf Steinar Sætre

**11**

Have you ever thought about all the revolutionary changes we've seen, just in the past few decades, in how we handle money? Ironically, we hardly even handle the stuff anymore, at least physically. We now use credit cards to charge our purchases, ATM cards to get quick cash, Internet banking to pay our regular bills, and direct deposit to send our salary right into our banking accounts. In addition, we trade stocks electronically, manage our finances online, and have banks compete for our loan business. But the banks are also changing—i.e. they are merging feverishly. Branch offices have been consolidated to the point where a trip to our neighborhood bank often means interacting with automated machines instead of human tellers.

But for all that consolidation, we still see some differences in banking practices, especially from one country to another. In Norway, banks haven't issued personal checks for over a decade. Checks are still used in the U.S., but even there, checkbooks are becoming obsolete. In September 2001, a Norwegian bank introduced SmartPay™ and SmartCash™, two systems that allow a cellphone to be used as a wallet. Now, when Norwegians want to buy a beverage from a vending machine or pay for parking, they simply type the needed information and hit a button on their cellphone. These extraordinary changes in the banking and finance industry have occurred largely thanks to information and communication technologies (ICTs).

*These extraordinary changes in the banking and finance industry have occurred largely thanks to information and communication technologies.*

While consumers can certainly see the changes, so can their bankers, even those located in more rural communities. In this case, you will meet one of them: Elaine Galvin, the chief financial officer (CFO) of a small community bank that services some 8,000 residents. It's a part of America that remains dominated by ranches. In fact, Ms. Galvin, who lives with her family in the country, drives past 20 ranches every day just to get to work. But you'd never guess that she lives on a ranch when she is working in the bank. Dressed in the latest dark-colored business suit and conservative low-heeled shoes, her middle-aged body projects an image that is all business. In this rural community, her job responsibilities place her in the highest ranks of women—in fact, she's thought by some to be one of the two most influential women in town. While rising through the ranks, she has successfully raised a family and is proud to be a role model for other women and men. With two decades experience in the banking industry, she has watched major shifts occur. In the profile that follows, Ms. Galvin explains how ICTs have changed the way she does her job, the very banking industry itself, and the need for a new sales culture in her neighborhood bank.

### A CFO's ICT Use

As CFO for Celeron National Bank, Ms. Galvin oversees its investment portfolio, all major purchases, and human resources. To accomplish her administrative duties she employs a mix of ICTs, especially asynchronous ones such as email and the Web, since they provide documentation and are less intrusive than other media. Besides these ICTs, though, she also finds face-to-face communication occasionally essential.

### Extensive Use of Email

Ms. Galvin makes no bones about preferring email. "If I can email a file to someone, that's what I do," she says. "And everybody I deal with pretty much knows that. I love doing business that way. I have been doing it for a while, and I'm trying to get everybody else on board." She finds that email is replacing the fax. "In fact," she says, "I don't even fax that much anymore. I use email. That's the first thing I ask somebody: 'Do you have email?' More and more people do, and they prefer it." And she especially prefers email to the telephone, saying: "When I take a phone call from the person at the other branch [of the bank], he's going to want to catch up on things. And he's going to want to tell me all about this and that, and it's so much easier just to say, 'Okay, just send me an Excel spreadsheet or an email. If I have a question I'll let you know.'"

Email is also ideal for documentation purposes, she says, even when the communicators are in the same location: "This [email] is from someone in the bank explaining that we're having a problem. He's right on the other side of the bank, but see, using email he was able to send this to me and a couple other people, all at the same time." She explains that email is "easier and instantaneous. We've got a DSL line. So I get the information right away. And it's better quality than a fax. If it's a project that I'm working on, they can send me a file that I can do something to." That ability to modify an electronic document gives email a big advantage over the fax.

Another big advantage to email, Ms. Galvin says, is the flexibility it offers you when filing and retrieving information:

*I keep all my stuff in folders and divide it up according to [task]. I can go back and look, you know, six months, a year back and say, "Okay, I knew I got some*

*email on this [concerning] what one organization was saying about the mar-
ket." Now I know what actually happened, I want to go back and see. I do
some look-backs.*

"Look-backs" is her term for searching through mail folders. She uses Microsoft
Outlook and routinely moves things from her inbox into separate folders. This
simplifies her organizing the documentation she finds so valuable.

For Ms. Galvin, as for the rest of us, being able to access the Internet is the
critical first step in accessing email. Since she lives in a rural community, there are
times when email and the Internet aren't working:

*When the Internet is down, I have to put a lot of my stuff on hold or on stop—
I use it that much. That's the down side of technology—you're at the mercy of
your service provider. If you're in a bigger town, you'll probably pay a lot more,
but you aren't at the mercy of a "mom and pop" service provider that may decide to
do maintenance one day.*

She says that while her small-town Internet service is improving, its reliability will
never equal what customers enjoy in major metropolitan areas because competing
providers as well as competing types of service create more robust systems.

## Occasional Use of Other Media

There are times, though, when Ms. Galvin knows that email shouldn't be used.
Here's how she decides:

*What I look at first is: Can I do it by email? I also look at what kind of trans-
action, what kind of business, it is. If I am wanting something from that
person, okay, I would rather be face-to-face because I think that email can be
more task-oriented. It's more like you're trying to get something back quickly
and both of you agree that that's what you want to do. Face-to-face is more for
sales or for dealing with a problem.*

Specifically, Ms. Galvin uses face-to-face communication with customers and
when developing relationships among her employees. "Face-to-face tends to be
with people I don't know, in terms of people outside the bank," she says. She recognizes that rich face-to-face interactions are critical to building banking relationships, especially in a business context. She also uses "management by walking
around" (meaning that she does not try to manage her employees from behind a
desk, but rather, she physically travels to their location) as a way to oversee her
employees and learn about their challenges. She explains, "There is a value to
face-to-face when you're team-building and are managing by walking around. You
have to see what's happening—because I have a tendency to want to sit in here at
my computer and not talk to anyone else."

While acknowledging that face-to-face is useful for certain situations, she's
much less enthusiastic about the telephone. "If I can do it by email as opposed to
telephone," she says, "I'd rather do that." The telephone makes for information

overload: "I get too many phone calls to handle them all. In fact, if we weren't doing a services-and-sales business, I would turn my phone off and just answer voicemails." She appreciates the efficiency of voicemail: "Yeah, I love those. I don't like getting them, but I like having it. I like having it because, like in email, I say what I want. You have to be concise and spell it out." Another reason she dislikes the telephone is that it can leave her looking out of control, clueless: "When I get emails I know what they want. I can go and get it. I can call them back with a response. If you get a phone call, you're like, 'Well, let me go get that other file or old paper like bank and administrative stuff or regulatory reports we have filed.'" When she's put on the spot and needs time to respond to a request, she feels frustrated. Not only does the request make her look ill-prepared, but it also forces her to take time right then to find the information and respond to the person. Since the telephone doesn't work for her, she says her media choice "usually boils down to face-to-face or email."

### Extensive Use of the Web in Her Job

The theme of 'keep it electronic' extends beyond Ms. Galvin's communication preferences and into administrative and information-gathering areas. One of her administrative responsibilities is to file reports of many types. "Whatever I can, I file online," she says. "I generally file online because you have more time and it's just easier. I know it's gone and it's out there. Every regulatory report we can, we file online."

Ms. Galvin's desire for up-to-date computer technology is driven by her job requirements. She is responsible for investing the bank's money in safe and high-return investments. Before having an Internet connection, she says, "there were so many things, especially on the investment side, that I was running into a problem. We were doing a lot of instant investments, and it was taking up a lot of time. I would have something I was looking at and trying to do some research on, and by the time I could go through calling and doing, it would be gone."

Access to the Internet provides so many trading options for Ms. Galvin that she's surprised by all the changes just in the last two years. Trading is progressing toward a system that is exclusively delivered online, and it matches her need for speed: "You can go out and get [immediately] what you need on the Internet. The phone is just impossible for me because the trade is gone by the time you get your answer. So that is a big deal." While she does not actually place trades using automatic Internet software, she does email brokers:

> I'll tell them, "I've got X dollars I need to place, this is what I'm looking for, and as soon as you can find it email me back. Find three or four different [invest-ments] for me to look at." I'll look at those and I'll email back and say, "Buy so much of this." We're never on the phone. We're strictly initiating these purchases [of stocks, bonds, or funds] over email.

Ms. Galvin explains that when banks need access to money, the Internet provides increased options. Many state-government funding opportunities have moved online, some to synchronous bidding systems. This means that an organization like, say, the State of Texas will electronically send a notice to the banks explaining that they will have a chance to bid against one another for money. As Ms. Galvin explains the system, "All the banks have to be online at a certain time and you actually have three opportunities to bid. It works great. And you know right away if you got the bid because it's real time." This is important for banks loaning money, since delays might mean losing loan business.

Besides government sources of money, there are also private funds waiting to be bought and sold. Many of the private sources will pool money from several resources and then provide them as consolidated funds. Ms. Galvin explains how one company has automated this process: "There's a company called 'Bank Oxygen' that goes out and actually buys consolidated funds. They've made a list of 50 banks. And they post their rates. It's moving away from phone calls and heading toward the Internet—all those things paperless, and away from the telephone." From these posted real-time rates, banks can make much faster decisions that affect their ability to loan money to their clients.

In addition to her administrative duties, Ms. Galvin regularly searches for information, primarily on the Web. "I use Google because it's fast," she says. But she's less enthusiastic about some of the Websites it turns up: "I don't go to sites that are loaded up and covered up with banners. I don't like them. I will make a mental note not to go back. And if it's hard to get around [on a site], I'll find another way to do it. If it's one of those that you can't go back, you're stuck, I will make a mental note and I will *never* go back to that site." Once again, we see that speed and efficiency drive many of Ms. Galvin's decisions about ICT use.

Her preference for Websites that are simple and navigable is reflected in the Website for her own bank. She's proud of it; she thinks it's highly functional and appealing. Others agree. In fact, the Web interface makes it so easy to use that some customers use the site as their portal to the Internet since it provides many services, including regular stock quotes. Though it's a small, rural bank, Ms. Galvin enjoys pointing out that it began offering its customers online banking before many of the larger banks, and most of her customers use the online services. The bank itself is profiting, too, by getting new business from its Website. "We get 60 requests for new accounts each day," she reports with a smile. She also notes that some customers have found that when they leave this rural community and "move their account to a big city bank, they can't get the service. They come back here, and they bank here."

Another Web-related tool that Ms. Galvin finds useful is her Palm Pilot—a personal digital assistant (PDA). She uses this portable device to download information from the Web and then access it when she's away from the office, running personal errands:

> I decided to get a Palm to save time, because I didn't want to be wired to the Internet or anything when I am out of the office. I use it when I go to doctor's

*The common theme found throughout Ms. Galvin's use of the PDA and the Web in general is that business is happening faster and she is getting ever more efficient.*

*appointments and have time waiting in their lobby. Before I go, I'll download a couple of magazines just for our [the Bank's] sake, and some for personal use, including* Rolling Stone Magazine. *I'll also download parts of the* Wall Street Journal— *and even entire books.*

She claims that this technology is fast and allows her to multi-task. The common theme found throughout Ms. Galvin's use of the PDA and the Web in general is that business is happening faster and she is getting ever more efficient.

### ICT Preference Differences Are OK

Though Ms. Galvin strongly prefers more asynchronous ICTs, she grants that preferences can and should differ, just as people's talents and personalities will. "Some people are more machine-technology-oriented," she says, "and a lot of times those people are not your best salespeople." She's learned that bank employees in different jobs tend to use ICTs very differently:

> *I have found that it's really rare to find a sales [or] good marketing person that is also good at using technology. It's such a left-brain, right-brain thing. So I realize that I'm never going to get our best lender up to speed. But I don't know that I want him to be. I'd rather he focus on establishing relationships and selling and doing what he does best. While I'd like everybody to be like me, I realize that it would be real boring if the office didn't have diversity. You know, it's okay that they are different.*

Ms. Galvin values the business relationships that her salespeople develop, and she recognizes that face-to-face communication is a key part of sales. It generates business for the bank, so she supports it. As much as she's dedicated to efficiency, she acknowledges the value of the "soft" skills in others. This evinces her flexibility as a leader. That flexibility is essential, she says, given the rapid changes in today's banking industry.

### Banking Changes Create a Need for a New Banking Culture

Historically, banks have served a given physical community, like a town or city. Developing friendly relationships with key members of the community—the "good-old-boy" network—has been a big part of how they've attempted to keep and gradually grow their business. But loan officers and new account representatives have basically thought of themselves as providing *service*, but not *selling* anything. Today's banks, on the other hand, have Websites and use automated bank-account management, so that part of it is more anonymous. And it's also a more aggressive sales culture. It's no different at Ms. Galvin's bank. Though she's in a rural community, she too feels the pressure to modify her banking culture to acknowledge these changes.

As accounts have moved to the Web, they've forced the culture of the bank to change. "We are going through a change right now in the bank to more of a sales culture," Ms. Galvin says. "It's the hardest thing because you have to re-train people. They don't think of themselves as having products to sell. So we have moved to a call center and personal bankers. It's just really hard for them to make the shift mentally, but we are trying to change to [a system] where we're open and trying to sell. Like Wells Fargo, they sell."

The real challenge, she says, is that bank employees haven't been trained to sell. As she puts it, they've been "order-takers rather than order-getters." Instead of passively taking orders from their customers, bankers now need to be proactive—that is, aggressively seek and get orders for services from their customers. While this is routine in many types of selling, the bank, historically a setting of quiet dignity and con- servatism, is finding the shift in mindset difficult.

*We are going through a change right now in the bank to more of a sales culture.*

Since, among her other duties, Ms. Galvin oversees Celeron's human resources, it falls to her to establish standards for how her employees will sell. She defines successful salespeople as those who build relationships and who aren't afraid to walk away from a sale that won't benefit both parties. Her understanding of what defines a good salesperson has developed over time. As CFO of Celeron, she interacts with many outside salespeople and makes final purchasing decisions. "A lot of times these salespeople come in and when they're face-to-face they over- promise and underdeliver," she says. Salespeople tend to fall into two camps, she says: "One camp of salespeople are the ones who are really slick. They're always willing to say they can do anything." Her bank will only do business with the other camp—people who admit that they don't know how to do everything. This is the camp where she wants her own salespeople to be—the relationship-oriented one:

> These are the salespeople who attend a meeting and are willing to say, "I don't know but I'll find the answer," or "My technical specialist knows how to do that." Sometimes they become proactive and say, "Can we do a conference call right here and now and we'll get an answer to that question?"

Her wanting her salespeople to be direct stems from her varied experience as a buyer. She will do business only with honest salespeople, even on-line. She looks for salespeople who value a long-term relationship.

As a businesswoman who's advanced to a position of significant power in a small-town bank, Ms. Galvin also confesses that she favors working with female salespersons—as long as they "don't have a chip on their shoulder and think that they can't work with technology." If they do, she says flatly, "they can't work with me and they can't work in the business world adequately." Most of the brokers that she uses for purchasing investments are women. She has followed at least two of the women through multiple companies because she wants to do business with them over and above the company they represent. "I think the fact that we're fe- males leads to a significant advantage," she says, "particularly when we start talk- ing about building partnerships. It impacts the emails that they send and the way that they talk in person and on the phone. Ultimately, it impacts the amount of business that those people get." She believes that they're more successful because they take more of a "let's-listen-to-your-needs kind of an approach to doing business."

One problem in her bank is that her employees have not been exposed to a sales experience focused on customer needs. The retraining is very tough, she concedes:

> They're really facing a pretty serious situation where they're going to have to shift that culture. We had some people that were not ready to make that change— just didn't want to get on board with that. And our bank is very big at getting buy-in—to try to make that change happen easily.

"Buy-in" refers to the mental and physical acts that demonstrate an employee's willingness to embrace organizational changes. She explains that those who don't "buy in"—the inflexible employees—lose their jobs, and she anticipates that more changes will happen before the bank achieves the new sales culture.

As this case illustrates, the banking industry culture has changed radically, mostly because of the extensive use of ICTs. Employees have had to become "order-getters," or salespeople, despite their lack of prior training. Banks have also shifted to an electronic communication mode with one another and with the finance community. While Ms. Galvin's preferences for email and Web-based communication are largely driven by her perception of her job needs, not to mention her personal love of efficiency, banking customers are also making that same shift to a preference for online banking.

*Employees have had to become "order-getters," or salespeople, despite their lack of prior training.*

## Conclusion

Does this mean that the need for face-to-face communication in this relationship-oriented industry will vanish? We don't think so. But the traditional business model is already changing. While face-to-face communication remains viable in high-end customer relationships, banks will need to carefully select customers when they use richer communication. This is the same process of targeting customers that is being used in many industries, since salespeople cost far more than automated electronic systems. Banks might find that they need to hire differently; instead of finance majors who enjoy working with numbers and systems, like Ms. Galvin, they will need loan officers and account representatives who enjoy working with people and getting the sale.

**Questions for Review or Discussion**

1. How do you get the right mix of face-to-face and ICT skills?

2. Consider your own skill-set. Would your talents match Ms. Galvin's expectations?

3. In what ways have changes in the banking industry created a new organizational culture?

4. Create a strategy for retraining people from ICT expertise toward face-to-face skills. What would be major considerations in such a plan? Now consider the reverse. How do we train people with face-to-face skills to use different ICTs?

5. Given Ms. Galvin's desire to use ICTs that promote her efficiency, how might this affect her credibility?

# From Blunt Talk to Kid Gloves:
# The Importance of Adaptability Across Culture

Jan-Oddvar Sørnes & Larry D. Browning

**12**

Chief Information Officers (CIOs) may be among the most important—and most underappreciated—executives in a company's talent pool.

They normally have three critical responsibilities. First, they're responsible for acquiring fresh information on their company for both internal and external consumption—information on such matters as company performance, product safety, personnel issues, and acquisitions. Second, they're expected to show all that information in such a way that people's impressions of the company are positive. Third, they must ensure that the information that gets disseminated does not violate insider-trading laws.

These are daunting responsibilities, to be sure, but it turns out that they're especially daunting at NorFood, a Norwegian-based agricultural firm. The Chief Information Officer there is Karen Einarson, an engaging, attractive woman in her late 30's. Because her company operates multinationally, with operations in markets as far-flung as Chile, the U.S., and Indonesia, she faces the challenge of "speaking to" highly disparate audiences. But she also has disparate audiences right within her own company, an amalgam of dozens of formerly independent small companies.

Actually, more and more CIOs are facing a situation similar to Karen's. Today's world has shrunk so much that a big company like NorFood will find many of their customers based in other countries, often with widely different cultures and thus widely different customs. So how does someone in, say, Norway acquire the global sophistication needed to deal with these differences, and how does this sophistication show itself in the work that a person like Karen does? We will attempt to shed light on these fundamental questions.

First, though, let's look at some challenges specific to Karen at NorFood. Our interview turned up three major ones: the company's need to be open about ecological practices affecting its products, the need to establish a company culture based on strong leadership and ethical standards, and Karen's internal and external communication strategies.

A recurring theme of Karen's story is the adaptation and planning required to get NorFood's multicultural and multiethnical workforce to operate effectively. She is concerned about cultural differences across national boundaries, revealing what she considers ethnocentricity—how manners, customs, and communication practices in Norway are a mismatch with, or often misunderstood by, people from other countries. Here is how she describes one part of the problem:

> The challenge for Norwegians is the way we are, the way we talk to each other, and the lack of politeness that we have among ourselves. It is not understood as being rude here [in Norway]. But immediately when we get to England, Belgium, or the USA we are understood as being very rude, because we haven't learned to stop and say, "Hi, good morning! How are you?" We'll just say "hi" as we pass by and then it's right to the matter.

What works fine as a conversational custom among Norwegians themselves is viewed very differently by other cultures within the NorFood operation.

This brusqueness will often seem especially offensive, Karen says, when a Norwegian needs to ask for help or ask someone to complete a task. To themselves, Norwegians will sound just direct, not rude. When one Norwegian makes a request of another, "We just say that we want this or that done and it is considered totally fine"—including that the task be done by a particular time. This is very different, Karen says, from the extended preliminary rituals that people in other cultures use when making a request of someone. For example, they'll first check on the "possibility" of another person's fulfilling a request; then the other person will respond with some statement about their availability for complying; and then—and only then—the actual request will be made. Karen calls this cultural knowledge "social intelligence," and she sees the need for it as one of her company's challenges. She says, "You *must* know to consider the cultural differences—you *must* be aware of them." Karen believes that such awareness can be taught not only by corporate training but by having the company's main communicators both follow and promote a "communication consciousness."

*The challenge for Norwegians is the way we are, the way we talk to each other, and the lack of politeness that we have among ourselves.*

## Openness About Ecological Practices

A mainstay of this "communication consciousness" is NorFood's principle of openness in making information about the company and its practices as widely available as possible. Since its key customers are professional buyers who themselves monitor the production process and make purchasing decisions based on whether there are problems in any of the stages involved, that openness is a requirement that NorFood has little choice but to meet. And it drops down to their subsidiary companies, too—the ones that actually market brand names in Europe and the U.S. In fact, these companies specialize in good communication with their customers. At NorFood, the information given to professional buyers focuses on "information about the [safe] raw materials and how the food is produced," Karen says. "And the sales part is done by those who are really good at it." Since these products—all agriculturally based—depend on a clean environment, many things can go wrong with production. As one safeguard, NorFood has an active question-and-answer program on its corporate Website. Karen says, "There are many questions from customers, consumers, and journalists which concern the environment, feeding regimen, and Sellafield.[1]" Questions about these topics are posted as FAQs[2] on the Website.

One reason for NorFood's focus on ecology is that the surrounding environment for the production of food is "unbelievably important, and new issues come up constantly," Karen explains, citing problems like "Mad Cow Disease, dioxins, and emissions of radioactivity from Sellafield."

Given the ecological problems faced in production, Karen says that it's essential for NorFood to maintain a good environment: "We have to keep it clean. Otherwise, it is not economical." Karen ties ecology to good business practices. For this CIO, the way to face the problems of producing safe products is to provide leadership in the ecological area. "We deliver a product that *we* know is safe and that our customers know is safe," she says. "We have been leading the pack— we employed the first environmental consultant [in this industry] in Norway in 1999 and started with an environmental approval of all the facilities." One issue NorFood has had to face was not of its own making. Owing to Mad Cow Disease in the late 1990s, concern for food safety automatically drifted into other industries and left it no choice but to actively get out in front of any problems. Another important audience for their communication is environmental groups. Karen says: "Now the pressure has come from the outside concerning environmental security. The environmental organizations have become much more active. But we feel that we have been in the lead." She sees much work ahead, "but we have been aware that the demands were coming and we have tried to stay ahead."

Not only has information about NorFood's ecological practices been disseminated to the public, but Karen has made sure to insert it in the materials going out to company employees. One of her goals is to have everyone in the company, no matter what their location or task, understand and talk about problems in the same way. She says, "Wherever people have questions, either in Norway, the U.S., or Chile, we give the same answer throughout the company, so that one customer talking with two salespeople doesn't get two different answers to the same question." This shows NorFood's desire to establish a common frame of reference about the ecological challenges it's facing, in order to offer professional customer relations management (CRM).

## Creating a New Corporate Culture at NorFood

Karen talks in detail about NorFood's corporate communication project, which was started in January 1999. This initiative, called the "Leadership Training Project," began with a series of three-day seminars that resulted in a set of ethical rules for

---

[1] UK nuclear power plant
[2] Frequently Asked Questions

the company. "It was drafted," she says, "to show how management should work with employees, and how colleagues at the same level should work with each other— what one is allowed to do or not do, and how one behaves." The seminar's purpose was to develop a clear position on what the company stands for. Karen calls these position statements "the foundational pillars." They address the company's values, goals, and strategies, and are intended to be actualized in a variety of communication practices, including "how one interacts with the other." She sees these practices as leading to concrete behavior:

> We have ethical rules for what we are allowed to do internally and externally. It is important to make sure that this information is out in the open, understood by all, and that everyone agrees that a common frame of reference is important.

She is also clear about what leads to people's understanding of what is expected of them in relation to these values. Expectations, she says, must be emphasized through supervisory training of employees until they become common practice: "It must be repeated and repeated until it sticks."

The corporate communication policy also contains an "information policy for the whole company," she says, "and it lays out a change in the structure of how we are going to work internally with information." This strategy includes the important authoritative element that specifies "who is allowed to say what, including who has the responsibility for making the information accessible." The program also includes the charge to build up an information library, to update information bases constantly, "so that it's easier for the rest of the organization to get correct information." The goal is to develop a policy in enough detail that whenever employees have questions and are wondering about something, "they will know who to contact and who is responsible."

*"In such a large company as this we don't demand that everyone think alike, but they should have a similar basic attitude, at least."*

Karen's confidence in this policy results from her work on the ethical rules that the company has completed and handed out to all employees. Her interview shows that not only does she buy into the policy but, because of her role in the company, she sees herself as a promoter and a spokesperson for it. "My goal is to build the culture," she says. While free to talk about the need for a common understanding and for knowing the same technical information in the same way, Karen stops short of seeing the need for everyone to think entirely alike. She leaves the door ajar for appreciating cultural differences:

> In such a large company as this we don't demand that everyone think alike, but they should have a similar basic attitude, at least. A Chilean will never think like a Norwegian, because the backgrounds are so different, but we wish for the understanding about the company to be the same.

### Karen's Communication Strategies

One of Karen's main tasks is preparing information material that is used throughout NorFood. She is responsible for all content on the company Website—

especially how information is used technically within the business. Part of her satisfaction with doing this job is how easy email makes it for her to communicate worldwide. "We are such a large company, and you have time differences," she says, "so it's very nice to send an email and know that in six hours they can read it in Chile and there will be an answer waiting for me the next morning." One reason for focusing on the homepage as a source of information is so she can send out press statements via the Internet. She sees the NorFood Website as one of the most affordable ways for outsiders to get information. If people want to read a press statement, they merely go on the Website, and when they click on it they come directly into the news page.

She also uses Intrafarm's Website—both the English and Norwegian edition— to check if there is something happening in the market that's of interest to employees. Intrafarm is a Norwegian-based company providing news for and about actors in the industry in general, in addition to technical, editorial, and design services for actors such as NorFood. NorFood has outsourced these tasks to Intrafarm, who essentially provides a clipping service, selecting items in which NorFood is mentioned by name or that refer to the lowest market price for their products. One edition of the company's Website is a technical source that covers the Norwegian production industry and provides much of the information she needs. There are also several analytic publications for which NorFood has subscriptions, including weekly and monthly financial newspapers that provide relevant information.

Karen is also responsible for the company's Internet newsletter called *Norpress*. To generate items for it she makes a round of phone calls each Friday morning so the paper can be sent out by 2:00 p.m. that same day. She has a dependable network of contributors that she either calls or emails for items and then takes two or three hours to structure what she receives into a newsletter. Approximately one-third of the material is taken as is, with Karen contributing only the copyediting that's needed to go to press. The remainder she writes herself. The target audience for the newsletter are employees in Norway and Denmark as well as Chile and the U.S.

This newsletter goes out to the entire company, including the 3,000 workers at the production facilities who don't have an Internet connection on the job. For these people, who make up two-thirds of the company, newsletters are sent out in PDF format via email to the department offices. The managers receive this email, and then print it out so that all employees will have their own copy. Because there is no time for employees to read the newsletter during work hours, the newsletter is handed out to them as they leave work so they can read it either right then or when they get home.

One of Karen's responsibilities is keeping up with all that's going on in the company. She maintains a lot of contact with people within the company, and she also goes through the various newspapers and checks Internet news sources two or three times a week to see if something relevant has happened. It's very important for her to be up-to-date on things in the event that a journalist should call, so she will know what answer to give and whom to refer them to. She uses the Internet actively to monitor what is going on with other forces in the industry: "I use these trade pages—you have environmental organizations' pages where they publish reports and make assertions. I regularly check them to see what might affect the industry. I also use special-interest organizations."

Karen's role as a corporate communicator makes her conscious of a key rule of impression management: keep a step ahead of your audience by anticipating what they might ask about and have an answer prepared for it. Her work habits show how she does this, because the first thing she does at work is to learn what is going on: "It is the first thing I do in the morning—to use 20 minutes on the Internet to check if something has happened since I was last in." She makes a point of being connected to the company's informal network, too, so that "when I have heard a rumor about something that has happened, then I can go looking. Or if I'm sitting working with something, I get needed background material. Or if I get questions from people in the organization who need things which I'm not sure about, then I search."

*Karen's role as a corporate communicator makes her conscious of a key rule of impression management.*

One of her most critical roles requiring a strategy involves protecting confidential information at NorFood. Another newsletter, called *NorFood Magazine*, primarily targeting the media and the general public, is also Karen's responsibility. Beyond the logistics of putting the newsletter together, she pays particular attention to the boundary issues involved in releasing information about the company to employees or to external audiences. For example, on news items concerning the stock market, "anything that might be stock sensitive" is limited, she explains, in that she cannot say anything about the economics of a topic "unless it is already known." To ensure that this important rule is followed, when *NorFood Magazine* is finished, she sends "it out to four people who read through it to have an extra check in relationship to stock sensitivity." The most certain way to ensure that inside information is not given out is to list information only after it is known on the Oslo Stock Exchange. She also has to be aware of traders who have inside knowledge but who have signed a silence agreement and who can't buy stocks until results are made public. The down-side of this carefulness is that the newsletter does not contain as much interesting and specific information as it would if stock market information weren't an issue. But it's a trade-off she makes for the newsletter. Karen has dealt with this issue so frequently that it doesn't cause her much worry. She uses a common-sense rule of thumb as her guide to selecting content for the paper: "If this can be used to raise or lower the rate, you drop it."

## Communicating With People To Demonstrate Their Value

Another of Karen's communication strategies is to maintain close contact with NorFood employees so as to nurture them as sources of information. She regularly gets queries from outside the firm. If possible, she'll use information from the Norwegian version of their homepage to answer them, but she'll turn to employees when necessary. Once she gets an answer to the question and sends it out, she'll follow up with a phone call to ensure that things are understood. Occasionally she gets a question that requires maybe a week to answer. If the question and the question-asker are important enough, she'll ensure that a NorFood person is "sent on location to answer them." But Karen also likes to meet people face-to-face routinely. As she says, "I go and 'fish' a little—I go to ask what they are working with lately, and what moves them." She also understands the principle of information reciprocity—that to get information, you have to give it—and when people come to her office, she makes it a point to "greet them to get a feeling of what's happening." Her sensitivity to communicating with people within the organization extends to her consciousness of how people from the field perceive how those from headquarters might act superior to them and she tells of carefully avoiding this trap. She says, "When they come here, they will feel welcome." She makes sure

**Key Issue** ⊕
Information
collecting
strategy

> that they don't come to the main office where there are just a few important people sitting and working. We are of equal value—equal value in the job we do—so I think that is very important. It is also great to know people, to have a little chat with them—hand-shake, match a face with a name. Then it is much easier later to call and say "Hi! How are you" when I need help.

And the final point of Karen's seeking information from employees is her humility about what she knows and her continuing need to learn the details of the company. "The little I know has come with time," she says. "I always ask when there is something I don't understand. I have learned along the way because I ask."

In keeping with communicating the value of employee information are Karen's remarks about the value of employees as people. For example, when asked about the culture of NorFood, she balks a bit at the word's implication of homogeneity: "The culture of NorFood? Because the development of the company has happened so quickly, and we have become so large over such a short period of time, we haven't really gotten that 'we' feeling in all parts of the company. It is still 'us' and 'them.'" She sees people from the different cultural regions, even within Norway, as being distinct and different, but thinks that the different "regions should consider themselves part of the same 'we,' not 'us' and 'them.'" Her belief is this "we-ness" comes, again, from understanding the nature of the company in the same way:

*"My goal is to get us to become a large family and to know collectively what we work for."*

> So part of the goal is for everyone to know what NorFood stands for, which involves the environmental aspect, which involves the personal aspect, which attitudes we have internally in the business—all the way from the top to the bottom. My goal is to get us to become a large family and to know collectively what *we work for.*

While focusing on collective understanding, she acknowledges that the company's culture comprises people from different parts of the world, and their differences require consideration when interacting. "One of the challenges is that you try to do it on the *premises* of the nation in which you will spread information," she says, citing their Chilean operation as an example. There had been a great deal of sick leave there, she recalls, and NorFood researched the issue. It discovered poor health conditions among their Chilean employees. Because of the national health care program in Norway, this would have never been an issue at home, but such a program did not exist in Chile, so it fell to the corporation to provide health care to employees' families. "The workers had toothaches or their kids had toothaches, so they had to stay at home," Karen says. "So we set up a dentist's office that was open for employees and their families, and they got drastic reductions in sick leave." She understands that to empathize with, and understand, one's audience increases the likelihood of success with them. Despite having cross-cultural training as part of her formal education in economics, or through her IT background, she is very careful when dealing with other cultures. "I am open-minded and I read a lot," she says. "I would rather get to know them before I do too much out of myself—before I go in and put expectations on them. I want to know what they stand for."

Karen moves from this grand goal of common understanding again to her own communication practices that lead to such familiarity. She sees that this is accomplished in two ways: (1) gentle repetition and (2) using clear language that everyone will understand. Karen uses repetition in her messages because she is not certain that employees will have remembered her last internal newsletter: "To be sure they do, I go ahead and repeat it—maybe not so thoroughly, but I repeat it and refer to the fact that we have dealt with it in an earlier edition." Achieving simplicity is not always easy because much of what she communicates about must be addressed in specific, technical terms. But she keeps in mind that many of the NorFood employees are in hands-on working jobs and that simple, clear information is required. To identify with them, she has even worked as a technician. She says, "It is clearly a challenge. But what I see as a starting point is that the majority of the technicians and skilled workers are also those with the least knowledge of the company." She resists the desire to play to the favor of those like herself, and instead keeps her message focused on those who need to understand it.

*Karen's role as a communicator crosses several boundaries including legal, technical, educational, and national borders.*

## Conclusion

Karen's role as a communicator crosses several boundaries including legal, technical, educational, and national borders. She works hard to employ a careful communication style that acknowledges her own culture's practices and adapts to the needs of different circumstances.

Her cautious style reflects the way she selects different ICTs to communicate with people and when searching for information.

## Questions for Review or Discussion

1. What are the advantages and disadvantages of being in a corporation that is undergoing a cultural change?

2. How does this example of cultural change compare to the other culture-change stories in this book?

3. What are the differences between managing individual impressions and doing so for an international corporation?

4. In addition to the principles mentioned in this case, such as not listing information before it has been made public to the stock market, what criteria would you add for making information public?

5. What are the implications of making information available to all employees via different ICTs?

# Slowing Down in the Fast Lane

**13**

Larry D. Browning & Alf Steinar Sætre

Gina is a brilliant—and brilliantly outspoken—consultant in a prestigious international consulting firm that we'll call "Northwest Associates." The firm offers strategic advice to companies planning various business ventures. Her case shows how she uses ICTs efficiently—and how she coaxes those with whom she works to follow her lead. A blunt, pragmatic woman, she says that in the 10-year period prior to 2001, the use of ICTs became manic and counterproductive in the wild rush to business success. This whole environment changed, she believes, after the American tragedy known as "9/11." Our interview with her, completed just six months after the terrorist attack on the U.S., found her noticing that people now focus on a less materialistic definition of success and are finally primed to learning how to use ICTs more sensibly—a lesson she is more than happy to represent.

*People now focus on a less materialistic definition of success and are finally primed to learning how to use ICTs more sensibly.*

Gina brings a particularly sophisticated background to this interview on ICTs because, in her own work as a consultant, she has done similar studies of technology use. In the early 1990s, she was part of a team composed of a psychologist, technologists, and business professionals, that was researching new software products that were compatible with her own company's major product and other standard ICTs. Hoping to find a niche for some software product of their own invention, this team inventoried the best features of existing products and also asked end-users what features they most needed. While, for confidentiality reasons, Gina doesn't disclose the product that came out of this work, she notes that the research experience taught her a crucial lesson about ICT's—that their whole raison d'etre is efficiency. *Actual* efficiency, not bogus efficiency. This, in fact, is a constant theme in her story. She put it this way:

*It's all about the end result. It's all about the impact.*

> I think the impact the Web had on me might not necessarily be the impact it had on a lot of other people. Because for me it taught me how to be very efficient with it, and I know when to use it and when not to use it. I mean, it's all about the end result. It's all about the impact.

147

Gina's quest for efficiency is driven by her commitments. She has a demanding job as a high-level consultant in Northwest Associates. Yet, like many American professional women, she also manages her own household, which includes a husband and child. To keep her husband organized, she confesses that she clears out his old personal items and simply throws them away if he doesn't miss them. "I take bags upstairs into the attic," she says, laughing. "I leave them there for six months. If he has absolutely no mental recall, I take them to Goodwill. My husband doesn't even know that I've thrown away six bags of his clothes!" She's similarly organized when it comes to using ICTs to supply her household online. "I go on there [the Internet], I do my groceries, I buy books, I buy toys, I get diapers," she says. "So I don't have to spend seven hours at the store. I will pay a hundred dollars [in service fees] to have the privilege of doing that. That's how I use the Internet."

She's no less obsessed with efficiency in the workplace, as seen in her impatience with people who use ICTs in clumsy ways:

> I get emails from people, and I am just like, "What? What do you want? I don't understand what you're talking about!" I send people emails—it's like, "Hi, hope you're well, here's what's happening, here's what I need, 1, 2, 3. Please get to me by X date," or "I received your message. Here's my answer. " It's because I am so structured.

*"When people send me dissertations on email, it just drives me crazy—always has, always will."*

She is offended by someone who sends a message simply because it is convenient for them to do so, even though it will clearly require a lot of time for her to respond. For example, "When people send me dissertations on email, it just drives me crazy—always has, always will." Her voice rises in the interview when she reports what she finds herself mentally yelling at some people about their ICT use: "Why would you *do* that? What would possess you to do something like that?"

A later theme in this case is her critique of others' inane need to be using ICTs non-stop. She blames the economic boom of the '90s for making the technology available that in turn made it fatally easy for people to message each other mindlessly. "People don't know what to do," she says. "People do not know how to behave, because technology has been so transaction-oriented for them. Like email: it goes, it comes back." Her transaction metaphor likens sending an email to spending small change, which can be done so quickly that it's almost without thought.

*"I've seen over the last ten years . . . an increase in volume of communication, the increase in people being busy, the increase in everything."*

One thing resulting from a transaction orientation—where interactions come and go quickly—is an astounding volume of ICTs. "I've seen over the last ten years . . . an increase in volume of communication, the increase in people being busy, the increase in *everything*," Gina says. She estimates the amount of the increase as "more than double" and suggests a cause: "I see differences in age segments, because even the generation at Northwest Associates that's coming in as business analysts that are 22 or 23 years old use technology much differently than I ever will." These young professionals have a "constant need to be online or have the cellphone or have the Instant Messenger up and their email up. They thrive on that type of an energy of communication."

Gina is happy to contrast herself with these avid users, and she's adamant about preserving the boundary between work and home. Our interview with her happened to be completed on a Sunday evening, a time that Gina is normally very protective of. She says:

> My cellphone is off right now. It is off. There is nobody on the East Coast that needs to call me right now. I'll check it later if there's an emergency. But it is just off. I do not want to hear from anybody right now.

Gina even has a theory about what saves some of the users in her communication network from becoming ICT addicts: "I find that people who I think are much more confident and secure with themselves are able to turn things off." She also frets about the use of ICTs that override or minimize the importance of face-to-face communication. When the technology first became available, she says, people would arrive at meetings and open up their notebook computers on the desk and no one could see who was across the table, and if things got slow, people would check their email. She says this doesn't happen as much today: "In my company now, you don't do that unless you're in the team room with your team and you're working [together] on a project." This example shows the trial-and-error necessary with a new technology to discover the norms that fit with day-to-day practice.

> "I find that people who I think are much more confident and secure with themselves are able to turn things off."

As someone who has enjoyed a front-row seat on the technological development of the Web, Gina says she's struck by how little it has changed since email became popular: "I mean, the move to email [itself] was massive. When I had the realization that I had been using this for *10 years*, I thought, nothing's different! The enhancements are so incremental that they're not massive." The biggest change, she says, is in how efficient people have become at using ICTs: "You get better at it, right?"

In our entire set of cases, Gina proved to be the most prescriptive—and most commonsensical—evangelist of enlightened ICT use. Were her advice to be summarized and her reasons all laid out, the lessons might look something like this:

**Prescription**
Enlightened
ICT use

## Be Conscious of the Person Receiving Your Communication

Gina is quite conscious, for example, of the preferences and abilities of high-level executives, both in client firms and in her own, and in her experience it does not pay to expect too much from them. Even at Northwest Associates, she finds some of the local practices to be curiously retro but nonetheless respected. For instance, her firm is "very voicemail centered. Because technologists are in the minority, people just use technology as an enabler. It is not front and center in terms of anybody's life except for the research-and-information people." As a result, she has learned that partners within her firm seldom consider what is conve-

*"If they are a director," she says with resignation, "I know that they're incapable of clicking the Reply button, so I leave them a voicemail."*

nient for her, but instead stay in their own comfort zone and do what they've done in the past. "If they are a director," she says with resignation, "I know that they're incapable of clicking the Reply button, so I leave them a voicemail."

In her company, consultants also are on the road traveling much of the time, so their contact with the home office is hurried and offered on the run. Because of these conditions, the consultants use the phone for almost all information purposes. At times, she says, it gets ludicrous:

> *Partners will leave comments to an entire deck [of PowerPoint transparencies] on voicemail! "Here are my changes. On page two, do this. On page three, do this." And that could go on for 30 minutes. It usually doesn't go that long.*

Her adaptability extends to novel situations where she has no information and can only guess what is needed. As an example, she tells us about a new director at Northwest Associates with whom she had just begun working. In her initial phone conversation with him, she sensed from his accent and his attention to politeness that he was a "southern gentleman." From this she assumed that he was probably not very good with email, so from then on she automatically copied his office assistant on everything she sent to him. Her assumption proved correct, and the relationship prospered since any details that needed working out could be handled with his assistant.

### Choose an ICT that is Adaptive and Move On

Gina's underlying strategy is to combine speed with adaptability. She prides herself on developing a "very quick perspective" on what she thinks will work best. Because Northwest Associates' clients are usually global, she prefers using asynchronous communication, like email, to span the different time zones and to minimize language problems that often involve hard-to-understand accents. Were she on the phone with a client, she might have to say, "Can you repeat that question? I don't understand you." But over email, she needn't worry about asking for "translations." Email, she says, helps her to avoid "insulting people and—it's much safer."

*Email, she says, helps her to avoid "insulting people and—it's much safer."*

### Shape the Behavior of Peers to Match Your Preferences

One of Gina's strategies, unprecedented in our interviews, is to control the behavior of those she is working with in order to bring their practices in line with her own. While she is flexible in some instances, she says she's quite willing to "force them to do what I want them to do." She is comfortable with giving explicit directions to those she is working with because she thinks many people's ICT practices occur without thought. "I will redirect people on purpose," she says. "When people start something in a voicemail communication that really needs to be an email, I'll respond by email and force them to do what I want them to do." Since people use ICTs so mindlessly, if Gina switches from one medium to another, she is assured that the other person will follow her lead. "I know what they'll do," she says. "They'll just reply to whatever you send. Most people will just continue the status quo—respond in the form that you received." In this example, she received a voicemail in which the person was vague and droned on pointlessly, she responded via email to get them to be clear. If the person happens to be a traveling consultant, on the other hand, she'll shift from email to voice because she knows the person is overloaded and "the only way the task is going to be completed is to move it to the convenience of voice mail."

**Key Issue**

Redirecting mindless medium choice

## Have Strategies to Get You Better Information

For all her emphasis on efficiency, Gina does not overlook the value of a face-to-face encounter, even if it is often a costly way to communicate. "I mean, it's all about the end result," she explains. "It's all about the impact." She will use any of the ICTs, she says pragmatically, "if it's going to get me more than I would have gotten otherwise." She values developing a relationship with a person and will take the time to send them a piece of information that is not immediately task-related just because she knows they have a personal interest in it. "I use email to do that very often," she says. For example, she'll write to a professional friend and say, "I found this article; I thought you'd like it." When her purpose is relationship development, she'll try to understand the context of her audience and give them as many choices as possible. For example, she says,

> I sent an email to a former client in January and said, "I don't know if you're back from your maternity leave or if you're checking your messages, but I hope Conrad is doing well. Would love to have lunch whenever." She responded a week later. Said, "You know, so great to hear from you. Let's do end of February."

This illustrates her selecting from among ICTs to allow the other person to respond in a way that's most convenient. Gina continues: "I would have never left her a voicemail because I know she just came back from maternity leave. The last thing she needs is a voicemail from me. But she can respond to email in a comfortable time period."

Giving the receiver a choice of when and how to respond is very important to Gina because the consideration behind such a strategy allows her to get information that she would not have gotten otherwise. She sees this as a primary strength of email.

*Select from a variety of ICTs to allow the other person to respond in a way that's most convenient.*

She also seeks information by asking for a little and providing the opportunity for others to eventually give a lot. For example, she contacted a person who she'd heard could help her on a project and said, "I've heard you know something about questions two and three, which would be really helpful to us." But she also sends the full list of questions beyond two and three with the hope that the person will also comment on them. She'll say, "If you have any comments on the others, that would be helpful, too." Gina compares this email example to trying to elicit such voluntary help on the phone, where, she surmises, she'd only get the specific question answered. By laying out the opportunity through email, she gives a person some options—as she puts it, speaking for that other person, "whether I choose to do it and when I choose to do it. Because now it's in email." But after getting such help from email, she often follows it up with a phone call because the information has placed her in a position to ask still more substantive questions.

## Communicate Efficiently in a Slowed-Down World

While Gina is focused on efficiency, she is also conscious of the change in the business climate at the turn of the 21$^{st}$ Century. She sees that her world has "slowed down" and that the level of activity makes more sense now that we're past the hype of the 1990's, when "people were just doing, doing, doing, doing. Again, I think it was the environment." During that period of hyper-activity, she says, people represented themselves as if to crow, "I'm so busy, I'm so busy, I'm so important, I'm so important." Then this norm spread so that "everybody had to do that." This created a level of such useless activity that a single communication could take up to "half a dozen transactions." They now have been reduced to only two.

*The world has "slowed down" and the level of activity makes more sense now that we're past the hype of the 1990's, when "people were just doing, doing, doing, doing."*

## Conclusion

In the five strategies just enumerated, Gina reaffirms her emphasis on reading the opportunity correctly, being flexible to a superior's requirements, pushing for norms of practice that are mindful rather than automatic, and doing as much as possible to develop a meaningful understanding of the ICT environment. Her case also provides a look at ICT use that emphasizes efficiency and adaptability to the power of different receivers, what they have to offer, and their ICT preferences. She is careful to meet the preferences of clients. Gina disciplines peers who use ICTs mindlessly without attention to what is being accomplished.

## Questions for Review or Discussion

1.  The balance between work and private life is different between national cultures. In what way does this case illustrate or disagree with your own cultures?

2.  If you worked with Gina, and she used the control techniques she displays in this case, what influence would they have on you?

3.  What do you learn from seeing Gina adapt to different people when using ICTs?

4.  Gina's solution is efficiency. Using the Garbage Can Theory as a guide, what problems does she solve?

5.  In this case Gina senses the need to copy an executive's assistant on all information. What dimension(s) of impression management is she invoking?

# Serving the Customer Locally Without Moving There: How to Use ICTs to Project a Local Presence

## 14

Alf Steinar Sætre & Keri K. Stephens

This is a David-and-Goliath story, but with a twist: it involves multiple Goliaths, not just one. The David here is "InterStock," a small Norwegian Internet brokerage firm. While operating in foreign European markets, it managed to do the impossible. In a span of less than five years, it outperformed far larger, more established competitors. And it accomplished this task with minimal resources. More miraculous still, it did so even without physically showing up! Not only that, but it managed to triumph even as the dotcom bubble burst in 2000-2001.

The brilliant individual you'll meet in this remarkable story is Rune Karlsen, a platinum blond 33-year-old smiling Norwegian, whose brain works so fast that he speaks like a machine gun. Rune is in charge of all their international activity as they enter new markets, a job that involves recruiting employees and making whatever system adaptations prove necessary with each new country they do business in. For example, at the time of our interview, Rune had just completed a deal with an American broker allowing InterStock to make purchases on the New York Stock Exchange for their Norwegian and Danish customers. He is currently working on securing InterStock membership on the Frankfurt Stock Exchange so it can enter the German market. This involves his completing membership applications at the Frankfurt exchange, then organizing the financial settlements of their German customers' stock trades with a large bank that will handle both cash and credit settlements for them. Trading in Germany is different than in Norway because German laws require that banks, not brokerage firms, handle stock transactions. To meet this requirement and to support their organizational goal of showing a local presence in all their operations outside of Norway, InterStock is partnering with a German Bank.

## Working Across Different Business Cultures and National Regulations

Each stock market has its own rules of engagement, making life more difficult for people like Rune. The Frankfurt Stock Exchange, though, wins his applause for posting its idiosyncrasies and protocols right on its own Website: "They [The

Frankfurt Stock Exchange] have all you need for documentation—application forms and the whole nine yards." Since it's all plainly there on the Website, a prospective customer need only sign on as a user, download the information needed, fill out the application on paper, sign it, and send it in by snail-mail, as an original signature is required—the only time paper is involved. Once the application is approved, the communication returns to the electronic mode—in this case, email.

Besides its automated application process, the Frankfurt Exchange offers, again via the Internet, training courses on various topics, such as trading in the German market. These courses are also available in a traditional classroom setting, but they cost more there, so the Frankfurt Exchange clearly employs market incentives to drive users towards technology. In fact, Rune says, "The only thing that is not via the Net is the concrete agreements that I get in my lap, and there are only a few of these, because most of the agreements are on the Net as well." Rune sees the German model as an exemplar of how to use the Internet to streamline a standardized but rigorous process. The Frankfurt Exchange's extensive use of the Internet facilitates the process of becoming a member for foreign brokerage firms.

Because countries differ in how money, stocks, and shares will flow, Rune's job is to set the specifications for each system and to define the account routines for how trading will occur in each particular market. To speed up this process, he works from a generic platform that he helped create for InterStock when it was entering the Danish market; it enables him to move quickly into a different language and establish InterStock in yet another country. And for each such market he also creates a Web homepage. Because he uses the material previously created (now boilerplate), he needs to develop only about 20% fresh content. As he says, with a grin, "There is no reason to reinvent the wheel." For example, he identifies a group of 12 German Net brokers and then maps out a plan for how InterStock should approach the German market. This is based on the generic structure that most of the existing Internet brokers are using. When the Website concept is complete, his work is sent on to InterStock's systems-development group.

*Because he uses the material previously created (now boilerplate), he needs to develop only about 20% fresh content. As he says, with a grin, "There is no reason to reinvent the wheel."*

That group numbers 22 employees, most of whom live in Oslo, Norway, and specialize in setting up the servers and the associated technology. Rune regularly uses Microsoft programs—PowerPoint, Word, Excel—since he knows that standardization is important. Once he specifies how the page needs to look, he lists his work on what is called the "Task Execution System," which displays the project he's working on and automatically invites help from others in finishing it. He says, "You put in desired tasks that you want solved, and then everybody has access to it—both on the technical and the non-technical side." The Task Execution System allows those responsible on the development side to distribute tasks to be completed.

Of course, when something is unclear, which often happens when programmers tackle content in a foreign language and have little grasp of stock trading, follow-up is needed. The translation issues for InterStock's German application, for example, are requiring a fair amount of interaction. His staff, Rune says, "will not quite get what it says," so the project will require some close monitoring by individuals versed in German. "The problem is that a system developer does not necessarily have an intuitive understanding of how, for example, a stock transaction takes place at the Frankfurt Exchange. You have to explain this in relatively explicit detail." So while the Frankfurt Exchange is very good when it comes to design, it has a bit more difficulty explaining "both what is happening and what it says."

There are other ways for InterStock's systems-development personnel to work around the language obstacles arising when aligning their technology for the German market. Since none of the Norwegians in Rune's Oslo office speaks German except him, they are currently hiring more German-speaking technicians in Norway to work on the project. Fortunately, the Frankfurt Exchange is also offered in the English language, which is a lifesaver for some of InterStock's technicians. In fact, there are people who work in the support group in Germany who speak no German at all! This focus on English is "of course related to the fact that the Frankfurt exchange has many non-German customers and brokers," Rune explains. "Almost one-third of the brokers are not located in Frankfurt."

Access to the U.S. stock exchanges introduces new challenges since financial settlements are handled much differently in the U.S. than in Europe. InterStock's goal with an American partner was to establish "one-stop shopping." But that was not easy for two reasons. First, the U.S. firms that make desirable partners are large organizations with whom it's difficult to establish a working relationship from a distance. Second, InterStock is not likely to generate much business by the standards of American brokerage firms. As Rune notes, with a smile, InterStock's one-day high trading record "corresponded to about 8 seconds on the NASDAQ." But InterStock did manage to make a workable pricing agreement with a large U.S. broker. It was no small triumph, Rune says, since "we are a small actor in the U.S., and on a good day we have only about 60 to 70 trades in the American market, so of course you don't get max attention from the big brokers. That much is self-evident." But because InterStock now offers all their Scandinavian clients the opportunity to buy on NASDAQ and NYSE, this agreement with a large foreign broker in the U.S. perfectly fits their needs.

*"Even though it seems to us a very genial and likable country and that they are like us, still they are fundamentally different in some areas—in particular, in business etiquette."*

Once the relationship between InterStock and the various international stock exchanges was established, the ICTs currently in use all came into play. Rune says that communication "takes place in part by phone; otherwise we communicate through Internet solutions. We have a few applications that allow us to go in and check account status and transactions." In addition to consulting the daily status reports from their partners, Rune can directly monitor the current activity level that their customers generate with those partners.

From its effort at global business, InterStock has learned that "cultural differences are much larger than they appear on the surface." Just as Canadians and Americans can seem virtually interchangeable yet actually show subtle differences that prove decidedly important, so it is, Rune says, with Norway and its neighbor Denmark: "Even though it seems to us a very genial and likable country and that they are like us, still they are fundamentally different in some areas—in particular, in business etiquette. That is, how you build relations, how you maintain these, how you make agreements."

For all the cultural differences, Rune says, "there are also greater industry differences—that is, a given industry will have a common codex and culture, and it's stronger than geography, in this context." In other words, ironically there may be greater differences between a broker and a regulatory agency in one country than there are between two brokers from different countries. Even though industry differences are greater than national differences, InterStock has concluded that national differences, although at times subtle, can't be ignored. Rune thinks that most Norwegians imagine doing business with Danes is easy because "we are so similar." Not so, he says. In Norway, "it is normal procedure that we communicate via email and that's it. But, for example, already in Denmark it is very different." There you "cannot continue in a process until you have met them personally." In his mind it is crucial to be aware of such differences.

### Projecting a Local Presence

*Having local partners helps to keep the cost of market entry down, and it also gives them both greater credibility and a broader market impact. Most important, however, is that it fits hand-in-glove with their ambition of projecting a local presence.*

InterStock's efforts to operate outside Norway's boundaries are more developed in Denmark than in Germany. In Denmark, InterStock has "been up and running" for a while, and they are a member of the Copenhagen Exchange. In Germany, they partner with a Danish stockowners' association (DSA). Rune says, "We have collaboratively rolled out campaigns with very low prices for members of DSA, and we have marketed ourselves in their magazine and on their pages, and then we have run joint marketing campaigns in large newspapers. Those are our primary collaborative partners in Denmark."

Not only does InterStock use German Banks for credit and settlement statements, but it also has a relationship with several large stock clubs and stock owners' associations. "German stock clubs have membership of about 20,000-25,000," Rune says. "We will make some cooperative agreements there, both to gain credibility for ourselves and to gain access to customers." Having local partners helps to keep the cost of market entry down, and it also gives them both greater credibility and a broader market impact. Most important, however, is that it fits hand-in-glove with their ambition of projecting a local presence.

In the case of Denmark, the projection of a local presence has been enhanced by hiring a Dane to be responsible for much of InterStock's efforts there. After Rune handled the application and certification, InterStock was "very lucky and managed to recruit a trading manager—the trading manager from our largest competitor in Denmark—and he brought a mountain of networks and competencies with him." Turning the Danish operations over to a Dane suited Rune because his next task was to focus on the U.S. market.

Rune knows that being close to InterStock's different markets is important. "In my case," he says, "I am in Germany a great deal in order to gain certain closeness to the market." InterStock learned this lesson early from watching the failure of an American Internet broker that entered the Scandinavian market and tried to control everything remotely. InterStock has a different approach: "We establish a branch office, we have an address, the Germans are calling German phone numbers, the Danes are calling Danish phone numbers, they send mail to local addresses. So, for the customer we are perceived as local." As opposed to their technical staff, all their customer service people always "speak the native language." He continues: "You can say that we are compensating for the lack of closeness as much as we can by using these methods." Behind the scenes, all the mail and all the phone calls are automatically forwarded to Oslo, as that's where all of InterStock's employees "in these countries" are located. Meanwhile, all the mail from InterStock to its Danish and eventually, German customers is mailed with Danish and German stamps and postmarks, though it originates in Oslo.

*One major part of communicating, or projecting, a local presence involves having people who not only speak the language, but are natives.*

One major part of communicating, or projecting, a local presence involves having people who not only speak the language, but are natives. InterStock knows this. So all calls that are made to local numbers in Denmark and Germany get answered by Danish and German customer-service representatives respectively—and they are all sitting physically in Oslo!

**Key Issue**
Ethics

InterStock is well aware, too, that there are ethical issues at play when communicating a local presence. Rune says that the careful observer will find information about the company's true location on their Website, though to the casual observer the company appears Danish or German. In this way InterStock is perceived to be more present in their local markets than they actually are.

## Distance and Media Usage

Although advantageous in many ways, not being physically present in a market has other "costs" associated with it, Rune says: "You can say that what you lose, then, is the more informal relationship-building that is not planned but that often happens by coincidence." Meeting someone new in an unplanned fashion can often be valuable, but it is hard to estimate this value, Rune concedes: "How important is that? Difficult to say, really."

As the physical distance is increased, electronic communication media become increasingly important, even in the world of the already digitized Internet stock brokers. But the closeness to the market that rich face-to-face communication affords cannot be overlooked. The minus with InterStock's innovative approach is that "you don't have the closeness to the market that you would want during an internationalization process," Rune says. "The core in all internationalization is that you should be close to the market." InterStock's Danish Head of Operations understands this all

*The core in all internationalization is that you should be close to the market.*

too well himself, "because he cannot have these small informal meetings that you can have if you are, for example, sitting in Copenhagen," says Rune. With InterStock's approach, they "have to plan to a much greater extent, and the cost—well, you don't know what a meeting will bring and therefore it is difficult to budget it, because you don't buy airfare for USD 1,000.00 just to have coffee for an hour with a journalist." But Rune feels that "you can still build a relation towards a local market by traveling a great deal. In my case I am in Germany a great deal in order to gain a certain closeness to the market." Getting that closeness though, might just take a little longer.

In business it is common practice that the smaller firm will visit the larger firm, not vice versa, but with InterStock's U.S. deal-making, the opposite occurred. Rather than little InterStock going to the U.S. for acceptance, representatives of the U.S. brokerage firm traveled to Oslo—to "check out" the applicant. Rune explains: "They actually want to see who they have as clients. They know very well what they are selling, and they want to know who we are. They wanted to get an impression both of the person they were talking to and also the organization." Rather than viewing face-to-face meetings as some soft, interpersonal preference by the Americans, Rune sees them as entirely sensible—and a reflection of American business practice:

*In Norway we stick to the issues and manage to exchange information via the Internet, mail, or telephone.*

> *The Americans display a very rational behavior. They shall build relations, and they shall only be built where they can obtain the maximum amount of information—when you have the personal contact. So it is actually a rational affair. If you think about it, it is the right way to do things.*

By traveling to Oslo, the U.S. brokerage firm not only met with the people they would have met if InterStock had traveled to the U.S., they also got to see InterStock's facilities and its operations.

Rune reports that Norwegians see themselves as cooler and more factual in their interactions, so they think they have less of a need than Americans for such a face-to-face encounter. "This is also a cultural issue," he says. "In Norway it is much stricter—we communicate via email and that's it. In Norway we stick to the issues and manage to exchange information via the Internet, mail, or telephone." But in its effort to become a global company, InterStock discovered that Germany and Denmark, much like the U.S., preferred face-to-face communication as part of the engagement process. Rune says, "In Denmark they have a very fixed opinion that you cannot continue in a process until you have met them personally. In terms of being stringent, then, Denmark is strongest when it comes to personal relations. Then [comes] the U.S., and then Germany."

*In Denmark they have a very fixed opinion that you cannot continue in a process until you have met them personally.*

## Organizational Learning and Emergent Strategy

InterStock, like most dotcoms, had great expansion plans around year 2000 "that we fortunately were not able to realize." Rather than executing these plans,

Rune says, InterStock "focused on consolidation in Norway, trimmed the organization, prepared a completely different strategy in connection with market entry, and still wanted to enter new markets, but wanted a totally different cost profile." Its original plan was to set up actual offices with a new group of people which would incur a cost profile with a great deal of fixed costs, but they quickly halted these plans. One of their competitors, who was not that agile, "entered with a huge staff of 60 people in Frankfurt alone, and managed to acquire a small number of clients," Rune recalls. "In the time they were there they burned several millions and pulled back out."

*We have an extremely low marginal cost when we enter a new market—we only need a couple of hundred trades in order to break even, actually.*

InterStock opted for a different strategy in the face of a reclining economy and a bursting dotcom bubble. Now they focused on cost. InterStock's basis for entering Denmark was that everything was run from Oslo. Rune claims that this led them to "have an extremely low marginal cost when we enter a new market—we only need a couple of hundred trades in order to break even, actually." This strategy is radically different from the dotcom economic model of pouring in resources to capture market share rapidly. Rune says that InterStock's current strategy "enables us to enter new markets with a very low exposure, test out the systems, and quietly and carefully grow." This more careful approach has afforded InterStock continued growth in a reclining economy.

The Internet brokerage business is facing not only a declining economy but intense competition within its own industry. Rune says proudly, "We are the price leader—well, actually not quite as well as we thought. We do have a competitor that offers free trading."[1] When asked how InterStock is still managing to beat a rival that is making stock trades for free, Rune confesses:

> That surprised us as well. But it has to do with different things. We have very good systems, to begin with. They also have that, in a way. But our customer service is extremely good. The follow-up of customers is very quick if it is through email. Or if they pick up the phone, they get a very competent and sympathetic person at the other end.

InterStock might have the best technical solutions and outstanding customer service, but Rune suspects that their success against this competitor might also be explained by some customers' fear of being duped:

> We are wondering if free is suspect—that it might be perceived as more honest to have a discount, or a favorable price, because then the customer feels that, OK, then it is less. You very often get negative associations when it comes to a free offer. It gives a negative feeling: What is wrong with this? *Right?*

The result is that InterStock has "totally kicked their ass in market share."

When probed further on their strategy for market entry, Rune admits that it was not as premeditated as it may seem. Actually, he says, "we toyed with the idea

---

[1] In other words, their competitor does not charge a brokerage fee.

*InterStock is using a clever combination of ICTs to shape their market entry strategy so as to project a local presence.*

[of having no brokerage fee] as well. Then they came before us and we couldn't very well do the same, so we set the price at a low level, but still not free." Now that they're outperforming their non-charging competitor, they're in the ironic position of having been "saved by our competitor, because we were considering the same strategy!" This again shows how InterStock pragmatically adapts to both changing environmental conditions and competitive situations. At InterStock they are extremely quick and flexible learners.

### Conclusion

InterStock is using a clever combination of ICTs to shape their market entry strategy so as to project a local presence—in today's terms, a virtual presence—instead of physically building one. Using ICTs instead of bricks and mortar has also significantly reduced their cost of operations, while allowing them to exploit the commonalities between their different markets. Knowing that trading slows in a declining (bear) market and that their revenues depend on trading volume, InterStock has adopted a more cautious and cost-effective approach, which has helped make it a survivor where its Goliath competitors have stumbled.

**Questions for Review or Discussion**

1. What are the implications of trying to be as similar to your customer as possible with the hope of increasing your own credibility in order to get their business?

2. How do you use a combination of ICTs to bridge time and space, thus communicating a local presence?

3. How would it affect your satisfaction as a customer to be given the impression that you were talking to a local person and to later learn that they were in fact a global representative?

4. What are the impression management and credibility issues involved in representing yourself as a German broker to a German customer?

5. What are the top three impression management issues found in this case?

# Overloaded But Not Overwhelmed: Communication in Inter-Organizational Relationships

**15**

Keri K. Stephens & Alf Steinar Sætre

For the past 14 years Stan Silverthorne has been a salesperson in the semiconductor industry. Stan is a work-hard, play-hard, type of guy – basically a big kid who has never grown up. He works with his clients in the morning and water-skis in the afternoon, and finds this combination to be a perfect balance. With such long tenure in a tumultuous industry, Stan can call himself a seasoned professional. He owes his success, he says, to his view of the communication process: "The more communication you have, the better that communication is, and if that communication is very honest, the better your chances will be [in making the sale]." He has a gift for negotiating his way through the diversity of communication channels and choosing efficient ways to gather and share information. But in the process, he finds that the biggest hurdle he faces is managing all that information. In this case, we will explore what causes information overload and how Stan deals with it.

## What Causes Information Overload?

In sales, communication happens in several directions simultaneously. Within their own organization, salespeople communicate with managers and their sales colleagues. They also need to gather and share information from organizational units such as marketing, engineering, and customer support. Salespeople also uncover and selectively communicate information externally with their customers. Stan explains his job as having two sides:

*Information overload happens because we are communicating in several directions simultaneously.*

> *Gathering information is one side, and the other side is communicating information. Gathering information is just talking to customers, being in meetings, trying to understand what's going on. And there can be some gathering information internally. And then communicating information is really taking that information and processing it and trying to understand.*

He asks himself these questions: "Does this [information] change my strategy? Is it in line with my strategy?" And then his job is "communicating that effectively internally to make sure that all of the people that support you understand and agree. And it helps them justify what they need to do."

*Availability of technology.* In the communication process, Stan explains that he has a host of ICTs available to him—actually, "too many," he says. "I think in today's day and age, it is very complicated. Having all those means of communication—it's great, but I think it makes it difficult. Let me start with my phone. I have a phone in my office, a phone at SemiProduct [his key account], and a phone on my hip." Two of these three phones have voicemail boxes. He also has a voicemail box located some 1500 miles away from him in his company's California corporate headquarters. Plus he has a pager. Even though the pager is not user as much today, one of his major clients manufactured pagers; thus, he adopted this technology at the request of his client. Plus he has a Palm Pilot, which he uses "for scheduling and for phone numbers." Finally, he has a laptop computer, multiple email accounts, and almost daily face-to-face meetings. All these ICTs—multiple telephones, a pager, a Palm Pilot, a laptop computer, email, and face-to-face—can lead to information overload. So Stan has evolved some rules for how they should be used.

*In the communication process, Stan explains that he has a host of ICTs available to him—actually, "too many."*

For the latter, he says he has an ironclad policy:

*If a customer has any sort of emotion, if it's a subject that's emotional, whether positive or negative, I'll go see him [in person]. Internally, if I'm in the proximity of that person, I'd rather go see him. I think personal visits are the most productive way to communicate. The only time I use email with a customer is to send them some information that I'd promised them. It's an effective means to transfer information that we've already talked about. Maybe quick questions on voicemail too—quick questions that are very unemotional, very unimportant.*

Asked why he has this rule, he replies, "Because in sales every decision is emotional. In reality it is. If someone likes something, they will go and justify it in other ways. So, relative to that, I think the personal aspect of talking to people is very important."

*Different expectations.* Stan explains that:

*In my industry, internal [communication]—voicemail and picking up the phone and talking to someone—is the most efficient and effective way to communicate. I think if you leave a voicemail for somebody, you should expect someone to get back to you that day, as compared to if you page them or something like that. The reason for this is because people's email loads up very, very quickly. You may get a hundred emails a day. And people tend to go down the list and say, 'I'll read this one, this one and this one.' They may miss your message.*

Stan insists, then, that "if you really want a message heard, at a minimum you need to talk to the person directly because the industry is at such a fast pace. Emails are OK," he says, "if they refer to tasks that need completion but aren't necessarily all that important. Email thus serves more as a reminder." But if the information is crucial, he says, he will "definitely talk to the person as well as maybe even follow up [that telephone or face-to-face conversation] with an email. I think that is a nature of the business. Not necessarily common practice throughout all industries, but in our industry it's pretty important."

The main reason that multiple ICTs must be used to ensure successful communication is that email is "overused and abused," Stan says. "People use it to cover themselves [and then say], 'I sent you an email.' And in my book, that's an excuse." This overuse of email creates for Stan, and his customers, a serious information overload.

*Multiple ICTs must be used to ensure successful communication because email is overused and abused.*

He prefers the telephone, chiefly for its reliability. "If someone leaves me a voicemail, I will get it. I will guarantee I'll get it that same day and I will listen to it. Probably I'll get it within an hour or so. But with email—if I'm traveling and don't get a chance to log on, it can be several days. Email is just not as efficient." Stan's view shows how perceptions of a given channel will reflect a culture, organization, or even an individual's habits. For example, whereas he doesn't insist on checking his email daily, other road warriors might even pause in airport terminals to check their email. Some people who sit at their desks all day may send and receive emails almost nonstop. While Stan's ICT uses reflect his needs and life as a salesperson, he acknowledges that other people may well have entirely different needs and preferences. "If we're communicating with somebody internal who does not have external customers, they think that email is absolutely the right way to go. Because they like everything *documented*; they are rigid. Also, their schedules allow them to sit at their desk and read emails all day." But people in sales, like himself, are vastly more mobile and are constantly out meeting with customers, so voicemail is preferable. It lets them check messages anytime and anyplace, he says. He further explains that responding to email is a function of the mobility of the job: "If someone sends me an email and I don't get to it for two or three days, I don't feel bad. But if I send an email to someone internally and they don't answer me within a day, then [I know] something's wrong. So it depends on the person's responsibility." But, he says, regardless of a person's job, voicemail trumps email: "Whether it's internal or someone in sales, everybody agrees that they'll get the voicemail. And get it very quickly."

*Stan has a strategy for handling all his voicemail boxes and controlling overload.*

Thus far, Stan has explained that he has many ICTs to juggle. Let's turn now to the strategies that he has developed to help him avoid becoming overwhelmed with information.

## Strategies for Handling Overload

*Adjustments made to compensate for overload.* With so many voicemail boxes, Stan needed a strategy for checking them, and he has one:

> I have a box in California I call once a day, so that's easy. My voicemail on my cellphone goes off and I answer it right away. I usually check my office voicemail box four times a day: morning, mid-morning, afternoon, and then maybe when

*I get home at night. And actually, the one at my customer site does not have a voicemail box. They asked me if I would like one [and I said no].*

Why? It would have made just one more box to check, and it might not have many messages anyway.

He confesses he's in love with his compact pager. "The best thing ever invented!" he exclaims. "I love this thing because I can communicate internally, locally, in California, or with my customer—anyplace I am, whether I'm in a meeting or not." A pager functions much like text messaging or SMS does on a cellular telephone. In the U.S., pagers are used frequently in several industries. His own is one of these. Stan knows that his customers have little time to spend with salespeople, so he uses his pager to respect that reality: "It's the most efficient communication device I have because our customers are always busy. And our customers are always in meetings. Trying to catch them on the phone and asking them to call you back is—well, you're taking a chance of even catching them, number one. Asking them to call you back is a *task* for them that they have to go and do. You know, I think it's unfair [to ask that of them]. Our customers fortunately carry the same pager and are disciplined enough to call you back as soon as they get the page. No matter where they are, I get a response. So it is very efficient."

*Adjusting communication with customers to avoid overload.* In sales it's important to understand how best to communicate with various customers. Stan says he adjusts the ICTs he uses based on how well he knows the customer. For example, he says, "I will spend a lot more personal time with somebody I don't know. I will very rarely page a new customer." Stan prefers to talk to new customers directly, either in person or over the phone. He explains that he "will rarely send them emails until I get to know them. Basically, what I'm trying to do is build confidence and trust within that individual." Once a strong relationship is established—and, along with it, trust—Stan thinks that "it's acceptable to send them pages, send voicemails, or emails. But I try to keep that to a minimum until I really feel comfortable with them as well as vice versa." Sometimes that's difficult he says, because he has customers who live out of state, "so I may just travel there for no other reason than to go to lunch with somebody. And in the long term it is worth it."

*Stan says that if you ignore the customer's desires, the customer won't communicate with you. Preferences vary a lot.*

Stan also finds that customers have different ICT communication preferences, which he tries to accommodate: "Some people say, 'Send me an email on everything you want to communicate because I'm very disciplined about reading my email.' That's fine, and that's what I'll do. Other people say, 'Page me and I'll always call you back.' That's fine, too." One main reason it's important to learn about these preferences, he says, is that if you ignore the customer's desires, the customer won't communicate with you. Preferences vary a lot, he says. For example, "I had one customer—I could leave him three voicemails a day, he never talked to me. Page him and he'll be back to me in 30 seconds!"

The information-overload management strategies that Stan has adopted help him maintain strong customer relationships. As seen throughout this case, when possible he consciously creates systems, such as handling all his voicemail boxes, that provide structure to his routine. But he does not mindlessly superimpose this structure on his customers. He'll talk with them, learn their ICT preferences, and adjust his communication accordingly.

*Delegating information-searching to others and to technology.* Besides the various personal strategies Stan has adopted to handle overload, he also delegates information searches. His job demands constant searches. "If I need the information quickly, I'll do it myself," he says. "That is the benefit of the Net. I can get on and get the information and then get out of there." But for less urgent or more involved information searches, Stan finds someone else to do it. For example, he says, "If we're trying to confirm the spending patterns for a company over many, many years, then we'll have somebody else do that work for us."

Recently his sales team wanted 10 year's data on SemiProduct, his major account, so they hired a new college graduate to look it up—"all on the Net," he says. "It was very interesting because it confirmed what we thought." This is valuable information for Stan's sales team since it enhances their credibility with their management team: "It convinces not only our team but also senior management that when we say, 'Our market share is X and here are some patterns of spending from our key account,' we are knowledgeable." Stan says it's particularly gladdening when the numbers gathered from the Web agree with "what we [the sales team] have said over the last several years." This makes upper management believe what the sales team is saying because they have data to prove their claims.

Besides often delegating information-collection to others inside their own organization, Stan's team has learned to use technology efficiently to collect and organize data:

> We have a search engine that pulls together all of the press releases in our industry and compiles them into a list, usually in chronological order. And then you can just scan through them or you can search for a specific company's name and you can read all of the press releases for that particular company.

This tool, available on their corporate Intranet, lets them look up past or current information at any time.

It's an important tool in a market as dynamically linked as the semiconductor industry. Stan often needs to understand more complex business relationships such as his customer's customer or joint ventures, because "that's going to drive their demand and in turn drive our demand." Besides understanding his customer's customer, he needs to know which companies are entering into joint ventures: "If there's a joint venture coming up [involving] one of our specific customers with another customer, it gives us a lot of insight, and then our two groups at our company will start working together. And as a matter of fact, we are [organized] based on that."

*Information-sharing.* Stan can also search for technical information housed inside his own organization. "We have a technical library," he says, "and you can access anything that the company is working on except for those projects that are considered proprietary." What he calls his company's "library" is actually a database where information is collected and shared. The database focuses on collecting engineering information, since there are roughly 15 different engineering groups scattered around the world. The library is useful because, as Stan explains, "Some issues are common, and an individual thinks, 'Geez, someone had to look at this and do this work before.' They can go to the library and find the information without going to track down the individual who actually did the work." This saves considerable time.

Sharing engineering information is useful, but sales data and tips are much harder to share. Stan says because "the information that sales people have relative to their customers is sometimes proprietary—and some things you shouldn't even know about." The proprietary information remains in his head. Were others in his organization to learn about it, he feels it could be "very dangerous" both to his customers and to his business: "Another group of people may not understand the sensitivity of it [the proprietary information] and use it in a way that's incorrect. Before you know it, trust and confidence are broken down." Thus, many times he doesn't share the information—especially in writing. If it is shared, even partially, it is done so orally.

When sharing non-proprietary information, Stan says, email is his ICT of choice: "Email is extremely valuable because we can target exactly who we want to have know it. In a lot of cases, that information just goes to those people and it can't be transferred any further." Stan explains that even though he does not typically lock his email to prevent its being forwarded, experience tells him that people normally honor requests to not forward messages.

Interestingly enough, salespeople view some of the information they receive from customers as confidential, and they don't share it even with other departments of their own organization, such as engineering: "Even if [the information] may not be confidential, we really don't want engineering and maybe some other people in the company to know it because then they start trying to use that information to justify what they do." Salespeople visit customers and learn about their specific needs and wants. In an ideal world, that information could be shared with engineering. But in his experience that information is often used for personal gain, not with the customers' interests in mind. To avoid this problem, Stan explains, "People in sales will communicate some of the critical information about a customer or a customer's needs or what we are seeing [when visiting customers] to corporate marketing."

## Conclusion

This case illustrates just how many communication decisions good salespeople may make. Not only must they consider the ICTs used inside their own organizations, but they must also respect the ICT needs and options of their customers. This can result in information overload. Stan provides us examples of how one salesperson handles the problem. He creates systems that provide him structure in handling all his communication devices. While he uses this structure, he also listens to customer preferences and cheerfully adapts to them. This strategy saves him time, just as delegating information searches does. He also selectively shares information with individuals inside and outside his organization.

## Questions for Review or Discussion

1.  How do you adapt to in-house and customer preferences across time-zones.

2.  What strategies do you use to manage your needs to check various ICTs such as mobile phones, email accounts, voicemails, etc.?

3.  You have been asked to write your top five recommendations for managing multiple information sources. Using this case as a guide, what would those be?

4.  What are the implications of this case for communicating with workers in distributed environments?

5.  Imagine that your livelihood depended on your ability to adapt to your customers' ICT preferences. If you had customers that were early adopters, how would you adjust to meet their needs?

# Depending on the Kindness of Strangers: Using Newsgroups for Just-in-Time Learning

Keri K. Stephens & Jan-Oddvar Sørnes

In the past decade, computer technology has revolutionized how we conduct business. Technology gurus—hardware experts, software developers, helpdesk personnel—often know an encyclopedic amount of information essential to their jobs. But given the constant changes in the technology they support, they're always having to play catch-up. How do they manage to stay current?

This narrative will introduce you to several gurus and their just-in-time learning method—Internet newsgroups. Here, we use the term broadly to represent both Internet-based discussions posted to a central location as well as those distributed via email. Essentially, newsgroups—an ICT—are used to solve the problems created by rapid technological change whether in the workplace or the home. They are also critical learning links for individuals in small organizations since they have more limited infrastructure. These newsgroup participants depend on recommendations of total strangers located around the world, and they'll often make strategic business decisions based on this advice. This is networking on a grand scale, crossing cultural boundaries as well as national ones. What is created from all this amounts to a community of digital philanthropy.

**Key Concept** Newsgroups are a great source of expert information: also known as just-in-time learning.

## Just-in-Time Learning

There are two sides to newsgroups: receiving expert information and offering responses to queries. We refer to the first type as "just-in-time learning" (JIT), since many techies describe newsgroups as one of their prime sources for the latest information, troubleshooting problems, and best practices. Not only are user groups helpful for work situations, but all the newsgroup users in this narrative consult them for their hobbies as well. Allen, one of the interviewees, explains that finding relevant newsgroups is fairly easy: "You must just look at what they are called and what type of discussion is going on in them. It is really pretty self-explanatory."

Newsgroups seem to be most useful for very specific questions. That he tends to use newsgroups only during certain stages of a project:

> We use newsgroups to a certain extent, but more for specific things that typically come later in the project. For example, say I can't get something to function in a certain way or don't know how I should solve it. By posting a question in a newsgroup, I usually get an answer.

He says that "early in the project the information-gathering is much broader—you don't collect many specific details." This is a time, he says, to use books, or search the Internet.

The key reason that techies prefer newsgroups over other technologies is that they provide access to rapid, specific, and accurate responses. Tom explains: "When you have a completely concrete issue that needs solving, you use newsgroups because as a rule, you get answers relatively quickly." While the number of responses varies, Tom says, "On average I would say I get between five and ten responses, and of those, two to four are real answers to your question. Then you typically have follow-up questions that can be a good part of it." Other interviewees explain that some of the less useful responses are from individuals offering third-party accounts of how to solve an issue. For example, some newsgroup participants will say things like, "I heard that if you hold down the Shift key while typing the letter *J*, on some computers you will get the technical symbol you need." Usually, such tips prove incorrect. What is most helpful is the response based on personal experience. When people have actually tried to find the needed technical symbol themselves, their response is usually correct.

> Having access to experts around the world offers another advantage to newsgroups. Allen explains: Let's say you have a problem with WindowsNT— a server problem that is such-and-such. You go to the newsgroup that discusses subjects that are under that area, you ask the question, and it's likely you will get an answer. If you post your questions in an international newsgroup, you will be guaranteed an answer.

Another interviewee explained the value of international reach this way: "It is indeed fantastic. Here there are colossal numbers of people around the whole world who have encountered the very same issues and have published solutions on the Net someplace or another. You skip having to invent gunpowder again." These ICT users see their participation in a virtual international group as vital and transparent. Since many newsgroups converse in English, the interviewees claim that language barriers are rare. The same goes for cultural barriers. Allen says, "You don't really think about where people are from. It all takes place in English. If it is possible to learn, it really is inconsequential where they come from."

### Asking Questions on a Newsgroup

To best use newsgroups, it helps to know how to ask a question clearly. While it might appear very straightforward—you simply locate a relevant newsgroup, type in your question, and wait for a response—the quality of the response often depends on several more subtle considerations. For example, is the newsgroup moderated? Moderated newsgroups have a person(s) who filters all the questions and responses, thereby eliminating irrelevant or commercial-type queries. These newsgroups typically have fewer comments that are completely off-topic. A non-moderated newsgroup, on the other hand, has no *policeman*, so every communiqué gets posted. But while you'd think that non-moderated newsgroups would quickly become overloaded with irrelevant information, that does not seem to happen very often. The main reason is that they appear to have powerful sets of rules—not always concrete—that govern their users. In this way, newsgroups have a type of self-justice since they reward and punish their members.

*Newsgroups have a type of self-justice since they reward and punish their members.*

## Role of Culture

*It is pretty unique and it reflects a little of the old Internet culture sort of that the Internet is "for everybody, and free of charge." Like it still is in the Linux world. —Norwegian software developer*

Linux is an operating system that remains free and that enjoys an extensive following in the software-developer community. When the Internet was created, it operated on the belief that anyone could participate and share information using this vast virtual network. People have referred to this view as a "Culture"—one that functions as an open, egalitarian system. But, you find, even in an open culture, rules serve important roles, one of which is to create order.

Rules typically fall into two categories: formal and informal. With newsgroups, formal rules are tough to enforce since the participants are from all around the world, are often anonymous, and are normally transient. So the rules that typically govern a newsgroup take the form of a strong, yet informal, culture. By "culture" we mean a collective phenomenon that provides individuals with accepted ways to express and affirm their beliefs. For example, one of our interviewees participates in a newsgroup consisting of people fascinated with flight simulators. Most of these individuals are both hobbyists and professional pilots. He describes the self-enforcing culture of his newsgroup this way: "Really, the way that we communicate, what is allowed and what isn't allowed—the unwritten rules—matter. In our newsgroup, no one talks about flight simulation as a *game*." Many actual pilots are active in the newsgroup, he says, and accidents are not a game. Empathy is expressed over accidents, and "there is a great sensitivity and discussion on what air safety really is." The newsgroups usually deliver high-quality answers, he says: "If you throw in a question about a problem that you have, you get 10 answers—nice answers, at once." The norm of the group is to be responsive. This norm intrinsically conveys unspoken but strong rules about how people should communicate in the forum.

When asking questions in a newsgroup, another consideration is whether that particular group is receptive to how newcomers ask both basic and more advanced questions. For example, Allen explains how he searches newsgroup archives before posting a question. Newsgroup archives are where members can scroll back and review responses to prior questions and answers: "You must look at whether there is someone who has posted the same problem before and search a little to see if you find anything. If not, you put up a new question." Allen projects a sense of courtesy for the current members because he believes this is part of the culture of that both groups and individuals communicate behavioral expectations to each other.

### Socialization of Fresh Newsgroup Members

How do newcomers learn the unwritten rules of a newsgroup? The interviewees in this narrative say that they actively socialize newcomers by publicly punishing any member who acts out. Here we use the term "socialization" to describe the often spontaneous way that group "members of established cultures communicate to newcomers systematic sets of expectations for how they should behave" (Trice & Beyer, 1993, p. 130).

**Key Concept**
Socialization is the often spontaneous way that groups communicate their expectations to newcomers.

This socialization-through-punishment approach is viewed as enjoyable by some newsgroup members, who relish the chance to reassert the group's norms by shaming anyone who oversteps the line. Allen likes being an enforcer:

*The fun thing is that when someone does that, there is a storm towards these persons with questions like, "What are they doing here?" This is not the kind of fellowship we want. We help people. We develop each other's skills. We develop each other's interests. And if you don't have anything else to contribute with, then you better stay away.*

In moderated newsgroups, a conscious effort is normally made to shelter members from inappropriate emails. But sometimes the moderator will allow improper questions and responses to be displayed as a reminder to all members of what is unacceptable. Allen describes a situation where a participant from another country once asked for help in obtaining an illegal copy of expensive software: "We have a very straight attitude. For example, no pirate copying." People have come onto the newsgroups, he says, and actually asked if they need to purchase software or if perhaps a member could just send them a copy for free. Newsgroup members quickly respond and re-establish the group norms.

Sometimes newsgroup members will shift their information-sharing approach to a commercial venture. For example, Allen describes one member of his aviation newsgroup who had a hobby Website where he provided copyrighted maps that people could download for free. This individual had contacted the copyright owners of the maps and had gotten their permission to use the maps, provided that he "mark it with 'Not for real aviation' and that he didn't take money for it." This was fine for a while, but then the hobbyist decided to start a business. "The free map site went so well that he started a company and sold CD-ROMs." Allen says that almost immediately the map copyright owner used the newsgroup to publicly expose the hobbyist's inappropriate business. The entire legal battle took place right on the newsgroup's site and sent a strong message to its members that illegal activity is not tolerated, even on a hobby-based newsgroup. Once again, we see that newsgroups rely on a type of self-justice.

Despite a newsgroup's readiness to punish members who violate their unspoken rules, the culture on these sites is often almost purely philanthropic. Allen describes several newsgroups as having an "unbelievable strong identity on the Net when it comes to such things—an amazing kind of helpfulness. Everybody helps one other." One interviewee explains that bonds are created, and simply calling them newsgroups doesn't do them justice: "No, these are not newsgroups, but real discussion-groups on the Net, connected to this air-fellowship."

This fellowship extends beyond the virtual newsgroup and into physical connections. One interviewee provides an example of how generosity permeates the Web community. In his newsgroup, there was an American "who said he had come across a bookstore that sold cheap navigation maps because they were outdated," and who then asked if anyone was interested in having them. As it happened, the interviewee himself was very interested. So he wrote the American a personal email and told him that he was from Tromsø in Norway and that he would love to have the maps. The American agreed to mail them to him. Several days later, they arrived as promised. Such is the philanthropy that is fostered by newsgroups.

## Conflicting Rules

*How do you participate in a newsgroup without giving away company secrets?*

Since newsgroups are virtual, the participants are formally connected to other organizations, such as their employing business. Many employers themselves have rules concerning what information is fit to be shared. The challenge for people participating in a newsgroup is how to indulge their sharing impulse without violating any confidentiality rules. Allen explains: "You try to include as much information as you can, without making available information that you shouldn't give out. We can't, as a rule, give out information about customers, but we can talk about the technology in general." This illustrates how users will walk the line.

## Who Are the Digital Philanthropists?

With people constantly posting messages to newsgroups, one might assume that they are also avid responders. This does not seem to be the case. The digital philanthropists—those answering queries and expecting nothing in return—are somewhat rare. Allen explains:

> There are people who spend an insane amount of time on the newsgroups, and you are very thankful to them——they have a fantastic expertise. Typically, you recognize five to 10 names, and you see that they usually answer 10 to 20 inquiries a week.

The interviewees speculate that the responders are developers, university students, and "so-called 'nerds in the basement' who get damned interested in a certain specific area, so they sit with the newsgroup up there [on their computer screen]...when something pops up." Since their computer already has the newsgroup visible, it makes it fairly simple to reply. But it is really their passion and expertise that drive their participation.

Even though most of our interviewees claim that they rarely contribute to newsgroups in a work context, they are more active participants in their hobby-oriented newsgroups. We can only speculate why this occurs, but one reason might be their on-going needs. Many interviewees in this study work on many projects, so they never become a focused expert in one small area. They selectively use the newsgroups, but they don't need to become an active participant. Perhaps this participation explains why the interviewees wanted to talk more about their hobby newsgroups. It is plausible that as individuals actively contribute, they also follow more of the on-going dialog. They can also articulate the values and culture of a newsgroup where they are a more active participant.

## Conclusion

In this narrative we have seen how organizational members seek information outside their organization to fulfill their needs for just-in-time learning. A key way this is accomplished is through accessing various newsgroups. Individuals also will contribute back to newsgroups, and since they expect nothing in return, this is a type of digital philanthropy. Managers might want to pay more attention to this ICT because it can serve as a valuable resource. The people in our narrative shared some rules of how and when to use newsgroups. We can also see how virtual cultures develop and actually shape the behavior of newsgroup members and newcomers.

## Questions for Review or Discussion

1.  Now that information is so easily accessible through the diffusion of the Internet, what are the implications for business practices?

2.  How do you learn best? As an observer? As an active participant? How does that affect your ICT choices?

3.  Why do you think that many people take advantage of information (free riders), but fail to contribute in return? What are three useful criteria that might guide participation?

4.  When using the Internet as an information source, how do you determine credibility?

5.  How can a newsgroup newcomer learn the unspoken cultural rules?

# Building a Medical Community Using Remote Diagnosis: The Story of DocNet

## 17

Alf Steinar Sætre & Jan-Oddvar Sørnes

Even though the Internet has now gained near-universal acceptance in western societies, Norwegian hospitals continue to resist using it. They have been wary of permitting Internet access on their computers out of concern for security and the confidentiality of patient records.

This story concerns a small group of pathologists who, quite unaware of the many obstacles facing them, formed an organization they call "DocNet," a Web-based service for pathologists in Norway. On the DocNet Website they post, for learning purposes, the "diagnostic case of the month," and they are gradually building a diagnostic database using electronic images of tissue samples and the corresponding diagnosis.

One challenge facing these entrepreneurial medical professionals is the low level of technological awareness among their most senior colleagues. Although growing their digital community has been slower and more obstacle-ridden than they could ever have imagined, the founders of DocNet are today beginning to see the positive effects of their professional community-building efforts.

The story told in this case is based on two separate interviews. First we interviewed Dr. Tor Hemne, a 30-year-old native Laplander who is a teaching doctor at a university hospital in Norway. Dr. Hemne started telling us the story of DocNet. From this conversation we learned about the "pioneering figure" behind DocNet, Dr. Inge Nerdrum, a former colleague of Dr. Hemne who had recently moved to the Norwegian University of Science and Technology's (NTNU) Medical School and St. Olaf Hospital in Trondheim. Currently an Associate Professor at NTNU's School of Medicine, Dr. Nerdrum has a part time-position as Chief of Pathology at St. Olaf Hospital, and also a part-time position at the National Center for Telemedicine (NST) in Tromsø. Our second interview was conducted with him, and he was happy to show off the latest technology in his office.

Both doctors find pathology a challenging profession because it often requires access to an inordinate amount of information to produce a correct diagnosis. The need for information stems from such a wide range of issues that it is "difficult to have everything fresh in one's memory at any given time," says Dr. Hemne. As a result, both doctors follow the medical tradition of spending a lot of time with medical reference books in their department and university libraries.

Their research techniques have changed in the past few years as they have begun to make use of Internet-based services to gather information. The Internet is used not only to search for information, but also to consult with colleagues outside their own hospitals when confronting a particularly enigmatic case. The vast majority of cases, though, are mundane.

"There are so many banalities because we insert tubes in so many cavities and organs of people," says Dr. Nerdrum. Once an instrument is inserted into a patient, doctors tend to take more samples than are strictly required to ensure they have a good sampling of material, so "there is an incredible number of commonplace samples to look at," says Dr. Nerdrum.

These mundane samples constitute 95% of their total case load; the remaining 5%, however, are "special cases" that require consultation, and it was that need that drove the establishment of DocNet. Using Internet technology both to build a database of routine cases and to share expertise across the relatively small pathology units at various Norwegian hospitals struck a few entrepreneurial pathologists as a smart idea.

## Starting DocNet

The project began very informally. DocNet was started by a few enthusiastic young doctors—well, "maybe one enthusiast [Dr. Nerdrum] who 'shanghaied' those who he thought had some clue about computers," Dr. Hemne says. Dr. Hemne says that it was this selection criterion that led Dr. Nerdrum to invite him into the project, because he had "seen a computer before, and had seen the Internet, specifically." This became an important criterion since there were many—and still are many—pathologists who operate at a "Stone-Age level" when it comes to computers, says Dr. Nerdrum. He is confident that this reluctance has less to do with age than with their attitude towards ICTs. An example from the interview shows that his diagnosis of his colleagues seems well-founded. "I don't understand it," laughs Dr. Nerdrum. "If they have MS Word up and then are going to go to another program, then they—for crying out loud—*close* Word in order to open that other program! It's unbelievable!" Despite this obvious drawback, DocNet entrepreneurs were enthusiastic about the project. But they were also unaware of the real obstacles, technical and social, they would soon face.

*The project began very informally. DocNet was started by a few enthusiastic young doctors.*

Yet NST and their "remote diagnosis" was a starting point for building DocNet. The University Hospital in Tromsø already served some of the regional hospitals in northern Norway with remote pathological diagnosis using the existing telephone lines, which provided at least a partial substitute for a local pathologist. If a surgeon at the local hospital decided that something needed further analysis while the patient was still anesthetized, he or she provided a frozen cross section during surgery to be analyzed remotely.

The surgeon cuts a small sample of the tissue he wants analyzed. Then technicians at the local hospital quickly make small slides, freeze the sample in nitrogen, and place it in a microscope. A pathologist in Tromsø then remotely controls the microscope using existing telecommunication lines and communicates his diagnosis directly via speakerphone to the doctor who's performing the surgery. Despite all the long-distance coordination this requires, Dr. Hemne is quite pleased with the process and says, "We get good results doing the job that way." These experiences showed the potential of long-distance medicine.

*They discovered that the results were very similar to what they got when pathologists analyzed "live" samples and decided that working with digital images could be a useful methodology.*

Through NST's network, the doctors who started DocNet had access to discussion partners with relevant expertise. The initial thought behind DocNet was to build a Web-based solution—using digital still photographs—that facilitated consulting colleagues who were physically located elsewhere. Before going online, they did a pilot project at the Nordland Central Hospital to test the diagnostic reliability when using still photographs. They discovered that the results were very similar to what they got when pathologists analyzed "live" samples and decided that working with digital images could be a useful methodology. Their insight was that if diagnosis with digital images through a microscope works in real time, then it should also work with digital still photographs, which would allow remote consulting with more challenging cases.

ICTs have the potential for greatly increasing the collaboration among diagnosticians. In Norway, there are 18 hospital pathology departments with approximately 150 doctors of pathology and assistants, and many other technicians—an environment totaling some 400–500 individuals. Dr. Nerdrum's experience that "several heads together think better than several heads separately" served as an impetus for starting DocNet in Norway. The DocNet would also be of great importance at more remote hospitals where pathologists often work alone.

The remote diagnosis, aka "real-time telemedicine," using remote-controlled microscopes, had been established for a while. The development of DocNet was a natural extension of this. Dr. Nerdrum observed that "people sat and did a great deal of their thinking at various places, in parallel, without drawing on each other's know-how—in a way, duplicating work." His idea was to develop a venue—a Web portal—through which they could "share experiences."

They also had some secondary motives for exploring the possibility of using the Web to achieve fast diagnosis of still photos. For example, they wanted to get "the pathologists more favorable towards switching to Internet-based knowledge acquisition," says Dr. Hemne. Using the Internet would provide more contemporary information than reference books would provide. Using email and the Internet allowed them to access the expertise of well-known researchers throughout the world. Even though this was a great opportunity, Dr. Hemne viewed it as a real challenge because he perceived the pathology community in Norway as being "not especially young and dynamic." The pathology profession

*Getting doctors to use DocNet was a real challenge because the pathology community in Norway was not especially young and dynamic.*

can be characterized as a "mature" profession—that is, in Dr. Hemne's words, composed of "a number of well-situated men with positions" who are not the easiest group of people to change. Their specialty was perceived by medical students and young doctors alike as stale and boring, he says, but once the project got underway, students and other doctors realized "it was actually exciting."

### Excitement in Spite of Struggles

Despite early struggles and disappointments with the slow progress, DocNet's founders remained enthusiastic because they were attempting to create something truly revolutionary in their field. They began by establishing the parameters needed for the Website. Creating this framework took great effort and it also established the definition for their product. Once this was done, "a software supplier surfaced, who seemed to have a number of good solutions that we adopted," says Dr. Hemne. Once the concept was tied to specific technological solutions, the viability of the project became palpable. They subsequently received public support in the form of a government grant in order to customize these solutions for DocNet.

DocNet currently includes a public Webpage where the "editors" of DocNet control what is published. In addition, they have a password-protected site open to all the pathology departments at all the hospitals in Norway. This password-protected "Intranet" site constitutes the core of DocNet, and all its regular members have the opportunity to freely access and publish information on it.

Whereas they previously thought of using the Internet to aid in using world experts for diagnosing difficult cases, they realized that it is also the ultimate medium for storing this knowledge through case archives.[1] These cases consist of a number of pictures and accompanying text containing basic patient information. There are many still pictures associated with each case to compensate for the different magnification levels and adjustments that a sample in a microscope allows.

### Defining the Success of DocNet

*The thorough planning and thoughtfulness that went into the project made it attractive for others to copy. The basic structure is now being developed for other professional Webs-eye, ear, nose, throat.*

As they planned DocNet, they paid particular attention to the preferences of the doctors who would be using it. Says Dr. Hemne, "We have thought a great deal about the wishes one could have as physicians." The users were heavily involved—"maybe not in the technical solutions behind the product, but in the use of it—the functionality" of it, he says. The thorough planning and thoughtfulness that went into the project made it attractive for others to copy. The basic structure is now being "developed for other professional Webs—eye, ear, nose, throat," says Dr. Hemne. They simply fill the architecture of DocNet with their own content, but at its core it is the same product. This use of a "boilerplate" shows the ease of taking successfully established ICTs—in

---

[1] The development of their case archive was made possible, in part, by a grant from the Norwegian Industry and Regional Development Fund. This grant enabled them to work with an external contractor who develops Web-based solutions.

this case, a Web-based solution—and readily transferring them to other settings. ICTs are thus increasing the ease of technology transfer. Dr. Hemne says with some pride that his "stale" profession now "has contributed to breaking new ground." The National Center of Telemedicine, a recognized leader in the field of telemedicine, "thinks it [DocNet] is one of its greatest successes," says Dr. Hemne. This shows that it is possible for professions that are some distance away from technology's leading edge to make major innovative contributions.

But Dr. Nerdrum feels that DocNet is used less than he had thought or hoped it would be. At least part of the reason for this, he speculates, is that in the majority of the 18 pathology departments in Norway, the doctors must still go to a separate PC room in order to use DocNet. "So there are many who don't have access," he says. "And with a tool that one should use daily, one shouldn't have to go into the next room in order to log on. It should be accessible by Alt-Tab, really." His focus on convenience goes straight to a crucial issue in the diffusion of innovations.

When considering the number of members actively involved in contributing content and those using DocNet as a resource, the pathologists themselves "are not so sure if it has been an overwhelming success," says Dr. Hemne. But one of DocNet's purposes was to link Norway's small and scattered community of pathologists. In this regard, Dr. Hemne thinks that DocNet has had some success:

> I think we have broken a little new ground and tied scattered departments to each other, created a better information flow. And in that manner we are involved with quality assurance in the nation's pathology departments. So we have done some good.

The Internet has proven a useful tool in sharing the expertise across the various pathology departments in Norway. It has also increased awareness of the location of the expertise in each of the subfields of pathology, which makes it easier for a doctor to locate the best talent available for any given problem.

Even so, recognition of their work has been slow in coming. Ironically DocNet "has been applauded more abroad than in Norway," says Dr. Nerdrum. He thinks that one reason for the slow adoption and recognition is what he calls the "north-of-the-Sinsen-intersection phenomenon," a reference to what Oslo natives previously thought of as the city's northern limit. Everything north of this intersection used to be (and still is, to a certain extent) considered "uninhabitable" by many in Oslo. The fact that the National Center for Telemedicine is located as far north as Tromsø[2] has, according to Dr. Nerdrum, impeded its acceptance in the medical community, and therefore—by association—also DocNet's proliferation. "I am sure that if they had been located at the Radium Hospital in Oslo, they would have been used more," says Dr. Nerdrum. This kind of a cultural parochialism shows some of the obstacles to disseminating innovative practices.

---

[2] Tromsø, a city of about 60,000, is situated about 700 miles north of Oslo and 200 miles north of the Arctic Circle

## Sharing of Knowledge

When sending out requests for information on a puzzling case, doctors experience few if any barriers to sharing knowledge. When facing a diagnostic challenge, "we of course go first and foremost in-house and consult with colleagues," says Dr. Nerdrum. Dr. Hemne concurs, saying that he has "never gotten a negative response" to such a request. "There is nothing that pleases one with expertise more than ladling out one's knowledge. It is even one's greatest wish—to really be able to pour out one's expertise on fresh assistant doctors." These experts have little difficulty in sharing their knowledge—whether by computer-mediated communication or by face-to-face communication—with those less knowledgeable than themselves. The reluctance of some of the more senior members of the medical community to use DocNet, then, is not a resistance to sharing knowledge but, perhaps, simply a resistance to new technology.

*There is nothing that pleases one with expertise more than ladling out one's knowledge. It is even one's greatest wish-to really be able to pour out one's expertise on fresh assistant doctors.*

Whenever consulting their most immediate colleagues orally doesn't resolve an issue, they will send a sample (tissue on a glass slide) to "the Radium Hospital or some other place where one has confidence that the people can give you a reasonable second opinion," says Dr. Nerdrum. In addition, he says, some of the pathologists send digital images by shooting "a number of pictures [through the microscope] and sending them by email or uploading them directly to servers." Using digital imagery allows local pathologists to access experts world-wide. They can log on to an Internet site like American Research Institute for Pathology in Washington, D.C., free of charge, and "fill out a form, and upload the picture files, and then get an answer back in a matter of a few days." These evaluations also provide details on how they were done. This "methodological" description not only permits the local pathologists to assess the credibility of the analysis, it adds a great deal of value and further enhances the dissemination of knowledge.

The reputation of the institution and the individual giving the remote evaluation determines its credibility. For the Norwegian pathologists to trust such a remote diagnosis, they need to know how the evaluation was performed and by whom. Dr. Nerdrum expects that the institutions that have credibility, employing the leading experts in their fields, will soon begin charging for this kind of service, as they are providing medical services of great value to doctors and patients all over the world through the Internet.

## Security Issues

One obstacle facing the entrepreneurial doctors behind DocNet was the regulatory restrictions imposed on them by the Norwegian Data Protection Authority (DPA), which limited Internet access from Norwegian hospitals. Most departments previously operated with as little as one shared Internet PC with a common username, which dramatically reduced the use of the Internet. Bergen's Haukeland Hospital was the first facility to allow free use of email and the Internet for its employees, but not without controversy. Haukeland "quickly got the Data Protection Authority (DPA) on their back—this was not allowed," says Dr. Hemne. The problem, of course, was that having sensitive information about patients on the same computer that had Internet access was a breach of security. In spite of the "heat" from DPA, the need for Internet access to the most up-to-date medical information has led other hospitals to follow this controversial example. St. Olaf's University Hospital in Trondheim, Rikshospitalet University Hospital in Oslo, and the University Hospital in Northern Norway have all followed suit. Thus far every user with Internet access has two PCs in their office—one with Internet access, and the other an in-hospital PC that does not have access to an outside network. Dr. Nerdrum therefore has one PC for diagnostic output and one for university-related work. But the hospital's IT department is now working on solutions so that each doctor will need only one PC instead of two, again simplifying and streamlining the use of ICTs. The hospital administrators who were willing to take the legal risk of pushing the envelope against DPA contributed to the speed of adoption of Internet-related services in Norwegian hospitals.

> **Key Issue** 🎯
> Keeping sensitive patient information on a PC with Internet access posed a security breach.

Information security for personal information remains an important regulatory topic in Norway. In the fall of 2001 doctors were required to read many internal directives and to sign several guidelines in order to use the Internet. Dr. Hemne thinks it ironic that "the guidelines and information were very similar to those we had made and used when we started up." He fears that the standards now being imposed are too strict—now doctors are effectively told to sign a contract to "never do anything wrong," and all information on the computers belongs to the hospital, meaning that the hospital can at any time check the activities on each computer. This is a thorny issue for doctors, says Dr. Hemne:

> *I think it is difficult that all the information on each PC belongs to the hospital. I don't really give a cat's ass about the data department seeing that I have a picture of boobs on the PC. What I think is more alarming is that they can go into my machine—on my domain—to see things that I have produced myself. I mean, this is my intellectual achievement. I don't really think it [the rule] belongs.*

Most doctors have signed the contract, but they resent having to do so. They feel that this agreement not only invades their privacy but jeopardizes the security and integrity of their own research. Despite these technical and legal obstacles, DocNet has survived owing to the enthusiasm of its founders and the willingness of pathologists to share their expertise.

## Conclusion

The story of DocNet shows that in spite of the heavy reliance on technology in their effort to build a community of pathologists across Norway, "it is the organization that is important, and technology is just an aid," says Dr. Nerdrum. Thus far, their community-building efforts have been hampered by both technical and legal obstacles, but as medical professionals across Norway gain improved access to the Internet, and as security issues are further resolved, the community-building effects of DocNet will continue to grow.

### Questions for Review or Discussion

1. How would you feel about having images of cells in your body used for teaching and diagnostic purposes over the Internet?

2. What, in your mind, are the reasons why the diffusion of DocNet's innovative approach has been so slow?

3. Review the characteristics of the Diffusion of Innovations and identify why this innovation does work and why it doesn't.

4. What are the credibility risks involved when sharing knowledge with other experts?

5. In Garbage Can terms, DocNet has provided a solution. Now identify the problems, participants, and choice opportunities to which it might be attached.

# Don't Get Between Me and My Customer: How Changing Jobs Shifts ICT Use

Keri K. Stephens & Jan-Oddvar Sørnes

**18**

Quite often we'll assume that as we discover newer, faster, and better ICTs, we'll automatically want to adopt those technologies. What's forgotten in this diffusion—adoption—curve assumption is that sometimes it works in reverse: people will abandon state-of-the-art ICTs because they no longer serve their purpose. These people aren't Luddites. No, they simply believe that ICTs ought to enhance, not hinder, communication efforts. They change ICT's for functional and symbolic reasons.

In this case, you will meet Darrell Urbanski, an aggressive ICT user who recently changed ICTs due to a career change. Darrell has a powerful voice and the ability to captivate any audience. Although a "techie," he has the ability to make technology transparent to others. His focus on community is demonstrated by the fact that he'll buy 50 copies of a book that he finds interesting and pass them out to colleagues to appreciate.

Formerly, Darrell had been director of a technology-training organization that sought corporate members and acted as a unified industry trade group. In that role, he had traveled almost constantly, meeting with various U.S.-based companies that were either current or potential members of the group. Darrell's training organization offered them three main services: (1) it collected and distributed the latest technology-training information, (2) it was a voice for the industry on policy concerns, and (3) it held conferences where members could meet either physically or virtually. Besides being a recruiter, Darrell served as a keynote speaker at many conferences where he represented the trade organization. Known by most people in the industry, he was considered a "technology guru." This was due in part to Darrell's prior work as a technical trainer for computer and hardware organizations.

But after deciding that the constant travel was sabotaging his personal relationships, Darrell began searching for another position. In the course of his search, he found a Web-based training organization headquartered in Scotland that was looking for someone to expand its operation into the U.S. The company was called WebTrain, and its first product was a Web-based questionnaire that helps corporations train their employees. Similar to a personality-styles individual assessment, WebTrain provides employees insight into their own learning styles where people are categorized into similar personality styles. Since many organizations provide their employees training, and since there are many training options today, this tool focuses on helping employees learn most efficiently. For example, if a company provides safety training to its employees in two different ways—via traditional classroom or via CDROM—the WebTrain learning assessment tool will let the employee know which type of course best fits his or her own learning style.

WebTrain is known as a "distributed organization," since the CEO and executive staff are headquartered in the U.K., while the executive who runs North American operations lives in Vancouver, Canada. Darrell saw this as his opportunity to cut down his travel and handle the U.S. operations for a growing company. Darrell got the job and soon started to establish the U.S. base, where he was responsible for finding, hiring, and training affiliates and independent contractors to work closely with him to develop the U.S. market. Despite the legally independent relationship between these contractors and WebTrain, "we treat them as if they were a part of WebTrain," he says. "It's a pretty tight relationship. We do all their marketing reports, invoicing, collections—I mean, the whole nine yards."

Despite his affiliation with this training organization, he is in many ways an entrepreneur. Unlike in his prior job, he does not have a company-provided office and staff. He's expected to build the U.S. operations from the ground up, using his prior contacts and his own resources.

## Working in the Virtual Office

Becoming an entrepreneur forced Darrell to rethink the types of ICTs he'd use—and for various reasons. First, he no longer enjoyed a company-owned laptop computer and mobile phone. Second, he no longer had administrative support for such tedious tasks as marketing and billing. Third, he had to train himself in how to efficiently manage his growing business alone.

*Becoming an entrepreneur forced Darrell to rethink the types of ICTs he'd use.*

To cope with these changes, Darrell invested in advanced ICTs. Now less than six months after starting the U.S. base, Darrell has himself a thoroughly networked home. "Since we are on a cable modem in the house," he explains, "we actually have six computers in the house: four Macintoshs and two PCs. We also have two Ethernet hubs." These Ethernet hubs enable him to share information between his computers. This highly computerized, 1,400-square-foot home creates an environment where work is constant. The first thing Darrell does in the morning is check his email, and since all six computers support his business, they run 24 hours a day.

After checking the email, he launches a software program called Human Click that allows him to have real-time interactions with visitors to his Website. Since this tool is only useful when he is working on his computer, he leaves it off when he's not physically present. When someone visits his Website, a computer alerts him by playing a doorbell sound. This lets him "track where they go on the site, and engage that person in live chat while visiting," he explains. His software functions almost like a business partner. And its tracking ability lets him see what the visitor's Internet protocol or address is, which yields him valuable marketing information. Quite often he can see the name of company that the visitor works for, and with this knowledge, he has sales leads. He calls it "a phenomenal human interaction" because he can both communicate in real time with the prospective customer and also gather marketing data.

Besides launching the morning by establishing links with potential customers, he also uses his Web browser to catch up on world-wide news. He describes himself as a "rake": "And as I surf, I grab things and they stay with me. I visit BBCnews.com, ABCnews.com, and MSNBC.com about three to four times a day." You will notice that most of his sites report global news. He explains that he wants "to know what's going on in the U.K. on a regular basis, and in the rest of Europe." Concerned with the variability of Internet access in the U.K., he is watching for changes so his company can exploit a strong market potential in the Web-based training industry.

As with general news, he finds that most personal and business information is now available on the Web, so he doesn't read magazines anymore or watch much TV:

> I used to read Fast Company *religiously. I just don't bother anymore. I think it takes too much time to sit down and flip through a magazine. And yet I probably do the equivalent of that everyday on the Internet. We get* Business Week, *we get* Fast Company, *we get a couple of other leisure magazines, and I just don't ever look at them.*

In working with customers, Darrell says he relies on the e-fax electronic faxing service, e-stamps for his postage, and accounting software: "I have an interfax number that people can fax to me from, and it goes right into my [email] in-box. I fax from a computer that has a scanner attached." Though he confesses that he still needs a regular fax machine, this electronic system helps him stay better organized, he says. Since the e-fax system automatically creates a digital document for incoming faxes, he can immediately organize and archive his faxes on his computer. He also uses Stamps.com "exclusively for all of our mailings." This is a private service that purchases postage from the U.S. Government. "You pay the service a fee every month based on how much postage you use or a minimum value," he says. In addition to e-faxes and e-stamps, Darrell also uses computer accounting software. On a computer not connected to the network, Darrell uses Quickbooks for his invoicing and accounting. These ICT-based tools have helped him grow his business despite his lack of people resources.

*Darrell also uses the Web to get and sustain business.*

## Using ICTs for Sales and Marketing

While his home office serves as his business infrastructure, Darrell also uses the Web to get and sustain business. One way that he and his associates find and acquire new customers is through the use of trial offers. When the

WebTrain affiliates attend trade-shows or prospect for new customers, they provide the prospect a Website address where they can complete a WebTrain assessment. Once the assessment is completed, Darrell receives the raw data from this Website and processes it into a report that is sent back to the prospect. He explains the value of this trial offer: "One belief about our marketing is that people will be more inclined to purchase our product if they've seen it used with up to three samples of people in their organization. So we give up to three away to every decision-maker."

While this Web-based trial offer is a useful prospecting tool, Darrel also uses other ICTs to prospect. He believes that one of the biggest predictors of success for his business is his ability to follow up with raw leads that he gets from trial offers, email, telephone, and face-to-face. "I have a lady at a Fortune 500 firm in Denver who has completed a report, and I haven't gotten back to her," he says. "She was all excited, all interested, and so my follow-up with her is important." Such leads sometimes generate his face-to-face sales calls.

*Before he visits a customer face-to-face, he uses the Web to do some detective work and provide him background information about the prospect.*

But before he visits a customer face-to-face, he uses the Web to do some detective work and provide him background information about the prospect:

*Yesterday I had a meeting with a company called Elotopics. Never heard of them. Always if I have that situation, I go to their Website. I do extensive research in the "about us" or the "corporate information" section because I want to know who their CEO is—who their chief executives are—what their experience is.*

He also reads enough on the Website to understand what they sell, to whom they sell, and something about the people who work there. To help him understand their "people values," he looks at their employment pages. He believes that this is a great place to learn about organizational culture, since he can see just how they sell themselves to potential employees. He also finds the Website helpful for office locations and press releases. He wants "to know what they've been talking about lately—what are their hot topics." Once he looks over their site, he doesn't "typically look outside of that. I just go to their Website. I can get exactly what I need, because all I'm trying to get is a feel for their culture." This strategy works for him because he rarely deals with companies that don't have a Website.

His strategy is quite different when he is meeting with companies that he has worked with in the past: "I know a lot about XYZ semiconductor company because they're local. I know a lot about PCMaker because I've done a lot of business with them. So I know their culture. But, you know, I've never been to their Website." To prove his point on the value of knowing culture, Darrell explains how one of his clients has "a very conservative culture, typically very Provo. I mean it's *very* Provo. And when you know anything about Utah—Utah Country—it is probably the most conservative country in the world." He tells a story about a good friend of his who was not Mormon and who moved to Provo to start a new job. His first day at the office he asked where he could find a cup of coffee. Well, this company had a core value that it would not serve tea or coffee on site since both contain caffeine. This company value mirrored a Mormon belief that consuming caffeine is taboo. "So he had to walk—for coffee—across the street to the gas station to get a cup. Once you understand those culture issues, you don't bother researching a lot from there." His existing knowledge is enough without using the Web for market research.

While understanding company culture is critical before a face-to-face meeting, Darrell reserves final judgment until he has actually visited the company. On the Website "I can get what they want it [culture] to be. But when I talk to the people and connect with them and understand what it is that they really need, that is where it becomes crystal [clear] for me." He essentially feels that organizations might project one image electronically and act differently in person. He is not able to offer an explanation for this behavior, but he does explain that people should be aware that the differences can exist.

*Darrell has given up his PDA because it creates an emotional barrier between him and his customer when he is face-to-face.*

## ICT Changes Resulting from a Different Career

In the process of making connections with customers, Darrell has changed the ICTs he uses. "Interestingly enough," he says, "I keep my entire schedule on a paper Day-timer now, instead of online. The primary reason is that when I am with a customer and they want to know my availability, I don't have to go into my laptop." For the last six years, he says, he had kept his schedule in his computer. In his prior work he had needed to share his schedule with others, and the best way to do it was electronically. But while it was useful then, "in this particular new situation, where I'm out on sales calls with customers, I put all my notes in my Day-timer." This saves him time and allows him to stay connected with his customer during the conversation.

In the past Darrell also used a Palm Pilot, a PDA (Personal Digital Assistant) is a device that many professionals use to store information about customers and scheduling. While talking about his paper Day-timer, he mentions that this Palm was "under those papers somewhere." He explains, "I'm not using it at all now. I used it in my previous job, primarily because of a business need for synchronizing with our membership database. We had 800 member companies that I needed to synchronize with." But as his need for constant connection outside of the office changed with his new job, he found that the Palm Pilot did not fit his needs.

> I couldn't write notes. I even had a keyboard, but it was too bulky to carry out and to use. So instead of using that, I started using paper of some kind, but I would never transcribe it back in. So I basically decided when I got this—my Day-timer—I said I wasn't going to do it any more. So I haven't been using it since.

In addition to the functional constraints of his new work environment, requiring that he be face-to-face with customers, he also suggests that there are symbolic reasons to abandon his Palm Pilot. He claims that it isn't as fast as jotting things in a paper Day-timer, and time really matters when you're face-to-face with a prospect. The extra time creates an emotional barrier between him and his customer. For someone who focuses all his sales and marketing efforts on trying to understand and adapt to his customer's culture, it isn't surprising that he has stopped using the Palm Pilot. "I will probably give it away to a friend," he says, "because it is more appropriate for his work environment than it is for mine. He doesn't do a lot of client meetings like I do."

Even though Darrell has abandoned his Palm Pilot, it's no sign that he is becoming a technology laggard (or that the rest of the world is either—in fact, a lot of people don't own one). Actually, one of his top desires when he hires sales affiliates is that they be technologically literate. He views technology as the way to keep his dispersed organization connected. One technology that he is trying to integrate into WebTrain is a Web-conferencing system. This technology uses a Web browser to virtually connect participants, potentially throughout the world. This is not a new technology—it has been used for about five years now—but the quality of the experience when conducting a Web-conference often rides on the speed of the user's Internet connection.

*When all of his affiliates attend a Web-conference simultaneously, he needs to convey information only once.*

The issue of Internet connection has already caused some tension between Darrell and several of his affiliates:

> One of them in particular is convinced that this is the stupidest thing in the world. And I've explained to her that she needs to switch Internet providers. She is on an Internet provider that's cutting her out every five minutes, and so it doesn't disconnect her, just cuts her audio out.

This has soured her on the communication process, ironically all due to the connection-speed aspect of a technology designed to enhance communication. Another affiliate has "computers with no sound card, speakers, or microphone," so Darrell must upgrade the affiliate's computers so she can participate in the Web-conferences.

Despite these challenges, he is not giving up on using technology to enhance communication: "There is too much that you can't communicate in an asynchronous fashion [such as email]. We can't communicate new product training updates in an asynchronous fashion when we can demonstrate them by PowerPoint in a synchronous environment." He explains that by using technology he saves time when sharing information. When all of his affiliates attend a Web-conference simultaneously, he need convey information only once. Without technology he must meet one-on-one with each affiliate. That is time-consuming and would involve extensive travel, which was his primary reason for changing jobs in the first place.

In addition to his regular communication with the affiliates, Darrell often needs to contact the offices in Vancouver and Scotland. The interesting variable that determines how he contacts these individuals is time-zone compatibility: "Honestly, with the folks in the U.K., it's almost all email, because every time I think to call them, it's always after they're already in bed. I've called them, but [in the past] every time I did it, no one was there that I needed to talk to. In the Vancouver office, I do a tremendous amount of phone conversations. Typically if I have question for someone in Canada, I call. And it is just as easy. I have a discounted long distance [service] for U.K. and Canada. And it's like 10 cents a minute."

Darrell admits that his extensive use of asynchronous communication with the CEO in the U.K. has a downside: "we both acknowledge that we miss the interaction and the connection." Fortunately, these two individuals have a strong relationship that overcomes their less-than-ideal communication patterns. While they communicate via email once or twice a week, Darrell says that they talk voice-to-voice only once every two or three months. He also notes that their telephone contact tends to increase right after they have been in a face-to-face environment. For example, they recently met in Toronto for a weekend to discuss U.S. operations. After returning to their respective countries, they had four more telephone conversations that week. So there appears to be a need for synchronous communication, even if that need doesn't always outweigh the time-zone differences.

## Conclusion

Darrell's case sheds light on the issue of reconfiguring technology use to meet changing needs. Sometimes these needs are driven by function, such as opening a new business and running it out of their home. In the process, there are times to adopt technologies to improve the efficiency of communication between business partners. Other times, a savvy technology user will selectively abandon technologies that inhibit business or personal goals. This case exemplifies a customer-driven sales-and-marketing strategy. It might have been easier for Darrell to continue using the same ICTs in his new position, but his focus on the customer compelled him to adapt, and he has learned to do so happily.

**Questions for Review or Discussion**

1.  What are the symbolic and practical implications of using ICTs during a face-to-face conversation?

2.  What implications does this case illustrate for your own personal practice? Have you ever abandoned an ICT to accommodate others' preferences?

3.  How do you enact a work environment in your home? What sensemaking is involved in this arrangement?

4.  How do laggards and early adopters find common ground in their ICT use?

5.  How are needs to communicate across distances met by different ICTs?

# Fighting Uncertainty With Intelligence[*]

## 19

Jan-Oddvar Sørnes & Larry D. Browning

One irony of the Digital Age is that the more information we manage to acquire, the greater our uncertainty about what we actually know. Why? Because each new piece of information can seem to undermine, or at least qualify, what we knew yesterday—or even ten minutes ago. With high-tech companies, operating in highly volatile markets, this problem has become acute. How are they to know what, exactly, their competitors are doing?

To meet the challenge, many companies now find themselves forming units whose sole function is to investigate competitors and give decision-makers advice on how to retain market share.

Trond Horn is a senior consultant who works in such a unit at NorthCell, a Norwegian cellphone provider. A 35-year-old robust urbanite, Trond has clearly spent a lot of time in the weight room, and he has an intensity that makes you believe that he eats, sleeps, and breathes his specialty: competitive intelligence. This is the story of the various strategies and tools he uses in researching—and attempting to outwit—his competitors. And there now are many of them, whereas only a few years ago NorthCell enjoyed a monopoly. The industry is experiencing rapid change owing to Norway's recent deregulation and privatization of both phone service and its infrastructure. This has allowed both domestic and foreign competitors to flood the market.

**Key Issue** Rapid change in the telephone industry is due to the recent deregulation and and privatization of phone service and its infra- structure.

A prime tool in Trond's work is the Internet. ICTs are prominent in this case because the Internet has fundamentally altered how businesses select, process, analyze, and distribute highly specific and timely information concerning industry rivals. Trond, who has lived through this transformation, says: "The market for cellular services has changed dramatically the past few years. Last year we had only one competitor. Now we have nine. This obviously has some impact on the way we do business." Operating in a market with so many competitors, NorthCell must pay as much attention to what their rivals are doing as to their own mission.

---

[*] The authors wish to thank Frode Soelberg, Bodø Graduate School of Business, for his valuable input to this chapter.

## NorthCell's Challenge

NorthCell is the largest telephone-service provider in Norway, and was a government-owned monopoly until the late 1990's, so it enjoyed a huge head start over its smaller competitors. But the question is: will it be able to sustain its market share?

Early on, NorthCell made a few clumsy attempts to fight off competitors by trying to exploit its strong market position. For example, it tried, unsuccessfully, to squeeze out competitors by building strategic alliances with cellphone manufacturers and nationwide retail chains. It also tried to impose switching barriers on its customers. The switching barrier, later declared illegal, was designed to prevent customers from using their cellphones with another provider before their service contract (normally 12-18 months) had expired. Despite such maneuvers, most people still viewed NorthCell as *the* service provider, thanks mainly to a successful pricing policy.

**⊕ Key Issue**
Management is constantly dealing with new market entrants.

NorthCell's management is constantly dealing with new entrants, though, and according to Trond the threat is real. "It's all about competitive ability in a market that is becoming big and aggressive," he says. "In such a heated environment, where new entrants and new technology threaten to undermine NorthCell's dominant position, competitive intelligence is of vital importance."

## The Nature of Competitive Intelligence

Competitive intelligence, known in the trade by its acronym, "CI," is the process of ethically collecting, analyzing, and disseminating useful intelligence about the implications of the business environment, competitors, and the organization itself. Such intelligence is deemed "useful" only if it is accurate, specific, relevant, timely, foresighted, and actionable.

*NorthCell's very life depends on agilely reacting to changing circumstances.*

NorthCell's strategy, as carried out by Trond and his CI unit, resembles a chess match. It aims to devise business plans based on what it predicts its competitors will do in response to NorthCell's own actions, and then what each side will likely do after that, in an ongoing act-and-reaction sequence. NorthCell's very life depends on agilely reacting to changing circumstances, and one key to its agility is its CI unit, which functions as both an adaptive and proactive force in NorthCell's business environment. For the CI group to be effective, besides collecting, analyzing, and disseminating information, it must be visionary—that is, it must decide where the business stands and where it should go, and it must communicate this information persuasively to its own organization so that its decision-makers (upper management) and operations groups are compelled to act on it. Trond recognizes the huge challenges his group faces. Producing really useful information is a daunting, ongoing task. "It is very difficult to forecast in this business," he concedes. "It's like science fiction."

## Ambiguity and Uncertainty

Trond's tasks seldom have textbook answers. In fact, often his work is like shooting at a moving target, for technological developments in this particular industry change so fast that his facts, figures, and estimates are soon dated. As Trond describes it, "New technologies are being implemented constantly, new competitors surfacing, others disappearing, so one day is not similar to the other." The changes may not appear significant when one looks at each incident separately, but "this business works sort of like a domino, and a small change in one place might have a dramatic impact in another place." To stay ahead of competitors in such a volatile market, Trond and his colleagues face a relentless pressure from management to deliver quality CI quickly. "Time of delivery and reliability are always critical to success," Trond says.

How Trond attacks a given task will vary. "It depends on the complexity of the problem," he explains. "If I were assigned to find out what one of our competitor's turnover was for the last quarter, I would just access their homepage to find out. But not all problems are that simple." Trond's work entails more than just presenting hard numbers. "Surveys are very quantitatively focused," he says, "whereas we are more qualitatively focused. We look at a survey and try to understand what it really *means*, beyond the fact that eight out of ten think so." Trond's analysis and judgment represent value, often well beyond statistical figures by themselves, because usually such statistics are available even to their competitors. Since these competitors might try head-hunting top CI staff from their rivals to get inside information, NorthCell has taken some precautions: "Here at NorthCell we have quarantine regulations, and that is security enough for us," he says. "Besides, the information in this business gets old very quickly, so hiring somebody from the competitor for that reason alone would not be worthwhile."

Once plain data has been turned into valuable CI, it is often graded and given to only a few individuals within the NorthCell organization. According to Trond, there are two reasons for this: (1) It's crucial that NorthCell's competitors don't get access to it, and (2) NorthCell must comply with the laws dealing with "insider information" since it's now a stockmarket-listed company. "We have to be more restrictive about how information is shared and the flow of information in general," Trond says, "and that means that we must follow certain guidelines about to whom, how, when, and what type of information we can release."

As a result, NorthCell has a media strategy that allows only certain people to make statements to the press and to other stakeholders. "Being listed [on the stock market] means that we cannot spread information internally, as we used to," Trond explains. "The different access levels for information on the intranet will have to be revised." This information policy has implications for Trond and the CI team, as they are forced to keep a lid on their strategic alliances and outsourcing partners. "Another change for us," he says, "is that we will have to get used to being constantly measured on what we do. Everything will be aimed at getting good results." The cumulative effect of all these changes makes Trond's work anything but predictable.

**Key Issue**
Sensitivity
to insider
information

## Responding to the Requirements of Uncertainty and Speed

Trond and his colleagues have taken certain steps to be ahead of the game when responding to some of these challenges and uncertainties. Let's take a closer look at these.

*The physical work environment.* NorthCell's CI unit is composed of just Trond himself and three colleagues. Their work area is ingeniously designed to simplify information-sharing. "We have intentionally placed ourselves in a star formation around a circular table at work, where we have our computers and a little personal workspace," Trond says. The whole idea, he explains, is to have visual contact and free-flowing conversation, for that intimacy is valued by all four colleagues. "It often happens that I throw out a piece of information, and my colleagues across the table correct it or add further insight," he explains. "Our ability to interact and communicate throughout the day is essential to what we do." Team members depend on each other for reliable information, and they believe success occurs because they always have somebody to ask.

> *We have intentionally placed ourselves in a star formation around a circular table at work.*

*Ad hoc team formation.* Depending on the task, teams are often formed by combining people from CI with two other units at NorthCell: (1) Business and Price Analysis, which focuses on NorthCell's pricing, versus its competitors, for comparable services, and (2) Market Analysis, which surveys customers and the general public on various issues, including brand value. The rationale for combining people from different units is that each person has special skills that are valuable to other units. Trond explains that NorthCell will often "create teams with people from Market Analysis, Business and Price, and one from Competitive Intelligence." Once a team is formed, their first job is to determine exactly how to respond to the particular task assigned them. "When doing this," Trond says, "we try to estimate how much time it will take to do the job, based on the degree of detail and the complexity of the task."

In the early stages of the team formation, face-to-face communication is important, but in later stages of a project, most communication is carried out electronically because they simply don't have time to meet face-to-face. But being so focused on task often carries a price. It is quite normal, and even encouraged, to have some disagreement within the group on how to approach the task, "so we will have to agree on the strategy before proceeding with the problem," Trond explains. In short, they want their conflicts earlier rather that later in the decision process. Once a decision is made, each team member is expected to carry out the tasks assigned them. They place a lot of attention on combining the right people for tasks, as this creates diversity by including input experts from several areas.

> *They place a lot of attention on combining the right people for tasks, as this creates diversity by including input experts from several areas.*

*Setting his own agenda.* Trond explains that tasks may be either self-selected or assigned by top-management—"usually a 40/60 split, in that order." This means that he is "constantly being assigned new projects, usually with a very short deadline, and new teams are generated based on the problem at hand." But tasks are also self-assigned, Trond says: "A lot of times we actually set the agenda ourselves— we at CI. It is our job to be able to determine what is important and what is not." This puts a huge responsibility on the shoulders of each CI team member. But it also has certain advantages. By anticipating what would really help decision-makers, as opposed to simply waiting for assigned tasks, they are better able to shape the strategy from their own point of view. This reduces uncertainty for the CI team.

*Standard procedure for creating CI.* While there is some variability in task, completion time, and complexity, Trond and his colleagues normally follow a specific procedure when gathering CI that is the protocol described in the classical competitive strategy literature. It involves four steps:

1.   Planning and direction—estimating information needs, resources, and directions for the task.

2.   Data gathering—accessing various information sources.

3.   Analysis and production—deciphering large amount of raw data and turning it into actionable intelligence/information.

4.   Dissemination—presenting the results to stakeholders internally and externally.

The process always begins and ends with decision-makers—usually top management at NorthCell, as they both assign tasks and make final judgments about possible actions. Trond's job is thus to produce information that enables management to make sound decisions. The CI team has standard material that they can bring together, and even with only little added, it can genuinely help decision-makers. Given the rapid changes in the market, new information must be added regularly to make the CI on target.

*Information search, storage and processing.* Trond uses various ways to access primary and secondary sources of information, both inside NorthCell (internal sources) and outside of it (external sources). According to classical competitive-strategy literature, primary information sources could include interviews with internal experts (colleagues), a company's own customers and suppliers, marketplace surveys, and tailored industry analysis. Secondary information sources, meanwhile, could include both internal and external databases, industry and government reports, statistical sources, newspapers and magazines, and trade publications. The chief difference between the two kinds of sources is that information from a secondary source was originally collected for a different purpose. For example, an internal archive of completed projects would typify a secondary source.

**Key Issue**

*Since speed is crucial, the information-retrieval process itself is a key to providing timely and reliable intelligence for decision-making.*

How and where the information is retrieved will depend on cost, availability, and the problem at hand, but several information sources and strategies are regularly used. Since speed is crucial, the information-retrieval process itself is a key to providing timely and reliable intelligence for decision-making.

Let's now look at the specific sources, strategies, and tools that Trond uses when gathering CI.

*Primary sources.* When searching for information, Trond emphasizes his abilities to network internally. By talking to his immediate colleagues (CI team), and by constantly being assigned to help out people from other internal units, he learns his colleagues' areas of particular competence and how they can help him:

> *Sometimes it is enough just to know that a person has dealt with something close to what you are working on, and they can usually help you or point you in the right direction. But it's impossible to have a foolproof system and know exactly who knows what. It really has to do with your own ability to network internally.*

As previously explained, the physical layout of the CI office space is designed to enable continual dialogue between the team members, and they do indeed depend on each other since their skills don't entirely overlap. This illustrates the value of face-to-face interaction in the information-search process.

Another primary source is the information gleaned from their nationwide chain of retail stores. To Trond this is invaluable because he can get fresh updates on customers' buying behavior and attitudes. "It's really all about getting the most out of the vast amount of data we have collected about our customers," he says. Trond explains that they "try to identify what a 'good customer' is, and strive to direct our marketing to attract more customers that fit that predefined category." To achieve this, they "try to map how people use their cellular [phone] and how much money they spend on the various services." Much of this information is publicly available, "but customer data is just ours, and naturally an advantage since our competitors do not have access to it." His access to market data gives him an advantage when predicting customer trends. This information can be accessed quickly and illustrates the value of internal information passed on electronically to the CI team to overcome physical distances.

Yet another primary source of information are the many professional CI agencies. "We subscribe to several national and international services," Trond says, "that provide us with data and analysis based on *our* specifications." Since he and his colleagues set the parameters, this information is not available to their competitors or the general public. Trond is satisfied with the quality of that information, but the most important factor is that everything is done electronically on the Internet. "I can access a database in London and get information then and there," he says, "whereas six years ago I would have received the information by express mail the next day."

**Key Issue**
The value of primary information sources.

Using information from primary sources makes the process of generating intelligence easier. Trond explains:

> *Our primary sources of information already have a seal of quality associated*

*with them —that's why we chose them in the first place.... [Also,] a person soon develops a good nose for what is trustworthy or not. And besides, everything that is produced here is thoroughly checked for quality.*

The value of primary information sources is at least twofold: (1) the information is not publicly available, since it is collected exclusively for or by the CI team, and (2) the information is perceived by the CI team as more reliable because the team can control the entire process.

*Secondary sources.* Information from secondary sources— information not originally generated for the task at hand—represents a substantial asset for Trond and his colleagues. In fact, he says, "Using existing information is the key to success with the deadlines we are facing." They frequently use an internal secondary source they call "personal folders," where information is collected from the various projects that individuals and teams have completed at NorthCell. As Trond explains, "The first thing I do is access our own databases and see if we have anything that could be useful for the problem at hand—previous analyses, background information for analyses, presentations, et cetera." These "personal folders" are searchable and can be accessed through the company intranet. And the collection of information is huge. "It would probably take many months to browse through it all," Trond says, "so to navigate it requires some knowledge about what we do and have been doing for the past few years." To enable easy access, he explains, "We have a policy where we try to label this type of information in a way that others can navigate and find what they are looking for by using keywords." Since this archived information is such a vital source of intelligence, they take steps to keep it structured. About twice a year they inspect their archives to ensure that folders and files have self-explanatory, accurate labels. Trond likes to make these "personal folders" as complete a possible. Throughout the workday, he is meticulous about documenting all kinds of information for future use. While searching for relevant information to solve a specific problem, he is constantly on the lookout for valuable information:

*I usually have a pretty good nose for picking up stuff that is not relevant at the moment but will be of help down the road.*

> *I scan and search a lot of resources and databases throughout the day, and it is impossible not to pick up something useful along the way. I usually have a pretty good nose for picking up stuff that is not relevant at the moment but will be of help down the road.*

This attention to possibility is a good example of their policy on "knowledge-sharing." Trond says: "If I have attended a conference, I am responsible for putting relevant information on our intranet. I usually write up a short summary to make it easier for the reader to decide if the information is valuable or not." The reason why they put so much effort into structuring and storing this information is simple: "We are fortunate to have a lot of very clever and experienced people here, and it just makes common sense to tap into their personal database first." Here again, he takes advantage of NorthCell's size by keeping its mountain of data well organized for quick retrieval.

The Internet is central in both searching and accessing the kind of information Trond is seeking. He primarily looks for "mergers, strategic alliances, new products, campaigns/promotions, issue of stock, and change of ownership." Such information is readily available on the Internet.

Competitors webpages are a highly valued source in this regard, but he recognizes that they are a double-edged sword for himself and competitors alike. He explains that the most valuable information on competitors webpages is the kind of sales pitch they use to attract customers, but he also realizes that NorthCell is similarly vulnerable: "Our competitors need to get this information out to potential customers, so it's easy for us to get access to it. But they can also get this from us, too." So while learning competitors' approaches is generally accomplished simply by accessing their sites on the Internet, NorthCell's CI team members, trained to be cautious, always treat such information as "very questionable."

The Internet also affords Trond instantaneous updates from publicly available sites such as the Oslo Stock Exchange. Thus, Trond explains, "From some of our competitors, at least the ones listed on the stock exchange, we can get fresh numbers daily, and that is good information for us." The Internet also allows information searches—using search engines to seek out information on key words or phrases. It's a common strategy Trond often uses, but he admits it's imperfect: "I seldom find that 'golden nugget,' but usually something that is helpful and can point me in the right direction." So his experiences with searching the Internet have taught him what he can expect and how he can build on what he learns.

When dealing with information from secondary sources, Trond is extra cautious. One reason is that such information is harder to verify. To ensure its reliability, Trond explains, it is "important to find out the origin of the information and who the sender is." But sometimes this isn't so easy. While some information is factually based and easy to verify, other information aims to advocate a certain position and is biased. Trond notes that some of NorthCell's competitors use this type of information purposefully: "It seems like some companies have press releases as part of their information strategy. This strategy works for some, but getting lots of publicity in the newspapers does not necessarily mean that you are a good company or have a good product." Trond likes to think that NorthCell has a more sophisticated approach. It entails working actively through their nationwide network of dealers to influence public opinion and to induce customers to choose their product.

**⊕ Key Issue**

It seems like some companies have press releases as part of their information strategy.

Hence, the required information is first sought within the CI unit and the NorthCell organization, and only if it fails to provide a satisfactory answer does the search continue externally. Further, secondary sources, such as data in their own databases, are consulted and scanned thoroughly before primary market research is even mentioned. Obviously, this helps keep costs down, but primarily it's an issue of time.

So while there are clear advantages to relying on the Internet—its speed, ease of use, and low cost in acquiring information—there are also disadvantages. One is that NorthCell's competitors can access it too. Another is that the information it provides isn't necessarily reliable. Indeed, some of it may prove untrue. Yet Trond and his colleagues sometimes have no choice but to use suspect information to make strategic business decisions that are based only on predictions about competitors' position, performance, capabilities, and intentions. The key is finding a balance between quality of information and speed of delivery.

*The key is finding a balance between quality of information and speed of delivery.*

## CI Information Dissemination and Media Choice

Trond explains how his CI team presents the information they gathered to decision-makers:

> Lots of times it is just a matter of getting it out on our intranet. Some information, such as customer polls, statistical data, or other market information, is routinely passed on to top management. Other times we have to spend some time figuring out who would benefit from the information, and then send it out on email or publish it on the intranet. In such instances, we often add our advice to the existing piece of information before we pass it on.

When information is presented face-to-face, on the other hand, it needs to be short and to the point. Their product—the bare bones of all the information they have gathered—is usually a presentation in PowerPoint or some other digital form, so it's efficient for them to share information and communicate digitally. Another major part of his work, Trond explains, "is to do presentations and lectures within the NorthCell corporate system about our competitiveness and what trends we see coming in the market." He also does presentations and lectures outside the NorthCell system, and he finds this to be "strategically important, but at the same time we must be cautious about who we talk to. It's important for us to be visible internally as well as externally." This illustrates the need to disseminate information to various internal and external audiences without revealing business intelligence to competitors.

*The information often presented as "fresh" may be nothing more than reinterpreted archival data.*

Yet Trond wishes he had more time to consult alternative sources in printed form. There is so much information to choose from, he says, and there is finally "no time to consult textbooks, periodicals, or conventional literature reviews, even if they would yield valuable and sometimes better information." So he runs a constant battle between information quality and "freshness." "Fresh" information connotes newness, but actually, Trond confesses, the information often presented as "fresh" may be nothing more than reinterpreted archival data:

> We are very good at recycling and reshaping good information, and I could probably put together a 30-page PowerPoint presentation—on anything—and have it completed by tomorrow, and the audience would most likely think it was made from scratch.

As that admission shows, effective style, or merely looking original, can help CI be convincing. But it also shows the value of good information, as it may be recycled and reshaped, yet still be called "fresh."

## Conclusion

This case illustrates the methods used by Trond and his colleagues to keep NorthCell robustly competitive. While the quality and outcome of their work can sometimes be hard to measure, given the uncertainties and volatility of their business environment, they have taken several steps to reduce uncertainty. This case also illustrates the constant pressure to provide "fresh" information and how an artful presentation by Trond and his CI team can legitimize their work with decision-makers. While Trond emphasized the need to constantly unearth new and reliable information, in reality the information his team passes along is sometimes little more than old archival data in a fresh wrapping. This case also illustrates the durability of good information, which usually comes from primary sources such as colleagues, or secondary sources such as "personal folders" or old case files. The role of the Internet may therefore be overstated as a source for information, but its value as a channel for dissemination is unquestionable. It may seem that Trond's effort is hard to measure and to precisely value. But he certainly feels valued. "A good indication for me is that colleagues come back, time after time, and ask me for information," he says with some pride. "That legitimizes my work."

## Questions for Review or Discussion

1. Does information change in value rapidly, or does the value of a fact remain fixed? Please support your position.

2. This case shows the value of having different team members contribute to a solution. What is the best team you have ever been a part of?

3. Now that we have so much more access to current information via the Internet, what are the challenges we face in organizing and structuring all this information?

4. This case identifies a high-pressure, speed-driven environment. What strengths and weaknesses would you bring to such a workplace? Would you be tempted to take shortcuts to accomplish objectives, and what would those be?

5. Identify a situation where you have used speed to manage an impression. If you took shortcuts to accomplish objectives, what were they?

# Close Up . . . From a Distance: Using ICTs for Managing International Manufacturing

Larry D. Browning & Alf Steinar Sætre

**20**

Jeff is an electrical engineer in his 40's who's now working as a procurement specialist for PRINT-IT, an American company that purchases computer products from Asia and then puts its own logo on them. His main job is working with the Asian manufacturer that supplies the printers. PRINT-IT in turn sells and distributes them to major computer companies around the world. PRINT-IT thus serves as a kind of subcontractor for computer giants that prefer being spared the hassles that go with overseeing an elaborate production process.

Because much of Jeff's work is coordinating a production process that is several time-zones away, he spends 35–40 percent of his day on the Internet. Much of this time he's using an ingenious new software program generically known as "supplier-vendor management software" ("SVMS") that allows a vendor like PRINT-IT to delay taking goods on inventory until they have been sold to a customer. Another feature of the program helps reduce the turn-around time, or "inventory turn," that a product sits on PRINT-IT's inventory sheet. The program also helps suppliers manage their own production more efficiently because they now get to enjoy real-time access to information on PRINT-IT's inventory and sales. This means that a manufacturer, after using a password to log on, can look up PRINT-IT's use of its product without waiting for an official report. Monitoring consumption on-line proves invaluable because one of the toughest challenges for suppliers is sudden production changes from a buyer.

*Much of this time he's using an ingenious new software program generically known as "supplier-vendor management software" that allows a vendor to delay taking goods on inventory until they have been sold to a customer.*

### Using a Third Party to Manage Confidentiality

For the printer part of its business, there are actually three parties involved in PRINT-IT's Web-based production-information loop: (1) PRINT-IT itself; (2) its Asian supplier; and (3) a virtual trading company—PRINT-IT's own cyber middle-man—which manages the PRINT-IT warehouse and buffers confidential information between the supplier and PRINT-IT. The trading company has separate confidentiality understandings with both

PRINT-IT and the supplier, so while all three parties are in the information loop, only the trading company gets to see the total picture on its computer screen:

1. PRINT-IT's sales.

2. PRINT-IT's total inventory (what is in its distribution center).

3. The manufacturer's inventory (the printers still being made).

4. The inventory controlled by the virtual trading company.

PRINT-IT's use of a middle-man requires an explanation, since in contemporary business practice, the more direct the process, the better—it saves time and coordination efforts, hence money. But here, previous sales and mergers affecting both PRINT-IT and the supplier had created such confusion that neither company retained the ability to perform all of its transactions independently. Experts had moved from one company to another, and international transactions were significantly reduced for one of the companies, meaning it no longer benefited from economies of scale. So both parties agreed to work through a middleman.

*There are actually three parties involved in PRINT-IT's Web-based production-information loop: the company, its supplier, and a virtual trading company which manages the warehouse and buffers confidential information between the supplier and PRINT-IT.*

These three groups' different access to this information via SVMS works like this: Let's say Jeff needs to buy 5,000 printers from the Asian supplier. But how long will it take to get all these printers built and shipped to America? Before SVMS, any forecast that Jeff made was basically frozen for six months from the time of the order because some suppliers use very unique and proprietary raw materials—some of which have lead-times of nine months. Suppliers keep only an adequate amount of these materials on hand for fear that they'll have more on their inventory shelves than they really need. With this new software, however, Jeff's lead-time is cut in half. Because his order information is listed on the screen, it gives the supplier more updated information on Jeff's needs.

Why is the screen information faster than the traditional fax? Previous communication was structured to allow each party enough time to perform their analyses of the numbers. The flow of information moved very slowly since Jeff might send his fax to the middleman who might not look at it until a few days before they review the numbers before forwarding them to the supplier. Now that the supplier has more of a real-time view of Jeff's situation, they do not have to wait for the middleman. Additionally, they can be monitoring Jeff's situation on-line and "hedging" on what they think that he'll eventually ask for—in effect, starting their planning process (without actually committing to it) based upon what they think that Jeff will request of them. So while he still has an official lead time of six months, in fact he can go on screen and make changes that his supplier can react to immediately, not just once a month as in the past.

### An Example of the Order Process

On a typical day Jeff gets information that, for example, says he has two days' stock in his distribution center. If he thinks that's not enough, then he can hit the automatic pulse key on his computer that will generate a purchase order with his supplier. The program then virtually moves the product from the supplier onto his inventory, which is across an imaginary "yellow line" in the virtual warehouse. The action pulls the product, Jeff says, "from one side of the line into my side."

*So while he still has an official lead time of six months, in fact he can go on screen and make changes that his supplier can react to immediately, not just once a month as in the past.*

These transactions occur each evening during an "automatic dump" into PRINT-IT's portal Website. The "yellow line" display informs Jeff he's moved product and tells the vendor it's now safe to invoice him for it. Once the supplier has listed the invoice number and date, all that information is automatically listed back on the portal Website. "It tells me that I've been invoiced," Jeff says. "And it tells the manufacturer that it's off their books and that the trading company has invoiced them. The manufacturer then can decide, 'That's not anything unexpected, I don't need to adjust my manufacturing because of it.'"

While all this information exchange lets the different players know what has been completed, it also allows them to proactively make rescheduling decisions based on what the Website portal displays. Jeff offers a hypothetical:

> *Say it's June 15th. The manufacturer can do a quick extrapolation and say, "It's now 50% of the way through the month, and Jeff has sold only 20% of his volumes. I don't think that he's going to sell his full 100%, and I need that production capacity for Company B, so I'm going to go ahead and start shifting production and kind of take a gamble."*

While the supplier is still contractually responsible for meeting Jeff's volumes, it can quickly reallocate its resources. This information set-up gives all the players comfort with the information so that "nobody's going to overreact," Jeff explains. "If, five days into the month, you've only sold a few pieces, you don't start slashing production. You put some common sense into it." This shows how ICTs not only provide greater lead-time but also flexibility to do things differently with regular information.

PRINT-IT and its Asian supplier rely on this method comprehensively, and they spend considerable time each day going over the numbers posted on the Website because they know everyone is treating this as the official word. Jeff, who is not prone to hyperbole, says that this use of the Internet "has really changed the way we do business" because it has halved the lead-time for making commitments to the supplier from six months to three. In the production world, a shorter lead-time means that PRINT-IT's money is not tied up in product that isn't showing a profit. He says, "That's huge when you consider we're buying probably in the neighborhood of $300 to $400 million [in printers] a year." So here's a case where the efficiency of an ICT produces major savings, thanks to real-time monitoring and improved predictability.

The effects of an increased lead-time and the flexibility to adjust schedules are fairly significant not just for PRINT-IT but also their Asian supplier, because that supplier does its production scheduling quarterly to give it longer lead-times with

*The effects of an increased lead-time and the flexibility to adjust schedules are fairly significant for PRINT-IT and their Asian supplier, because that supplier does its production scheduling quarterly to give it longer lead-times with its own raw-materials suppliers.*

its own raw-materials suppliers, located in the Far East and in Europe. As Jeff says, "Those guys [the raw-materials suppliers] have lead-times with their manufacturers, too, and they don't want to adjust their production like the American companies do—constantly on the fly." The additional access to information for suppliers down the food chain allows them to mimic the flexibility demonstrated above them. With this more real-time information, Jeff says, PRINT-IT's Asian supplier has been able to say, "Okay, I can start doing some of the things that maybe the Western companies do and actually feed that information back to our raw-materials suppliers."

Jeff offers an example of how additional information in the supply chain works. His Asian supplier buys a core component from a company in Belgium. That company now gets on the same kind of Web portal that his direct manufacturer does. This access to information about both plans and daily use of product causes everyone in the chain to feel more self-control and ownership of a manufacturing process that is geographically scattered. Jeff hopes this access to information can be extended still further down the chain to his suppliers, his suppliers' suppliers, etc. so that the process will produce the same result it has in other instances, reducing lead-time still further. He wants it to be halved yet again, from six to three "down to one-and-a-half months, thanks to the additional information available."

## Selective Communication and the Need to Know

Even with this additional access to each other's information that allows them to plan and deliver product in a more efficient way, all parties are pledged to communicate selectively only to parties that need to know. Jeff is careful not to "jump levels in communication." He also knows that there is lots of information in the chain that he has no right to see. "I primarily respond to a trading company" he says. "Whatever that trading company does to get information to the manufacturing company and then on to their core suppliers is their business," he says. Jeff also holds details close to his vest because he doesn't want to release information that's proprietary. The several participants in these relationships occupy different roles, and it's important that they avoid overlapping them. He says:

> I don't want the manufacturing company to know what the trading company sells the product [component] at. That was at the request of the trading company. It's handled as a totally separate company. They don't want the manufacturing company to know what the mark-up is. Similarly, the manufacturing company doesn't want the core suppliers to know what the mark-ups are. So that's held very close.

There is also confidentiality within the Website because it contains information on pricing and lead-times. He says, "I don't want a major competitor to know what I'm paying. I don't want a major competitor to know how fast I can react, either."

Firms have different pricing arrangements with different customers for all sorts of reasons, including (a) when the contract was made, (b) the volume of product purchased, and (c) whether there is some kind of partnership arrangement in place. But even with these different circumstances, when the product price is altered for different customers, dissatisfaction on someone's part is likely if this information becomes public. PRINT-IT uses dealers as middlemen to move their products to the end consumer. For example, if the University of Texas needs a printer, they are obligated to buy it from a local dealer. However, they want the best deal that they can get so they shop from one dealer to another (in some cases, even buying from dealers in foreign countries if the currency benefit justifies it). PRINT-IT is careful to assure that all dealers are being treated fairly so that end consumers don't pinch one of their dealers out of business. He is also concerned that if the details of production schedules get out, the information will be used to manipulate supply and demand: "I don't want Company B coming in and saying, 'Hey, I know that Company A can't respond for six months; therefore, I'm going to try and create an artificial demand and they won't be able to react and I can go in and steal their business.'" These concerns about trusting partners are, in fact, hypothetical, and Jeff is confident that different pieces of production are carefully controlled for a specific need to know.

*"I don't want Company B coming in and saying, 'Hey, I know that Company A can't respond for six months; therefore, I'm going to try and create an artificial demand and they won't be able to react and I can go in and steal their business.'"*

## Communication Within His Own Company

Jeff also uses ICTs to communicate within his own company because his boss doesn't want to spend valuable time on a portal Website reviewing scheduling decisions. Jeff says, "I have to tell my people who are interested what my inventory terms are going to be." There are lots of details to keep his boss abreast of because someone unfamiliar with its workings can easily misinterpret the data from the Web portal. For example, PRINT-IT's demand for production from the Pacific Rim can be volatile, and in some months they'll get what appears on the Web portal to be a 200% increase in demand that would require—oh, mercy!—a five-month back order for product from the supplier. But what that information actually means requires Jeff's expert interpretation. And he can correct any confusion by assuring his boss that they'll recover from these anomalies in a matter of days.

Beyond his own boss, Jeff also uses ICTs to communicate with the director of PRINT-IT's supply chain and with the trading company. As his remarks prove, Jeff is an unusual combination of technical know-how (he's a math whiz) and savvy regarding human behavior. For example, he is very systematic about matching a message to the comfort level of a given audience:

*Beyond his own boss, Jeff also uses ICTs to communicate with the director of PRINT-IT's supply chain and with the trading company.*

> If I'm doing a presentation, even if it's a Web conference, I like to go high level
> to down level. So I'll give them all a high-level detail on PowerPoint. And if

> *I see that they have questions or they're hitting their calculators a lot, then I just bring up an Excel file that shows them the math so they don't need to sit in the meeting and do the math to figure out how I did it. If there's even more concern, we'll dig one layer deeper and go through all the math. But typically we do very high-level bullets, then see if there are any questions.*

In some instances, he'll go down still another level and include the raw data on which the math was based.

Even though much of his day-to-day communication over the Internet handles the regular performance issues that arise, face-to-face interaction remains significant, Jeff says. He and some PRINT-IT colleagues schedule a quarterly meeting in person with their Asian supplier "just because communication and relationships are so important." His comment suggests that these meetings are primarily ritualistic—a symbolic bonding. And they also offer gratifying opportunities to celebrate achievements previously reported over the computer.

Face-to-face meetings are held quarterly within PRINT-IT, too. Ostensibly, they're meant for addressing major problems, though in fact they're typically used to review, and finalize, only the results of previous problem-solving. Jeff will say to his superiors, "Here's how we handled them [the problems]. Here's the status of them. You can consider them closed." But as he and his colleagues continue to be effective communicators using ICTs, he sees less need for these pro forma meetings:

> *Maybe those will go to once every six months and then once every year just for comfort. Because they're seeing that we're not getting a whole lot of value. All we're doing is we're learning how you close the problems. And they don't really care about that. They care that we close the problems.*

He anticipates the meetings in the Far East continuing, however, because relationship maintenance is so important in Asian cultures. Also, because the Pacific Rim company is the supplier, keeping projected needs and current capacities at the forefront remains critically important. Jeff ruefully recalls an incident that taught them a lot:

> *Truthfully, we got burned one time and we vowed we'd never get burned again. We had a supplier who couldn't come up the start-up curve fast enough on a new manufacturing site. They said it was going to take them maybe six months. Well, it took them 14 months. And even when they came up in 14 months they didn't have the exact equipment that was needed."*

*He anticipates the meetings in the Far East continuing because relationship maintenance is so important in Asian cultures.*

Manufacturing a printer is a chemically intensive and a very specific process, and small differences in equipment and materials can have huge effects on the final product's performance. So these kinds of manufacturing details are covered in face-to-face meetings—usually in the plant, Jeff says. The PRINT-IT folks will say, "Show me with a walk-through. What's different about your plant? Are you using the same inventory software system?"

## Deciding When to Use Different ICTs

While the importance of these technical manufacturing issues often makes the expense of face-to-face communication necessary, as this case shows, many of these specific details can be handled via ICTs. For instance, every three or four weeks they'll do a Web conference in conjunction with a videoconference. This is accomplished, Jeff explains, by having "PowerPoint or Excel presentations that everybody in the world sees at one time." They also establish some controls so that everyone will literally be on the same page. As Jeff says, with a smile, "We've eliminated this business of, 'Here's a 40-page packet, I want you to be on the third page and you're already scanning to the 20th.' That's a huge help."

*Every three or four weeks they'll do a Web conference in conjunction with a videoconference.*

Yet video conferencing via the Internet is still far away from producing ideal benefits. Because the images come across as snapshots that get refreshed every 20 seconds, the movements are jerky. Also, Jeff says, "I can't tell somebody's reaction like I can from sitting across the table." Jeff then brings up the cultural myth about how the Japanese make a sucking-air noise when they hear something they don't like. He says he finds the myth contains just enough grains of truth that he takes it seriously, and since he cannot hear this noise through a video conference, he feels disadvantaged there. "Body language is huge for me," he says.

PRINT-IT also handles cross-cultural differences by seeking help from someone within their own firm who has experience with a particular person. "After a meeting," Jeff says, "our directors will always go to the people who have known that specific Japanese person the longest" to learn what that person may have really been thinking. Jeff offers an example:

I deal with the same supplier that somebody else in my company does. They ask me to sit in on that meeting because I've known the guy for six years. And they say, "What do you think he really thought?" Because a Japanese person will make a statement like, "Yes, I can do that'" because they can't say no.

Jeff also has learned to use other kinds of cues to assess what is going on. He's found that at supplier meetings in Asia, people sit according to a power structure, with the key person sitting at the center of the table and everyone else in a "downward hierarchical tree from there." Also, if more people are called into a meeting, and "if there is lots of background talk and the sounds of sucking air, then you can estimate that more is going on than is being communicated through the emails."

While Jeff seems to make extensive use of data that can only be gained at an in-person meeting, PRINT-IT still makes effective use of ICTs, even for technical reviews of manufacturing processes that are incredibly intricate. For example, when a new manufacturing process is being set up in the U.S. that duplicates one from the Pacific Rim, they'll ask the Asian manufacturer to have some engineer walk through the plant alongside a video specialist with digital camcorder on his shoulder and videotape the entire process, explaining things all the while. This video, which costs just $3,000 to produce, will be placed in a file on the Web so

**Key Issue**

*So Jeff relies on three kinds of ICTs-face-to-face meetings, electronic communication, and video. Each has its limits, of course.*

"everyone can go out and look at it." The idea here is to capture, in detail, each last step. Jeff says, "In a chemical process you have things that are basically hidden. It's almost like a black box." Given the intricacies involved, the voice on the videotape is essential for talking the viewer through all the details being documented. Jeff says, "So we get a better feel walking through their process. We are familiar with the chemical processes, but sometimes they'll subtly alter a process, and what they [actually] decided to use can have drastically different results from what we thought they were using." For the cost of that $3,000 videotape, they can accomplish what it would "cost to fly 30 people to the Far East to understand every element of it."

So Jeff relies on three kinds of ICTs—face-to-face meetings, electronic communication, and video. Each has its limits, of course. But were he to summarize the advantages of each, they might look like this:

*Face-to-face:* Given the high costs of travel, only a small part of the total worktime occurs face-to-face, but that time is crucial because:

- People seem less likely to lie to you in person.

- Local dynamics (e.g., a group's power structure) are more discernable in person.

- Celebrations of accomplishments have more meaning in person.

*Electronic communication:* The telephone and the Web are prominent because:

- Reports of production planning and accomplishment can be listed.

- Monitoring daily change is possible.

- Human dynamics can be detected through phone calls.

*Video:*

- The most efficient way to observe, and document graphically, a step-by-step sequence of production.

## Conclusion

Jeff's case illustrates how an intricate manufacturing process can be managed from afar, even if the process contains many engineering details. He uses a variety of methods with an eye on history, culture, and effectiveness. He is skilled at providing technical information while monitoring interpersonal details.

## Questions for Review or Discussion

1.  What are the ICT choices for managing manufacturing in a global environment?

2.  When using ICTs to substitute and supplement face-to-face efforts, what are the advantages and trade-offs?

3.  What are the cultural assumptions Jeff Smith is making about his Asian partners?

4.  When Jeff Smith observes that Asian managers take out their calculators to check his math, and he compensates by providing more detail in future meetings, how is he managing impressions?

5.  Using the complexity reading as a guide, map the communication exchanges in this case. To what extent do they mirror complexity theory?

# Over the Hill but on Top of the World: An Atypical Salesperson

Alf Steinar Sætre & Keri K. Stephens

**21**

When Ron Klein, a recently retired high-school science teacher, started his little water-purification business in the remote town of Rico, Kansas, few people, even Ron himself, would have given him much chance of major success. Typically garbed in blue jeans and faded shirt, he's a hard-working man in his late 50's without any formal sales training. He founded his company on a business he'd acquired from an 80-year-old friend. And he acquired some major problems with it, too. The business was stagnant, the inventory was mostly outdated, and the nearest supplier for new inventory was located over 100 miles away.

But Ron had three things going for him, besides optimism. First, he was adaptable. All those years in the classroom had taught him how to tailor technical explanations to non-technical audiences. Second, he was rigorously honest. Unlike the stereotypical salesperson, he was quite willing to walk away from a prospective sale if he felt his integrity was compromised. Third, he was resourceful. So whenever he had a business problem, such as geographical remoteness from his suppliers, he'd somehow find a solution—one that sometimes involved his learning to use the latest ICTs.

## Overcoming the Odds with Adaptability and Honesty

*You're the worst salesperson I ever met, but you sure get everybody's business.*
—a long-time customer of Ron Klein

The water-purification business, Ron explains, includes "everything having to do with storage, transfer, and the treatment of water," including a "variety of different types of pumps, storage tanks, water softeners, reverse osmosis units, and components for all those." Even though Ron has been in business full-time for only three years, he has more work than he can handle, most of it acquired by referral. Customers are thrilled with the service he provides, and they're impressed with his savvy about water purification. Ron has a chemistry and physics background, and also holds a master's degree in educational counseling. He taught high-school science for over 25 years before starting his company. In addition, he had worked part-time in water-purification services for over 15 years. Yet he is not a typical salesperson. He wins business by searching for expert information and then genially teaching it to his customers.

**Key Issue**

*He wins business by searching for expert information and then genially teaching it to his customers.*

Ron sums up his approach to selling this way: "I am a teacher, not a salesperson. I have learned how to explain complex information to a non-technical audience." In the process, he encounters many highly educated professionals who are curious about how water purification works. "I love explaining what I do to doctors," he says, smiling. "I explain the reverse-osmosis process is just like dialysis. Furthermore, they understand [the need] for check valves because the heart is just a great big pump."

Having customers clearly understand what they need is a critical part of Ron's sales philosophy. He's willing to walk away from business if the customer is unwilling to purchase a long-term solution. Sometimes a customer will stubbornly reject his advice, saying, "Well, I really don't want that piece of equipment." While Ron could simply deliver what they think they need, he instead tells them:

> I'm sorry. You will not be pleased with the system I would put in if I leave that out. And if you really feel that strongly about it, you need to go to one of my competitors, because I will not put in a system that I cannot stand behind.

His customers might at first be taken aback, but, Ron says, "They very quickly will sit back and evaluate. And they may say, 'Now, once again, why do you really feel that I have to have that?'" Then he explains again—and uses documentation to validate what he is saying. Ron claims that he has "never lost a sale by doing that." That he also draws retirement income probably affects his willingness to send customers to his competitors. Nevertheless, helping customers understand their real needs is one of the things that determines Ron's success.

*Having customers clearly understand what they need is a critical part of Ron's sales philosophy.*

In the process of making customers understand their needs, Ron feels that his ability "to answer questions that people ask" is critical. Sometimes he finds himself getting unnecessarily technical and "giving too much information," but even this hasn't dampened most customers' enthusiasm for his approach, because "nearly always what the people will come back with is, 'Well, it's better than the people we used to do business with. They treated us like idiots and wouldn't answer any questions that we had.'" Ron says this is a common complaint. In his own approach to water purification, he feels that his "experience as a teacher is extremely valuable."

Ron's "sales pitch" is nonstandard, to say the least. He'll typically start off this way:

> You need to understand that I am a retired schoolteacher and I consider myself to have been an effective schoolteacher. And in order for me to communicate with you better and explain better, I'd like to know something about your educational background.

This approach raises a few eyebrows, he says, and "some people, they kind of chuckle. It startles them a little bit because they've never had anybody approach them that way. But then they will go ahead and tell me." His approach is very much in line with the First Commandment of effective communication: "Know thy audience."

Ron also has some customers that no one else wants to do business with because they're viewed as being "very difficult." As Ron puts it:

> I love to deal with those people because they are also confrontational a lot of times. And I love to have them put me on the spot. I love to have them think "Hey, that's not right," and have them challenge me on things. And I thoroughly enjoy being challenged.

Ron explains that while doctors are technically oriented people and are often considered difficult customers, he uses his communication skills to meet the challenge. When working with physicians, he simply relates water purification to the human body:

> I sold a water softener here in town to a husband and wife, both doctors, and I was selling her the idea of the reverse- osmosis unit. And she said, "Well, what does it do?" And I said, "It's nothing more and nothing less than a dialysis membrane, and it accomplishes the same thing.

After listening to Ron's detailed technical explanation, she bought the system.

These technically oriented people, when faced with Ron's approach, wind up being very good customers. Confrontational, inquisitive people are actually easier to handle, he finds, than non-technical people:

> The problem with non–technically oriented people who have limited education is that they feel threatened, and they're in a position where they feel they have to act like they're authorities on everything. And so they're the hardest of all to deal with.

Since Ron is willing to invest the time to explain details to a customer, he finds it results in a trusting relationship. Because of this, he can, if necessary, install some "extra" pieces of equipment without asking first: "With most of my customers, if it's something that doesn't involve over a few hundred dollars I go ahead and do it, bill them, and then give them an explanation as to why it had to be done." When this extra piece of equipment is really expensive, Ron is concerned that customers might feel price-gouged, so sometimes he won't mark up the price on the extra item, but instead openly state his wholesale costs. Such behavior contributes to his reputation as a fair and knowledgeable water-treatment supplier and serviceman.

## Resourceful Usage of ICTs

But even the most well-respected businessperson also faces challenges when he's located over 100 miles from the nearest metropolitan area. If a customer's water pump breaks on Monday, that person will typically expect to have Ron install a replacement part the next day. Ron can't go to the local hardware store to buy the part, so he needs to maintain a considerable inventory as well as effective purchasing relationships with suppliers located time-zones away. Ron's remoteness stems not only from his being located far from a large city, but also from the fact that his business is a one-man show, so he's rarely in his "office."

Ron has overcome those problems by employing a mix of ICTs. As we'll see over the next few pages, Ron has developed practices that allow him to get the most out of the communication media available to him. Actually his computer competence has helped him build strategic partnerships with other local businesses. Several of his suppliers like to receive orders by fax, so he does his business with them using this communication channel. His customers, predominately well-educated and wealthy home-owners, prefer to be billed by email. His dominant business telephone number is his cellphone number. But his technical support team, the people he turns to for expert advice, are located all over the world—on the World Wide Web.

⊕ **Key Issue**

*Ron has overcome those problems by employing a mix of ICTs.*

### Strategies for Overcoming Remoteness

Because Ron lives in a small, rural town, "you simply don't have availability," he says. When purchasing online, he has to pay shipping, but Ron says that "sometimes online I can find a better price than what I could just walking into a place anyway." Shipping costs, however, are not the only concern. If Ron drives to the nearest major city that has specialty suppliers, he loses an entire workday. His time is valuable, so he says, "Forget it. I can afford to pay a little bit more—if I have to—[but I] usually don't. I can pay shipping a lot easier than I can drive and get things." So being able to purchase online makes sense to him as a matter of both economics and convenience.

One way that Ron lightens his online costs is by allying himself with plumbers, electricians, and garden-maintenance businesses in his community. Many of these informal partners don't use computers at all. Since Ron has both a computer and Web skills, he's become a valuable ally to them. His centrality in this informal collaborative network gets him a fair amount of referral business, which allows him to be selective about what projects he undertakes. Ron uses his valued Web skills to order in bulk from suppliers, saving money on shipping and the items themselves. He says, "I have two people that I buy materials for—pumps and such. Also get 'em price updates, information concerning availability of the pumps, and other things. And so I am, to a small extent, a supplier, also." These bulk-ordering services that he provides to his informal partners strengthen their relationships and help them all overcome their remoteness.

*His centrality in this informal collaborative network gets him a fair amount of referral business, which allows him to be selective about what projects he undertakes.*

Ron proactively uses ICTs to manage customer relationships well. Once the workday begins, Ron says he is always "in the field." On a typical day, he awakens at 5 a.m. and checks his email. For some of his customers, especially those with non-urgent requests, email works well. "I have quite a few customers who want to be billed by email, so I just send my invoices in an attachment," he says. But "the majority of contact with customers is by telephone—the overwhelming majority." This is a necessity since, by late morning, Ron will have left his office and begun working on customer sites. "All my customers have my cellphone number," he says, "and that's their number one way to contact me." Through his use of email and the cellphone, Ron overcomes the fact that he is a one-man show.

## Optimizing Media Usage with Suppliers

While the heavy use of the cellphone helps customers reach Ron, when working with suppliers he has adapted to meet their communication media preferences and schedules. He uses the fax to place orders with suppliers, because "if I can get an order faxed in on Monday morning by, say, 7:30 [or] 8:00 o'clock—by the time they open in the city—by mid-afternoon I can have any pump or anything that I need." Ron uses the fax to place orders simply because "the first thing they process is faxes, and a lot of time I'll have that confirmation that way before I even get away from the house in the morning." He has found that email doesn't work for placing orders: "There's so much garbage. I've had things that I've done by email that they said they never received and I know that they did. And basically when they were going through culling out garbage, it got culled out." But, as he explains, "if they receive it in hard-copy form to begin with, there's not much way for that to happen."

Besides having his email order being deleted along with the spam, Ron has other concerns about using email for placing orders. When he's urgently awaiting a part, he wants to make sure that his supplier receives his order in a timely manner. Sometimes it takes several days before he hears back. "I don't know if they don't check their email that often or what," he says. As if this weren't enough, Ron has also experienced what might be called the e-brush-off. For example, several times he has emailed a supplier with questions and found his email ignored. Nowadays when he calls to follow up,

> I tell them I feel that they just brushed me off because I am a new business. And then they have a lot of trouble just brushing me off on the phone when they can easily brush off an email.

Ron's willingness and ability to work with a diverse set of communication media, necessitated by his being a one-man show, lend credibility to the conclusion that the most functional communication media with suppliers in the water-purification business is the fax machine, outdated as it may be. It would seem that some of these companies realize that they are not quite up to speed when it comes to the use of digital media, so they

> assign you your own particular salesperson to ask for every single time. At XYZ Water Supply, Laura is my contact person. And I asked her about faxing my

*"There's so much garbage. I've had things that I've done by email that they said they never received and I know that they did. And basically when they were going through culling out garbage, it got culled out."*

*orders, since everything from them I really know what I'm ordering, to begin with. And she says, 'That's my preferred way to receive it.'*

This seems to further validate that the fax is the preferred channel for placing orders in this industry, at least in this area of the world.

In addition to using the fax, Ron also orders supplies online—sometimes successfully but often problematically. As he puts it, "I'm much more likely to go ahead and order online ... if they have a good Website with online pricing and all available." But if the site is not well structured, he finds ordering frustrating. Ron offers this example:

*I ordered the humidifier in there from [a national chain], and I spent nearly two hours trying to figure out how to finally get my order placed. There was just one little thing that you had to click on there that was not prominent, like at that point it really should have been. So on some of the Websites, the quality is really not there.*

In fact, he says, "there's a real problem with a lot of the Websites this way."

He says that when suppliers are updating their pages with prices and other information, then "the Website won't be down, but you'll have, 'This page is not available right now,' over and over and over. So that can be kind of frustrating." Not only is it a frustrating experience, but sometimes the site doesn't work at all. He explains that for the last two months his major water- softener supplier's Website has been down: "They've been updating based on a new catalogue that they have, and for two months it hasn't been working." Since Websites can be poorly organized and email often doesn't get a fast response, Ron prefers the fax.

## Key Issue

*Customers of this caliber "want answers, and they ask extremely intelligent questions, in some cases more than what any person could ever actually be able to answer right off the top of his head."*

### Using the Web to Enhance Credibility

While the Web is a mixed bag with respect to its usefulness for ordering, Ron finds it indispensable as an information source. The reasons are twofold: (1) he finds quick answers to technical issues that he has never previously encountered, and (2) the Web provides him with a tangible source of instant credibility.

As discussed earlier, Ron's customers are often perceived as being "difficult." "They're essentially all college graduates," he says, and wealthy, and they are looking for quality, their homes being "typically a million and a half up." Customers of this caliber "want answers, and they ask extremely intelligent questions, in some cases more than what any person could ever actually be able to answer right off the top of his head." Instead of being put off, or getting defensive, Ron has a different approach. He'll say, "Hey, that's a good question. I don't know what the answer is but I'll get it. Do you want me to email [the information] or fax it to you?" Being faced with this type of question is a common thing for Ron: "I mean, it's weekly, maybe a little more often than weekly."

Ron claims that he always finds what he needs on the Web, and then forwards this documentation to his customer. Furthermore, he often prints the information that he finds on the Web and provides customers with hardcopy proof that backs up his oral claims. Even though he's an expert, he acknowledges that documentation enhances his credibility and wins him many sales.

Having access to technical information on the Internet and backing up his claims with hard copies of that information give Ron "a tremendous amount of credibility. It gets me referrals." Given that most of his customers "are very definitely computer-literate people," being able to use the Internet in this manner puts Ron "in a position to be able to communicate a whole lot better with the type of customers that I have." Although he is new to this way of doing business, it has already become a habit: "What's amazing to me is that I'm so new to it, really—I mean, like only a little over two years, really. And now it's just second nature."

Although he is very familiar with the water-purification business, the information available online often surprises him. For example, he describes recently looking at a supplier's Website and finding a new gadget that he "had no idea they even manufactured a thing like that." Information that he finds serendipitously on the Web is often useful. For example, he says, he once downloaded a photo

*of a place where the owners had been gone for two weeks. They came back in, found they'd left dirty dishes in the dishwasher, and the first thing they did was turn the dishwasher on. Turned out it was filled with a mixture of hydrogen gas and air. Sparks exploded and it actually blew the dishwasher out about eight feet into the room!*

He used this picture to support his point of view in a discussion with a building contractor. The contractor received incorrect information from one of Ron's competitors concerning a water heater. Ron's proof from the Internet not only discredited his competitor, but it also established Ron as an expert.

## Conclusion

Who would have thought that schoolteacher training, personal integrity, and the use of the Web could bring someone more business than he can handle? This is not an obvious recipe for sales and business success. What this case illustrates is how ICTs—specifically the Web—can enhance personal characteristics and overcome obstacles. Integrating the resourceful use of ICTs with his personal characteristics has not only enabled Ron's business to grow by referral only, but it has virtually eliminated the natural drawbacks of doing business in remote location.

**Questions for Review or Discussion**

1.  How does Ron use ICTs to adjust to the needs of his customers?

2.  How can you use quick access to experts around the world (the Internet) to enhance your own credibility?

3.  Does Ron's selectivity for customers create a market niche or limit his market? How might he use impression management to change this?

4.  How does Ron enact his relationship with his customers?

5.  Review the Media Choice chapter and explain why Ron uses the various media available to him the way he does.

# The Role of ICTs in Maintaining Personal Relationships Across Distance and Cultures

## 22

Alf Steinar Sætre & Keri K. Stephens

ICTs are so commonplace these days that most of us barely think about them. We just use them. But we pay a price for our mindlessness. Far from simply using them, in many insidious ways we are run by them. Our phone rings? We grab it, even in a fine restaurant. Our email plings us? We turn to check the new message, even during a conversation. In fact, we will often answer it, even if we really don't have the time to do so.

This is why we need to meet Anna Eidsvik. Ms. Eidsvik, a young executive with Energia, a Norwegian energy-policy agency, has an almost preternatural consciousness about how ICTs have infected our culture. That awareness stems not just from her intellect, which is first-rate and beautifully schooled in Norway, the U.K., and the U.S., but, more importantly, from her network of professional contacts, literally spanning all five continents. She is so internationally connected that she can make most of her colleagues look a bit provincial. Anna lives the life of a true cosmopolitan, even living downtown in a large Norwegian city just so she needn't bother with owning a car.

Historically, Norway has had ample hydro-electrical power, so most Norwegians, Anna says, "have in their heads that the waterfalls are running, the water is pure and beautiful, and it's all quite unproblematic since it is renewable. They think, 'Why on earth should we conserve energy when we have so much of it?'" But in fact Norway's demand for power now exceeds its production, and at times it has to import its power from foreign coal and nuclear plants. So a major effort has begun to increase the national awareness of energy conservation. Anna Eidsvik is an energy-policy advisor at Energia, a newly established government agency charged with increasing the awareness in Norway of energy conservation and alternative energy sources. Holding graduate degrees from both British and American universities, she is fluent in other cultures, so it is not surprising that she was the one tasked with coordinating Energia's international efforts. As a member of the International Energy Agency and as a board member of the European Council of Energy

*Holding graduate degrees from both British and American universities, she is fluent in other cultures.*

*Anna has discovered that differences often are greater within a culture than between them.*

Efficient Economy, she has fostered relationships with members from numerous countries around the globe—Japan, the U.S., Canada, and Australia, to name just a few. In this case, you will learn how Anna uses ICTs to develop and maintain these relationships.

### Media Preferences Across Cultures

A professional cosmopolite, Anna says she has discovered that "differences often are greater within a culture than between them." Her personal network, almost improbably far-flung, includes people from

> *African countries, many from Southeast Asia, a large proportion from India, China, Hong Kong, Indonesia, Malaysia, the Philippines, Ghana, Nigeria, from all of South America, Chile, Central America, and the Caribbean. All of these people use the Internet and email and that type of communication as a matter of course.*

In fact, she claims that there is "no difference whatsoever" in terms of media preferences among all these people.

Anna also believes that there are implications for how we communicate that are specific to the work context. "Say you're a professor at a university," she says, citing just one example. "Then it is, in a way, your job and what you work with that determines how you relate to other people," rather than who you are or where on the globe you are. So, she says, it is the similarity in the work context, the educational level of the communicators, and the place of education that determine how she herself uses media with her vast personal network. She also realizes that if she visits, say, Ghana, she will see huge differences between a privileged person, who has the opportunity to get a doctorate in the U.S., and the average population. In other words, she feels that an individual's specific context and media availability are far more important than their national culture when it comes to media preference. Similarity of educational background and such personal similarities as sense of humor and political ideology are, according to Anna, also more important than cultural background in determining media usage.

Anna has actually met most of her international contacts. Meeting people face-to-face is important, she says, because "then [you] have a tie that makes it much easier to contact them later." Not only is it easier to communicate with a new colleague when you have met them in person, she explains, but it also helps you know how to approach a conversation, "because then you know what kind of guy this is—if the guy is very formal or informal." She will know, for example, if the person is someone she can banter with. "If you communicate with, say, some group in the U.S., then you know whom you can and whom you can't joke with when it comes to [the President]." This is important to know, because if you don't, "you should not take the chance either."

*Meeting people face-to-face is important because then you have a tie that makes it much easier to contact them later.*

When returning to Norway after many years abroad, she noticed that while a few of her friends did not use the Internet or email, most of them used ICTs the same ways that she did. This again emphasizes her point that differences are often greater within cultures than between them—assuming, of course, that technology is comparably available.

## Distance and Media Choice

Most of us imagine that the greater the physical distance between people, the greater their propensity to use electronically mediated channels to communicate. But Anna's own experience proves otherwise. She uses email with people close at hand, and richer media with people farther away. She finds that whenever she moves away from her friends, she doesn't "communicate as much via email with them. I'd rather call." In her personal relationships, it seems that the greater the distance, the less important electronically mediated communication channels become in maintaining a relationship. This finding, decidedly counterintuitive, requires further explanation.

*Anna's own experience proves counterintuitive. She uses email with people close at hand, and richer media with people farther away.*

Anna says that when she doesn't have the constant personal contact that would otherwise let her know what is going on in a person's life, she feels a need to hear their voice rather than just send them an email. To indicate just how much contact she would be missing, she describes one of her current groups of friends. "We meet over a cup of coffee because we have breaks in the work, we meet for lunch, we go out together, we go to movies . . . We are friends outside work, and we are also together a lot in [our] work context." With so much interaction, she feels she knows "what is going on in each person's life." Because she doesn't need anything else, she feels comfortable just firing off a quick email saying something mundane like, "Want to see a movie Saturday night?" This suffices since there's no need to revalidate the relationship.

But there is also another side to using such lean asynchronous communication media with her more workaholic friends and colleagues. With such people "you don't necessarily have the opportunity to call, or you want the person to read the email when they have the opportunity." So email, by virtue of its very unobtrusiveness, is preferred, she says, when communicating with people who are extremely busy.

But when circumstances deprive her of daily contact with people, she finds email "a bit impersonal." So at least with people whom she considers close friends, she prefers to call instead "in order to hear the mood of the other person, because that is quite important to me—that is, to hear." This makes for a lot of phone calls, she says, explaining, "I have lived abroad for 12 years, so my friends are largely scattered all over the world."

## The Primacy of Email Over Other Media

Still, Anna admits, "I try to avoid talking on the phone." She finds the phone both intrusive and time-consuming. She clearly prefers electronically mediated communication: "If I am to rank in terms of technology, then it is email, text messages (if I am 'talking' to people in Norway), and then telephone, in that order." She likes SMS (Short Message Service) as an easy backup to email: "So if I don't get an answer on email, then I send text messages on the cellphone." Email and SMS are both asynchronous media, whereas a phone call is synchronous and thus more insistently intrusive. But Anna will use the telephone if she needs to. In short, while she has strong preferences when it comes to communication media, she has learned to be sensitive to what ICT is the most effective and efficient in each situation.

 **Key Issue**

*"If, in order to explain what you want to communicate, you have to spend a great deal of time on writing it down in an email, then that is not a particularly effective use of time."*

Her sensitivity towards what is efficient is apparent in statements like this one: "If, in order to explain what you want to communicate, you have to spend a great deal of time on writing it down in an email, then that is not a particularly effective use of time." In such cases, she will simply pick up the phone and call the person, because it is most efficient. She also chooses the phone whenever some ambiguity may be involved: "It is easier to call a person—to tell them, explain in the way that is normal to explain it—and then you get an immediate check if the person has understood what you actually are talking about." In this way she can ensure that her communication partner grasps each step of her reasoning and, if not, has a chance to reconcile any lingering ambiguities.

While Anna uses the phone as a backup to email and SMS, she also uses email as a backup to telephone conversations. Sometimes, she says, there will be "discussions back and forth on the phone, and then we sum up on email and say, 'OK, this is what we discussed.'" Summing up what was discussed and what was agreed upon helps avoid misunderstandings and confusion. By using email as a support of oral conversations, she says, "you have a common understanding of the problems." The emails also serve as later documentation of both the process and the products of these conversations.

One possible explanation for Anna's preference for asynchronous media lies in the demands of her job and her desire to be effective at everything she does. Synchronous media strike her as intrusive. She confesses, "It is quite annoying when others come to me and decide that now I have to relate to some problem they have." She feels that when you have a job that demands great focus, such extraneous interruptions take up much more time than the interruption itself, simply because you now have to spend time finding "your place" again. This is also true for phone calls, so Anna says she is "very good about switching the phone off and over to the voice messaging system." When she does this, she also turns off her cellphone, for "otherwise I won't get anything done."

*Synchronous media strike her as intrusive.*

## Managing Private Relationships

In all her years traveling abroad, Anna noticed some changes in how her parents communicated with her. In years past, she says, her father never wrote her letters: "He might call me to keep in touch, but I have never had any written communication from my father in all the years I have lived away from home." But one day her father acquired a personal computer and a modem, and soon she began receiving a stream of emails from him. Nowadays, electronically mediated communication is their predominant form of communication: "We communicate via email and text messages [on the cellphone] and by phone." Anna's mother, meanwhile, had regularly used handwritten letters to stay in touch with her daughter when she was abroad, but now that they are both in Norway again, she prefers the telephone. Actually she uses no computer-mediated communication channels at all, which is commonly the case with Norwegian women over 65.

Anna says that she is much more conscious of the communication technology she chooses for work purposes than when she uses ICTs in her private life. As she sees it, "when it is personal, it is more what is practical." Maybe so, but she still shows a high level of awareness of what she is doing even when it comes to personal relationships. Anna uses electronic media not only to maintain relationships but also to stay abreast of her field, and to share information with the people around the globe that she works with.

## The Internet as a Two-Way Source

Anna tracks what is going on in the international community mainly through the Internet. She has online subscriptions to The New York Times, The Guardian, and some Norwegian newspapers. She reads electronic journals, too, and downloads information from relevant databases and online libraries. For Anna it is "fairly simple to be dependent on the Internet as a source." She got her "addiction" to online information sources at the University of Delaware, which has won prizes for its computer systems.

*The members of IEA don't even get documents mailed to them. They download them.*

Besides the Internet, Anna also acquires information from other sources, such as her personal network, when she needs to review an issue or to give policy-related advice and recommendations. That is a big part of her job. She informs "politicians, people in the oil and energy department, and also others who work with implementation of projects at a regional level, national level, and local level." Not only does she gather her information largely from the Internet, but Anna and *Energia* also use the Internet as a medium for their policy reports. They are always mindful that "what we are producing will be uploaded to the Web."

Anna works a great deal internationally, and to a large extent she "will be the one that coordinates Energia's international engagement," since she's an active participant in the International Energy Agency (IEA) on behalf of Energia and Norway. As a member of IEA, Anna downloads "all the documents for the meeting and such." The members don't even get those documents mailed to them. "You just enter with a username and password," she explains, "and then you have all the meeting documents that you can download from their home page." Even if it doesn't save paper, it saves distribution time: "You usually print the documents to take with you to the meeting, but those who are disseminating the information don't have to keep sending it out." And it shifts more of the responsibility for keeping abreast onto the individual members.

This process of posting information on a Webpage where members log in and download only the information they deem relevant instead of getting everything emailed to them has other advantages as well. Say that Anna is asked to make a statement about a special case on behalf of Norway. Typically, she just "sends it to the secretariat and then it is posted on the Net immediately." This way, "everybody gets access as soon as we send it in." Another advantage of the system, as Anna sees it, is that "you are not dependent on getting ahold of someone in an office, for example, because here you are working with people in Japan, USA, Canada, Australia—all of the IEA membership countries." Also, this system overcomes all the time-zone issues since it is both asynchronous and constantly available anywhere there is Internet access.

## Email Etiquette

Working digitally as much as Anna does, she has developed a sense of electronic-communication etiquette. First, she believes that when you reply to an email, you should take the time to update the heading of the email so the recipient knows what it's about: "I get very irritated if people just reply with the same email, and then suddenly they have just used Reply, right, because they can't be bothered." She hates some people's "tendency to go to the most recent email they had from you and then click reply and not change the heading, even though now it is about something different." Anna will scan the headings of her emails to help her choose which ones deserve a reply.

*She believes that when you reply to an email, you should take the time to update the heading of the email so the recipient knows what it's about.*

Although she feels there is a certain minimum level of courtesy or etiquette when using email, she readily admits that "email is a very loose communication form"—much less formal than, for example, a traditional letter or even a phone call. Interestingly, she finds that "people say much more in an email than they would have over the phone, or in a letter." She feels that the threshold for what you can say in an email is lower "because you can be much more informal, and then you don't feel that you have to write in complete sentences, but you can be a bit quick and loose." But when she is writing a letter that needs a signature, "I am much more careful with formulations and how I construct sentences." She finds herself and others more accepting of typos and misspellings in an email. It is precisely because people feel less pressure to be correct when writing emails that they get a bit careless and sometimes reveal more than they otherwise would. This contributes to making email a potentially richer media than most people might realize.

**Key Issue**
Email: formal vs. informal, thresholds and courtesy.

The "looseness" of an email depends in part on the occasion and on who your communication partner is, says Anna: "If I am answering an official request—where they want our statement—then I am perhaps as formal also in an email." The level of formality in emails is also influenced by the maturity of the relationship. In fact, "there are quite a number of things that determine the level of formality." If you are requesting information from someone who is in a high-status position, she says, email can be quite formal. For example, when initiating a project with a power company to pilot-test a project, your email communication can initially be fairly formal. But once the project is underway and you are working together, things become much more informal. As Anna puts it, "it has to do with the maturing of relations."

*If you are requesting information from someone who is in a high-status position, she says, email can be quite formal.*

## The Richness of Face-To-Face Communication

Although Anna strongly prefers mediated communication, she will also exploit other media when it meets her particular needs. For example, when applying for grants, she wants to know as much as possible about the preferences of her readers, the decision-makers. This becomes what she calls a "fact-finding mission." In such instances she will use face-to-face communication if at all possible, "because if you are a bit intuitive and have some social antennas, then you can read an awful lot more out of a conversation where you talk with a person." This helps her ensure that when she later writes up her application, it goes straight to "that which is closest to that person's heart."

When the tables are turned and she finds herself evaluating applications from others, she expects them to have invested a similar effort. She wants applications carefully tailored. She gets "annoyed when I get applications that are not—it looks like they are taken right out of a context"—that is, they seem tangential to what was laid out in the funders' project description. With a copy of that description in front of you, it ought to be "so simple when one is writing an application, to then relate" the application to the description of the project being funded.

## On Being Constantly Available and Modern Office Spaces

Despite her comfort with electronically mediated communication, Anna acknowledges some negatives that often are associated with ICTs. She feels that in many ways they are tyrannically taking control of our lives. She notes, for example, an increasingly common habit of her colleagues: "Every time the inbox says 'pling,' even if they are not expecting anything, they have to dash in and see who they got mail from." She believes that becoming more efficient "has to do [not only] with how you use the technology, but also how you structure your day." Anna feels that it "is a bit sick that most people have that kind of relation" to their communication technologies. Realizing their addiction, she will sometimes email extremely busy people instead of calling them, because she's "guaranteed to have a quick response," even if she knows they would not have taken the time to talk to her on the phone. Such people, she concludes, "are governed by their ...ing inboxes, pardon the expression."

She thinks that if "you decide not to check email until 15.00 [i.e., 3:00 p.m.], for example," you get more accomplished in a day. But Anna herself admits to spending "too much time on email-checking." She feels less efficient than she could be, because "if one is to be more effective, one has to be more conscious of what one is doing and why one does it." To become more efficient, she says, she should make a list of her tasks, stick to those, and not check email until after lunch. But "Email is so easy, right? It is just quick. It requires little. So we procrastinate, right? We delay the heavier tasks because it is much easier to grab ahold of the stuff we know we can finish quickly." Hence the habit of checking for, and replying to, email continually. People welcome the excuse to procrastinate, rather than tackle their "serious" work.

Anna's work often involves reading, and digesting long, technical documents—tasks that are impeded by the constant interruption of incoming email. Having to hold a lot of complex thoughts in her head and then tie them together and write a coherent report on them requires Anna to focus hard for sustained stretches. Email is not, then, only a distraction. Her office environment itself is actually far worse.

> We work in a pen [office cubicle] landscape that I don't think works at all. It is absolutely terrible. You have umpteen cellphones buzzing constantly, you have telephones, and then you have people who have informal meetings [between cubicles], and then you have people who walk back and forth, and then you have . . .

She tosses her hands up as if to say, "Well, you get the idea." The constant buzz of such an open office landscape is, according to Anna, not conducive to getting any kind of deep thinking done. In this kind of hustle and bustle, she "cannot sit down and, for example, write." When writing is a major part of your job description, as it is hers, the open office landscape becomes an impediment to getting actual work done, simply because "there is so much input." Anna's solution to this problem? "I usually sit at the office until far into the night." After everyone has left, she finally finds the time to get work done. It makes for fiendishly long workdays. "Last week I almost did not go home one single time until one thirty at night," she says. But she still "starts working" at the regular time in the morning.

> **⊕ Key Issue**
>
> *The constant buzz of such an open office landscape is, according to Anna, not conducive to getting any kind of deep thinking done.*

Though blessed with high stamina, she has come to realize that this is an untenable situation, and she is "going to bring it up" with her colleagues. Anna is still living with some friends, so she does not have a home office; otherwise she would have "worked the first half [of the day] at home, doing some thinking work, then gone to work and done everything else that does not demand so much concentration," like checking email.

## Conclusion

Anna's high level of mindfulness regarding how she works—including her ICT usage and media choices—helps her to be more effective and thus very good at what she does. She maintains a vast international personal network, mostly work-related, that spans all continents and many national and regional cultures and languages. The way she uses email and the telephone might appear counterintuitive, but she has valuable insights into how distance relationships are maintained. Most ICT users can also learn from Anna's insight into how technology can control us and make us inefficient.

**Questions for Review or Discussion**

1. What factors contribute to "leveling" national culture differences?

2. Are there situations where you let technology control you rather than you controlling the technology?

3. If you were to design a questionnaire to determine ICT "addiction," what questions would you ask?

4. What other cases in this book provide insight into ICT "addiction?"

5. What theories would help explain "Anna's views" on various media?

# One in the Hand is Worth Two on the Web: Relying on Tradition When Selling Financial Services

**23**

Larry D. Browning & Jan-Oddvar Sørnes

Ed Smithers, a lanky, boyish-looking professional in his late 20's, owns a small financial services business. He sends out a weekly financial tipsheet in hopes of attracting clients to his investment services. But while he uses the Internet actively in that business, he is reserved about judging its effects. In fact, he confides that during the four years he's focused on e-business, he can point to only one client—"Just one!"—that he has made into a customer solely from Internet contact. So as a small-business owner, he naturally worries about the value he gets in relation to the cost he's paying for ICTs. He says, "Maybe we haven't been attractive enough on the Web. Maybe it's been too scattered. I have scratched my head and we've poured buckets of money out the window on this thing." For anyone who thinks that clients can simply be drawn to a Website to do business, and that the money will then pour in, Ed's experience is sobering. First of all, "very few people are going to cough up financial information about themselves." So to gain information about them, "you're going to pay dearly for it." He sees email as very effective as a direct mail forum, but "spamming via email and sending out a solicitation to millions of people? Ugh. Not happening." As he says, it's a "horrible waste of money from a marketing standpoint."

> **Key Issue** ⊕
>
> *He sees email as very effective as a direct mail forum, but spamming via email and sending out a solicitation to millions of people is not good business.*

## The Client Strategy

He talks in detail about his strategy for business over the Internet, how he uses the Net, and what effects he gets with it. He also talks about the parts of the business where he is less disciplined and what he hopes to do to change his practices.

As an investment counselor, he spends considerable effort using technology to generate information about the financial world and then posting it on his Website so that people can see what he's doing and what they might gain from his expertise. Ed had just purchased a high-speed connection and was relishing getting price quotes and all kinds of information in real-time, as opposed to delayed, access.

Because he operates a small business, he is cautious about expenses. He says, "we've only purchased and used the technology that has been useful for our business. And I think you can easily get out on that curve where you're buying things you don't need or you're not even using the whole package." While he is certain that subscribing to all the ICTs available to him would be a waste of money, purchasing a broadband link was an efficient move for him.

The high-speed connection allowed him to discontinue some of the quote services that he'd been purchasing at $800 a month just to get "good, real-time data." Now he collects the same data from a variety of free Internet sites, and he runs his entire investment business from these financial information sources. So in this case, speed means lowering the cost of doing business. Once he gets these data, he applies them to his own investment models. His strategy is to distribute the analyses he's completed from his formulas over the Internet to show Website visitors what they'd gain by using his service.

*His strategy is to distribute the analyses he's completed from his formulas over the Internet to show Website visitors what they'd gain by using his service.*

As with many service-oriented firms that use the Internet and its convenience as a major piece of their business, his pressing need is to develop a larger client base. One of his ways of doing this is gathering estimated retirement dates for potential clients and saying to them, "Happy retirement! Here are three things you need to be doing now." Most of his clients are 60 or older, and Ed, a young man who looks even younger than his age, knows that establishing credibility is essential to his securing clients and keeping them. As he says about personal contact, "That part of our business will never go away. It is still very relationship-oriented." He also collects clients' children's ages so he can approach them at age 21, when they graduate from college—though he's careful to have the parent's authorization.

Ed's identification of potential clients is only a part of his efforts. Most of his client development comes from office visits, face-to-face, where he creates a personal profile that focuses on potential customers' investment objectives. While our interview focused on the use of technology to run his business, Ed is clear that the face-to-face communication is crucial. Because he's handling other people's money, he is certain that trust, and purely trust, is a key component of his business, and it requires customers to answer this question of faith about him: "Do I trust you to act in my best interests?" One of his ways of developing and maintaining trust is to make "house calls," including out-of-state ones, at his own expense. Each such visit accomplishes two things: (1) it gives the client in-person information about what he is like, as an individual, and (2) it shows the client that he is "interested enough to fly out and meet them." The first purpose produces concrete information; the second purpose communicates "symbolic" information, or information about his commitment. After reviewing the information he's gathered, Ed arranges a follow-up interview and makes a recommendation based on his offerings. The client typically takes some time to review the offer and to make a decision on becoming a client.

**Key Issue**
Trust

So Ed's experience confirms one of the oldest assumptions of marketing and business: Few things are more powerful than face-to-face contact for important financial decisions.

## Displaying Information

Ed's business and marketing strategy is to display all the relevant parts of his business, including the performance of individual securities he personally owns, on his Website. He's saying to the potential client directly, "Here is our strategic performance. Look at the whole strategy. Here's what it's done." He sees his value-add as being his analysis, rather than just offering pure data. The strategy is effective in that it sells itself and it saves him time in closing agreements with clients, reducing his closure time to "a quarter of what it used to be." The time in closing a client is reduced because Ed's clients want to do their own research and their own examination in such detail that Ed has no need to explain it to them. He finds that the nature of the current investor is "a little bit more of a do-it-yourselfer." And they want to "hold everything—touch it and massage it before they buy it." But the do-it-yourselfers that get help from subscription services often fail to act on their beliefs. Ed estimates that 70% of them do not have the confidence to act on their own accounts, or that if they have, they have failed at it and are seeking help from a professional like him. Yet with the array of things he uses to attract clients, he ponders new ways to gain a customer. He says, "I think I have to throw them a bone. I have to maybe throw them a trial period or something and say, 'For those of you who are lurking out there, you know, we are going to offer you a trial offer.'"

## Website Interaction

Ed reviews the traffic on his Website monthly to determine which portions are getting heavy traffic and which are not being visited. He also posts weekly updates on his Website to get a measure of how sensitive people are to recent information. He sees a pattern of active use after he posts information on Thursdays only to see it subside fairly quickly. Visitors appear to have learned Ed's schedule for providing information and have adapted to it. Ed sees these postings as a requirement to keep the visitors he's attracted. "I know I'd better have it up there by Thursday night or I'm going to start losing readers," he says. He also makes Website postings after certain news events have happened. An event just prior to this data collection shows how Ed integrates the use of Web-based financial information with his own professional judgment.

## Learning From the Pizza Guy

In the fall of 2000, the U.S. Presidential election was delayed dramatically by the recount in the state of Florida, but after a torturous extension, it was finally resolved. There had already been public speculation about the effect of the election uncertainty on the stock market, and

> Key Issue
>
> *Few things are more powerful than face-to-face contact for important financial decisions.*

> *Ed reviews the traffic on his Website monthly to determine which portions are getting heavy traffic and which are not being visited.*

*Ed's purpose in making his prediction about the election was to communicate a surprise, to get his readers scratching their head saying, "I expected a rally."*

Ed saw the opportunity to make a Website posting because he knew his readers would be checking the site to see what he had to say. One of Ed's data points for judging the effect of the election was the pizza-delivery guy who always likes to talk about investments when he makes his delivery. Ed recalls the last delivery. The pizza guy arrived and said, "Should get a big pop out of the market, huh?" "Not any more, not now that you're telling me," Ed replied with a smile. He posted on his Website that the resolution of the election recount would have no effect on the market.

Ed reports that he uses the pizza guy as an indicator of the Man-on-the-Street whose opinion demonstrates that the market opportunity, if there was one, has definitely passed. He calls this piece of face-to-face information his "contrarian indicator"—meaning that if the pizza guy thinks it is a good idea, the assessment itself is proof that it is not. Some of Ed's clients serve the same purpose, and when he hears from them with concerned calls that they should be buying, it's proof to him that the time is not right for making a purchase. Ed's purpose in making his prediction about the election was to communicate a surprise, to get his readers "scratching their head saying, I expected a rally." Also, for this message to be powerful, it had to be available to his readers immediately.

### Increasing Website Visitors—Lurkers vs. Clients

One of Ed's dilemmas is how to induce Website visitors into becoming clients. His calculation is clear: "I have a regular amount of visitors—almost 4,000 visitors a month. And I have 200 clients. So who are these 3,800 individuals?" He doesn't know where they come from—whether they are the same people logging on and off every day, checking their balances, or simply new "lurkers." He says, "I don't know them and they don't know me. I've never spoken with them. But I think I have a substantial untapped pool of lurkers. And I don't know how to meet them."

*The problem of determining who the visitors are is complicated by Ed's conviction that they want to remain anonymous.*

The problem of determining who the visitors are is complicated by Ed's conviction that they want to remain anonymous. He invites them to send him their email, but they resist doing so. Ed's frustration is that only the old ways work, and that people come to his business by getting referred through a present user who, almost inadvertently, suggests they contact him. Ed offers an example: "I had a funny conversation with a guy yesterday who I barely knew. And he said that he talked to somebody who talked to somebody who talked to somebody who's been receiving my email. I've never heard of this person. So I think my emails that are going out are also being forwarded onto other people that I have no idea who they are." Marketing practices that are typical in Ed's industry tend to make potential clients cautious. He says, "A lot of people are now afraid, because of the gorilla marketing that's going on, to even make contact with a potential service provider. And they're afraid to reach out and say, 'Please send me information,' because they know they're going to get on some eternal mailing list that will spam them forever." With Ed's method, they can just anonymously log in.

Ed tries to attract clients to his service by offering them something of value for free, rather than just descriptive information on whether the market went up or down that day. In this interview he regularly mentions the strategy of disclosure as his key asset: "I think the fact that we are willing to lay everything out on the table and we've given them complete transparency to our business—well, they like that." He is especially careful about the fee structure and wants to make sure that there are no hidden fees because he's certain "they don't like hidden things." Ed maps out every fee they could potentially pay in the system so that the numbers are clear—"good, bad, or ugly." The information provided on the Website is intended to communicate the firm's honesty and to also show that he's been in the business for a while. As he says, "They see our picture. They know who I am." He sees such a display as part of his distinctive competence.

*"I think the fact that we are willing to lay everything out on the table and we've given them complete transparency to our business—well, they like that."*

One of the estimates Ed makes about the value of the Internet services he offers is about the client retention it achieves. In an industry that has a client loss rate of 10% to 12% a year, he has been able to reduce that to 6%. And he sees this client retention as a product of the amount of online services, the transparency he provides, and his effort to meet with everybody in person. Yet even this estimate is just a guess; as he says about client retention, "it's hard to quantify, though. Everybody lies. You ask them why they're leaving and they don't—they won't—tell you the truth."

## Partnerships

The changes in the financial industry are marked by the kinds of partnerships for information that are available, and Ed takes advantage of an institution like Schwab's "advisory platform" that allows him to do his trading for big blocks of accounts on the Web. In the past, he would dial directly into these sites; now it is all Web-based. Ed does business with six different institutions, and they post information directly on his Website. He sees this as a differentiator between him and his competition, and it also makes it easy for his clients to use his service. Clients prefer this consolidated service because it allows them to see all their accounts in one space, including their balances and their allocations. Ed thinks these kinds of partnerships are the future of small business advisors like him: "And to me, that's where the industry is going, to consolidation. And so we've taken a step out. And I've paid up for this to have this service done for us. And I think you're going to see many other advisors who are staying in business, are able to stay in business, providing these types of added value like a consolidation aggregation-type service." Another advantage of these partnerships is they allow a wider span of marketing for Ed's service: "Our data base through them allows me to market to other intermediaries like CPAs and even other advisors and say, 'Here are our strategies that are available to you. If you want to bring clients to us as a money manager you

*Everybody lies. You ask them why they're leaving and they don't—they won't—tell you the truth.*

can view through the Website just the accounts that you have with my firm.' It's just a standard hierarchical data base." Through these partnerships Ed is able to use a database as a marketing tool to intermediaries.

### The Structure of Ed's Firm and the Integration of His Personal Life

One of Ed's problems is getting a set of systems in his office to track and move clients into the stream. As he says in dismay, "If we ever get into a position where we've got more than two people to process at one time we're dead." And while he sees such a state of internal affairs as ridiculous, he sees it as the nature of a small business. As a small-business owner, he has particular doubts about his ability to process the clients through his office. He sees a need to be more systematic about potential customers he has met and arranging a database about them. He wants to be able to take a client who has called for information and take them "all the way through the chain," and assure nothing gets dropped before they are signed up for his service. As he says, "Somehow we have a knack for dropping the ball. It's unbelievable to me."

*"If we ever get into a position where we've got more than two people to process at one time we're dead."*

One of the effects of Ed's use of ICTs is his report on how it has reduced his time at work. He says: "I mean, I used to work a 10-, 12-hour day. I probably max work an eight-hour day. So yes, I'm getting my life back a little bit." He is conscious of the advantage the technology has given him and what advantages it provides: "I would just attribute it to sanity and say it's a trade. I pay more for technology but I gain in sanity."

### Conclusion

In conclusion, Ed's case shows that people who use the Web for business constantly still attempt to get the attention of users by looking for ways to increase the amount of face-to-face contact with them.

## Questions for Review or Discussion

1.  Have there been times when you have used an ICT to quickly send a message on an important matter, and you later realized that you would have gotten a better outcome if you had spent the time face-to-face? What would have been different if you would have chosen face-to-face over email?

2.  How do impression management and credibility fuse into a single issue in this case? What is that issue?

3.  How would you design a process for having employees contact customers to follow up an inquiry that began over the Internet?

4.  Is Ed's attempt to bolster his credibility ethical or unethical? Explain your view.

# Do What You Do Well and Outsource the Rest...
# Even Guarded Information

## 24

Larry D. Browning & Keri K. Stephens

John is a manager in FolkKind, an American software firm that provides business solutions such as accounting and procurement solutions. He runs a group called Strategic Marketing, which he refers to as the FolkKind "brand." He's engaging interpersonally and a good listener. He sees his role as defining and communicating the corporate position of FolkKind to three audiences (1) out in the market to customers, and partners; (2) internally to employees; and then (3) out to the financial and industry research analysts.

FolkKind's products are marketed through a direct sales force, but they also enlist system integrators and partners who recommend and help implement FolkKind software service products. While their sales are done directly between sales people and customers, the first place that anybody goes for information is the FolkKind Website. John sees a lot of changes in Websites recently. He says, "Websites a few years ago were really more of a brochure online. They just had a lot of information. And we're evolving that now so a Website visit is an interactive tour of Internet products that are built on our own technology."

*"A Website visit is an interactive tour of Internet products that are built on our own technology."*

This example illustrates the degree of change in how ICTs are used at FolkKind. Now, FolkKind uses their basic software over the Internet to both sell their product and service it once they gain customers. While a lot of personal contact continues to take place with the customer via phone and face-to-face communication, the Website allows customers to see products in action and to buy them directly. This change in the use of the Web has also affected salespersons demonstrating the product on-site with a prospective buyer. Earlier, a sales person would "pull out the magic computer with the magic software" and demonstrate a mock version that "everyone knew wasn't totally real. But it was a good example. Now we just do the real thing [live on the Internet]." As such, these "live Internet demos," are now plugged in through the customer's modem on site. This allows FolkKind sales people to show live demonstrations of a real product. John notes the difference in the customer's response when showing the real

**Key Issue**

*Once the customer is guided through the demonstration, then "they can actually do it themselves." This helps customers see immediate applications and their reaction results in sales.*

product on the net, with no special equipment, and the customer's own company data is used as an example for the demonstration. "Their jaws drop and they say, 'Okay, this is real.' You start from there and say, 'imagine this is you.'" Once the customer is guided through the demonstration, then "they can actually do it themselves." This helps customers see immediate applications and their reaction results in sales.

In addition to the Web-based communication, once a person or firm becomes a customer and licenses the software, as John says, FolkKind moves to a "push-type" communication, including email newsletters, and direct mail. They also have a "pull-type" polling system called "New Networks" that customers can log on to with a secure user I.D. and password. This allows them to get information about the company including fixes, patches, information on implementation, and new products and services. But the push-pull marketing becomes blurry after that, because after a customer is in their marketing system, FolkKind uses an "Approval Sales Strategy" for customers to sign on for additional services. Once customers have made this level of commitment, FolkKind initiates still other kinds of push communication including weekly calls, where the customer has direct conversations with FolkKind's strategy specialists.

## CommMeets as Useful ICTs

These conversations between FolkKind and customers—they call them "CommMeets"—take place over the phone with participants looking at a PowerPoint on a computer screen. CommMeets are organized around a mixture of emerging topics. For example, strategists researching new products might initiate some sessions. In the development process, they may encounter common themes among customer interests. In other instances, customer preferences drive these phone discussions directly based on topics they've submitted to talk about. John characterizes this latter mechanism as being "totally demand driven." Interested parties, from 20 to 100 people, dial in and participate in a question and answer session lead by one or two FolkKind spokespeople. The purpose and focus of these teleconferences vary—sometimes the topic is "selfish" and is driven by new products FolkKind wants to promote, and with a bit of luck, sell. In other instances, the sessions are driven by customer demand and are organized around problem solving. The strategists answer questions such as: "How do I connect these two applications together?"

**Key Issue**

*The audience views this PowerPoint over their own computers and they access verbal information via a teleconference.*

To broadcast the CommMeets, FolkKind uses a technology called "Web-ON" for the strategist's presentations. CommMeets represent the combination of two ICTs. There is a PowerPoint presentation given by a FolkKind strategist. The audience views this PowerPoint over their own computers and they access verbal information via a teleconference. John gives us a brief example of what this sounds and looks like: "Okay, let's take a look at slide seven. This is the diagram explaining XYZ."

While following these kinds of discussions, the audience can either download the presentations, or they can simply go to the Website and treat it like a slide show. The excitement for John here is how the mix of media allows for a vital conversation. He says, "we just about live on PowerPoint here." The success of this mixed use of ICTs propels future plans at FolkKind. One of their top five corporate priorities is to "drive all operations to the Web." An example of this commitment is found in their plan to cease paper production of a FolkKind annual report.

*"I'm a brand marketing guy and so I'm concerned about perception. You know, I want people to think of us as a company that is leading edge."*

John speaks of this corporate commitment to integrate a way of doing business with his own vision of the company. He says, "I'm a brand marketing guy and so I'm concerned about perception. You know, I want people to think of us as a company that is leading edge." One indicator of being on the forefront is how FolkKind does simple things that cause their customers to think, notice, and mimic their actions. He'd like to hear customers say, "Hey, that's a progressive way to do things, I should be doing that myself."

In addition to the perception/image value of FolkKind's technology practices, John recognizes the material value of implementing these ways of communicating and doing business in their own operation "as huge." He offers an example of their software procurement system: "It used to be if you wanted to buy ten new chairs for your office building you'd go through a purchasing manager at a supplier, such as Office Depot." They discovered that the cost of processing that purchase order—including "signing, sealing, faxing, mailing, credit processing, and getting it approved on both ends—used to be well over a hundred dollars." FolkKind has been able to reduce these steps into a single solution, he says, "We sell an application and also use it internally because it can cut that down to about ten dollars per process. So that's a 90 percent savings. And as a company gets bigger, those cost savings are just enormous."

The cost savings analysis also applies to the CommMeets. Prior to implementing multi-media use for meetings, they would simply hold a telephone conference, "which is good but not as rich, in terms of the media you can deliver." An earlier form of delivery for them included regional seminars with people traveling to these events, which was a "huge cost." When these meetings were service oriented and provided value, customers paid their own travel expenses to them, but when FolkKind targeted a buyer with a product for sale, they'd provide for the expenses including the customary wining and dining typically associated with a pure sales type event.

**Key Issue**
Time saved in traveling days

The CommMeets cut FolkKind's in-person meeting costs considerably because they use the underlying technology and people resources that they already have available for customers. These include things like the computer networks, software, and time of the one or two internal strategists to lead the CommMeets. For all participants, customers, and FolkKind representatives alike, the time saved in traveling days accounts for a major part of the efficiency of the CommMeets. A theme within FolkKind is to "practice what they preach" about technology. Consulting firms are notorious for being weak at the same management techniques they give advice on, but John claims that his company consistently uses its own products effectively.

## The Importance of Face-to-Face Communication in Sales

**Key Issue**
What closes the sale?

This case places lots of focus on face-to-face communication. Despite the technological availability, cost reduction, and time savings, John comments that FolkKind's sales process is largely still a "one-on-one, face-to-face type process." Sales efforts are developed as sales persons get leads produced through the Website or the telemarketing department. Once the sales person establishes a conversation and a need with a prospective buyer, "they'll go out and fly around the world and go meet those people in person." So even with the emphasis on the Web and the CommMeets, giving a PowerPoint presentation in a face-to-face environment usually makes sales.

The licensing agreements FolkKind sells commonly cost customers over a million dollars and John sees that it is only natural for the customer to want to meet not only the sales person, but a vertical slice of people in the FolkKind hierarchy as well. He says, about their software product, "people are paying well over a million dollars. And generally, if you're going to spend that kind of money, they're going to want to meet our sales people, our sales managers, our vice-president, and our executives." Because there may be little direct contact after the sale, the initial agreement and the trust it symbolizes is very important. John sees it this way: "Especially in our industry, there's a lot of CEOs who spend half their time just closing deals."

*Because there may be little direct contact after the sale, the initial agreement and the trust it symbolizes is very important.*

Face-to-face is also the ideal environment to share and ask for business references. Establishing a reference relationship is a powerful sales tool because it clearly demonstrates that other people have purchased this product and used it successfully. On the face-to-face visits, sales persons are their most persuasive when they are able to say, "Well, did you know that GO-FLY manages all its employees using our human resources software?" When the potential customers says, " I'd like to talk to that person at GO-FLY, you increase your chances for the sales." Once such a recommendation closes a deal, then that customer is added to the reference pool. John says, "that's golden," since references make sales.

### Partnering for Trust

The network of references and the use of ICTs to communicate with customers is a major part of their strategy, but they also work with partners to influence customers to consider FolkKind for a purchase. They have a highly developed relationship network in that they partner with the world's largest hardware and consulting service providers. These networks are maintained by teaching and educating their clients on the advantages of using FolkKind products and services. John sees the value of partnering with these industry mammoths because they are a third party, rather than just themselves, which helps to establish trust.

Another way to establish a kind of structural trust is to either take an equity interest in the customer's product or have them actually purchase FolkKind stock as part of the customer agreement. This "we're-all-in-the-same-boat" approach works especially well when the complimentarity is high and FolkKind will either buy or sell a significant amount of stock. "If it's a software company that's buying our software and we think that they're going to be complementary to us in the future, then we'll look into a large amount—maybe five percent." The willingness to make such an exchange of resources communicates, "that it's not a customer/vendor relationship—but a partner."

*John sees the value of partnering with these industry mammoths because they are a third party, rather than just themselves, which helps to establish trust.*

These partnerships often involve a substantial amount of face-to-face communication because, in addition to the size of the deal—which may involve auto makers with 30,000 suppliers—the complexity of the agreement requires that the ICT used to reach it be equally complex. This means more face-to-face communication to account for nuance and context in understanding. As John says, "I think it's the complexity and the size of the deals that warrant more actual personal touch."

One of the effects of this level of integration with partners—who are often much larger than FolkKind—is that FolkKind serves as a third party security provider for many of the bigger customers' financial data. This means these larger companies "outsource" the security of their financial data. As John says, FolkKind has "dozens of customers whose whole businesses—their information systems—are all housed here. They just go out to a Website, use their user name and a password and get in." This is another issue that requires the face-to-face contact: the complexity of a relationship where the outsider is trusted with financial information. "Imagine you're the CFO of a Fortune 500 company" John says, "and you're responsible for all the finances. It's a little scary to think about accessing your finances outside of your own domain and, you know, having all that competitive information out of your control." But FolkKind has been able to convince customers that FolkKind's storage and access parameters assure a security that is "more secure now than it was even in their own corporate environment." Because of the trust required for such a commitment, marketing such arrangements is "a big sell."

*"I think it's the complexity and the size of the deals that warrant more actual personal touch."*

When asked what percentage of FolkKind's programming effort is directed toward convincing customers of the security and reliability of the product, John answers adamantly, "All of them. A hundred percent—because people are running billions of dollars of operations." Much of this effort is directed toward service agreements that build redundancies upon redundancies to guarantee against breaches in security and power outages so the customer can survive with their information intact for months—even if the system goes down.

John accounts for these examples of communication and service as manifestations of the company culture. He says, "FolkKind is known within the information technology industry as a high-touch, customer-satisfaction oriented company." This effort may have a component of symbolism attached to it. Yet, John sees "high-touch" as a practical outcome of the delivery of their service. The personal planning involved in having a service representative come in as a consultant, sit down with the client for six months, and document how the customer is going to operate as s/he implements the software, "really does take a lot of personal touch."

*As in all of John's examples, he ties any act of human communication that requires time and effort, to a software solution that saves time and effort.*

As in all of John's examples, he ties any act of human communication that requires time and effort, to a software solution that saves time and effort. For example, personal touch is tied to Customer Relationship Management Solutions, a product that enables the application of software at call centers to accomplish the same thing as individuals talking in call centers. An additional focus on saving time and effort shows up in the business analysis tools that demonstrate where the application of resources would have a greater impact. For example, they also sell software that makes analyses of efficiency possible by identifying for a client the customers that are producing the most income and the ones that are losing money. They have similar applications for suppliers that allow for a breakdown of the ones that deliver on time for the right price and the ones that do not.

The zeal for innovation is consistent throughout this interview and John has lots of ideas for future products and services. He says "I'd love to be able to have software that lets our customers go through at least some of the service processes and some of the sales processes over a phone or over a Palm Pilot with wireless access. Some of this technology is already available at FolkKind and merely needs to be improved and made more usable to become "more consumerish."

*There are also times when face-to-face communication is absolutely necessary to initiate business relationships.*

### Conclusion

By listening to John, it is easy to conclude that many types of ICTs are useful and necessary for his business to grow. The Web serves a valuable purpose by getting new customers, easing the burden of servicing existing customers, facilitating the outsourcing of security, and helping salespeople sell. However, there are also times when face-to-face communication is absolutely necessary to initiate business relationships. With millions of dollars at stake, trust is necessary. And trust is built in a physical space.

## Questions for Review or Discussion

1. How do you handle the issue of information confidentiality?

2. What do you need to know about a company to feel comfortable about it handling your company's financial information?

3. What are the advantages and disadvantages of having a product that potential customers can scrutinize prior to purchasing it?

4. How does it influence credibility to have vice-presidents flying to meet with customers face-to-face to close deals?

5. John articulates a detailed description of his environment. In what way does his action match his description?

# Orchestrating Communication: The Process of Selling in the Semiconductor Market

## 25

Keri K. Stephens & Alf Steinar Sætre

Have you ever wondered how the microchips are made that run your computer, mobile phone, digital camera, and such other electronic devices? Behind the scenes of high-profile computer retailers like Dell and Apple, there are two other layers of companies involved in microchip production: chip producers and capital-equipment suppliers. That first background layer includes companies like Intel, AMD, and Freescale semiconductor—computer-chip producers that supply microchips to the computer retailers. There are relatively few such companies—approximately 30 internationally—because the cost of building a manufacturing facility can be a multi-billion dollar endeavor. One reason the cost is so high is that the manufacturing facilities need multi-million dollar pieces of capital equipment to produce the chips.

The second background layer includes companies that sell that pricey equipment. This narrative focuses on one such equipment producer, SemiSales. Their sales process is unique because they have very few customers, each generating hundreds of millions of dollars in sales. Obviously, SemiSales cannot afford to lose those customers, so they've developed an elaborate sales and customer-satisfaction process that involves many ICTs. Elliott McGuire, one of their technical sales specialists, shares responsibility for coordinating the disparate groups inside of SemiSales to keep the customer satisfied. His story is a behind-the-scenes look at how a global organization communicates internally to present a unified front to the external customer.

### The Web of Behind-the-Scenes Relationships

*Working with customers.* Elliott is a tall, lean man in his early 30's. A former engineering major in college, he transitioned into technical sales after five years at SemiSales. His current job involves both traveling to the customers' sites and working within his own organization. As a technical sales specialist, he is assigned specific customer accounts and is responsible for generating business with them. But to get that business, he finds he must also get involved in other non-sales issues, especially resolving any technical complaints. In this sales role, he says, good communication is essential:

> *The reason that communication is so important is that the processes inside of a company are not perfect, right? Because if they were, you could spend more time taking care of your customers' problems than communicating internally. [Good communication] is redundant; it's checks and balances so that nothing gets missed. And through communication I can always make sure that issues are ultimately solved.*

To best understand how Elliott coordinates communication at SemiSales, we will first explain the complex set of relationships involved in the behind-the-scenes communication web of the sales process. Figure 25-1 illustrates this web. Two groups are represented in this figure. First, there are all the people in sales who interact directly with customers—sales management, global account management, account managers, sales specialists, and service engineers. But these same sales-people—whom we're calling the "Sales Organization"—serve as a buffer separating the customer from other groups inside SemiSales. These "other groups" include global resources, marketing, parts, engineering, and service engineers. SemiSales' various salespeople typically interact with all these internal groups, acting as go-betweens. This can create communication gaps. Not everyone who should know something will always get the word. Information will "fall through the cracks," so they say.

The sales-specialist position (Elliott's) is more junior than the account managers who visit the same customers. The general account managers handle all non-technical sales issues for a specific account location. They negotiate purchase

*Figure 25-1*

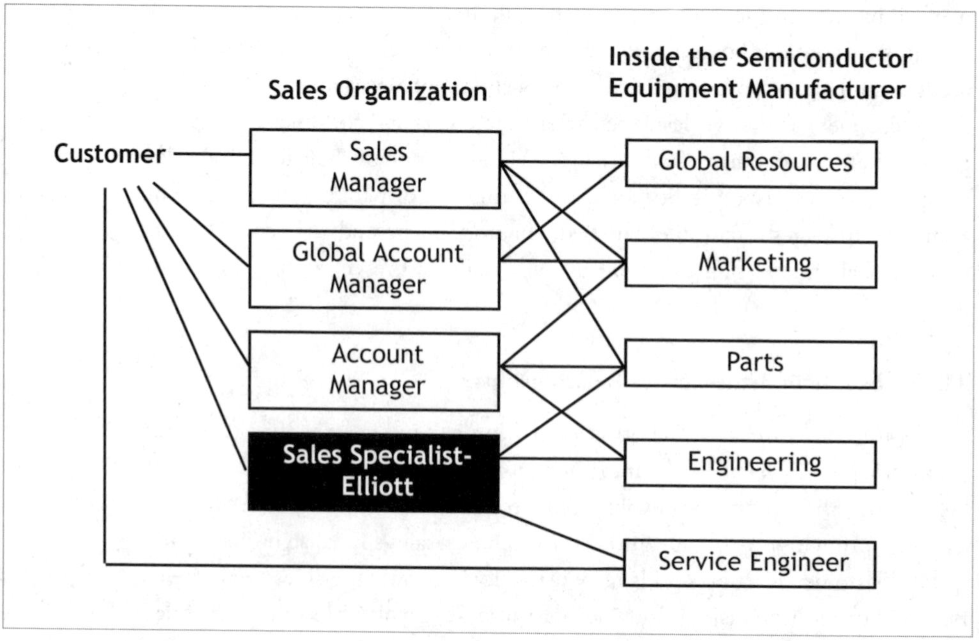

contracts on a local level. Global account managers, meanwhile, are still higher up in the SemiSales hierarchy because they manage global relationships with customers' key executives. In addition, they negotiate technology non-disclosure (confidentiality) agreements. They also establish global volume-purchase agreements that combine all purchases from a given customer.

So SemiSales will have several different people visiting each corporate customer: a sales specialist, an account manager, a global account manager, and a sales manager. Complicating matters still further, they are often visiting different people inside the customer's organization. Elliott's role is the most technical of these, so he communicates specifically between the technical groups and the customers.

*Engineers working with customers.* Besides the sales staff, SemiSales has two types of engineers that deal with customers. First are the service engineers who repair broken equipment, install replacement equipment, or upgrade existing systems. Depending on the size of a customer's facility, these engineers can spend so much time there that they become almost permanently assigned to it. Product and application engineers, meanwhile, provide the customer with technical advice. While they normally work in one of SemiSales' own research laboratories, they will sometimes accompany the company's salespeople when they visit customers.

*Communicating inside SemiSales.* Under most circumstances, the people mentioned so far are boundary spanners working both outside (with the customers) and inside SemiSales. But when Elliott handles customer issues, he often needs to contact people who work wholly inside his own organization—specifically, colleagues in the parts department, in marketing, and engineers in Japan.

The parts department provides a prime example of when "the [communication] system's not perfect." Elliott would like to not have to mess with parts issues. But when parts fail to arrive at the customer site on-time or when a customer complains that a part is too pricey, he can't help finding himself involved, even though such issues are not directly related to how his work is evaluated. He grants that his work involves "not just a sales process. It's part of managing the whole product." Still, side issues can take a lot of his time and while it's important for customer satisfaction, it's also frustrating because it cuts into time he'd rather devote to selling.

**Key Issue** ⊕

*Communication is not perfect. Elliott uses ICTs to achieve better communication through redundancy, frequency, and functionality.*

## Using ICTs to Overcome the Imperfect Organizational System

A major problem that Elliott faces is SemiSales' imperfect system of checks and balances with respect to both internal and external communication. To deal with this problem, Elliott uses ICTs creatively in three ways:

1. Redundantly (to overcome geography issues).

2. Frequently.

3. Functionally (to improve future communication attempts).

*Redundancy to overcome geography.* Geography, Elliott says, plays a big role in how he communicates internally to keep customers satisfied. With colleagues in his home office, he prefers face-to-face, but when they're in another country, he'll use combinations of ICTs. He explains:

> *I feel like I'm more effective if I go talk to a person face-to-face. I feel that way with customers, and I also feel that way with people [here]. I like to get up, grab my notebook, grab my PDA, pen, and walk across the building. I'll walk wherever I have to, to sit down and say, "Look, I have this problem; I need your help." I feel like I'm more effective that way.*

But Elliott also works with some of SemiSales' engineers located in Japan, many time zones away:

> *When I need help from Japan, I always send an email, and then I follow up on the email with a phone call. That's overkill—or should be overkill—but sometimes if someone's busy, it [my issue] isn't high on their priority list. And if it is that important, then I call and send an email.*

**Key Issue**
Face-to-face communication is still very important.

Besides redundantly using both email and the telephone with his Japanese counterparts, Elliott looks for excuses to hop a plane and actually visit Japan: "Whenever I get a chance to go to Japan, I make the most of that trip. Not just meeting people but going to dinner with them. They like doing that. Go get food, drink with them, get to know them and it makes this job a lot easier." During his tenure with SemiSales, he has flown to Japan four times. He believes that unless he has strong relationships with his overseas counterparts, his job will be very hard.

Elliott uses redundancy in his local communications as well: "A lot of times, even as you're sending email, you're in the same office, and when you see that person [you say] 'Did you see that email?'" That conversation in the hall often leads to additional face-to-face conversations: "They could say, 'Let's go downstairs and grab some coffee and talk a little more about it. I think I'm going to have some questions on this.'" He explains that even though he uses email as his first ICT, it doesn't eliminate the need for face-to-face conversations.

Elliott's redundant ICT use points up the fact that no single ICT is sufficient to communicate important or complex messages. ICTs well suited to communicate detail—e.g. email—don't necessarily communicate the priority level of the task. ICTs that communicate task priority—e.g. face-to-face—don't allow for detail and clear documentation. Elliott has learned to compensate for the disadvantages in each ICT by coupling ICTs to achieve his goals.

*The frequent use of ICTs.* Elliott uses ICTs frequently, almost addictively. He offers a snapshot of his daily routine.

> *Well, when I come in, in the morning, the first thing I do is I go to my Palm Pilot and I hit my to-do button. I go through it and I update everything that needs to be done today—urgent, not urgent—and I prioritize everything. Then*

*when I'm finished, I put this [my PDA] on the saddle, press this button, and it synchronizes my to-do list [with my computer contact list].*

*Elliott uses ICTs to gather data about his customers. This "helps you understand what questions you should ask and what questions you shouldn't ask."*

This ensures that his PDA and his laptop will be current when he leaves the office. After synchronizing his work tools, he checks his email: "I spend most of the day working on email because that is where you get a lot of your [new] things that you need to do." He receives emails from customers as well as colleagues inside his organization. Quite often these emails are so detailed that he can address an entire issue electronically. Elliott is proud that he uses the computer much more than paper. He even brags about sometimes having trouble locating a pen because so much of his work is computerized.

There are times when "computer communication," as Elliott calls it, is necessary: "I use email mainly for reporting, for communicating, specific requests that—well, it's not just only one [request], but many line-item requests. I look at email as really important for documentation purposes." For example, he may send an email to document a detailed customer problem that contains 10 or more to-do items.

Not only does he use email inside his organization, but customers also send him to-do lists by email. Often he'll forward these requests to others inside his organization:

*This morning…my customer sent me a list of three things that need to get done. They are pretty big items, so they are spelled out. The person that is going to be doing this work is out [of the office] in training, so I am going to forward it to him. And then I'll probably follow up with a phone call. I will forward the information with my instructions.*

This ease of forwarding information to the appropriate person is another key use of email. It allows for documentation, keeps all the involved parties informed, and saves time.

Another major part of Elliott's day is visiting customers on site. He takes his PDA with him everywhere because his laptop is often inconvenient: "Sometimes I'll take it [my laptop] to a customer site, but at ChipWare, for example, you have to check in the laptop at the security desk. It's such a pain that I just put my PDA in my pocket and take my [paper] notebook, write good notes down, and take them back to input the information." The laborious check-in process at the customer site involves pulling everything out of one's computer bag, turning on the computer, and letting security personnel verify that it is indeed a laptop computer and that no customer-confidential information is there. Despite this hassle, there are times when Elliott knows that a meeting will be note-taking intensive, so he'll endure the security check to save himself time during the subsequent meeting.

*ICTs facilitate customer information gathering.* As part of Elliott's sales efforts, he uses ICTs to help him learn more about his customers. The customer information "helps you understand what questions you should ask and what questions you shouldn't ask." And information is what he uses to frame his questions:

*I look at today as the Information Age. And if you don't have information, you're not going to be competitive. So if you have a lot of information today and the competitor does not have enough information, you're going to have a competitive advantage. I look at it more as "There is never too much." The more informed you are, the better position you're in for negotiation.*

He learns this information in several ways—by interacting with the marketing department, searching the Web himself, and using software to help him manage information. "Sometimes with an account," he says, "we want to find out about what product they're manufacturing and how strong they are in the marketplace." If the customer is well-established with SemiSales, Elliott knows much about their strengths and weaknesses. But with new customers or with established customers that change and move into new markets, he often needs to learn about both what is actually happening inside the customer organization and the market's perception of what is occurring. This information-gathering often happens face-to-face as Elliott and others in the sales organization meet with individuals in their customer organization. Elliott calls this the "old-fashioned way," but he says it usually works if he's trying to find out sensitive and subtle information.

For confidential or more speculative information, Elliott relies on his marketing department. The microchip producers, Elliott's customers, often decide to purchase new capital equipment when their stock prices are high. Market perceptions tend to drive many of these purchases. SemiSale's marketing department searches for the hints of these stock rises in press releases, technical papers describing core competencies, and market-research firms such as Data Quest or the Gartner Group. Not only do they look for chip producer account-specific information, but they find information on other chip producers, especially those that compete with one another. This information can reveal business potential since a competitor's actions often drive changes throughout the industry. Each day the marketing department combs these resources, and when they find something concerning Elliott's accounts, they send it to him. Much of this information is automatically distributed internally via email.

*These sales situations are often ethically complex. Elliott not only tries to gather as much information as possible about his potential clients but also control what information he gives out to customers.*

As he communicates with customers, one challenge for Elliott is deciding what information is public and what's private. Customers try to get information from their vendors, such as Elliott, that will give them a competitive advantage. Quite often they simply ask for industry information, or they might even suggest that if he wants their business, he needs to share some confidential information. Sometimes this information is about SemiSales or another of SemiSales' customers. These sales situations are often ethically complex. Elliott not only tries to gather as much information as possible about his potential clients but also control what information he gives out to customers.

*ICTs to improve future communication attempts.* While ICTs facilitate many communication activities within SemiSales, some areas inside the company have yet to be computerized. This makes for a lot of time-wasting communication, Elliott says, that ought to be automatic. He explains that automation through ICTs will "allow people to spend [more] time doing things they want to do." One challenge for salespeople, Elliott says, is that a customer views them as their problem-solver, regardless of the cause of the problem:

> *Typically, salespeople tend to be a contact person when the customer does not know who else to talk to. The salesperson is their problem-solver. So it is an opportunity for the salesperson to build a good relationship with the customer, solve his problem. And that's fine—that's a good opportunity for a salesperson. But when you get too much of that, it takes away from what the salesperson is really supposed to be doing—going out and getting new business and more market share.*

To streamline process, and ideally reduce such calls to the salesperson, SemiSales is now working to automatically identify and possibly repair equipment failures, Elliott says. "If there is a problem, a signal is sent to the engineer's desk. Maybe it is something where the engineer can send a command and the machine can fix itself." Since Elliott's customers can make money only when their chip-making equipment is running well, these automated trouble-shooting procedures are vitally important. Yet while this type of remote monitoring is common in other manufacturing industries, it is, curiously, still rare in the semiconductor market.

Besides using ICTs to spare the salesperson and handle hardware issues directly, Elliott envisions ICTs serving more of an e-commerce role as well. This might seem odd considering that the products he sells normally cost a million dollars per item and up, but he sees some opportunities to streamline sales processes. He believes that two areas can easily move to the Web: the purchase of replacement parts, and ordering duplicates of new equipment. Automating these processes, he says, would help make the salesperson's role more strategic and less tactical.

He also acknowledges that automation can affect jobs: "We wouldn't need as many sales specialists, but I think it would make the business more efficient." While this might be a new idea in the semiconductor market, other companies like Dell Computers, have devised entire business models around allowing their customers to "go direct" and use the Web for ordering. The big difference between Dell and SemiSales is that Elliott's typical sale is in the multi-million dollar range.

## Conclusion

In complex business relationships—often international—ICTs play a vital role that helps satisfy customers. Not only is it the salesperson's responsibility to meet with customers and take their orders, but customer satisfaction is often managed by the sales organization as well. With technical specialists spread throughout the world, salespeople use ICTs to connect ideas, solutions, and expertise with customers.

### Questions for Review or Discussion

1.  When using a combination of face-to-face and distance ICTs, what are the guiding principles? Do you want to use face-to-face more or less?

2.  Using the communication chart in this case as a guide, how complex is Elliott's communication environment as compared to the other cases in this book?

3.  What are the implications of inserting more ICTs—such as Web-based ordering—into the already complex communication web?

4.  A key part of structuration theory is managing time/space relations. What is the best example of this in Elliott's case?

5.  One of the claims made about ICTs and national culture is that ICTs perform a leveling function. Is that the situation in this case?

# Nothing Fishy Going on Here:
# Tracing the Quality of the Seafood Product

**26**

Jan-Oddvar Sørnes & Alf Steinar Sætre

In an ideal world, if you were to order some Norwegian salmon in an elegant Parisian restaurant and wanted assurance of its quality, the chef could produce for you its full pedigree—its age, provenance, nutritional value, when and where it was processed, and so forth. Polar Seafood, the second-largest fish-farming company in the world, aims to make this ideal an everyday reality. And it's experiencing considerable outside pressure to do so. Not only do its customers—restaurants, smoke houses, specialty stores—want this information, but so do regulatory agencies. Why? Mounting health concerns. Just as the beef industry has been periodically crippled by the Mad Cow Disease, the fish-farming industry has felt the effects of its own epidemics, caused by everything from algae attacks to ocean pollution. So it's essential that when an epidemic occurs, authorities can quickly determine its scope and trace the problem to its specific origin. This is known, in the trade, as "traceability." And solving the challenge of ensuring traceability at Polar Seafood falls squarely on the shoulders of a 32-year-old biologist named Arne Olsen. Arne is a slender, unassuming Norwegian whose personal ease and discipline match the story he tells in his interview.

## Fisheries: a Vital Part of Norway's Economy

Norway is a nation with a long fishing tradition, and next to the income generated from its vast fossil-fuel reserves, the fishing industry is its second largest source of income, hence an integral part of its economy. It's sure to remain so, too, especially after the fossil reserves get significantly depleted. As a result, Norway has from the mid-70's invested heavily, through seed-money and research programs, in growing its fish-farming industry to meet future demands. Due to this heavy investment, Norway is today one of the leading nations in fish-farming—a multi-billion dollar industry world-wide.

Polar Seafood, headquartered in a small coastal fishing community in northern Norway, just above the Arctic Circle, accounts for 10% of the world's annual production of farmed salmon, with production facilities scattered among four countries—Norway, Scotland, USA, and Chile. Its operation includes the production of eggs, brood, smolt/fry,[1] farmed fish, slaughtering, processing, selling, and marketing of Atlantic salmon.

*The fish-farming industry has traditionally employed a lot of manual labor.*

While off-shore fisheries in Norway employ state-of-the-art technology for all aspects of fishing, including navigation and fish-finding, the fish-farming industry has traditionally employed a lot of manual labor. This is changing, thanks to the introduction of advanced ICTs. So Polar Seafood finds itself in an epoch-making transition period. From his small Arctic office, lacking even a direct view of the ocean, Arne, the resident ICT expert, is helping to revamp conventional fish-farming practices for thousands of workers world-wide, most of whom spend their day on the ocean or at production facilities ashore.

While the industry is no doubt very prosperous, constant challenges confront Polar Seafood in its effort to stay ahead of the competition. Those challenges, which face its competitors as well, deal primarily with increased regulatory and policy issues, commercial pressures, and the implementation of state-of-the-art ICTs.

### The Regulatory Problem

*It's imperative that relevant information be collected at every stage so as to generate a traceable path of the history and the quality of the process, not just the end fish product.*

The fish-farming industry is confronting growing demands from regulatory authorities—both national and the European Union—for detailed information on the nature and origin of farmed fish products. To meet this demand, Polar Seafood has begun implementing a traceability system— a record-keeping procedure that shows the path of a particular batch of fish, from fish eggs to the dinner plate, through all the intermediate steps in the value chain. It's imperative that relevant information be collected at every stage so as to generate a traceable path of the history and the quality of the process, not just the end fish product. Traceability of all the steps in the value chain of such products has become not only a legal necessity but a commercial one as well.

### The Commercial Problem

Having accurate and timely information is particularly important when dealing with customers. For some, it's vital, and Arne mentions smokehouses and supermarkets as being especially fussy: "They are interested in all kinds of information about the quality of the smoked fish." Among Polar Seafood's most demanding customers is Worldfoods, which owns 25 supermarket chains around the world. Worldfood insists on having detailed documentation of production routines. For instance, Arne explains, "they like the ability to check the temperature [in the containers] of a certain transport phase as a measure of quality." Having fastidious customers like Worldfood actually helps Arne and his colleagues to stay

---

[1] Smolt/fry are young or newly hatched fish.

focused. For such customers, it is simply unacceptable to reply to a query, "We can get this information to you in two weeks."

While advanced ICTs have been indispensable in helping Polar meet both the commercial and regulatory challenges, just implementing state-of-the-art ICTs proved a challenge in itself. Let's look at that challenge now.

## The Technical Problem

Many technical and organizational obstacles must be overcome to meet these increasing demands. To enable traceability, which is vital for commercial and regulatory reasons, state-of-the-art ICTs are introduced to provide a more reliable system for ascertaining information about the production process. Until relatively recently, the methods for tracking products included simple hand-written labels, or labels printed by the production workers. Arne explains why that normally sufficed:

> Our fish-farming operations were small, family-owned companies with one or two licensed production facilities where everything was manageable. You had a Post-it® note which listed how much you had fed and how many [fish] had died, and that was really enough.

**Key Issue**

But the system was vulnerable to human error, "as it is easy to write 100 instead of 10, and 500 instead of 50." Arne says that such errors often occurred without much incident, "but if you do that often enough there will be big consequences." For the traceability system to work accurately, it must record the precise information through every stage in the value chain, which means that even the lowliest production workers must be absolutely responsible. To ensure that they are, training has become vital. Today, Arne explains, "the local caretakers at the productions facilities manage these systems, but there is a great inconsistency in both skill and ability." So Polar Seafood faces yet another problem: how to train their employees properly to handle the new ICTs?

*Today, Arne explains, "the local caretakers at the productions facilities manage these systems, but there is a great inconsistency in both skill and ability." So Polar Seafood faces yet another problem: how to train their employees properly to handle the new ICTs?*

Yet another problem facing Polar Seafood is that "70% of the technology is stand-alone solutions." In other words, the production workers at each facility must dial-up to a central computer in order to register feed, mortality, and treatment/vaccination of the fish. While this is very cumbersome, Arne admits, his real worry is about all the data that is registered and stored on the remote computers. Since these computers are not constantly online or networked with corporate headquarters, it's impossible to pull critical real-time information such as feeding, mortality, and other production-related information. So the problem with the existing method is the time-lag. Another problem is that "it is very costly to have a communication line open 24 hours a day to enable real-time monitoring." It is also an issue of information quality. Monitoring certain processes centrally has advantages in terms of quality control, but the more locations and people are involved, the greater the risk for human error. Currently, in some of the most remote facilities, like off the coast of Chile, this information is sent by regular mail on floppy disks! Arne's goal is to get most of the locations networked for real-time monitoring.

## Solutions

With support from the European Union and major research institutions in Norway, Arne and his colleagues are leading the way in implementing full traceability of the production processes through the entire value chain of their fish-farming operations. Arne explains that the three major concerns for all actors in the fish-farming industry are food safety, customer service, and the ability to stay competitive. For Polar Seafood, all three priorities have called for it to drastically restructure its organization. Arne has been a big part of that restructuring. He's responsible for integrating both existing and new ICTs into a fully networked, traceable-information system.

*The three major concerns for all actors in the fish-farming industry are food safety, customer service, and the ability to stay competitive.*

When designed correctly, a traceability system will provide:

1. Accurate identification of units/batches of all ingredients and products.

2. Information on when and where those units or batches are moved.

3. A system linking these data.

**Key Issue**
Traceability and the shift from push to pull ICTs.

At the heart of traceability is the shift from push to pull ICTs. As Arne explains, "Converting from push to pull information management entails a huge organizational shift for Polar Seafood." The push model automatically delivers data to the user based on some criterion, such as news, new products, price, subscription, etc., through technologies such as email. This contrasts with the pull model, in which the user specifically asks for something by performing a search or requesting an existing piece of information— on, for example, the Internet. When relating these concepts to the production process at Polar Seafood, the aim is slightly altered. Instead of transferring all the data to a central database at every stage in the production process (push), an information highway is created where transformation data[2] will "follow" the fish from beginning to end. As a result, every stage in the process is traceable, and information can be obtained at any time by anyone who has access to the data (pull). In a pull system, data is entered once and is "transformed" or updated at each point as it follows the batch from stage to stage. By looking at this transformation data, Arne explains, the customer will see the "family tree of the fish." This pedigree "shows where the fish has been." This gives Polar Seafood, as well as its customers, access to production data, whether "from only a single facility or all the facilities," Arne adds.

The traceability system enables both Polar Seafood and its customers to pull information at any stage, and it reduces the total amount of data and the time to

---

[2] Transformation data is entered at the first stage in the production process-the egg/brood stage-and follows the batch through its entire life-cycle.

produce it.[3] To the extent that customers recognize this increased product control, which is based on transformation data and the pull information system, it will create added value for Polar Seafood, and help it stay ahead of the competition. While their customers demand maximum traceability at all times, Arne's main goal is to ensure the "ability to trace things," which means that the necessary information must be available when required. Arne is, however, prepared for increasing demands, and explains that "if we are not able to provide full traceability, then we will become a B-level supplier." In other words, the technology for tracking becomes an integral part of the value of the product. Tracking the product and pulling information also meet the requirements of regulatory agencies.

*Once a mistake is discovered, they can find out within 30 minutes exactly where in the world those particular fish are-and recall only that batch.*

The advantage of the system is the ability to pull information in order to guarantee both food safety and increased effectiveness of recall and speed of information in the event of emergencies. For internal quality control, the transformational data is at the batch level, which is smaller than a production unit. There are typically about 10–15 batches, or fish cages, at each production unit. Having access to data at this level enables them to practice what they call "surgical removal." This has obvious advantages for customers as well. As Arne explains, if a batch of fish is "growing badly, we want to find out why." Once a mistake is discovered, they can find out within 30 minutes exactly where in the world those particular fish are—and recall only that batch. In the past, this was very expensive, as "an entire region was considered one batch," resulting in "recall of all the fish from the market." Arne hopes the system will give more control within the value chain, which should deliver safer food as well as better quality.

While state-of-the-art ICTs are vital to this revamping process, the need for a skilled workforce is equally important.

In order to achieve employee competence, Polar Seafood has formed a partnership with a local college and established the "Polar Seafood School." The intent there is to "run everybody through a basic ICT 101," Arne explains. While basic skills in ICT use are important, it's crucial that Polar Seafood's employees, both existing and new, understand the correct use of ICTs in relation to fish farming. Arne explains that it is important for the company to "create a much deeper understanding of using technology—not only to learn about the nuts and bolts, but to interpret the signals that are coming back from the technology in order to get a more optimal operation." Training of employees at Polar Seafood is important because they "have many people who are going to remain here, and if they don't reach the acceptable competence level that we need, then we will eventually lose the whole organization."

Besides needing to train existing employees, Polar Seafood wants of course to hire new people with the right qualifications. Arne expresses strong feelings about this issue: "I personally think that we need to begin to rewrite the position de-

---

[3] In the old system, data files were sent from stage to stage, but at each stage a new file was created in addition to the original files. This duplicated work and data in multiple files and created an enormous amount of data that was hard to track.

scriptions to obtain operations managers and middle managers with the necessary skills. After all, they manage values between 50-100 million (NOK)[4]." So while Polar Seafood now has an educational system in place, Arne says, "we have a long way to go when it comes to implementing the technology and getting the people with the right expertise in the right place." He explains that this same challenge faces the whole industry. At Polar Seafood they often get applications from exactly the type of people that they don't want to attract, such as "middle-aged men whose main skill is that they're very handy." So Polar Seafood now includes more detailed demands in the position descriptions, and targets people with a college background. This effort has paid off, Arne explains, as applicants now tend to be "young, creative, and with a biology background."

The process of training existing personnel and wanting to hire the best-qualified people in a changing industry is not that unusual, but at Polar Seafood it is not necessarily an uncontroversial process. "There are many small kings in a system like this," Arne says, smiling grimly, "and they are afraid to get expertise below them because they will be overtaken themselves." Arne is not surprised by this, as the company has undergone major changes in the past two to three years: "It has to do with the quick growth rate we have had. Last year [these people] worked in a little company, and suddenly they are a part of a worldwide international corporation. That transition is difficult." Consequently, Polar Seafood still has "a great number of the kind of people who think locally." The company has its subcultures, and they resist melding into a greater whole, Arne says: "Those who work in production have the clear impression that they are to produce fish. So all the things that go via ICTs are interfering elements that are forced on them as an extra burden." Granted, Arne says, there are no shortcuts for establishing common ground within the company, but the workers "should be educated to realize that they are a part of a large organization."

*"There are many small kings in a system like this."*

### The Value of Automating the Production Process

The change from manual labor to automated production processes at Polar Seafood has seemingly occurred almost overnight. The use of yellow Post-it® notes for record-keeping is now passé, and is being replaced by electronic tags (bar codes and radio frequency tags).

At a production facility yielding some 1,000-2000 metric tons[5] of fish per year, a lot of feed is needed. For an operation of this magnitude, Arne explains, "you need to have control of all the parameters." Until just a few years ago, before the feeding process was automated, "it was normal to stand there with buckets and spades and toss out the feed because there was enough capacity to do that." Back then, tracking the amount of feed manually was a manageable task. Today, however, "there are just two men who operate a facility, and automation is imperative, as they need to distribute three to four tons of feed per day." With feed being expensive (it constitutes 50% of

*The use of yellow Post-it® notes for record-keeping is now passé.*

---

[4] On currency exchanges, the two first letters denote the country and the last letter the name of the currency. In this case Norwegian Kroner (Crowns).
[5] One metric ton equals 2,204.6 Pounds

the total production costs), waste control becomes an issue. They'll confront questions like: What percentage of the feed is consumed by fish? How much is wasted? Arne says there are several ways of monitoring waste. Cameras are one way. So are electronic aids such as Doppler radar, which registers excess feed sinking towards the Doppler placed beneath each fish cage. Using this input, the technology can automatically adjust the speed of the feeding process.

To meet sudden changes in customer demands, Polar Seafood needs to know just how much fish it has in each of the various stages in the production process. For the sales department, such information is valuable because "they can sell fish of a known quality and quantity even before it is slaughtered." All of these processes are automated, Arne says, including the one calculating the weight/size registration of the fish: "We place a frame down in the water [in the fish cages] that the fish swim through and which registers the size, so that the whole time you know the development of the average weight and the weight breakdown." Having access to such detailed information is not only advantageous to Polar Seafood's customers but also to the company itself in maintaining an advantage over its competitors, who may not be able to offer such predictability.

*Even the most fundamental traceability information has considerable commercial value.*

## The Doubled-Edged Sword of Traceable Information

As mentioned, there is increasing commercial pressure from customers and food-safety regulators alike to disclose more and more information about products and production processes. But since such information has great value for its competitors, Polar Seafood has chosen not to make all their traceability information public. This is important, Arne explains, since "Polar Seafood has suppliers that our competitors also use." Even the most fundamental traceability information has considerable commercial value, since open access to it would reveal a firm's suppliers, markets, and trading patterns. So Polar Seafood needs to safeguard its ownership of this information and control the access to it. "We are going to differentiate the customers by giving them level-dependent access," Arne says. This means that everybody logging on to the Polar Seafood Website will be able to see a graphical display of the production process, and will receive the most basic information by "entering the batch-number on the fish package they have purchased." Then the system will run every "customer through a filter that results in them getting access to the information pertaining to their particular purchase." The information dealing with more intricate details in the production process will not be available at this level to individual customers. Customers needing more detailed information will be given access, while "other producers of salmon are not going to get into the system at all." The consequences for Polar Seafood could be serious if competitors got access to intricate details about production processes.

## Conclusion

As this case shows there is decisive value in information. Polar Seafood's ability to document every stage in the production process of salmon greatly augments its perceived quality and hence its value. The move from push to pull information systems has enabled the movement in this direction without choking the company with information overload. This change has offered technological as well as organizational challenges for Polar Seafood.

## Questions for Review or Discussion

1. What are the implications of using the Web to make quality-information public?

2. Using Garbage Can Theory, to what problem is traceability a solution? How are participants and choice opportunities involved?

3. What's the value of having more information about products easily available to consumers?

4. Is it fair for Polar Seafood to require workers to learn new skills, and to discard some of the very workers who built the company?

5. What is the difference between the credibility of a person and that of a company when communicating safety information?

# From Information to Emotion: The Changing Use of ICTs Following the 9/11 Tragedy

**27**

Larry D. Browning & Alf Steinar Sætre

Barbara works for "StrategyFirst," a renowned consulting firm in international technology and strategy that serves CEOs exclusively. One of her jobs is to write technical articles for the firm's Internet newsletter. Another, more all-encompassing job is to do information searches on the Internet that produce the content for these articles as well as providing the technical knowledge for her firm's front-line consultants, who bill their corporate clients directly. Barbara is a specialist in broad-band technology. This case shows both her use of ICTs for StrategyFirst and how she uses them in her own sideline business in real estate. The final section of the case shows how Barbara, who happened to be in New York City when the 9/11 attack occurred, used ICTs to contact and support friends who were affected by the disaster.

## The Case

Barbara has a Ph.D. in communication from an American university and is an expert in information technology. A born teacher, she also has a knack for articulating highly complex ideas in simple terms. Her focus over the last 20 years has been on predicting the use and value of global information and communication technology, with an emphasis on how different technologies, like those for the PC and TV, are integrated into a single information program. At StrategyFirst she offers expert knowledge about consumers using broadband communication, primarily in the home.

Though an expert in implementing new office technologies, Barbara continues to be amazed at (1) how much executives and consultants depend on original data sources for their decision-making, (2) how little their information searches have reduced the risk of that decision-making, and (3) the old-fashioned way that many older diehards still use for getting their information. Some executives continue to get new information primarily from peers, often another CEO or CFO from some other company, and frequently in an informal setting—during a round of golf, for instance. For corroborating details, the peer might then recommend a

Website or some other electronic information source. But in-person, face-to-face contact remains their prime way of getting information. One reason for this otherwise inefficient means of communication is that it makes the whole process of information acquisition less public, thereby reducing the threat of potentially embarrassing exposure for any executive who may still be learning about basic features of the problem or the technology.

## StrategyFirst's Work Culture

Many business consulting firms offer their prospective clients a contract specifying the work to be done and the estimated cost for each portion of it. Not so with StrategyFirst, which mimics law firms that bill clients by the hour—indeed, by one-tenth increments of an hour. Another noteworthy feature of StrategyFirst's work practice is its continuing dependence on the telephone as its primary way of providing high-level information to the client. This practice may reflect, in part, the fact that StrategyFirst began back in the 1920s, when the telephone suddenly became the high-tech business tool of its day. Since telephone discussions are crucial to their business, StrategyFirst provides its new consultants with informal guidance in how to be successful with this medium, but most of their success will rest on their persuasive skills in convincing a client to follow a recommended strategy. The telephone conversation supports the original trilogy of consulting: (1) develop useful information, (2) help the client decide what to do with that information, and (3) coach the client to remain committed to the plan once implementation has begun.

*Another noteworthy feature of StrategyFirst's work practice is its continuing dependence on the telephone as its primary way of providing high-level information to the client.*

## Barbara's Role in StrategyFirst

Barbara's role is both to discover position papers on the Internet and write them for publication on the company's own Website.

She works on teams of information-collection and decision-making about different parts of messages designed for clients. She has almost no client contact herself; instead, she is a consultant to StrategyFirst's consultants, and will spend perhaps 10 to 50 hours on an "understanding" (the firm's term for a working agreement with a client). To provide this support, she will have a conference call "maybe three times a week, often at six o'clock in the morning because I'm working with Europeans." The consultant's time on a customer's project might be ten times hers. While her time is billed to the client as expert advice supporting the business advice provided, she herself remains in the background. She also works with consultants when they themselves are doing research and sometimes puts their name at the top of publications for which she did much of the research and writing. As with any consultant, she wants to make her client look good, and her client is the StrategyFirst consultant who is working for the external client who is ultimately paying the bill. She is comfortable with this backseat role; if her client looks good to the external client, a fair kind of social exchange has taken place.

"There's a pretty organized way of doing assessments at Strategy-First," she says. "They're done twice a year. Messages are sent out to the people with whom I've worked. They're asked what impact I had—what were the positive and negative issues involved."

## Barbara's Use of the Internet

Her favorite search engine is Google because it helps her gauge the popularity of any given site—an important fact in legitimizing the information she provides for decision-making. "Google looks at how many times a Website is accessed," she says. "And so you always come up with the most used sites, which are usually the most useful sites." Since Google makes its searches from a vast database, part of Barbara's expertise rests in knowing what technical terms to plug in that will allow her to find useful information.

Despite her history with the ICT industry, Barbara continues to be amazed not only at the staggering amount of information available but how frequently older executives, some of whom had never allowed a typewriter on their desk, will use ICT information. Some diehards won't, of course. "But today there are very few of those old types," Barbara says. "They're just in pockets."

So for Barbara, the sheer amount of information, not the interpretation of it, is the most surprising feature of the ICT environment she serves. "If it weren't for Google," she says, "someone could just call and ask me for something and I would have to respond out of my background. Nowadays I'm never quite sure. Is my background really current? You know, what am I missing?" This comment suggests that while Barbara was once an "expert" who provided factual information, she now knows she has to regularly double check her facts to ensure that she's still up to date. And she also finds herself updating related knowledge during these double checks for accuracy. Even as a seasoned veteran in the world of ICTs, she is astonished at how accessible information is on the Internet and how valuable it is:

> So it's a matter of being able to go into this amazing world of information and find so much more than I would have ever dreamed, really. I mean, even though I knew that someday this would, quote, "happen"—you know, everything would be online and would be accessible—I really didn't understand how. And I didn't appreciate how powerful it would be.

A key finding of our study applies here. One of the most important uses of the Internet is to search for facts—especially facts that are so credible to an expert user that they will view the study as "ethical" (that is, trustworthy). Barbara's case illustrates the ethical theme. While the ethicality of any information is important, it is fairly easily determined. For Barbara, the most popular sources of the information are the most credible ones. In the democracy of information search, anyone can go anywhere to verify informa-

**Key Issue**
*As with any consultant, she wants to make her client look good, and her client is the Strategy-First consultant who is working for the external client who is ultimately paying the bill.*

*"Is my background really current? You know, what am I missing?"*

**Key Issue**
*For Barbara, the most popular sources of the information are the most credible ones.*

tion, so there is a larger system of selectivity and competence operating here; the most used way is usually the most correct way.

### Barbara's Private Business and Social Use of ICTs

As a sideline, Barbara buys and refurbishes cottages on the Texas coast. One of her favorite uses of the Internet is discovering information on the area's weather history. She and her husband, an equally adroit techie, have found a prodigious amount of detail on the impact of the last hurricane there and what building standards were necessary to respond to weather it. She says, "They are sending us the CD-ROM with all of this data and a really detailed analysis of the impact of the beach renourishment there. Well, that just wouldn't have been cost-effective before IT. It's not that these things weren't possible, but it's really brought the power of that."

She also tracks the effect of ICTs outside formal organizations and has noticed the surprising depth of relationships that people have achieved through their informal networks:

> Outside of organizations, the extent to which people carry on their personal relationships, their not-so-personal relationships, and their spirituality electronically—well, it just blows my mind. It's so amazing, so astounding. And I think part of it is just the convenience of broadband. I imagine a lot of it is driven by kids at the computer, and when you have broadband, you don't have to tell the kids to get off.

Barbara's remark shows how the power of the technology is a function of its availability. Broadband makes for a democratic technology.

One of Barbara's examples of how ICTs are affecting personal relationships is how she managed to connect with her high-school graduating class, which she had heard was planning a reunion. A particularly precocious student, she had graduated a year early, in 1965, "so it's always been hard for them to find me, and so I've missed a few reunions with my moving around. But they found me, and I found them. With Yahoo, there's this site you can go to to find your graduating class. I was astounded to track down over 250 people out of my class actively involved in a reunion in our Website. That was 250 out of 600. And it's grown since then. We're now up to about 400 on the Web now. I mean, this is Louisiana—not very wealthy Louisiana, right?" Barbara mentions the "wealth" of her home state because Internet use is less popular there than in more wealthy urban centers.

*She also tracks the effect of ICTs outside formal organizations and has noticed the surprising depth of relationships that people have achieved through their informal networks.*

### Barbara in New York City After 9/11

Her attention to these and other relationships has been heightened by the 9/11 disaster. She recalls:

> I was in New York City and it was clear that they were closing down the

*telecommunications, because if there were terrorists in the city they wanted to disrupt communications. So it was very hard to get through for a while—for the first 24, 48 hours.*

Telecommunications increased in the following week, with people not only able to reach out via ICTs but feeling a still-urgent need to. She says, "In the weeks after that I just got a lot more personal communications from people that I would not have gotten, and I sent a lot more." This use of ICTs created for Barbara a "bigger sense of community after September 11."

Because 9/11 had such an impact on New York and Boston, the impact there felt like a "cancer" because, as she put it, there is "only one degree of separation between you and somebody who lost somebody." That is, just about everyone knew someone who'd lost someone in the World Trade Center or at the Pentagon. Since she works in the community around New York and Boston, she automatically began any phone conversation or email after 9/11 acknowledging the possibility that the recipient had lost someone in the disaster. So just to acknowledge that the person might be dealing with that loss, she'd begin emails with "I hope your friends and family are OK. If you don't want to get back to me, either don't do it or tell me." Her intent was to give people the permission to either ignore her or to let her know when they'd get back to her. The words of support were not necessarily long or elaborate, but would usually contain a note of acknowledgment: "I would just say I find in my own messages and in other messages they're more likely to have some personal comments. 'I hope you're OK. I hope, you know, the people you love are OK.' There is a partner's brother-in-law here who's never been found." Some messages were simply never returned.

*Her attention to these and other relationships has been heightened by the 9/11 disaster.*

Given that the Internet was shut down for the first day following 9/11, Barbara kept in touch as best she could. The television proved invaluable: "This television thing has really had a big impact because it was just something—television was good. I did nothing for three days except watch television, because it was like my connection to the world. I didn't even want to talk to other people. I had lots of friends in New York, but I didn't call them. I just went to a little hotel room, the smaller the better. I had my television. I was by myself."

*"I hope your friends and family are OK. If you don't want to get back to me, either don't do it or tell me."*

This interview was completed six months after 9/11, and Barbara worries that the feelings and consciousness that surrounded 9/11 have slipped away very quickly. She laments, "We're losing that sense of spirituality. That's why I'm going to New York for Ash Wednesday, because I don't want to forget it. I want it to stay with me." She thinks the disaster holds lessons for us and worries that they will not stick. "I think the president wants people to get back to normal and start spending money and things like that," she says. "I don't know anyone who really wants to get back to normal."

*"I had lots of friends in New York, but I didn't call them. I just went to a little hotel room, the smaller the better."*

She also thinks the disaster could have had an even greater impact if the stock market decline and the 9/11 disaster had occurred closer in time to each other: "If the stock market had really crashed then, we could now be in a true depression, right? It would've happened much more precipitously instead of just being a kind of blip. So that could've been worse."

There was a complete standstill in business activity for three days, and even after that people began communicating very slowly. Her sense of herself was that she was a "non-functioning human being. I was just a ball of useless carbon. Just totally useless." She notes that the brusque city of New York has turned up a sensitive side: "I've been to New York almost every week since two weeks after. And people are definitely nicer. Things are definitely different."

*"If the stock market had really crashed then, we could now be in a true depression, right?"*

She sees 9/11 as carrying a bleak message: "Get used to this—this is the world." And her answer to this is that Americans need to learn more about their enemies: "See how much we've learned about Afghanistan? We have no reason to know anything about that part of the world. Nothing. No personal relationship to us. And then, all of a sudden, we have a very personal relationship." Barbara talks philosophically about our need to learn about the world and our willingness to do so:

> You know, the book sales! Oh my God, that's what I love about America: when confronted with a challenge we'll buy books and start reading and become informed and change our discourse. So, on balance, I think that it's going to be really good for us in the same way that Pearl Harbor was. The size of the devastation may be at least a fraction of what it might've been if it had been a biological attack or something like that, had it been more systematic. So while they were successful in making a symbolic hit, they weren't that successful in making a substantial hit.

A significant thing for Barbara is how vital ICTs have become: "It's been a big difference, and I think the Internet is even more important to people. It's a way of making connections that you just couldn't do otherwise. Other ways are just not efficient, but the Internet allows you to connect easily."

## Barbara in New York City After 9/11

Barbara's case shows how research from Web sources are used to legitimize executive decisions. It also demonstrates how technical specialists like herself add value to professional reports headed by front line consultants of the firm. Her case also shows the integration of personal and professional life at a moment of catastrophe.

## Questions for Review or Discussion

1.  What are the possible outcomes of communicating with clients only over the telephone?

2.  How did the 9/11 tragedy influence the way people communicate, including their ICT use?

3.  When workers are dispersed, what does this case suggest as a way to evaluate their performances?

4.  In what way does Barbara use ICTs to enhance her professional credibility?

5.  How has Barbara adapted her ICT use to match the culture of her organization?

# Give Me a Cellphone and I'll Give You Trouble: Technology Usage in a Young Start-Up

## 28

Alf Steinar Sætre & Jan-Oddvar Sørnes

Until recently, our workplace and home were kept rigidly separated. When we were "in the office," we were working; when we went home, we were strictly on our own time. But this is changing. A lot of us now have access to business-related ICTs at home, so today it's not uncommon for high-level professionals to work each evening at their home computer. Another thing that's driving the change is that intense competition has radically shortened many products' life-cycles. And this in turn has merely intensified the competition. One result of this high-velocity environment is that it puts companies in an almost perpetual crisis mode. What are they to do, then, when emergencies require the expertise of key employees who are off work? This is the story of how a young Norwegian high-tech company has tried to address just that challenge. It's a story about the use, and possible abuse, of ICTs.

*Until recently, our workplace and home were kept rigidly separated. When we were "in the office," we were working; when we went home, we were strictly on our own time.*

Portfolio Solutions provides large corporations with knowledge-management software. Portfolio was started in the spring of 2000 by three students at the Norwegian University of Science and Technology (NTNU) in Trondheim, Norway. One of the co-founders is Kjell Madsen, a 26-year-old civil engineering student in theoretical physics at NTNU. Though still an inexperienced manager, he appears both introspective and precocious. Like many entrepreneurs, he started his firm before finishing his university degree. The company chiefly employs fellow students of his—technology-oriented whizzes, all equipped with the latest and greatest information-and-communication technology.

Because Portfolio was founded just before the end of the dotcom heyday, it enjoyed easy access to capital, allowing it to grow rapidly. But within a year the dotcom bubble burst, and Portfolio got "the recent developments in the IT business straight in the face, as have most," Kjell ruefully recalls. "From 30 employees we are now down to 10." Their prospects are brightening, though. Portfolio has won two large contracts with important clients, so its workload is actually higher than ever.

Portfolio Solutions' chief product is a software tool for developing and managing human competencies in large corporations. According to Kjell, the product "has its basis in the so-called 'people-centric solution.'" Using Portfolio's products, employees get tools to document and visualize their professional competencies, making it easier for them to get matched to the right position. It's quite common, of course, for large organizations to have employees keep their competency profiles up-to-date so that new projects can be matched with employees' special interests and skills, and vice versa. But the tool provided by Portfolio facilitates this whole match-up process, and Kjell contends this "gives value-added for the company" by enhancing the company's "internal marketplaces for positions and projects."

When an organization anticipates needing certain skill-sets that it currently lacks, it will often buy training courses from external vendors, like Portfolio, that allow employees to augment their personal competencies while also allowing the organization to expand its pool of human resources. Portfolio specializes in this area. It offers various training modules that together form an integrated, seamless whole. One tool provides for performance-appraisal conversations between a leader and an associate. Another tool provides a systematic three-way evaluation of leaders—something known in the trade as a "360-degree evaluation." Leaders get evaluated from the perspective of those who work for them, from the perspective of their peers, and from the perspective of their own boss. These elements become part of a person's profile, Kjell says; the organization then uses this information to map competencies and make development plans for individual employees.

*All employees should have a tool for continually documenting their own competencies in a life-long learning perspective and have the opportunity to actively develop their own career.*

According to Kjell, Portfolio assumes that all employees should "have a tool for continually documenting their own competencies in a life-long learning perspective and have the opportunity to actively develop their own career." Because it's clearly in their self-interest to do so, employees have a big incentive to update the information on themselves. And the benefit extends beyond their current organization, since each update generates an electronic résumé that records their personal experience and skill-development. So both the individual employees and the employer get a better overview of employee competencies. Portfolio sees its product as a great way to integrate individual and organizational needs.

Let's now look at how this high-tech, ICT-intensive company uses its ICTs.

## Using Email and the Internet Productively

Portfolio's employees use all communication channels available to them. Email, especially, plays an important role there. Because it is both asynchronous and still fairly immediate, email helps keep the communication lines open once a client relationship has been established. One advantage of email, Kjell says, is that the Forwarding and Reply functions can provide a log of the electronic conversation, so any newcomers to a task are more easily brought up to speed. Furthermore, with email "you have a tendency to think things through," he says, whereas communicating by phone will sometimes tempt you to "talk faster than you think." So when Kjell desires preciseness, he prefers to write an email; he knows he'll have to carefully think about what he really aims to achieve with that message.

Besides using email to communicate with clients, Portfolio increasingly uses email internally. For example, when someone has been working with a client to set the specifications of a particular module, these specs are no longer allowed to be transmitted orally. As Kjell admits, "We have burned ourselves many times. The message either wasn't received or was misunderstood." Whenever important information arrives from the client via email, that same email gets forwarded to everyone involved in the project "so that it is traceable afterwards," Kjell says. No longer can anyone say "We didn't know that" or "We misunderstood."

Portfolio's use of email to document product requirements came about, Kjell says, because the young firm had seen "lots of quarrels" about who was responsible for mistakes that occurred. These quarrels would often get quite heated, "with dirt-throwing and accusations of various sorts" of what had gone wrong and who was at fault. Using email for documentation helps Portfolio avoid squandering precious time and goodwill on fruitless quarrels.

The company also relies heavily on the Internet to learn crucial information about potential clients, and also to keep up with current terminology. As we'll see, this information helps Portfolio know how best to approach a potential client.

Kjell frequently needs specific financial information about potential clients. He gets this data by going to Brønnøysundsregistrene (www.brreg.no). The Brønnøysund Register Center, which consists of several different national electronic databases, is Norway's central register authority and source of information. Here Kjell can obtain financial information such as a company's turnover, profits, and corporate officers. This information proves crucial when he's preparing a strategy for approaching potential clients.

In the human-resource and knowledge-management software business, the style of presentation—how you say it—can be as important as the substance. When asked to what extent Portfolio uses the Internet to search for information for product development, Kjell replies, "The most important contribution of the Internet to our organization is a high consciousness around—what shall I call it?—the jargon that is used within the 'competency' world." He smiles broadly, then adds that if you visit the home pages of Accenture or other large competitors, "you can adopt a terminology that is needed to communicate in the same language to a market." He maintains that a continual update is important because it is a terminology "in constant development." He even admits, "Often it is as much about finding [fancy] new terms as inventing new technology."

Besides monitoring the terms that are used by most important consultants in his industry, Kjell also monitors potential clients' Webpages to see which of the major consulting firms have consulted with them. Kjell indicates that he can

**Key Issue**

*Portfolio increasingly uses email internally. For example, when someone has been working with a client to set the specifications of a particular module, these specs are no longer allowed to be transmitted orally.*

pretty much tell inductively which consultants have been working for a given company: "You can often see much of what is done in a company—in particular, the large companies—by going in and just reading what is there. What is the focus? What words are they using?" The demands for understanding and adopting these terms seem to be fairly high. He likens these consultants to a school of fish, saying they "have an extremely well-developed ability to all turn in the same direction, and do that very quickly!" He regularly monitors both the Webpages of large corporations in Norway and the home pages of the consultant companies "that are supplying much of the premises for the terminology." Kjell may find new terminology on the Internet but it is confirmed in face-to-face meetings.

*He likens these consultants to a school of fish, saying they "have an extremely well-developed ability to all turn in the same direction, and do that very quickly!"*

The founding partners of Portfolio then use this information about clients—financial data, a list of officers, preferred buzz words, and so on—to formulate a strategy for how to approach that client: "We are very conscious when we approach, for example, Statoil, Telenor, or Hydro, or other large companies, that we must have a sizeable client plan." They need to know who the real decision-makers are and be able to "relate to the decision structures that are already in place" so that they can attack from "a position of knowledge rather than ignorance." Kjell spells out that it is important to know "something about the currents in the company, what strategy they have, for example, in the competency area. Does the technology correspond to the approach to the problem formulated in that strategy? If it does not, then we have to re-evaluate or sell them another packaging."

In sum, Kjell and his partners use all this information to evaluate the potential client and to devise a strategy, or "angle of attack," that they deem best tailored to that particular client. But they were not always so mindful of the use of communication technologies, and this had some unintended consequences.

### The Unintended Consequences of ICT Use

Because this is a start-up company, created by students, who then began employing other students nearly their own age, everyone at Portfolio has been simultaneously discovering how to be a company. The founders had no managerial experience, and the employees had virtually no work experience, yet the pressures to become quickly productive became intense. One of Portfolio's survival tactics was to develop ways to expand their access to their employees' abilities. So, for example, Portfolio provided each employee a high-end cellphone, hoping thereby to put its employees constantly on call. Kjell says, "Our motivation for giving employees cellphones is that we have a crystal-clear policy: when the cellphone is on, we can call them anytime, day or night." The policy worked, but it also created a new and perhaps bigger problem: it blurred any boundary between the public and private domains. In accepting the gift of the fancy cellphone, employees had also implicitly accepted a contract of availability.

**Key Issue**

*The founders had no managerial experience, and the employees had virtually no work experience, yet the pressures to become quickly productive became intense.*

The agreement between the company and the employees, Kjell says, is stunningly simple, seductive, and absolute: "Yes, you can call your friends on the company cellphone, but as long as your cellphone is on, you are available to us." Portfolio especially needed to increase the availability of its programmers. The cellphone arrangement gives Portfolio and its employees what Kjell terms "a mutual flexibility." He illustrates: "For example, if we have problems with a program and need one of the programmers, we call the number, and if the cellphone is on—which it often is if you use the number for all your friends as well—then we reach the person." Being able to reach the person who actually wrote the particular component of a problematic code is obviously much more efficient than having a new programmer sit down and look through the massive amount of code in search of an error.

The employees of Portfolio are primarily students who, being technology-oriented, are "relatively active users of both the Internet and SMS[1] and messenger and that kind of chat," Kjell says. This kind of communication technology can be a great aid in doing and coordinating work, but it can also become a distraction that impedes performance. The use, and abuse, of these communication technologies "interrupts the workday for people who sit and program relatively complex code." When they are "interrupted every 15 minutes by an incoming email or SMS, it has some consequences for how effective" they are, Kjell says. In fact, he says there's an "incredible amount of hours" wasted on messenger and SMS every week at Portfolio. This concerns him for two reasons. First, when such "intrusive" and "interruptive" communication is basically social (i.e., for keeping up with friends), then the communication is unproductive, at least as far as Portfolio is concerned. Second, even if such communication is job-related—which frequently it isn't at Portfolio—it interrupts the flow of work and therefore further reduces productivity.

One way that Kjell addressed the problem was to intervene directly when he saw excessive interruptions occur in their open office. He recalls: "We had a graphic designer that worked for us and sat behind me. As a graphic designer you primarily use the mouse when you sit and draw things." This graphic designer was an avid user of messenger, "and at regular intervals I hear her typing infernally—and then we are talking every 30 seconds on some days—then some movement on the mouse, and then back to the keyboard again." Kjell knew, based on what she was supposed to do, that her work should not include large amounts of text. By closely monitoring the sound coming from her desk, he soon realized that she could not possibly be very productive. Not only did these constant interruptions consume time and disrupt her work process, but they also led her machine to crash quite frequently when she was chatting on messenger. Kjell finally told her, " 'Now you have to cut it out.' She didn't talk to me for a few days, but she stopped doing it." Kjell realized, however, that he was not going to be able to monitor and comment on everyone's use of these ICTs.

> **Key Issue** ⊕
>
> *This kind of communication technology can be a great aid in doing and coordinating work, but it can also become a distraction that impedes performance.*

> *When they are interrupted every 15 minutes by an incoming email or SMS, it has some consequences for how effective they are.*

---

[1] SMS (short message service) is a text-messaging system used on cellphones.

Kjell and Portfolio are now addressing this issue with a new policy. It asks people to close "email applications for periods of the day, instead of having a 'pling' every time an email comes in." He feels that getting rid of this distraction will improve the productivity at Portfolio. He also acknowledges that "email should be the least problematic since it is asynchronous." But because everyone uses email and tends to answer messages throughout the day, it still interrupts work. As people fail to take advantage of email's asynchronicity and continuously respond, email becomes a distraction as well. Kjell states that even he will get "about 30-40 emails per day on some days." If you fall for the temptation of responding to all your emails as you receive them, "then you are down to relatively short periods of effective work." And if you also have a fair amount of SMS messages and messenger chatting on top of this, the problem can become acute.

*A new company policy now asks people to close email applications for periods of the day.*

## Communication Technologies in the Public and Private Domain

Internet-based communications, such as email and messenger, have not been the only disruptive technologies at Portfolio. Text messaging via cellular phones (SMS) has also become commonplace. SMS adds yet another level of convenience because people can send messages even when they are away from their desk and on the move. Because Kjell gets the bills for the company's cellphone use, he can easily monitor how much is spent on SMS versus on actual telephone calls. The problem, he says, is staggering: "We have employees who'll send 1,000 text messages a month on company cellphones!" Consider what all this means, he says. When sending SMS messages, you must use the phone keypad to type in letters, so "it takes time to send 1,000 text messages." And with the cost running at 60-70 øre (about 10 cents) per message, the aggregate cost of those 1,000 messages is considerable. But it doesn't stop there, Kjell says. If a person sends 1,000 SMS messages, then he or she will probably receive an equal number in return. One thousand SMS messages a month works out to roughly 35 messages a day. Figuring two minutes per message, all this adds up to just over an hour a day of using the cellphone keypad. Little wonder that Kjell is concerned if worktime is being squandered and if ICTs are an aid or a distraction!

**Key Issue**

*Email and messenger have not been the only disruptive technologies at Portfolio. Text messaging via cellular phones (SMS) has also become commonplace.*

A possible explanation for the "unproductive" use of ICTs at Portfolio is the youth and inexperience of employees and managers alike. Even when it had over 30 employees, their average age was about 25. While the company had planned to take advantage of these new ICTs, it was unprepared for the misuse that quickly appeared. "Many of these people had never been in a corporate setting before," Kjell recalls, so they "felt no responsibility to uphold some routines, no responsibility that the time spent was actually not their own." These individuals were still students, both literally and attitudinally. And some of them never managed to make the shift—or leap, if you will—from being a student to becoming an employee. As Kjell puts it, "The distinction between an 'every day' as a student and an 'every day' as an employee remained very blurred for some people." At Portfolio these new communication technologies became more of a nuisance than a productive aid, Kjell says, because people tended to "move the social sphere into work, in a situation where they have clearly defined deadlines and tasks."

After working at building Portfolio's business for over two years, Kjell sees the drawbacks of being constantly "wired" to communication technologies. "To be online is cool for a while," he says, "but when one has a lot to do, then technology becomes very tiring." As a result of this, "most of us try to show much greater respect for other people's time off than we did before—in spite of the cellphone policy that we have." In other words, the policy remains in place, but they have raised the threshold for invoking it.

*While the company had planned to take advantage of these new ICTs, it was unprepared for the misuse that quickly appeared.*

Given the incessant deadlines and the huge effort that goes into establishing a start-up, when someone finally gets some time off work, Portfolio now shows a greater respect for employees' privacy. The employees themselves do as well. Kjell will even "turn the phone off for a whole day." And when at work they are all now trying to spend more time "off-line" from ICTs in order to get more work done. The goal is to find the right balance. Although ICTs at Portfolio have shown their potential for being seriously disruptive, these same technologies—especially email and the Internet—are also enormously useful and productive, when used appropriately.

## Conclusion

Information and communication technologies are not inherently productive or disruptive; instead their use determines their productivity. When Portfolio tried to extend its corporate "domain" into the domain of employees' previously private lives, it quickly discovered that this boundary is permeable in both directions. Just as employees took their work with them into their private life, they very easily brought their private and social life to work.[2] Soon the infringement of its young employees' social life subverted rather than enhanced Portfolio's productivity. Kjell and Portfolio quickly recognized the need to be more mindful of how to use these technologies.

---

[2] We are not implying a direct causality here, since the blurring of the "boundary" between one's private life and one's work probably has multiple causes.

**Questions for Review or Discussion**

1. What freedoms do you gain and lose with mobile technologies?

2. If you are doing good work, does a company have a right to know where you are doing it?

3. Here's a young company with young leaders. How would they have behaved differently if they were five years older, with another five years' experience?

4. Two features of structuration theory are rules and resources. Please map the rules and resources surrounding the issues in this case.

5. How did the leaders of Portfolio enact their own media and work environments?

# Information Will Get You to Heaven

**29**

Keri K. Stephens & Larry D. Browning

In the constant quest for intellectual capital, we often forget that knowledge is a valuable asset even outside of government and business. In a small town, this asset is often called "history" and it suffers from many of the same challenges as those confronting the typical organization. Some of this information is confidential, hurtful, and even the source of legal battles. But it is also valued since it links the community's past with the present and future. The challenge is how best to collect and organize it when it is scattered and when the sources have dubious credibility.

In this narrative you will meet Reverend Harrison, a Protestant preacher in a close-knit community who has earned a reputation as the town historian. Like many ministers Rev. Harrison's "on-button" became stuck at an early age and he has not stopped talking since. Yet, his knowledge and charming demeanor make him a captivating speaker. Despite the fact that broadband is not even available in his town and his Internet connection is very slow, he uses ICTs in creative and expert ways.

*How do you get to heaven?*
*Information is the answer.*

You might imagine that if you ask a small-town preacher how to get to heaven he would reply, "Go to church every Sunday, tithe, and help others less fortunate." You might even expect him to recruit you to attend his next sermon, confess your sins, and ask for forgiveness. But Rev. Harrison has a different answer. He claims that information is the key to heaven, and he is doing everything in his power to capture it. In the pages that follow you will learn how Rev. Harrison has become the local historian in five short years, thanks to his phenomenal energy, devotion to accuracy, and the Internet. In the process he has earned the respect of the town leaders, even those who don't attend his church.

## Banned From Pursuing His Own Family Genealogy

Rev. Harrison developed an interest in his family genealogy about 10 years ago when he began piecing together information from relatives. But five years later he stumbled on a Website that carried some misinformation about his family. He recalls:

*I know that there was some [erroneous] stuff put up on my grandmother's family tree because this is what this woman [the Website coordinator] had heard all of her life. I remember emailing the coordinator and saying, 'You know, none of this is true. This is all a lie. I can prove every bit of it.' She said, 'Well—you know, that she had to leave it up there, dah, dah, dah.' And so I said, 'Well, fine. You know, just leave it up there, but it's all wrong.' And she said, 'Well, would you like to correct it?' And I said, 'Sure.' And so I corrected it. Then I get this family member who I had never seen and I don't know anything about, you know, who calls me on the phone and just chews the living fire out of me because I changed her quote, unquote, family stories and her family history. And I told her—I said, 'Well, I have a marriage license to prove all my stuff. You know, what do you have other than just family stories?' Well, because of that, unfortunately, I've gotten lots of nasty letters from this side of the family…and I was kind of threatened by a family member not to do anything else on the family tree until he died. And so I said, 'That's good enough for me. I don't care if he's an 85-year-old man. If he says no, I'm not doing it.'*

And so Rev. Harrison turned his genealogy interests away from his own family and toward his new community, Solidad, a small town in the southern U.S.

In many ways Rev. Harrison is an outsider in the community; but his wife's family has strong ties to it. He explains that his wife's mother and her four brothers all graduated from Solidad High School. He describes them as "people of integrity and honesty and character." This association with credible sources is only one thing that helps him collect data in his adopted community. The second is that he is an outsider—a definite advantage, he says: "I don't have any background here. I can look at everything objectively…. I don't know anything about these people." He hasn't heard the stories of the "town drunk." He doesn't know about the individuals who had to leave due to business scandals. He started as a clean slate, networking in the community, collecting information and photographs, and carefully piecing together the disparate pieces of information.

**Networking as a Key Source of Information**

Solidad was founded by a few college-educated families, a rarity in the late 1800's. These families, including the Solidads and their descendents, still control the town. They run the main businesses, attend the local churches, and participate heavily in volunteer groups such as the Rotary and Lions Club. Though Rev. Harrison is a preacher, it wasn't through his church that he developed relationships with these powerful people. Rather, it was through the volunteer clubs, where he took to giving "these little silly talks," as he calls them, accessing information on the Internet. Through these talks he believes he has established himself as a person of "integrity and character, especially as far as knowledge is concerned."

He explains that knowing the right people has helped him gather more information about Solidad. "It's not like I go to their house or we go out and eat supper together or anything like that," he says. "But I know the right people and they know who I am. And so far I haven't done anything that would indicate that I don't have credibility." These key families are proud of their heritage, and they cherish information and family photographs. They also value the fact that Rev. Harrison is willing to spend his time collecting and organizing the disparate information. They have given him their only copies of many historical photographs because he is capable of using ICTs to archive them. For example, he has a series of photographs taken atop the local hill looking down on the center of town. In one photograph, the founder sits looking out on a barren space with only a few houses, cattle, and grass. In the next photograph, taken 15 years later, the founder's son sits atop the same hill. Below him now lie a post office, some businesses, and many more houses. Rev. Harrison has collected about 10 such pictures that archive the development of this community over a 75-year time frame. Not all the pictures came from a single source, but together they are valuable to the community as a whole.

*Because Rev. Harrison can use ICTs to archive photos, he is trusted by many people to preserve Solidad's history.*

Knowing the right people and then "name-dropping" is another way that he gathers information. Quite often he will "write a letter to somebody who's an unknown to me—and I am unknown to them. But say, they know someone who's descended from the Solidads... I drop names all the time." This technique enhances his own credibility and increases the chance that people openly share information with him. This has made him a powerful person in the community, but controversial, too. "Probably unofficially I'm the Solidad historian," he says, but explains that there are official historians, too, which creates conflict and competition. One such "official historian," he says, is an older woman who is well-known in the community:

> *Because she has always perceived herself as the Solidad historian, I irritate her a lot. And one of the reasons I irritate her is because I'm on the Internet. And I'm sharing things for free. I don't charge. I never charge anything. All I want is information. I don't want money. I have to report money. I want information, because I'm writing things that are interesting to me and are curious to me, and I connect things that way.*

## Email for Sharing Information

One ramification of being the unofficial historian of Solidad is that many people from around the world now contact him for information on their family. He describes himself as providing a "service." Since most of this communication takes place exclusively via email, he explains that he is "kind of faceless anyway to people because all they know me by is my email address and maybe my name—that's maybe all."

*The challenge when responding to an email request for information is that the request is often quite general.*

The challenge when responding to an email request for information is that the request is often quite general—the type of question you might ask in a face-to-face environment when you know someone very well and are spending an afternoon with them. "I get lots of emails from people that say—well, as an example, 'Tell me everything you know about the Smith family.'" Rev. Harrison believes that this is an inappropriate question to ask via email because he now knows so much that he could type for days and probably not finish sharing "everything" about a given family. So he "most often sends a response back that just says very simply, 'Can you be more specific?' And I put my name and the town that I live in." Still, he receives these requests daily and enjoys responding to their requests—almost always via email.

**His Elaborate Storage and Backup System**

Besides having townspeople give out his name as a knowledgeable historian, he also receives requests from people who have seen his information posted on the Internet. "I really got into the email part of it really strong in April of 98. That's when I… sent a lot of things to an archival Website and uploaded a lot of things." The types of information that he has collected demonstrate his detail-oriented nature and his quest for accurate information.

*I transcribed two telephone books—I mean, I have all the telephone books from 1910 till about 1998, 99. And I've transcribed, oh, the 1874 school census, the 1881 school census, the 1913 school census, the 1912 school census. I know most of the people who taught school in Solidad, and Solidad County. I know all the schools in Solidad County that ever were. For most of them I've got pictures of the older school buildings in Solidad County. I've just got tons and tons and tons of history.*

Rev. Harrison frequently receives inquiries about information that he has in his files. He faces the challenge of needing to carefully verify the identity of the requester. During this validity check, he uses the opportunity to gather additional information for his files. "In order to claim an unclaimed marriage license, you have to tell me how you are kin to these people—how you descend from them. That's what the State requires." But besides asking for the same information that the State requires, he also asks for additional scraps of information: "What I find out is the husband's name, wife's name, where they were born, where they died, where they're buried, children's name, spouse's name, children's name, spouse's name, children's name, spouse's name till I get to the end. And then I find out, you know, name, address, date, ZIP, and an email address."

*Because he deals with sensitive family information, Rev. Harrison has a strategy to verify the identity of the requester.*

With all this information, storage becomes a critical consideration. He relies on dedicated hard drives, CD ROMs, print copies, and redundancy:

*Everything is burned [on a CD]. In fact, I have a hard drive, and then I have a backup CD in my house. And then I have a backup CD in my safety deposit box. And then I usually have a hard-copy of pictures, too. And I print them—usually I print them on a canvas paper so they'll last a long time. I didn't use archival inks; I use 25-year inks. And I have three filing cabinets that I have for hard copy stuff. And I have those in acid-free-envelopes. It's not what I would call a secure environment—but, you know, it does what I need it to do. I collect a lot of things from a lot of different sources.*

His office at the church is filled with hard-copy documents and photographs that are in the process of being archived. It is difficult to imagine that he ever sleeps because this is only his "hobby"—he also has a full-time job as a preacher.

## The Challenge of Collecting Credible Information

Rev. Harrison prides himself on collecting information from credible sources. He provides considerable insight into how he initially gathered the information, thus how credible it might be. Paper documents, sometimes digitally stored, hold the key. "There's a good chance that if it was written in a family Bible, it's probably more accurate because they've had time to think," he contends. Contrast this with the information found on a death certificate or funeral record. Even though such information is filled in by funeral home representatives, they get the data from the family. Now it might seem that the family is knowledgeable about the life of their loved one, but, as Rev. Harrison explains, "Death is a time of duress—[you] can't think straight. You can't think what's going on. And so they [the funeral home] say, 'Well, now, when were your parents married?' 'Oh, uh, uh.'" This is how many "official" documents get their information.

*Rev. Harrison prides himself on collecting information from credible sources.*

*"Family stories don't mean truth."*

He also finds that family stories can be of questionable veracity. "Family stories don't mean truth. I've heard their stories when they were younger and I've heard their stories when they were older, and the stories don't match." Stories also become embellished over time. Rev. Harrison recalls once receiving an email from a woman who claimed that her grandfather was Solidad County sheriff. Rev. Harrison checked his records and emailed her back saying no, he wasn't a sheriff:

*[She said,] 'Well, it may have been he was a deputy sheriff.' [Rev. Harrison thought,] 'Well, now, that's harder to prove.' And what I've done is, I've gone back in the County Commissioner records to see who they paid. And I said, 'No, he's not a deputy sheriff.' She said, 'Well, you know, in the time period Solidad County they used to call their chief of police the "marshal." And they called him "marshal" until the thirties.' And so then her argument was, he was the city marshal. And I said, 'No, wasn't city marshal. I've got a list of those.' She said, 'Well, then he was a city police officer.' And I said, 'During this time period? No, no, he wasn't. Not a city police officer.' I said, 'Where did he die?' 'Well, he died in Solidad County.' And I said, 'Oh, well I said, What date? What year was it?' 'Well, the year was about 1928, 1929.' I said, 'Oh, that's open records. We can look at that stuff.' And I said, 'I'll email you back in a few minutes what he was.' And so I looked in my records and emailed her back and said,*

*'Night watchman.' [She said] 'Oh, no, that couldn't be right.' [And I said] 'Well, that's what his death certificate says.' And I said,' That's what his obituary says—night watchman.' And she said, 'Well, we were always told he was a sheriff.' See? Family story.*

To overcome this issue with unreliable information, Rev. Harrison triangulates by using multiple sources. Many times he refers back to the local Solidad newspaper as a reliable primary source. "In those days," he explains, "the only reason a person bought the newspaper was to make sure the editor got it right. You know, they had given him a story and they wanted that story to be right. And that's the only reason they took the paper." Other sources, such as church records, provide different information than what is normally useful to a historian or researcher. Sometimes baptismal records are useful, but often their historical documentation is fairly incomplete. He explains, "I was doing some work in the old Methodist files the other day. And one of them—I think it's hilarious to me—but it says, 'Church broke up today because of gunfire.'" That is the end of what the church has documented. But what's more important to Rev. Harrison is, "Why was there gunfire?" For that information he looked in the Solidad newspaper and found out that it was a family feud.

*The real challenge with having access to credible information is that it can sometimes hurt others.*

Another source of credible information is the graveyard. The headstones often tell accurate birth and death information, but they are not always labeled, or the marker has been destroyed. To find unmarked graves, Rev. Harrison owns what he calls "probing rods." Admittedly, this is a rather unconventional way to find information—a way that often requires rubbing elbows with the law:

*I was out there the other day doing it and somebody called the police on me. You know, they came out there to ask me what I was doing. And they looked at me and they said, "Oh, it's you." My—I guess that's just part of the fun. But, you know, there's lots and lots of family history.*

The real challenge with having access to credible information is that it can sometimes hurt others. Rev. Harrison is very careful to only share information between consenting parties. He will often act as the go-between by putting his own email address as the contact point. But sometimes there is no third party to contact prior to sharing information. While Rev. Harrison carefully obeys the law, sometimes the information is shocking to the requester:

*One of the examples we ran into was an unclaimed marriage license—and I've learned a lot of lessons on those already. One of them that we did, she asked for a marriage license for dah, dah, dah, dah—it's her mother and father. Okay. And I said, 'I'll be glad to send that to you.' I said, 'Now, his name was so-and-so-and-so-and-so?' 'Yes, yes, his name was that,' she said. 'Okay,' I said. 'Well, now, do you have a brother or a sister?' She said, 'Well, yes, I have a brother.' Okay. Well, now, how old is your brother?" I said. "Well, he's X number of years old,' she replied. 'Okay,' I said. 'Well, do you want these other marriage licenses, too—your father's other marriage licenses?' And she said, 'Oh, no, he was only married once.' And I said, 'Okay. Well, you're probably right; I probably mis-read it, you know.' Well, about six months later I get a phone call from her and she said, 'Who was the other marriage license to?' And I said, 'Well, it's probably [incorrect information]...' And she said 'Well, I really want to know.' 'Well,' I said, 'it was to this [other] woman....you know, he had been married the first time, and his wife died and they had kin.' And come to find out all these years she had thought that they were brother and sister, and they were actually half-brother and half-sister. And they had never told her that story. And so they died without ever having told her. And I opened up a big can of worms, you know. Inadvertently.*

The interesting thing about this exchange is that every step in the conversation took place over email. "And, you know," he adds, "one of the things I think about communication and knowledge is it's one thing to have knowledge, but it's a whole different thing to know how to communicate the knowledge." Information can obviously be dangerous.

## Conclusion

Thus far we have learned about a preacher who has positioned himself as the information hub of his small Southern U.S. town. You might even say he is empire-building—certainly not a typical characteristic of a man of God. But he has one tangible use for this knowledge that reveals his true nature, and it's best explained in the context of a story that Rev. Harrison tells. He explains that one of his primary duties as a pastor is to visit older and often dying parishioners in nursing homes and the hospitals, for in their last few days they look to him for comfort. But instead of citing passages from the Bible that may or may not provide them the relief they seek, he talks with them about their family. Since he knows information for several generations back, he asks them about their parents and grandparents. Quite often he knows positive things about those relatives that the dying parishioner has never heard. He can tell them stories about their friends when they themselves were in high school. He knows about their children, their grandchildren. By sharing his valuable knowledge, he provides them cheering confidence that they will not be forgotten. Yes, they too will be remembered. They will be a part of stories for future generations.

## Questions for Review or Discussion

1.  How do you use ICTs to enhance your own personal credibility?

2.  Would you trust or distrust a minister who is constantly using the Internet for the development of parishioners' family histories to enhance his credibility?

3.  Please describe the minister's working environment and how he enacts it. Given the same environment, provide an alternative enactment strategy that also accomplishes his credibility objectives.

4.  Is there a difference between a researcher going to newspaper files to gain information and them getting information over the Internet?

5.  What would he be missing if he relied exclusively on the Internet as a source of information?

# Postscript: The Source of Our Stories

ps

The stories in this book were drawn from a larger set of interview data that was collected in the United States and Norway over two and a half years, from Fall 2000 through Spring 2003. Special effort was placed on identifying ICT users from a wide range of professions including farming, banking, the legal profession, university teachers, and various governmental and for-profit organizations, including high-tech firms. Apart from their relative uniformity in age (75% were under age 40), participants consisted of a cross-section of users representing different functions, ethnicity, professional and organizational tenure, and gender. We had two particularly relevant criteria for selecting participants: (a) all of them used ICTs extensively in their daily work, and (b) they frequently communicated with either internal or external customers. This last feature becomes important in our data set because few studies make an effort to collect data from sales and marketing (externally focused communication) as well as coordination and production (internally focused communication).

Data was collected using semi-structured, in-depth interviews, which can be readily adapted to each context and individual. We created an interview guide that focused on the interviewees' day-to-day ICT activities and then followed up with probes for details to produce specific responses. Interviewees were encouraged to tell the "story" of their technology use to ensure the inclusion of outlying details. To further ensure richness, participants were first informed about the study, then asked to think of one or more specific projects that they were currently working on or had recently completed. The interview focused on how participants use ICTs in their daily work as well as more general inquiries about collaborative processes with both internal and external customers.

Following this strategy, the four authors of this book—two American, two Norwegian—conducted a total of 68 individual interviews, including 34 in the United States and 34 in Norway. Each interview lasted 45-90 minutes and was audio-recorded. The recordings were then transcribed, resulting in approximately 2,500 pages of double-spaced text. To facilitate subsequent data analysis, the Norwegian data set was translated into English by one of the Norwegian interviewers and checked for semantic and contextual accuracy by the other. Both Norwegian researchers are native to that country, but both have advanced degrees from universities in the U.S.

The 20 stories in this book were selected from among the 67 interviews. We then pulled direct quotes from these stories, edited them slightly to make them clearer, and arranged them in a sequence to best convey the different points from the interview.

# Index

ABCnews.com 191
access 121, 223 *See also Internet: access*
    level-dependent access 265
accidents 96
account managers 252
accountability 65
accountants 105
accounting and procurement solutions 243
accuracy 262, 269, 283
action threshold switches (ATS) 80
ad hoc team formation 200
Adams, D.A. 110
adaptability 150, 217
Adaptive Structuration Theory (AST) 33, 88
    five tenets of 88
adoption 106, 189, 278
adoption, early majority 48
advertising 39
Afghanistan 272
Africa 226
agency 85, 89
agenda 200
agriculture 137
Allen, M.W. 65
allocative resources 87
ambiguity 198
AMD 251
American Research Institute for Pathology 186
Anderson, P. 97, 98
anonymity 238
apathy 122
Apple Computers 251
appropriation 89
Aristotle 37, 39
Arthur, Brian 94
artificial demand 211
assignment lists 121
asynchronous communication 128, 132, 150, 228, 276, 280
    channels 70
    downside of 195
attitudes 42
    adjusting 74
audience 42, 124
    being one step ahead of 142
authoritative vs. allocative resources 87
automated production 264
automatic dump 209
automation 131, 132, 264, 265
availability 166, 231, 270
Axelrod, R. 97

backup system 201, 286
balance 281
banking 127
Barley, S. 109
Barrios-Choplin, J.R. 31, 100
Barton, L. 40
BBCnews.com 191
behavior 65, 82, 98, 107, 150
Belgium 138, 210
Bendor, J. 57, 61
Benoit, W.L. 39
bifurcation 101, 103
body language 213
boilerplate 184
Bolino, M.C. 65
boosterism 52
bounded rationality 62
Bowlby, J. 38
Boyd, B. 110
Brewer, M.B. 38
broadband 236, 267, 270

Brønnøysund Register Center 277
Brown, S.L. 93
Browning, L.D. 57, 69, 86, 87, 115
budgeted bed occupancy rate (BBO) 80
Burger, J.M. 65
Burke, K. 67
business climate 152
business model 134
business objectives 109
business schools 119, 121
Business Week 191
buy-in 134

Cacioppo, J.T. 42
call centers 248
cameras 265
Cameron, G.T. 42
Canada 195
capacity, data carrying 32
capital-equipment suppliers 251
Capra, F. 97, 103
CAS (complex adaptive systems) 97, 98
CAS theory 94
Cassell, P. 91
cause map 76, 79, 80, 83
CD-ROM 176, 190, 270, 286
cellphone 105, 106, 149, 168, 197, 220, 221, 228, 275, 279
    company 280
    services 197
    usage policy 278, 281
CEO 106, 246, 267
CFO 127, 128, 267
Chaffee, S.H. 42
challenge 198
change 107, 112, 143, 190, 193
    deregulation and privatization 197
    dramatic organizational 103
    environmental 75, 76
    from the traditional business model 134
    in the banking industry 132
    industry 256
    organizational 103
    organizational culture and 107
chat 143, 191
chemicals 214
Cheraskin, L. 38
Chervany, N.L. 38
Chile 141, 144, 226, 260
China 226
chip producers 251
choice opportunities 61
CI (competitive intelligence) 205
CI team 198, 199
CIO (Chief Information Officer) 137
Classfronter 121, 122
clear language 144
client retention 239
client strategy 235
climate 107
clipping service 141
closeness 159
cognition-based trust 38
cognitive maps 98, 103
Cohen, M.D. 57, 58, 60, 61, 62, 63
collaborative network 220
collaborative software 96
collecting and organizing information 283
collective learning 125
collective understanding 143
commercial content 40
CommMeets 244
communicating knowledge 289

communication
    asynchronous 121, 228
    capability constraints 32
    channel 51, 53, 65, 165, 227
    channels, computer-mediated 229
    consciousness 138
    consequentiality of 78
    electronic 214
    email 29
    gaps 252
    interorganizational 109, 110, 211
    practices 112
    practices leading to familiarity 144
    preference of customers 221
    push-type 244
    serial 124
    skills 219
    strategy 138
    style 144
compatibility 53
competency 49, 107, 137, 239, 263, 270, 276
competition 210, 239, 265
    competitors 66, 161, 199, 204
competitive intelligence (CI) 198, 200, 201
competitive strategy
    competitive intelligence 201
complex adaptive systems 94, 96, 97, 101
complex business relationships 169, 257
complex systems 93, 95, 97
    analogy between organizations and 93
complexity 53, 93, 94, 96, 199, 247
    fundamentals of 96
complexity sciences 93, 100
complexity sciences. 93, 107, 121, 129, 139, 149, 157,
    167, 175, 183, 191, 199, 209, 219, 227, 237,
    245, 253, 261, 269, 277, 285
complexity theory xix, 101
computer networks 110
computer-mediated communication 29
computer-science 119
conference calls 133, 268
confidential information 170, 207
confidentiality 207, 256
conformity 49
Conrad, C. 85
consequences 51, 278
consideration 68
Constitution of Society, Giddens 85
constraints 82
consultant 148, 267, 268, 278
Contractor, N.S. 32, 52
contributing content 185
convenience 185
conventional literature 205
Coombs, W.T. 40
copyrighted 176
corporate culture 106, 109, 247
    *See also culture*
cosmopolite 49
cost
    effective 270
    marginal cost 161
    reduction 246
    savings 209, 245
courses 121, 123, 156
Cowden, K. 41
Crecine, J.P. 59, 60
credibility xviii, 41, 42, 43, 44, 70, 158, 186, 223, 236, 283, 287
    communicator xix
    media 41
    message 40
    source 269
critical mass 48
CSS 100, 101
CSS-type emergence 100
cubicle 232
culture 106, 107, 109, 111, 114, 116, 137, 175, 193, 226
    adaptation and planning 138
    African 226
    American 106
    American business practice 160
    Asian 212, 226
    awareness 138
    banking industry 134
    building corporate 140
    Central American 226
    conversational customs 138
    corporate 108, 143, 192, 247
    definition of 106, 111
    differences 112, 138, 140, 157
    four dimensions of 112
    French 106
    multi-cultural workforce 138
    national 116
    national values 112
    Norwegian 106
    occupational subcultures 110
    offensive 138
    organizational 116
    parochialism 185
    preliminary rituals 138
    selection of technology and 85
    shifting 134
    typical American 105
    unwritten rules 175
    work 268
Cummings, L.L. 38
customer 251
    CommMeets 244
    driven sales-and-marketing strategy 195
    emotion 166
    fear 161
    foreign 155
    investing time with 219
    issues 253
    needs 134, 218
    potential 236
    relations management 139
    relationship management solutions 248
    satisfaction 257
cyber middle-man 207

Daft, R.L. 28
damage control 70
Darrell Urbanski, 189
data gathering 201
Data Protection Authority 187
Data Quest 256
database 170, 201, 229, 240, 269
    intelligence from 203
day-timer *193*.
    *See also PDA (Personal Digital Assistant)*
De Mooij, M. 114, 115
decentralized diffusion systems 50
decision structures 278
decision-makers 198, 206, 278
decision-making 50, 61, 108, 112, 133, 138, 268
delegating 169
Deleuze, G. 95
delivery 40
Dell 251
demand driven 244
democracy of information 269
democratic technology 270
demonstration 244
Denmark 158, 159, 160, 161
deregulation 197
DeSanctis, G. 33, 88
designed transactions 86
determinism 27
deterministic and social constructionist perspective 33
devices 171
diagnostic database 181
dialectical processes 86
dialogue 70, 178
Diffusion of Innovations Theory 52, 54
digital
    community 181
    document 191
    images 183
    philanthropy 173, 177, 178
Dillard, C. 69
diplomacy 124
direct mail 235
disaster 271

discursive consciousness 87
discussion (newsgroup) 173
displaying information 237
disruptive technologies 280
dissemination 144, 201 *See also information disseminating*
dissertations on email 148
dissipative structure theory 101
dissipative structures 101, 103
distance 90, 159, 202, 227
       PDI 113
       projecting a local presence 158
DocNet 181, 184, 185
doctors 183
documentation 156, 214, 223, 255
      email for 128
      via database 203
Doppler radar 265
dotcom bubble 155
download 245
Downs, G.W. 51
dramaturgical contingencies 68
dramaturgical discipline 68
Dual Capacity Model 31, 43
duality 87
duality of structure 86, 88

e-commerce 257
e-fax 191
e-stamps 191
early adopters 48
ecological change 75, 76, 83
ecological practices 137, 139
economy 259
efficiency 113, 151, 152, 166, 210, 231, 257, 263
      actual 147
      adopting technology to improve 195
      communication channels 165
      of voicemail 130
      the telephone 228
Eidsvik, Anna 225
Einarson, Karen 137
Eisenberg, E.M. 32
electronic conversation 276
email 28, 30, 33, 34, 39, 86, 87, 96, 106, 123,
      148, 150, 151, 160, 166, 167, 177, 183, 186,
      191, 220, 226, 228, 230, 232, 235, 238, 254,
      255, 262, 277, 280, 289
      as a precursor to face-to-face 254
      as disruptive 280
      as documentation 128
      asynchronicity 280
      benefit of multiple recipients 128
      benefits of 276
      billing by 220
      communicating freely 120
      customer contact preferences 168
      detailed 255
      drawbacks of 221
      flexibility of 128
      for details 254
      for non-urgent requests 221
      for reporting 255
      forwarding 276
      headers 230
      ICT of preference 170
      impersonal 227
      inefficiency of 167
      maintaining a client relationship 276
      newsgroups distributed by 173
      no anonymity 238
      normal procedure in Norway 158
      overcoming language barrier 150
      overuse 167
      redundancy 228, 254
      reply option 150
      small change metaphor 148
      spamming 235
      temptation 280
      to overcome timezones 194
      transferable 170, 285
      virtual classroom 123
emergence 100

Emergent Strategy 160
emergent structures 103
emergent system 89
empathy 39
enactment xviii, 62, 73, 75, 76, 78, 79, 80, 83, 94
energy conservation 225
engineers 111, 207, 253
England 138
entrepreneurial pathologists 182
enunciation 40
environment 73, 74, 80, 83, 96, 139, 147, 246
      heated 198
      learning 122
      physical 200
      school 120
environmental constraint 103
equal access to information 123
equilibrium 97
equivocality 28
Erickson, 1968 38
ethernet hubs 190
ethics 38, 66, 68, 269
ethnic backgrounds 111
ethnocentricity 138
ethos 37
etiquette 68
      email 230
Europe 138, 157
European Union 262
exchange relationships 65
expectations 123, 166, 176
expertise xix, 43
experts 174
Extended Care Unit (ECU) 80
external pressure 93, 139

face-to-face 28, 29, 34, 37, 66, 91, 129, 151, 159,
      186, 192, 193, 200, 205, 226, 231, 238,
      243, 246, 268
      meetings for details 212
face-to-face communication 28, 29, 149
      benefits of 214
      drawbacks of 54
      essentialness of 128
      for courting potential clients 236
      for important decisions 237
      high end customer relationships and 134
      importance of 213
      in sales 246
      need for 134
      preferred in Denmark and Germany 160
      terminology and 278
      to communicate priority 254
      to demonstrate value 143
      value of 124, 202
facilitating customer information gathering 255
facilities 88
FAQ's 123, 139
Fast Company 191
faux pas 68
fax 103, 191, 208, 220, 221, 222, 245
feedback 70
feedback loops 83
feelings 69
Figure
      Composite Map of Three Cases 82
      Dual Capacity Model 31
      Factors Affecting Overall Perceptions 43
      Rate of Adoption 48
      Roos and Hall's Cause Map 81
      Sales Process Communication Web 252
      Sensemaking and Enactment 77
      Social Influence Model 30
      Visual Representation of Media Richness 28
financial industry 239
financial services 235, 237, 239, 240
firm structure 240
fish-farming industry 259
Flanagin, A.J. 41
flexibility 128, 279
      flexible learners 162
      flexible learning activities 123

fluctuations 103
Fluid Model Depicting Credibility Considerations 42
FolkKind 243
formal 231
formality 32
forwarding information (see email) 255
framing 79
freedom 122, 123
fresh information 206
freshness 205
friction of distance 91
Frink, D.D. 65
Fulk, J. 30, 110
functionally 253

Garbage Can theory xix, 57, 58, 59, 60, 61, 62
Gartner Group 256
Gass, R.H. 39
Gattiker, U. 32
GDSS (group-decision support systems) 86
Gell-Mann 98
genealogy 283
generating intelligence 202
gentle repetition 144
geography 210, 254
        geographical remoteness 217
        overcoming issues 253
Germany 155, 158, 160
gestures 68
Ghana 226
Giddens, Anthony 32, 85, 86, 87, 88, 90, 91
        Structuration Theory xviii
global sophistication 137
goals 80, 140
Goffman, E. 67, 68
        Impression Management xviii
        Interaction Ritual 67
        Presentation of self in every day life 67
        Rule of consideration 68
        Rule of self-respect 68
        The presentation of self in every day life, 67
golf 267
good business practices 139
goodwill 39, 43
Google 131, 269
Greenwood, R. 87
Gregory, K.L. 110
Griffin, D. 97
group collaboration 121
group decision support systems 86
group norms 107
group-think 107
groupware 50
Gudykunst, W.B. 116
guidelines 187
gurus 173
Guttari, F. 95

habits of thinking 107
Hall, R.I. 80
hard sciences 94
hard-copy form 221
heaven 283
Hemne, Dr. Tor 181
Henten, A. 50
Hewlett-Packard 106, 108
high-level information 268
high-speed connection 236
        see also Internet access
high-velocity environments 275
Hinings, B. 87
Hirsh, C. 87
historian 286
Hofstede, G. 110, 111, 112, 114, 115
        Hofstede's First Dimension 113
        Hofstede's Four Dimensions of Cultural Differences 112, 116
        Hofstede's Framework 112
        Hofstede's Perspective 111
Hogarth, R.M. 75
Holland, J. H. 97
homogeneity 143
honor 68

Horn, Trond 197
hospitals 181
Hovland, C.I. 37, 40
Huber, G. 113
Human Click 190
human error 261
human resources 133, 277
Hydro 278
hydro-electrical power 225

IBM 105, 106, 108
ICT
        Adaptive Structuration Theory and 89
        adoption 83
        combination of 162
        commonplace 225
        complexity and 93
        culture and 106
        effective use of 213
        efficient use of 149
        emergent structures and 103
        enactment and 74, 78
        enlightened use of 149
        implementation 106, 113
        implementation of 51
        impression management and 65
        improving future communication 256
        innovation and 54
        learning process and 125
        mix 220
        multiple 167
        overcoming distance 90
        peer and opinion leadership and 49
        preference 34, 85, 132
        preferences 152, 168
        reluctance to use 182
        role of in the workplace 112
        sales and 170, 191
        strategy 150
        structuration and 90
identity 177
IDV 112
        countries 114
        cultures 115
        Individualism/Collectivism (IDV) 114
IEA 230
imperfect organizational system 253
impersonal 227
implementing new office technologies 267
impression management 65, 66, 67, 69, 126, 142
        corporate 137
inconsistent and ill-defined preferences 57
indicator 238
individualistic vs. collectivistic (see IDV) 111, 114
informal 231
informal partners 220
information disseminating 137
information dissemination 139, 205
information gathering 165, 256, 268
        acquiring fresh information 137
        competitive intelligence 277
        credible data 287
        for decision making 267
        primary sources 202
        secondary sources 201, 203
        via the Internet 130, 182
information hub 289
information management framework 69
information overload 165, 168
information reciprocity 143
information storage 286
information-sharing 170
initial trust formation 38
innovation 50, 51, 52
innovators 48, 120
insider trading 199
Instant Messenger 149
insulting 150
integrated symbols 107

Intel 59, 108, 251
Interaction ritual, Goffman 67
internal communication 251
internal marketplaces 276
Internet 47, 130, 141, 177, 183, 191, 197, 204,
       213, 226, 229, 269, 271, 272, 277
       access 181, 191, 230
       access from a rural community 129
       as a source of news 141
       brokerage firm 155
       connection 194
       daily use in Norway 50
       daily use in U.S. 50
       information gathering 174
       instantaneous updates via 204
       its contribution 277
       live demos 243
       monitoring competitors 98
       monitoring industry forces 142
       no access 141
       paying bills 127
       services 239
       solutions 157
       training via 156
interorganizational linkages 110
interpersonal credibility 39
interpretation 269
interpretive processes 86
interpretive schemes 88
interruption 279
InterStock 155, 159
intranet 169, 184
inventory 207, 208, 220
irreversibility 101
Isaacs, W. 97
IT department 187

Japan 29, 108, 226
Jarvenpaa, S.L. 39, 113
Johnson, B. 101
just-in-time (JIT) 173
just-in-time learning 173, 178
       newsgroups 178

Karlsen, Rune 155
Kiousis, S. 42
knowledge 289
       See also competency
knowledge-based trust (see trust) 38
Kramer, R.M. 38
Kristenson, T.M. 50

laggards 48
language 156, 157
       language obstacles 157
       linguistic paradigms 107
laptop computer 95, 166, 190, 255
late majority adopters (see adoption) 48
laws 68
lead-time 210
leadership 65, 85, 132
       opinion 49
       peer 49
Leadership Training Project 139
lean media 69, 113
learning 122, 178, 181, 256, 276
       learning process 125
Leary, M.R. 65
lecture 123. See also learning; training
lecture (see learning or training)
       lecture notes 121
legal obstacles 187
legitimizing executive decisions 272
Leifer, R. 101
leisure content 40
Lengel, R.H. 28
letter 230
Levin, S. 100
Lewicki, R.J. 38
library 170

linear model diffusion 49
linking data 262
Linux 175
Lions Club 284
local market 160
local presence 155, 158, 162
long-distance medicine 183
look-backs 129
Lord, R.G. 65
low-priority response 32

Macintosh 190
Mad Cow Disease 139, 259
Madsen, Kjell 275
mail 159
       snail-mail 156
Maitland, C. 114
making connections 272
man-on-the-street opinion 238
management paradigms 62
managing impressions 66
       See also impression management
manual 125
March, J.G. 58, 62
market 141
       analysis 200
       entry 161
       incentives drive users to technology 156
       research 204, 256
marketing 119, 191, 236, 243, 253
       department 256
       push-pull 244
Markus, Bikson, El-Shinnawy, & Soe, 1992 110
Massey, J.E. 40
Materiality/Sociality Index (MSI) 111, 115
McCroskey, J.C. 38, 39
McGuire, Elliott 251
McKnight, Cummings, & Chervany, 1998 38
McKnight, D.H. 38
media 42, 142, 221
       choice 27, 129, 170, 205, 227, 232
       electronic media and cognitive maps 98
       mindless medium choice 150
       preference 98
       richness 28
       Richness Theory 28, 29, 31
       strategy 199
       symbolic carrying capacity of 32
       synchronous 228 See also synchronous
mediated communication 231
meetings 166
       See also face-to-face
mental models 107
message 40, 42, 43, 70, 238, 271
metaphors 107
Metzger, M.J. 40, 41, 42
Meyerson, D. 38
microchips 251
Microsoft 106, 156
       Excel 50, 90, 156
       Outlook 129
       PowerPoint 33, 50, 58, 73, 150, 194, 205, 211, 244, 245
       Word 50, 90, 156, 182
mindlessness 225
mindsets 111
mistakes 263
misuse 280
modern Sisyphus 120
modernity 91
monitoring cellphone use 280
moral constraints 68
Motorola 108, 251
MSI 112
MSNBC 191
multi-ethnical workforce 138
multi-media use 245
multiple sources 288

National Center of Telemedicine 185
national culture 106, 111, 116
       See also culture

natural selection 75
need to know 210
Nerdrum, Dr. Inge 181
nerds in the basement 178
NetMeeting 91
networks 89, 110, 141, 142, 183
    good-old-boy 132
    networking 284
new entrants 198, 199
New York 270
news page 141
newsgroups 111, 173, 174, 175, 176, 177
    asking questions on a newsgroup 174
    digital philanthropy 178
    hobby-oriented newsgroups 178
    moderated newsgroups 176
    non-moderated newsgroups 175
    socialization of members 176
    source of information 173
    unwritten rules 175
newsletter 141, 142
non-proprietary information 170
non-stop 148
non-technical audiences 217
non-urgent requests 220
nonlinearity 96, 97
nonverbal 67
nonverbal cues 29
Nordland Central Hospital 183
NorFood 141
normative contingencies 32
norms 88, 152
NorthCell 206
Northwest Airline's 41
Norway 51, 105, 113, 116, 127, 143,
    155, 160, 183, 198, 229, 260, 262
Noyce, Bob 59, 108
NST 183
NTNU, Trondheim Norway 181, 275

observability 53
obstacles for innovation
    technical and social 182
occupations 110
off-shore fisheries 260
off-the-shelf software 33
Office Depot 245
office landscape 232
office location 192
office spaces 231
Olsen, J.P. 62
On Rhetoric, Aristotle 37
one degree of separation 271
one-on-one 194
online
    banking 131
    filing regulatory reports 130
    information sources 229
    purchasing to save time 220
    state-government funding opportunities 131
    supplying the household 148
    trading 130, 155
openness vs. closedness 69
opinion leadership 49
optimizing 221
order process 208
organization
    external pressure and 96
organizational
    change 134
    citizenship 65
    climate 86
    communication 86
    culture xix, 106, 107 *See also culture*
    learning 160, 162
    shift 262
    subcultures 106
organizing 74, 148
Orlikowski, W.J. 33, 106
O'Sullivan, P.B. 69, 70

O'Sullivan's Model 69
outcomes 82
outsource 247
overload 167
    *See also information overload*

pager 105, 166, 168
    customer contact preferences 168
Palm Pilot 166, 193, 254
    drawbacks of 193
paradox 124
Parks, M.R. 29, 34
participants 60, 63, 121
participation 60
    fluid 58
partnerships 239, 240, 247
password-protected 184
pathology 181, 186
patterned repetition of human interaction 85
patterns of interaction 103
PC 185, 187, 190, 267
PDA (Personal Digital Assistant) 131, 193, 255
PDF format 141
PDI 112, 113
pedagogical model 125
pedagogy 120, 122
Pedersen, Gunnar 119
peer leadership 49, 50
peer networks 48
Pentagon 271
perception 245
performance criteria 80
personal integrity 223
personal network 226
personal relationships 227, 270
persuasion research 37
Peters, T. 58
Petty, R.E. 42
philanthropy 177
philosophy 107
phone 231 *See also telephone*
    calls 159
    discussions 244
    drawbacks of 227
    limitations 130
    message 70
photographs 183
    pathology 183
    picture files 186
physical distance 159, 227
    *See also distance*
pizza guy 237
planning 201
Polar Seafood 259, 260
policy 80, 105, 140, 166, 189, 280
politeness 138
Poole, M.S. 33, 89
Poole, Scott 88
portal 209
    *See also Web*
Portfolio Solutions 276
Post-it® notes 264
posting 121, 237
Power Distance Index (PDI) 111, 113
power structure 213
PowerPoint 33, 156, 205, 244
    *See also Microsoft PowerPoint*
practical consciousness 87
practices 150
    email marketing 238
press releases 192, 204
pride 68
Prigogine, Ilya 101
    Theory of Dissipative Structures 101
PRINT-IT 207
privacy 187
private domain communication 280
privatization 197
pro-innovation bias 52
problem 59, 62, 261
    identification 120
    problem-solving 51, 119
problem-oriented learning 121

problems 212
procedure 123
procrastinate 232
procrastination 232
production processes 262
production-information 208
productivity 276, 279
    and disruption 281
professor 124
psychoanalysis 47
public domain communication 280
public image 39
public relations 39
pull information systems 266
pull system 262
pull-type polling system 244
pulling critical real-time information 261
purchasing 220
push vs. pull 262

Quickbooks 191

radioactivity 139
Ranson, S. 87
Rao, A. 65
rate of adoption 48
    *See also adoption*
raw data 192, 212
real-time 236
    access 207
    information 210
    interactions, Human-Click 190
    monitoring 261
    telemedicine 183
    view 208
record-keeping 264
record-keeping procedure 260
recursive interplay 89
redundancy 253, 254, 286
reference information 40
reflexivity xix, 86, 116
regulatory challenges 261
regulatory problems 260
relationships 103, 228, 246, 270
    developing relationships 132
relative advantage 52
relativity 51
reliability 204, 247
remote diagnosis 182
remoteness 220
reply function 276
    *See also email*
reporting 255
resources 87, 88
    reallocating 209
    *See also human resources*
responsiveness 39
retention 75, 76
reverse-osmosis 218
Rice, R.E. 29, 32, 110
rich media 70
    *See also media: richness*
Ring, P.S. 78
risk 124
Ritz Carlton Hotel 69
Rogers, E.M. 50, 51, 52, 53, 54
    Diffusion of Innovations Theory xviii, 47, 55
Ron Klein 217
Roos, L.L. 80
root metaphors 107
Roper Organization 41
Ross, D.N. 106
Rotary Club 284
Rousseau, D.M. 38
routines 103, 156
rules 34, 68, 87, 103, 107, 175, 177
    conflicting 177
    moral 88

Sætre, A.S. 95, 115

sales 83, 133, 160, 165, 167, 170, 191, 218, 257
    and marketing 39
    direct 243
    face-to-face communication 246
    lead-time 210
    people 170, 252, 257
    pitch 218
    process 252
Schein, E.H. 107
schemata 100
Schmitz, J. 30
Scotland 260
Scott, C.R. 110
search 169, 256
    search engine 169
    searchable 203
secrets 69
securing clients 236
security 247
    issues 188
selection 75, 76
self-control 69
self-organization 87, 96, 97
self-organized structures 100
self-respect 68
Sellnow, T.L. 41
Sematech 108
semiconductor industry 165, 192
seminars 140
sensemaking 73, 76, 78, 83
sensitivity 143, 198
service-oriented 236
Shapiro, S.P. 38
Shared meanings 107
sharing 170, 203
    information via email 285
Sheppard, B.H. 38
Sherriton, J. 109
Shetler, J. 100
Shin, J.H. 42
Short, J. 28
simplicity 144
Sitkin, S.B. 31, 58, 100
skill level 63
skilled workforce 263
    *See also competency*
small kings 264
small organizations and limited infrastructure 173
small-business owners 235
small-town preacher 283
SmartCash 127
SmartPay 127
Smircich, L. 74
Smithers, Ed 235
SMS 39, 47, 98, 105, 168, 228, 279, 280
social
    accessibility 49
    actors 76
    construction 27, 33
    constructionist perspectives 33
    context 51
    encounters 90
    influence 30
    influence model 30, 31
    intelligence 138
    interaction 32
    presence 69
    structures 85
    systems 90
    use 270
    use of ICTs 270
Social Influence Model 30, 31, 32
societal cultures 106
society 85, 91, 114
Soelberg, Frode 197
soft sciences 94
software 90, 176, 243, 247
    solution 248
    supplier-vendor management 207
solutions 59
Sørnes, J.O. 115
sound card 194
source 42

source credibility 37, 39
sources of credible information 288
sources of information 142
spamming 221, 235
speech rate 40
squandering worktime on SMS 280
St. Olaf Hospital, Trondheim 181
St. Olaf's University Hospital 187
Stacey, Griffith & Shaw, 2000 98
Stacey, R.H. 93, 98, 101
Stamps.com 191
Stan Silverthorne 165
stand-alone solutions 261
Starbuck, W.H. 78
start-up 278, 281
Statoil 278
status conferral 52
status reports 157
Stein, E.W. 32
Steinfield, C.W. 30
Stephens, K.K. 115
stereotype 124
stock exchange 142, 157
         Frankfurt exchange 156, 157
         NASDAQ 157
         NYSE 155, 157
         U.S. 157
Stohl, C. 52, 60
strategic alliances 199
Strategic Marketing group, FolkKind's 243
strategy 82, 140, 161, 165, 237, 244
         communication 140, 150
         customer communication 246
         for getting better information 151
         market entry 161
StrategyFirst 267
Straub, D.W. 29
streamline 257
Structuration 32
Structuration Theory 32, 91
         See also Giddens, Anthony: Structuration Theory
structurational influences 32
structure 40
structures 103
structuring the day 231, 240
Stubbart, C. 74
students 121
subcultural influence 109
subculture 106, 109
         See also culture
subscription services 237
supplier-vendor management software 207
suppliers 220
supply chain 211
suppressing emotions 69
Sutcliffe, K.M. 31, 100
SVMS 207, 208
symbolic meaning 31, 100, 236
symmetry 103
synchronous communication 195
         bidding systems 131
         media 228
         Web-conferencing 194
systems-development 157


Table
         Four Characteristics of CAS 99
         Norwegian and U.S. scores on Hofstede's 113
         Seven Properties of Sensemaking 77
         The Formation of Dissipative Structure 102
task contingencies 32
task execution system 156
task management 33
Taylor, J.R. 78
teaching 217
         material 121
         synchronous collaboration 121
         teacher 119, 121
         undergraduate and graduate students 119
         via video conference 120
team formation 200
teamwork 32

techies 119, 173, 174
technological determinism 28
technological innovation 51
technology 62
         awareness 181
         practices 245
         See also ICT: innovation and
telecommunication 183, 271
telecommunications 50
telemedicine 185
Telenor 106, 278
telephone 166, 214, 221, 228, 230, 232, 254, 268
         efficiency of 166
         follow-up 152
         for high level information 268
         increased use after face-to-face 195
         reliability of 167
tension 103
terminology 277
Teven, J.J. 39
Texas 131
Texas Instruments 108
text messaging 96, 228, 280
text-messaging 278
Theory of Organizing 74
third party security provider 247
time savings 246
time-space relations 90
time-zone compatibility 194
timely information 260
Timmerman, C.E. 110
TQM 58
traceability 261, 262, 263
traceability system 260
traceable information 265
tracking products 261
tradition 235, 237, 239, 240
traditional classroom 120
traditional classroom setting 156
training 190, 217, 261
         cross-cultural 144
         employees 263
         of employees 140
         participatory learning 125
         safety 190
         salespeople 134
         via the Internet 156
transaction-oriented 148
translation 150
transparency 66
Trevino, L.K. 28, 32
trialability 53
Trice, H.M. 106, 107, 109
Tromsø, Norway 185
trust 38, 121, 168, 211, 219, 236, 246, 247, 248
         customer 236
         economics or calculative-based 38
         institution-based 38
         knowledge-based 38
         personality-based 38
         trustworthiness xix, 37, 43, 269
turn-around time 207
TV 267, 271


U.K. 195, 225
UAI 112
         countries 114
         cultures 114
         Uncertainty Avoidance Index 111, 113
uncertainty 112, 198
uncertainty avoidance 112
         See also UAI
unclear technology 57
unconscious 87
understanding 39
unintended consequences of ICT use 278
university 267
University Hospital in Tromsø 182
unnecessarily technical 218
USA 113, 137, 138, 160, 207, 243, 260, 289

value chain 261
values 140
    espoused 107
    national cultural 112
Van Birgelen, A. 115
Van Maanen, J. 109
Veiga, J.F. 113, 114
verbal 67
video 213, 214
video conferencing 106, 120, 213
videotape 214
virtual classroom 119, 121
    Classfronter 121, 122
    pedagogical model 125
    virtual studying 120
virtual international group 174
visitors 238
visual representation of Media Richness Theory 28
voice messaging 228
voice-to-voice 195
voicemail 39, 96, 98, 106, 130, 150, 151, 166, 167, 168
    strategy for checking 167
    trumps email for sales 167
volume of communication 148
volume of information 269
Von Meier, A. 109

Waldrop, M.M. 94
Walther, J.B. 29, 34, 69
waste control 265
water-treatment 219
Web 41, 101, 120, 122, 124, 147, 213, 222, 223, 251
    based production information loop 207
    bifurcation 101
    classroom and 120
    credibility and 222
    finding background information using 192
    for market research 193
    for technical support 220
    information gathering 169
    shopping 125
    technical development of 149
    to achieve a fast diagnosis 183
    to increase credibility 223
    use of on the job 130
    wealth and usage 270
    winning customers 248
Web community 177
Web conference 211
Web learning 122
Web portal 209
    *See also Website*
Web sources 272
Web traffic 237
Web Train 190
Web-based learning 121
Web-based questionnaire 190
Web-based solution 185
Web-based training 189
Web-conference 194
Web-ON 244
Webpage 41, 122, 125, 230, 278
    competitive intelligence and 204
Website 38, 66, 122, 141, 156, 192, 209, 222, 235, 236, 239, 268, 286
    competitors 204 *See also CI (competitive intelligence)*
    customer relations management 139
    frequently asked questions 123
    interaction 237
    intranet parameters 184
    traffic 237
    using Human-Click 190
    virtual classroom 122
    Web portal 183, 209, 211
Webster, J. 32
Weick, Karl 38, 73, 74, 75, 76, 80, 83, 94
    Organizational Enactment xviii
    Sensemaking in Organizations 77
    Social Psychology of Organizing 74
    Theory of Organizing 74, 75

wired 281
Wood, R. 98
work
    boundary between home and 149
    context 226
    culture 268
    day 124
    environment 73
    fiendishly long workdays 232
    ICT adoption in the workplace 83
    multicultural workforce 138
    office 220
    practice 268
    units 95
    virtual office 190
workaholic 227
workflow, interruption 279
workplace 275
    excessive interruptions 279
    office landscape 232
    Web a mainstay in 101
World Trade Center 271
world-wide news 191
World-Wide-Web (WWW) 47, 106
    *See also Web*

Yahoo 270
yellow line 209

# About the Authors

Larry D. Browning (Ph.D., Ohio State) is a Professor of organizational communication in the Department of Communication Studies and the John T. Jones Centennial Fellow in Communication, College of Communication, University of Texas at Austin. His research areas include the role of lists and stories in organizations, information-communication technology and narratives, cooperation and competition in organizations, and grounded theory as a research strategy. In addition to over 50 articles and book chapters, he, along with his co-author, Judy Shetler, wrote: *Sematech: Saving the U.S. Semiconductor Industry*. College Station, TX: Texas A & M University Press (2000).

Alf Steinar Sætre (Ph.D., University of Texas at Austin) is an Associate Professor in the Department of Industrial Economics and Technology Management at The Norwegian University of Science and Technology. His research interests include information and communication technologies, organizing, communication, information management, innovation, and new venture creation. He has published articles in such journals as: *Venture Capital, The International Journal of Enterpreneurship and Innovation*, and *Informing Science*. Alf Steinar has a Ph.D. in Organizational Communication from The University of Texas at Austin.

Keri K. Stephens (Ph.D., University of Texas at Austin) is an Assistant Professor at the University of Texas at Austin. Keri's research examines how people use information and communication technologies (ICTs) at work. Her published work appears in *Communication Theory, Journal of Business Communication, Journal of Health Communication, Informing Science*, and several book chapters. She has also won several top paper and teaching awards. She has a BS in biochemistry from Texas A&M University and prior to returning to academia, Kery worked in technology-related industries for eight years.

Jan-Oddvar Sørnes, (Ph.D., Norwegian University of Science and Technology, 2004) is an Associate Professor and Vice Dean at Bodø Graduate School of Business, Norway. Jan's research focus is on organizational communication, specifically how ICTs are used in organizations. He has 10 years of experience with e-learning and ICT use in higher education. His published Work as appeared in *Informing Science Journal, Qualitative Inquiry, Case Studies in Organizations: Ethical Perspectives and Practices,* and several other edited books. Jan teaches undergraduate and graduate courses in computer science, organizational communication, technology management, energy management and qualitative research methods.